Also edited by McKinsey & Company

Reimagining Japan: The Quest for a Future That Works

REIMAGINING
INDIA

UNLOCKING THE POTENTIAL
OF ASIA'S NEXT SUPERPOWER

CLAY CHANDLER AND ADIL ZAINULBHAI

EDITORS

MCKINSEY & COMPANY

Simon & Schuster

New York London Toronto Sydney New Delhi

Simon & Schuster
1230 Avenue of the Americas
New York, NY 10020

First Simon & Schuster hardcover edition November 2013

SIMON & SCHUSTER and colophon are registered trademarks
of Simon & Schuster, Inc.

For information about special discounts for bulk purchases,
please contact Simon & Schuster Special Sales at 1-866-506-1949
or business@simonandschuster.com.

The Simon & Schuster Speakers Bureau can bring authors to your
live event. For more information or to book an event, contact the
Simon & Schuster Speakers Bureau at 1-866-248-3049 or visit our
website at www.simonspeakers.com.

Interior design by Nancy Singer
Jacket design by Tom McKeveny

Manufactured in the United States of America

10 9 8 7 6 5 4 3 2 1

Library of Congress Cataloging-in-Publication Data
    Reimagining India : unlocking the potential of Asia's next
superpower / Clay Chandler and Adil Zainulbhai, editors,
McKinsey & Company. — First Edition.
    pages cm
    1. Economic development—India. 2. India—Economic
policy—21st century. 3. India—Social conditions—21st
century. 4. India—Politics and government—21st century.
I. Chandler, Clay, 1960– editor of compilation. II. Zainulbhai,
Adil, editor of compilation.
    HC435.3.R435 2013
    330.954—dc23
    2013025055
ISBN 978-1-4767-3530-6
ISBN 978-1-4767-3532-0 (ebook)

The difference between what we do and what we are capable of doing would suffice to solve most of the world's problems.

—*Mahatma Gandhi*

contents

chapter three. business & technology 113

chapter four. challenges 197

REIMAGINING
INDIA

foreword
Dominic Barton and Noshir Kaka

By the time Alexander the Great reached the Indus River Valley in 326 BCE, he had vanquished three formidable empires: Syria, Egypt, and Persia. But on a rainswept night on the banks of the Jhelum, an Indus tributary, the Macedonian conqueror's quest for global domination collapsed at the hands of a Hindu king. Greek historians called Alexander's Indian foe Porus. According to their record, he stood seven feet tall and commanded an army of thirty thousand soldiers and two hundred war elephants. After an all-night battle waged in a howling monsoon, Alexander eventually forced Porus to surrender. But it was a hollow triumph. By Indian standards, Porus was a minor raja. The Magadha emperor, who ruled the lower Ganges River to the east, had many times more men and elephants. Alexander's men, exhausted and terrified by the prospect of battling another giant Indian army, mutinied, compelling Alexander, the most successful military commander in ancient history, to turn back home.

Modern visitors, too, can find India overwhelming. Passengers disembarking at Indira Gandhi International Airport's gleaming new third terminal are greeted by the Nine Mudras, an installation of colossal metallic hands looming above the Immigration counter. The hands, according to their designers, are arranged in delicate gestures from yoga and Indian classical dance to symbolize reassurance, benevolence, "the oncoming of novel tidings," and the "linkage between the individual . . . and the ever-throbbing life force of the universe." Travelers proceed under the Mudras, through baggage claim and customs, along the air-conditioned arrival hall adorned with posters celebrating "Incredible India" and then out onto the curbside, where they are plunged headlong into "ever-throbbing" life—and plenty of it.

An abundance of life—vibrant, chaotic, and tumultuous—has long been India's foremost asset. As Western economies struggle to recover from global recession, India's multitudes earn it a place alongside China as one of the world's two indispensable emerging markets. India, with 1.2 billion people, half of them under the age of twenty-five, is expected to overtake China as the world's most populous nation before 2025. In good years, India's sprawling economy has shown itself capable of growing as rapidly as China's; in 2006 and 2007, Indian GDP surged 8.5 percent. In 2012, according to the Organisation of Economic Cooperation and Development, India likely eclipsed Japan as the world's third-largest economy.

> An abundance of life—vibrant, chaotic, and tumultuous— has long been India's foremost asset.

Asia's "other superpower" has many strengths. Indian business leaders, unlike their Chinese counterparts, are at ease in global markets; many, if not most, are fluent in English and graduates of leading business schools in the United States and Europe. With increasing confidence, CEOs of India's leading companies are venturing overseas, making headlines with high-profile acquisitions such as Tata Group's purchase of Jaguar and Land Rover or Bharti Airtel's acquisition of Zain's African telecommunications business. Indian software giants like TCS, Wipro, and Infosys have emerged as global technology leaders, thanks partly to the skills of the thousands of world-class engineers who graduate each year from the country's famed Indian Institutes of Technology. Indian companies are thriving in other key sectors such as pharmaceuticals, petrochemicals, and steel, demonstrating a capacity for efficiency and innovation that is changing the global competitive landscape. India's banking system and equity markets are well regulated and far more open to foreign participation than China's. India's currency, unlike China's, trades freely. It is often argued that India, with its wildly pluralistic society, fractious democratic political system, and boisterous independent media, has the potential to show the world's other emerging markets that ethnic homogeneity and authoritarianism aren't the only—or even the best—path to successful economic development.

But there it is, that word "potential"; it crops up all too often in conversations about India. As consultants we hear it again and again, from business executives, government officials, and opinion leaders inside and outside India. Today, almost seventy years since shaking off the yoke of British imperialism, India is reclaiming its historical prominence in the world economy. It has congratulated itself for "rising" and "shining"— but is it doing so as quickly or as brightly as it should?

As *Reimagining India* goes to print, there is growing anxiety, fueled by a severe market downturn, that the burst of economic liberation of the 1990s and the decade of rapid growth that followed have given way to deadlock and complacency. Manmohan Singh, the celebrated architect of the 1990 reforms and now India's prime minister, has vowed to "take all possible steps" and do "whatever is necessary" to curb government spending and stabilize the economy. But the questions linger: What steps are possible for India? What is the nation's true potential? And what can be done to unlock it?

This book is an effort to encourage discussion and debate about those questions. *Reimagining India* follows the spirit and format of *Reimagining Japan*, a McKinsey-edited essay collection published in the wake of the "triple disasters" of earthquake, tsunami, and nuclear crisis that struck Japan in 2011. As with the Japan book, we have sought wisdom from many dimensions, social and cultural as well as economic and political. We have solicited essays from India's leading business executives, CEOs of some of the world's largest multinationals, economists, investors, entrepreneurs, scholars, journalists, artists, and athletes. Readers will, of course, find essays here on the strengths and weaknesses of India's political system; growth prospects for India's economy; the competitiveness of Indian firms; and Indian foreign policy. Other con-

> There is mounting frustration that the burst of economic liberalization of the 1990s and the rapid growth in the first decade of this century have given way to deadlock and complacency.

tributions explore how India might harness the power of new technologies, improve its infrastructure, expand access to health care, revamp its educational system, rethink its energy strategy, and halt destruction of its environment. But there are also essays on "softer" topics such as Bollywood, cricket, Indian cuisine, chess, classical dance, and India's bid for a stronger performance in the Olympics. The result, we think, is a collection of ideas and expertise without parallel in any other volume.

These are independent voices. McKinsey made no effort to censor or influence the views of any contributors other than to press them to express their ideas as sharply and clearly as possible. While McKinsey consultants have contributed a few essays to this volume, *Reimagining India* is not the product of a McKinsey study; neither is it meant as a "white paper" nor coherent set of policy proposals. Rather, our aim was to create a platform for others to engage in an open, free-wheeling debate about India's future.

No vision for India's future can be complete without an awareness of India's extraordinary past. The subcontinent was home to some of the most sophisticated early human civilizations. Critics of India's modern infrastructure would do well to recall that inhabitants of Mohenjo-Daro and Rakhigarhi built the world's first-known urban sanitation systems five thousand years ago and may have been the first to use wheeled transport. For centuries after Alexander's departure, India was governed by powerful Hindu dynasties who patronized the arts and took keen interest in religion, philosophy, and practical science. Megasthenes, the first Western historian to venture beyond the Punjab into the Gangetic plain, described a land so verdant and fertile that "famine has never visited India and there has never been a general scarcity in the supply of nourishing food."[1] Venetian traveler Marco Polo, who claimed to have visited several ports in India during his 1292 voyage from China to Persia, declared Malabar (now Kerala) on India's southwest coast to be the "richest and most splendid province in the world."

---

[1] J. W. McCrindle, *Ancient India as Described by Megasthenes and Arrian* (Trubner & Co., 1877), p. 32.

In 1603, when English merchant John Mildenhall presented himself at the court of Akbar, the Mughal emperor, clutching a letter of introduction from Queen Elizabeth, Mughal India was the world's richest nation, accounting for as much as a quarter of the global economy.[2] Akbar, whose empire stretched from Kabul in the north to the Deccan Plateau in the south, was by far the world's most powerful man. At his court in Fatehpur Sikri, notes British historian Alex von Tunzelmann, Akbar lived in "unmatched opulence . . . in rooms done out with marble, sandalwood and mother-of-pearl, cooled by the gentle fanning of peacock feathers." By comparison, Elizabeth was "a weak and feeble woman" who ruled over a "grubby, unsophisticated, cold, dismal little kingdom."[3]

And yet, a century and a half later, that dismal little kingdom was a rising naval power and the Mughals in disarray. By 1757, the East India Company, the fledgling British firm Elizabeth granted a royal charter to trade with India, was strong enough to seize control of the entire subcontinent. Direct administrative authority for India was transferred to the British crown after a bloody uprising in 1857, where it remained until India emerged as an independent nation in 1947.

Many of our authors cite the transition from colony to nation as India's original act of imagination. With its riot of different races, religions, languages, and castes, India was, in its first decades, mostly an idea in the minds of its founders. As Fareed Zakaria reminds us in this volume's opening essay, pre-independence India was a loose confederation of shifting power centers, alliances, and local traditions—nothing like the single-religion, single-culture nations of Europe. There was no guarantee modern India would hold together. The efforts of Jawaharlal Nehru, India's first prime minister, to portray India as a diverse but unified polity, tracing a line from the early years of Indus Valley civilizations all the way to modern day, were mostly wishful thinking.

In its first three decades, India was beset by wars on multiple borders

---

[2] Angus Madison, *The World Economy*, vols. 1-2 (OECD Publishing, 2006), p. 638.
[3] Alex von Tunzelmann, *Indian Summer: The Secret History of the End of an Empire* (Henry Holt, 2007), p. 13.

and numerous tribal insurgencies and separatist movements that threatened to pull the nation asunder. The overwhelming preoccupation of its leaders was consolidating control of the central government. That effort overreached most spectacularly under the prime ministership of Nehru's daughter, Indira Gandhi, whose efforts to weaken regional political rivals and tighten the central government's grip only fanned the flames of rebellion.

Early approaches to economic policy followed a similar dynamic. Nehru's thinking about the relationship between the state and private enterprise was steeped in ideas of Fabian socialism that had captivated him as an undergraduate at Cambridge; he was an ardent admirer of Soviet-style central planning. Indian business leaders contributing to this volume can attest to the difficulties of trying to run a business under India's "license raj," the elaborate tangle of permits, permissions, and regulatory red tape that stifled nearly any form of entrepreneurial activity in the first four decades after independence. A 1991 balance of payments crisis—and the humiliation of the Reserve Bank of India being required to airlift sixty-seven tons of gold to London to secure an emergency loan from the International Monetary Fund—forced the government of Prime Minister Narasimha Rao to loosen its stranglehold on a host of key industries.

Those reforms may have been compelled by crisis but, as Reliance CEO Mukesh Ambani points out, they were "visionary and bold"—as the rapid growth of Reliance itself underscores. Indeed, liberalization, and the burst of entrepreneurialism and growth that followed, can be described as India's first effort to "reimagine" itself.

The premise of this book is that powerful forces at work since the 1991 reforms—and partly accelerated by them—have created another moment for "visionary and bold" change. Growth, globalization, and the spread of technology are bringing India together in a way that facilitates new conversations about a collective national future—conversations that might not have resonated twenty or even ten years ago. Zakaria is one of many observers who hails the expansion of India's middle class—a group "whose interests transcend region, caste and religion"—as a powerful force for unification; indeed, he sees the recent spate of mass demonstrations in India, protesting official corruption and the brutal rape of a young woman in Delhi, as calls by a unified middle class for the Indian government to fulfill its basic duties. Popular culture, too, has played an important role in bringing Indians together, as explored in the essays by writer Jerry Pinto on Bollywood and sports broadcaster Harsha Bhogle on cricket.

But it must also be said that the idea of India itself has inherent power. Over time, Indians have embraced the notion that, whatever their other differences, they are part of a single nation. Brown University political science professor Ashutosh Varshney argues in his essay that "regional diversity no longer poses an existential threat to India. The primary objective of India's federal design was to weave a nation out of its many diverse parts and protect national integrity. In that, India's federalism has largely succeeded." As *Indian Express* editor Shekhar Gupta puts it: "It is only now when India has subsumed its many rebellions and moved on from the politics of anger and grievance to the politics of hope and aspiration, that our nation is in a position to leverage its success as a liberal, diverse democracy."

What better moment, then, for a new round of reimagining?

The essays in this volume make clear India has no shortage of urgent challenges. Among the issues raised by our contributors:

The role of the state: Gurcharan Das, a libertarian and former head of Procter & Gamble's India operations, argues that India can't fully unleash the creative power of its businesses and entrepreneurs without help from a strong liberal state. For decades, he argues, India's private sector has celebrated its ability to succeed despite overregulation and bureaucratic meddling, an idea expressed in the aphorism that "India grows at night" when the government is sleeping. "How," he asks, "can a nation maintain robust economic growth with a weak, flailing state? Shouldn't India also grow during the day? . . . Succeeding despite the state may be heroic, but it is not sustainable."

Morgan Stanley emerging markets expert Ruchir Sharma, however, argues that the solution for India is further decentralization. India's states and regions must be left to pursue their own economic policies, he contends. "The rise of the states is a sign of India's maturity. . . . In an increasingly federal nation, the dynamism of the state leaders is countering the ineffectiveness of the center." Industrialist Anand Mahindra agrees: "The best way to propel the economy may be to encourage different parts of the country to go their own way."

MIT scholar Yasheng Huang, for his part, takes issue with the oft-heard assertion that the reason China's economy has grown more rapidly than India's is that the former has one-party rule and an authoritarian government while the latter is a democracy. Democracy does no harm to growth, Huang insists; he dismisses the notion that authoritarian regimes are better able to engineer economic miracles as a "fable" predicated on a flawed analysis of political and economic data.

Embracing competition: Many contributors lament India's ambivalence about competition. Several note India's reluctance to allow foreign multinationals into Indian markets. But Harsha Bhogle's essay on cricket examines how creating greater equality of opportunity helped make India a global superpower in the game. Geet Sethi considers what it will take for India to field a contingent of truly competitive Olympic athletes. Novelist Manu Joseph, meanwhile, highlights the hypocrisy of India's middle classes, who decry family patronage in politics and reservations for members of disadvantaged castes, while they themselves live in a "paradise" of entitlement and protected privileges.

The quest for inclusive growth: A recurrent theme in many essays is the importance of ensuring that the benefits of economic growth are widely shared. Authors acknowledge there are no easy solutions to this challenge, but many express hope that technology can help India close the gap between rich and poor. Education is one area where technology has vast potential to reduce inequality. Digital educators Salman Khan and Shantanu Sinha contend the world is on the verge of another "printing press moment," which will break the elite's grip on the essentials of education, making available to millions of aspiring learners online knowledge and ideas once restricted to the lecture halls of Harvard or Stanford. K. Srinath Reddy sees similar possibilities in health care, citing the example of the Swasthya Slate, a tablet device that enables users to perform various diagnostic tests including electrocardiograms, as well as blood sugar, blood pressure, and heart rate readings. Former Infosys CEO Nandan Nilekani, now head of the government's unique identity program, explains how his agency is using digital and biometric technologies to help low-income Indians gain access to government services and benefits to which they are entitled.

Innovation and leapfrogging: Venture capitalist Vinod Khosla is one of a number of authors who argue that as a developing nation India should employ a "leapfrog mentality" to find unique new pathways to a better future—not only in education and health, but in areas like energy and infrastructure. So, for example, rather than blindly following in the footsteps of developed countries by trying to build more highways to accommodate more cars, India should think about what would be the best transportation system for self-driving vehicles. Khosla is one of several authors who urge India to do more to help new players and entrepreneurs rather than simply conferring benefits on established firms.

Sustainable development: Former Shell Oil executive Vikram Singh Mehta deplores India's counterproductive, contradictory energy policies. Vedanta chairman Anil Agarwal wonders why India lags so far behind in exploring its vast mineral wealth. Historian Ramachandra Guha counters that over the past twenty years India has rolled back many of the sustainable environmental policies it had begun to put in place, and is encouraging a Western-style consumer culture that imperils the planet's future. "India today," he writes, "is an environmental basket case, marked by polluted skies, dead rivers, falling water tables, ever-increasing amounts of untreated wastes, disappearing forests."

Finding India's place in the world: We are delighted to be able to feature in this volume essays by an extraordinary lineup of foreign policy thinkers.

Bill Emmott urges India to revive Nehru's expansive vision for India as regional leader in Asia. Stephen P. Cohen, Ahmed Rashid, and Bruce Riedel offer specific advice on how to fine-tune India's relations with, respectively, Pakistan, Afghanistan, and the United States.

A team of McKinsey consultants makes the case that India's companies, too, must take a more expansive international role—and offers a number of specific suggestions for how they might do so. Aditya Birla Group CEO Kumar Mangalam Birla shares his experiences leading one of Indian's most successful global transformations—and confides that one of his most unexpected challenges was deciding whether to put meat on the menu in company cafeterias.

Menus are also on the mind of restaurateur Rohini Dey, who offers a ringing manifesto for transforming foreign perceptions of Indian food, banishing "$8.99 all-you-can-eat buffets" with "mushy, overcooked fare swimming in oil and nuclear food dyes" so that Indian food may take its rightful place as a genuinely global cuisine. Ogilvy CEO Christopher J. Graves, meanwhile, shares his thoughts about "Brand India," arguing that the "Incredible !ndia" campaign could use a dose of credibility.

Defining India's identity: Anand Giridharadas explores a different dimension of the Indian identity. The focus of his interest is not national but individual—how Indians are reimagining themselves. For individuals, he argues, the Indian dream is "the dream of self-invention: of having the freedom and the means of authoring yourself into being. Your caste, your class, your native place, your religion, your parents' occupation, your family dietary habits—all these things be damned. It is the dream of becoming yourself, free of history and judgment and guilt."

In a way, India as a nation is engaged in something like that. Some of the deepest questions in Indian religion and philosophy swirl around the idea of karma. In its most simplistic form, the notion of karma suggests one's destiny is fated, predetermined by some prior act in another existence. But karma also provides for free will and the possibility that through one's own choices and actions, one can influence the trajectory of fate. What we find so heartening about all the essays in this volume is that they remind us that modern India is in control of its own destiny. India's people hold the power to unlock their nation's full potential.

Achieving that vision, however, will require all Indians to work together. Bill Gates, in his essay, recounts how India's people did exactly that in fighting polio. About that effort, he writes: "India has shown the world that when its people set an ambitious goal, mobilize the country, and measure the impact, India's promise is endless. . . . India has miles to go in this quest, by any measure, but it has shown it has the will and means to realize its full potential."

We couldn't agree more.

—August 2013

chapter one

reimagining

the rediscovery of india
Fareed Zakaria

Is India even a country? It's not an outlandish question. "India is merely a geographical expression," Winston Churchill said in exasperation. "It is no more a single country than the Equator." The founder of Singapore, Lee Kuan Yew, recently echoed that sentiment, arguing that "India is not a real country. Instead it is thirty-two separate nations that happen to be arrayed along the British rail line."

India gives diversity new meaning. The country contains at least fifteen major languages, hundreds of dialects, several major religions, and thousands of tribes, castes, and subcastes. A Tamil-speaking Brahmin from the south shares little with a Sikh from Punjab; each has his own language, religion, ethnicity, tradition, and mode of life. Look at a picture of independent India's first cabinet and you will see a collection of people, each dressed in regional or religious garb, each with a distinct title that applies only to members of his or her community (Pandit, Sardar, Maulana, Babu, Rajkumari).

Or look at Indian politics today. After every parliamentary election over the last two decades, commentators have searched in vain for a national trend or theme. In fact, local issues and personalities dominate from state to state. The majority of India's states are now governed by regional parties—defined on linguistic or caste lines—that are strong in one state but have little draw in any other. The two national parties, the

Fareed Zakaria is host of CNN's Fareed Zakaria GPS, *an editor-at-large for* Time *magazine, and author of* The Post-American World.

Indian National Congress and the BJP, are now largely confined in their appeal to about ten states each.

And yet, there are those who passionately believe that there is an essential "oneness" about India. Perhaps the most passionate and articulate of them was Jawaharlal Nehru, India's first prime minister. During one of his many stints in jail, fighting for Indian independence, he wrote *The Discovery of India*, a personal interpretation of Indian history but one with a political agenda. In the book, Nehru details a basic continuity in India's history, starting with the Indus Valley civilization of 4500 BCE, running through Ashoka's kingdom in the third century BCE, through the Mughal era, and all the way to modern India. He describes an India that was always diverse and enriched by its varied influences, from Buddhism to Islam to Christianity.

Nehru well understood India's immense diversity—and its disunity. He had to deal with it every day in trying to create a national political movement. The country's chief divide, between Hindus and Muslims, was to create havoc with his and Mahatma Gandhi's dreams for a united India. But he was making the intellectual case for India as a nation as the essential background for its national independence. And he had a good case to make. India has existed as a coherent geographical and political entity, comprising large parts of what is modern India, for thousands of years. Despite its dizzying diversity, the country has its own distinct culture. Perhaps that's why, for all its troubles, India has endured.

Where Nehru and Churchill were both wrong was in their political conception of the nation-state itself. India could not follow the example of the European single-ethnic, single-religion nations that sprouted up in the nineteenth century. The British unified India using technology—the railroad—and arms. That nationalizing trend produced, in turn, a unified national opposition to British rule in the Indian National Congress, bringing together all India's communities against foreign rule. But all this was a historical aberration. India had existed as a loose confederation for much of its history. Even when there had been a ruler in the national capital, he had exercised power by co-opting vassals, allowing regions autonomy, letting local traditions flourish. It was a laissez-faire nation in every sense. Despite the rise and fall of dynasties, the entry and exit of empires, village life in India was remarkably continuous—and unaffected by national politics. "India has historically been a strong society with a weak state," says Gurcharan Das, the CEO turned author and philosopher.

Modern India went down a different path. Nehru and many of his contemporaries were deeply influenced by nineteenth-century European nationalism and twentieth-century European socialism. They could not conceive of modern India without a powerful national government. The centralizing impulses were more forceful in the economic than in the political sphere, where local leaders were often strong and autonomous. Even so, by the late 1960s, the Congress started losing ground to regional parties, first in the south on linguistic grounds and then later to caste-based parties in the north. The harder the Congress tried to fight this tendency, the greater the local backlash. This opposition to New Delhi reached its zenith under Nehru's daughter, Indira Gandhi, who as prime minister attempted an extreme form of centralized rule in the 1970s, dismissing dozens of local governments, hoping to crush or co-opt regional parties. The result was half a dozen violent secessionist movements in the north, south, east, and west, one of which claimed her life in 1984.

Over the last twenty years, India has been moving toward a different model of nationhood. The power of regions and regional parties is now undisputed. Starting in the early 1990s, New Delhi has been overturning the license-permit-quota raj and opening up the economy. The result is an India that is quite different from the one its founders might have imagined—a motley collection of communities, languages, and ethnicities living together in an open political and economic space. Some older nationalists find this new India too marketized, decentral-

> Over the last twenty years, India has been moving toward a different model of nationhood; the power of regions and regional parties is now undisputed.

ized, noisy, vulgar, and messy, but it reflects India's realities and, for that reason, it has tremendous resilience.

Now, without central plan or direction, there are forces pushing India toward a greater sense of nationalism than before. Economic liberalization has created a national economy, and technology is creating a national culture. While there has been a proliferation of regional television channels for news and entertainment, there is also a growing set of national programs and media events. From cricket to Bollywood, a common popular culture pervades every Indian's life. As India grows, its people will discover that there is much that distinguishes them from other Asian countries—and that binds them together.

Economic growth has created one more common element in the country—an urban middle class whose interests transcend region, caste, and religion.

This is already having political consequences. Between 2011 and 2013, millions of Indians took to the streets to protest, first against corruption and then against the brutal gang rape and murder of a twenty-three-year-old woman in Delhi. The people marching came from cities and towns. In the past, mass agitations in India often originated in the countryside, with farmers petitioning for government largesse or some groups—defined by caste or religion—asking for special rights. The recent protests have a different quality: They ask the government to fulfill its basic duties. They seek an end to the corruption that is rife throughout the Indian political and bureaucratic system. They ask not for special government programs for women but rather simply that the police and courts function efficiently so that rape victims actually get the justice they deserve.

Most of India's wealth is generated from its cities and towns. Urban India accounts for almost 70 percent of the country's GDP. But almost 70 percent of its people still live in rural India. "As a consequence," writes Ashutosh Varshney of Brown University, "for politicians, the city has primarily become a site of extraction, and the countryside is predominantly a site of legitimacy and power. The countryside is where the vote is; the city is where the money is."

The United States is a middle-class society. Most of the country considers itself middle class and politicians cater to that vast group in every speech and policy proposal. In India, politicians have generally pandered to the villager. No party has a serious urban agenda, but all have elaborate rural schemes. Popular culture used to reinforce this divide. Village life in traditional Bollywood movies reflected simplicity and virtue. Cities were centers of crime and conflict, controlled by a small, wealthy, often debauched elite.

This focus on the rural poor has, ironically, been one of the major obstacles to alleviating poverty. For decades the national political parties handed out lavish subsidies for work, food, and energy—among other things—thus distorting all these markets and perpetuating many of India's basic economic problems. Even after India's economic reforms started, these patronage schemes continued and this mentality has often taken precedence over good governance, efficient regulations, and fiscal sanity. Policies that actually alleviate poverty by promoting economic growth are often enacted quietly and are even guiltily called "stealth reform" by their advocates. In a broader sense, too much of the political elite still thinks of India as a poor, third-world country, a victim of larger global forces rather than one of the world's emerging great powers that could and should be governed by the highest standards.

The middle class itself has played into this narrative, traditionally thinking it was politically irrelevant and so adopting an apolitical stance. Its response to India's problems was to expect little of government. Rather than demanding better government schools, they sent their kids to expensive private academies. Rather than trusting the police, they hired security guards for their homes and neighborhoods. Rather than running for office themselves, they didn't bother to vote and pined for the authoritarian efficiency of Singapore or, now, China.

But twenty years of strong economic growth have transformed the country. The Indian middle class now numbers more than 250 million; over 30 percent of the population of 1.2 billion lives in urban areas. And these numbers are growing fast. Indian movies are now often focused on this group, seen as young, aspiring, and filled with idealism and ambition.

Globalization has raised the expectations that this new urban middle class has for itself and its government. The opening of the Indian economy has exposed them to a new world—a world in which other countries like India are growing fast, building modern infrastructure, and establishing efficient government. Whereas they used to assume that to get rich one needed political connections, today they can dare simply to have good ideas and work hard. India is still a parochial country—for good reason, given its size and internal complexity—but this middle class sees no reason why its democracy shouldn't work for them too.

Globalization has raised the expectations of India's new urban middle class.

Technology is giving them the power to make their voices heard, even when outnumbered by other interest groups. India is unusual in combining the growth of an emerging market with the openness of a freewheeling democracy. (China has the former but not the latter.) The result has been an information explosion. The country boasts more than 170 television news channels, in dozens of languages. Three-quarters of the population has mobile phones. Texting and similar methods have now become a routine way to petition government, organize protests, and raise awareness. The Aadhaar program (*aadhaar* means "foundation" in Hindi), spearheaded by India's tech pioneer Nandan Nilekani, which will give every Indian a unique biometric identity, could have a much larger impact than imagined. Its stated goal is to make it possible for Indians to get the rights and benefits they deserve, without middlemen, corruption, or inefficiency blocking their path. But it could also make it possible for Indians to think of themselves for the first time as individuals, not merely members of a religion, caste, or tribe.

Many foreign observers, particularly Western businesspeople, look at India today and despair. The country simply cannot reform at the pace necessary to fulfill its ambitions for growth and progress. Everything gets mired in political paralysis, and the governing class remains committed to a politics of patronage and pandering. This is all true and deeply unfortunate. But it is a snapshot of today's reality, not a moving picture of an evolving society. In states as disparate as Gujarat, Odisha, and Bihar, state governments are aggressively promoting economic growth. And this is not simply a story about Narendra Modi, the controversial chief minister of Gujarat. That state of sixty million people has grown faster than China over the last two decades—with three different chief ministers. India itself, for all its problems, has been one of the fastest-growing large economies in the world over that period.

Can the country live up to its potential? If so, it will happen only because of a bottom-up process of protest and politics that forces change in New Delhi. India will never be a China, a country where the population is homogeneous and where a ruling elite directs the nation's economic and political development. In China, the great question is whether the new president, Xi Jinping, is a reformer—he will need to order change, top-down, for that country.

In India, the questions are different: Are Indians reformers? Can millions of people mobilize and petition and clamor for change? Can they persist in a way that makes reform inevitable? That is the only way change will come in a big, open, raucous democracy like India. And when that change comes, it is likely to be more integrated into the fabric of the country and thus more durable.

I remain optimistic. We are watching the birth of a new sense of nationhood in India, drawn from the aspiring middle classes in its cities and towns, who are linked together by commerce and technology. They have common aspirations and ambitions, a common Indian dream—rising standards of living, good government, and a celebration of India's diversity. That might not be as romantic a basis for nationalism as in days of old, but it is a powerful and durable base for a modern country that seeks to make its mark on the world.

breakout or washout?
Ruchir Sharma

On the new highway into Ahmedabad, the largest city of the western state of Gujarat, the sun sets red in your eyes, just as it does in the polluted industrial zones of China. The city ranks alongside Chengdu and Chongqing as one of the fastest growing in the world. Factories sprout from the farmlands on its outskirts: Gujarat generates about 40 percent of its income from industry, more like China than India as a whole. The state is home to many of the largest ports in India, just as China is now home to most of the largest ports in the world.

Narendra Modi, Gujarati Chief Minister since 2001, is seen as a can-do autocrat, admired by businesspeople but loathed by human rights activists because of the deadly 2002 riots against the state's Muslim minority. Now touted as a potential prime minister, Modi has inspired fears among many liberal-minded Indians that he would make the country more like China: more growth oriented but also more centrally controlled and possibly less democratic.

But because of India's natural social fabric, with its incredible diversity and numerous distinct identities, the future of India looks less likely to unfold on the uniform China model than the looser, pluralistic European model—not the debt-strangled Europe of the last two years but the successful Europe of the postwar years, a federation that brought peace, political stability, and widespread prosperity to a diverse continent.

Ruchir Sharma is head of the emerging markets equity team at Morgan Stanley Investment Management and the author of Breakout Nations: In Pursuit of the Next Economic Miracles.

Since India began to grow at a reasonably fast speed in the early 1990s, it has come to see itself as the democratic world's answer to China, potentially both prosperous and free. It can still achieve that dream, but to do so it cannot go back to the centrally controlled model that failed to produce strong growth in the early decades after independence in 1947.

For India to become what I have called a "breakout nation"—one that grows faster than rival economies in the same per capita income class, and posts consistently higher growth rates than investors expect for economies in that bracket—it must abandon its tendency to become self-satisfied and make excuses. Ever since India left behind the sluggish "Hindu rate of growth" three decades ago, it has portrayed itself as an ambitious nation, with a growing middle class eager to rise up in the global ranks. But as the poorest of the big emerging markets, with a per capita income of just $1,500, India is hardly overachieving; it is always easier to grow fast from a low base. Since the early 1980s, when the government cut back its monopoly on most imports and started easing rules about who could manufacture what and in which quantities, India has finished each decade with an average GDP growth rate about 1 to 2 percentage points faster than the emerging market average. That is unusually consistent but not particularly impressive—it's standard for emerging nations in India's low-income class.

After two strong decades, India's economy has slowed down this decade, ebbing along with the world economy. Once again, India is floating with the global tide, but this is not inevitable. China, Taiwan, Korea, and Japan have shown that it is possible to grow at a near double-digit pace for three or more decades, regardless of whether the global economy is hot or cold. They did so with policies that promoted rapid urbanization and the rise of manufacturing, as India should now. For thirty years after Deng Xiaoping came to power, China pushed reform in good times and bad, outperforming the global economy by a consistently impressive margin, with its economy growing at an annual pace of 4 to 5 percentage points faster than the emerging market average.

India has been typical of most other developing countries, which reform only in a crisis and fritter away the gains when things are going well. In India, this boom-crisis-reform cycle has followed a steady pattern, going back to the crippling stagflation of the late 1970s, which inspired the first reforms of the so-called license raj early in the next decade. Now the cycle is turning again. As the rupee weakens and ratings agencies threaten to downgrade India's debt to junk status, India is slipping in the emerging market GDP growth and inflation rankings. That has forced Prime Minister Manmohan Singh—the architect of India's early 1990s liberalization of the economy—to start reforming again, this time lowering fuel subsidies and further opening sectors such as retail and civil aviation to foreign companies.

India has been typical of most other developing countries, which reform only in a crisis and fritter away the gains when things are going well.

It's not clear these reforms will be enough to put India on a self-sustaining growth path. Singh has tended to dismiss India's growing problems with corruption and inflation as the natural side effects of rapid growth, even though these problems are much worse in India than in other nations at the same stage of development.

Other Indian policy makers explain away the government's failure to pursue economic reform as consistently as China by saying that a democracy can't command change the way an autocracy can. But plenty of democracies have gotten reform right, including Poland and the Czech Republic since they broke free of the Soviet empire. The general rule is clear: In the 124 nations that, since 1980, generated growth faster than 5 percent a year for at least a decade, about half were democracies and half were authoritarian regimes. Democracy is no excuse for a failure to act.

Still others claim India can't sustain tough reform because its people are not disciplined and predictable like the apparently dull East Europeans. Indians are more chaotic, colorful, and moody. But economists used cultural explanations to write off Mao's China in the 1960s as a Confucian society too wedded to traditional ways to modernize fast, and look how that turned out.

India tends to overreact to both good times and bad. It seriously misread the strong growth of the 2000s as a sign of sure prosperity to come. In fact, this was a highly unusual decade, when virtually all the emerging economies started to grow quickly as they recovered from the serial financial crises of the 1990s, with a huge boost from easy money flowing out of the United States and Europe. India was lifted by this global boom, not by the managerial genius of New Delhi. History shows that only a third of all emerging nations are likely to post growth faster than 5 percent in any given decade, much less for two or three decades. The longer a boom lasts, the less likely it is to continue. The result is that over time, emerging markets are not "catching up" to the rich, as many seem to think. Their average incomes are the same relative to rich nation incomes as in 1950.

In the last decade, some of India's policy moves reduced the likelihood of another good decade. The ruling elite focused its energy on trying to build a welfare state that India can't really afford. The Congress government has been throwing money at expensive populist schemes like the one that guarantees every poor Indian at least one hundred days a year of paid work. Over the past decade, even after adjusting for inflation, government spending has doubled—a trend that is simply not sustainable.

It's no accident that, despite its steady GDP growth, India has fallen dramatically in rankings of the size of government deficits and inflation rates, the cancer that has killed growth in many star economies of the emerging world. On the IMF ranking of nations by rate of inflation, India plunged to 122nd in 2012, from an average ranking of 65 between 1980 and 2010. This isn't a natural side effect of fast growth, as Singh would have it. Low inflation has been the hallmark of sustained economic success from Japan in the 1960s to China in recent times, because strong investment creates the capacity that allows the economy to meet rising demand without higher prices. India now spends a relatively healthy 7.5 percent of GDP on investment in infrastructure, but mostly by the government, which hardly does a great job of building capacity.

Another manifestation of this increasingly top-heavy central government is the spread of crony capitalism. Indian politicians often dismiss this problem, too, as a standard and expected offshoot of growth, but it is possible to judge whether a country is abnormally corrupt. Corruption should decline as a country gets less poor, yet on various international surveys, corruption appears to be getting worse in India, which has fallen on the Transparency International rankings from seventy-second in 2007 to ninety-fourth in 2012. The rise of crony capitalism is also reflected on the *Forbes* lists of top billionaires, which shows very little turnover in recent years, with most of the newcomers emerging from politically connected industries like mining and real estate.

Headlines often celebrate when Indian companies "go global," but this may also suggest that businesses are fleeing a corrupt and stagnant market at home. The signals are mixed for India, but at least two key indicators send a warning: Indian firms are investing more heavily in foreign markets, and spending much more to acquire foreign firms, than foreign companies are investing and spending in India. With its vast and largely untapped consumer market, India should be much more attractive to investors, Indian and foreign. It is particularly important for India to generate more investment in manufacturing—the foundation for job growth in most emerging economies. Manufacturing represents an anemic 13 percent of the economy, at least 6 percentage points below where it should be at India's stage of development.

> Corruption should decline as a country gets less poor, yet it appears to be getting worse in India.

India's current administration has been in power nine years, the point at which even some of the best governments tend to lose their way as economic managers. For inspiration, leaders in Delhi should be studying how an increasing number of smart, dynamic chief ministers are using the power granted to them since the fall of the license raj to ignite state economies. Voters are rewarding these leaders with multiple terms in office. There are now about half a dozen chief ministers who have been in office at least three terms—a feat virtually unheard of in the 1980s and 1990s—and they are returning India to its natural condition: a federation of diverse states like Europe. This was the state of affairs in the seventeenth century, when what we now call India was at the height of its Mughal power—an empire of many autonomous states.

Before independence in 1947, India was divided into eleven large provinces and hundreds of princely states, all with varying degrees of autonomy. Afterward, independence leader Jawaharlal Nehru tried to unify a nation riven by secessionist movements and deep poverty by imposing Soviet-style central planning. He got unity, but with desperately inadequate economic growth of just 3 percent a year. Thankful to the founding Nehru-Gandhi dynasty and its Congress party for liberating their nation, Indians resigned themselves to enduring poverty.

But times changed. The advent of satellite TV and the Internet began feeding Indian aspirations for a richer life. Slow growth made it difficult for India to earn the foreign currency it needed to pay for imports, leading to the financial crisis in 1991 that forced the Congress party to start lifting central controls—which gave state leaders more freedom to push economic development. Before this turn, the chief ministers had focused on building political support through appeals to religion and caste, the touchstones of Indian identity. Afterward, they realized that they could create a more enduring support base by catering to rising economic aspirations, which cut across caste boundaries. Now, these mass-based regional leaders are building strong state economies from Gujarat on the Arabian Sea all the way to Bihar on the Nepalese border.

The successful ones are pursuing economic growth strategies that fit the unique competitive advantages of each region. In Odisha, Naveen Patnaik is building steel industries on the local deposits of iron ore and bauxite. In Bihar, Nitish Kumar is focused on improving the yields of the state's fertile soil and moving up the chain from growing food to processing packaged food for a higher price.

There is no European-style debate pitting the free market versus government, because in India the issues are still very basic. It's about moving from "povertarian" politics—arguing over which patron has done more to help the poor—to creating the roads, the schools, and the bedrock of macroeconomic stability that will encourage businesses to invest. One of the main reasons India's federal deficit has been growing and is now about 5 percent of GDP, while state deficits have been shrinking and now average 2.5 percent of state GDP, is that the strong governments on the state level have the clout to make tough economic decisions.

The first states to prosper from the fall of the license raj were the richest ones of the south and west coasts, which already had strong industrial bases. Now the center of rapid growth is shifting north and inland, to formerly backward states where popular autocrats are taking charge. That includes Bihar, Odisha, Chhattisgarh, Madhya Pradesh, and others. The average growth rate of those northern states accelerated from 2.2 percent in the 1990s to 9.1 percent over the past decade, while India's national growth rate gained just two percentage points.

If anything, the rise of the states is a sign of India's maturity. Voters no longer worry about the country falling apart and focus instead on pushing India to develop. In an increasingly federal nation, the dynamism of the state leaders is countering the ineffectiveness of the center and changing the economic map of India. In response to their current economic difficulties, most European leaders are pushing for more central power. But India is more likely to break out with less.

toward a uniquely indian growth model
Anand Mahindra

When I listen to pundits, economists, and multinational CEOs talk about India, often I detect a familiar note of frustration. India, they insist, should be blasting upward like a rocket, its growth rate ascending higher and higher, bypassing that of a slowing China's. India's population is younger than that of its Asian rival and still growing. Its democratic government enjoys greater legitimacy; its businesspeople are more internationally adept. And yet the Indian rocket continues to sputter in a low-altitude orbit—growing respectably at 5 to 7 percent each year but never breaking through to sustained double-digit growth.

According to this way of thinking, India is an underachiever, perversely holding itself back—and needs only to fire some particular afterburner in order to get its rocket to full speed. The government needs to go on an infrastructure building spree, or open the door to big-box retailers. Political parties need to crack down on corruption and nepotism. Farmers need to adopt smartphones. *Something* will trigger the long-awaited boom, and the billions in foreign direct investment (FDI) that have flowed to China over the last two decades will at last head south.

If we continue to judge India's progress by China's, using metrics like FDI and GDP growth, or statistics like the kilometers of highway and millions of apartments built, we will continue to be branded a laggard. India's messy coalition governments are not suddenly about to become as efficient and decisive as China's technocrat-led Politburo. Nor should that be the goal.

Anand Mahindra is chairman and managing director of the Mahindra Group.

Moreover, India simply cannot afford to grow like China has over the last two decades. In authoritarian, tightly controlled China, the costs of that headlong economic expansion are obvious. Unbreathable air and undrinkable milk, slick-palmed officials and oppressive factory bosses provoke tens of thousands of protests each year. In a society as diverse as India's—riven by religious, community, and caste divides—those kinds of tensions can easily erupt in violence and disorder. Already the battle between haves and have-nots is driving a powerful rural insurgency across nearly a third of the country. Labor riots can turn into religious pogroms. Farmer protests can turn into class wars.

For India's economy to expand as rapidly and yet more sustainably than China's, we need to make our differences into virtues rather than vulnerabilities. For too long we have clung to a mind-set shaped by the early independence years, when the areas in the northwest and northeast had become Pakistan, and India's first government was struggling to weave a patchwork of provinces and maharaja-run kingdoms into a nation. In those days, the risk that India might break apart was very real. One of India's great accomplishments is that no one worries about that anymore. Indeed, the idea of a united India runs so broad and deep that it allows us to consider a counterintuitive way of thinking about growth—that the best way to propel the economy may be to encourage different parts of the country to go their own way.

> We need to make our differences into virtues rather than vulnerabilities.

I'm not suggesting secession, of course. But there's no sense in pretending that "India" is a single investment destination or even a coherent, unified economic entity. India's twenty-eight states and seven territories are as different from one another—as varied in language, food, culture, and level of development—as the nations of Europe. In some ways, Gujarat has more in common with Germany than with Bihar. Companies understand this. When they make decisions about where to locate factories or R&D hubs, they're looking at the tax policies, physical and legal infrastructure, or labor costs in the particular state they're considering—not at some mythical "India" visible only at Davos. We should be celebrating and encouraging these differences.

Certain states will be able to exploit these new powers better than others, of course, just as certain provinces on China's eastern seaboard have raced ahead of compatriots inland. But in India, success can inspire competition and push laggards to reform—as Bihar, say, has begun to. Though it started from a very low base, the Bihar government's focus on improving basic governance by providing security and enforcing the rule of law has made a remarkable difference. For years, Bihar and three other troubled north Indian states—Madhya Pradesh, Rajasthan, and Uttar Pradesh—were collectively dismissed as BIMARU. The acronym, formed from the first letters of each state, was a wry put-down because it sounded like the Hindi word *bimar*, or "sick." These days, the term no longer serves; not only does Bihar show new vigor, but Madhya Pradesh is now regularly included in rankings of India's best-run states.

> There's no sense in pretending that "India" is a single investment destination or even a coherent, unified economic entity.

All Indian states will have to improve their infrastructure and climate for doing business if they want to contend for major projects. In this way, investment will drive innovation and changes to the system much more efficiently than any edict from Delhi could. Tata Motors' decision to shift its Nano project from West Bengal to Gujarat illustrates the point.

We should encourage a similar competition between cities as well as states. India's biggest long-term challenge, like China's, is to figure out how to urbanize a population of more than a billion people. Millions have already migrated to the cities in the last two decades, and tens of millions more will soon follow. We cannot hope to stem this flow. Nor should we want to—urbanized societies produce an array of positive outcomes, from higher literacy rates to lower infant mortality. At the same time, if we don't slow the influx of migrants to a dozen or so key urban centers, our already volatile and overburdened cities will collapse under the strain.

India needs to find a way to *distribute* growth—to create new urban hubs all over the country that can attract talent and money. Even if government had the power to bulldoze neighborhoods and erect forests of skyscrapers, as some seem to wish, it would struggle to surmount the challenges currently facing big cities like Mumbai and Bangalore. At double or triple the population, those megacities would become ungovernable. We need to break these problems into manageable pieces, developing hundreds, even thousands of smaller cities around the country where the problems of water, transit, power, and governance can be negotiated at the local level. India's sprawling subcontinent can never become a plus-size Singapore. But perhaps we can weave together an urban web that is the equivalent of a thousand Singapores.

Technology is making this more than a fantasy. Given how much India has benefited from the way fiber-optic cables have already shrunk the world, we should be quick to see the opportunities in shrinking the subcontinent, too. With widespread 4G connectivity, many businesses will be able to operate from anywhere. That will create an advantage for locations emphasizing efficiency and livability. Workers will be able to perform their tasks closer to home, if not actually at home, thus relieving pressure on India's roads and bridges. Even manufacturing can be distributed, once technologies like 3-D printing become more widespread. Populations of laborers will no longer need to cluster around big factories. Indeed, once every home can become a manufacturing hub, the kind of small enterprises that have been the backbone of the traditional Indian economy could find ways to thrive in the modern world.

Forced to compete for talent and for business, cities will have to experiment and innovate. Several corporations, including Mahindra, have begun exploring new ways to live, work, and play in planned enclaves like Mahindra World City outside Chennai. While these efforts are continuing, the government too should foster and support such experimentation as a matter of urban policy. Already the government taxes coal and fossil fuels used in the power and transportation industries, and offers tax incentives for renewable energy and nonpolluting vehicles. But we can go farther, finding new ways to use technology to improve and expand the delivery of government services. The government's Unique Identification project, which uses biometric data such as photographs, fingerprints, and retinal scans to create cost-effective and easily verifiable ID numbers for all Indian residents, is an excellent example of how government can leverage technology to help India's citizens. These new numbers will make it easier for Indians to pay taxes, collect government benefits, and receive other government services. They also will help prevent fraud, bribery, vote rigging, and illegal immigration, as well as facilitate the delivery of many private sector services.

India's new cities will be its afterburners, the catalysts sparking new bursts of growth. The innovations developed in each scattered enclave will be emulated and improved upon elsewhere, and thus give rise to innovation. Rather than directing where capital should go, or funding white-elephant infrastructure projects, the central government should set the rules of the game and then step back.

What India needs from the world as much as investment dollars are bold thinkers who can help to define these new ways of living. We should seek out these visionaries, give them a platform to test their theories, and invite them not to build gaudy skyscrapers but to help develop new ways for the human race to live. Foreign direct *ideas* should be as valued a commodity as traditional FDI.

The world has a stake in India's success—and not just because of the need for someone to pick up the slack from a slowing China. Much of the developing world faces the same challenges India does. The solutions developed here—the answers to almost metaphysical questions about how societies should work and grow—will have worldwide relevance.

For better or worse, India is where the future will be made. Let's get it right.

how to grow during the day
Gurcharan Das

The economic rise of India has been the defining event of my life. It is not only good news for 1.2 billion Indians, but it is also reshaping the world. At a time when Western economies are faltering, a large nation is rising in the East based on political and economic liberty, proving once again that open societies, free trade, and multiplying connections to the global economy are pathways to lasting prosperity and national success.

India and its people, however, have achieved this prosperity in the face of their nation's appalling governance. Indians despair over the state's inability to deliver the most basic public services—law and order, education, health, and clean water. Where it is not needed, however, the bureaucracy is hyperactive, tying people in miles of red tape. Indians cynically sum up this paradox of private success and public failure with an aphorism: "India grows at night while the government sleeps." But how can a nation maintain robust economic growth with a weak, flailing state? Shouldn't India also grow during the day? The recent economic slowdown may indicate that India has begun to experience the limits of growing in the shadows.

india needs a strong liberal state

While India's economic rise has been a remarkable success, lifting tens of millions out of abject poverty, GDP growth is not sufficient for the development of a modern nation. India also needs honest police officers,

Gurcharan Das is an author and commentator. His latest book is India Grows at Night: A Liberal Case for a Strong State.

diligent officials, functioning schools, and primary health-care centers. In short, India needs a strong liberal state with three core elements: the authority to take quick and decisive action, a transparent rule of law to ensure that such action is legitimate, and accountability to the people. This was the original conception of the state as imagined by the classical liberal thinkers who inspired both America's and India's founding fathers, but building a state with all three elements is not easy, as each tends to undermine the other.

Part of the challenge is the citizens' low expectations. In India we seem to have forgotten that the state was created to act: It should not take eight years to build a road when it takes three elsewhere; it should not take ten years to get justice instead of two. Executive decision-making is paralyzed, parliamentary gridlock prevails, and the courts routinely dictate action to the executive. An aggressive civil society and media have enhanced accountability in India, but at the expense of enfeebling the executive.

As a libertarian, for a long time I viewed the weakness of the state with equanimity, for I dismissed the state as a "second-order phenomenon." I believed that while it could and should protect people in private life and in civil society, a state might also destroy those freedoms. As India began its remarkable rise twenty years ago, I celebrated the fact that it was rising despite the government. In the past few years I have come to recognize that the state is in fact of "first-order" importance, essential if its citizens are to flourish. Succeeding despite the state may be heroic, but it is not sustainable.

Furthermore, the state played a greater role in India's rise than is often recognized. India and its people created prosperity thanks to the state, not despite it, because the state quietly provided a modicum of protection for property rights, a degree of personal security, and an acceptable level of law and order. Today, however, that minimal performance is no longer sufficient if India is even to approach its true potential.

What India needs now is a strong, efficient, and enabling state with a robust rule of law and greater accountability. A strong liberal state is efficient in the sense that it enforces fairly and forcefully the rule of law.

It is strong because it has independent regulators who are tough on corruption and ensure that no one is above the law. It is enabling because it delivers services honestly to all citizens. It is a rules-based order with a light, invisible touch over citizens' lives.

the indian state was historically weak

It is a mistake to think that the Indian state was weakened in recent times because of coalition politics, feckless leadership, and economic liberalization. India historically had a weak state, though one counterbalanced by a strong society—the mirror image of China. India's history is one of political disunity with constant struggles among kingdoms, unlike China's history of strong empires. The type of despotic and intrusive governments that emerged in China and divested people of their property and their rights has never existed in India.

India historically had a weak state, counterbalanced by a strong society—the mirror image of China.

The king in Indian history was a distant figure who hardly touched the life of the ordinary person. The law, dharma, preceded the state and placed limits on the king's power in premodern India. The king also did not interpret the law, unlike in China; the Brahmin, a scholar class, assumed that function. This division of powers may have contributed to a weak Indian state at birth, but it also prevented oppression by the state.

The modern Indian state is also a product of British rule, which beginning in the mid-nineteenth century imposed a rule of law with explicit codes and regulations. Though efficient, that state was not accountable to its citizens. That changed in 1947, as independent India took those institutions of governance and made them accountable by developing into a vibrant, if untidy, democracy.

In the twenty-first century, true to its history, India is rising economically from below, quite unlike China, whose success has been scripted from above by an amazing technocratic state. It is also not surprising that India's traditionally strong society is evolving into a vibrant civil one. The mass movement led by the political activist Anna Hazare, which forced India's political elite to consider a strong anticorruption law in 2011, is only the most recent example of a historically weak state colliding with a strong society. A successful nation needs both a strong state and strong society to keep a check on each other.

what is to be done?

Unfortunately, Anna Hazare's movement, with its chanting multitudes inspired by a mystical faith in the collective popular will, might awaken people to the need for reform, but it cannot execute the hard work necessary to transform India's tottering state into a strong, liberal one. The passage of a sweeping anticorruption law was important, but it was only a first step. It will take patient, determined efforts to reform the key institutions of governance—the bureaucracy, judiciary, police, and parliament—along well-known lines articulated by numerous committees. The federal trend, which is shifting power away from the center and to the states, is a virtuous one, as is the slow decentralizing of power and funds downward to foster vigorous, local self-government in villages and municipalities.

But those trends do not address the central issue of how to reform the state institutions. If it is lucky, India might throw up a strong leader who is a reformer of institutions. But Indira Gandhi was a strong leader, and she turned out to be a destroyer of institutions. The next best hope is that the electorate will simply demand reform. The aspiring younger generation, now about a third of the population—and destined to make up half of the electorate in a decade—has no one to vote for because few politicians speak the language of good governance and the common good. The existing parties treat voters as poor, ignorant masses who need to be appeased briefly at election time with populist giveaways and appeal to the victim in the voter.

> The aspiring young are puzzled as to why India offers astonishing religious and political freedom but fails in economic freedom.

With high growth, mobility, and a demographic revolution, Indians who aspire to a better life will soon outnumber those who see themselves as victims. Pew surveys show that a majority of Indians believe that they are better off than their parents and that their children will do even better. The person who got the 900 millionth cell phone number was a village migrant from Uttar Pradesh, one of India's most impoverished states, and no one in India's political life captures his hopes. This rising youthful cohort will no longer accept a civic life shaped by those who are powerful and corrupt. Young Indians also have shown considerable ability in mobilizing media and employing the new technology of social media. Political life is thus set to change.

filling india's political void

Who will fill the empty secular political space at the right of center in Indian politics? The aspiring young are puzzled by the fact that their tolerant nation offers astonishing religious and political freedom but at the same time fails to provide economic freedom. In a country where two out of five people are self-employed, it takes forty-two days to start a business, and the entrepreneur is a victim of endless red tape and corrupt inspectors. No wonder India ranks 119 on the global Index of Economic Freedom and 132 on the World Bank's ease of doing business index.

India reforms furtively because no political party has bothered to explain the difference between being promarket and probusiness, leaving people with the impression that liberal reforms help mostly the rich. They don't understand that a promarket economy fosters competition, which helps keep prices low, raises the quality of products, and leads to a rules-based capitalism that serves everyone. The probusiness mind-set, on the contrary, allows politicians and officials to distort the market's authority over economic decisions, leading to crony capitalism. This confusion explains the timidity of reform and why India does not perform to its potential.

If no existing party can fill the empty space, aspiring India may well demand a new liberal party that trusts markets rather than officials for economic outcomes and relentlessly focuses on the reform of institutions. Such a party may not win votes quickly, but it will bring governance reform to center stage and gradually prove to voters that open markets and rules-based government are the only civilized ways to lift living standards and achieve shared prosperity.

finding india's new moral core

Reforming corrupt government institutions is always difficult but is particularly so in India with its tradition of a weak state. Fortunately, history is not destiny, and people in the end obey the law when they think it is fair and just and because they become morally habituated to it. Obeying the law then becomes a form of self-restraint and character. Therefore, the demand for governance reform must also emerge out of a reinvigorated Indian moral core. The notion of dharma imposed this moral core in premodern India. The task for India's twenty-first-century politics is to recover constitutional morality.

Early in the freedom struggle, Mohandas Gandhi discovered that the liberal language of constitutional morality did not resonate with the masses, but the moral language of dharma did. So, the consummate mythmaker resuscitated the universal ethic of *sadharana dharma*, not unlike the Buddhist emperor Ashoka in the third century BCE, who embarked on a program to build new "habits of the heart" based on *dhamma* (*dharma* in Pali). Gandhi was not able to end untouchability, but he breathed life into the freedom movement. In the same manner, our challenge is make the Constitution a moral mirror by transmitting its ideas to the young as part of a broad citizenship project until they also become habits of the heart.

Impatient voices in India today clamor for a civil war to bring accountability into public life. Although urgent, the current crisis should be addressed not through mobs on the street but through politics and institutional reform. The cautionary message we all should draw from the success of Anna Hazare and his followers in bringing change is that if the political class is not ready to embrace governance as a central platform, then it better be prepared for an uglier revolt.

in search of the indian dream
Anand Giridharadas

Must a country aspiring to significance possess its own bespoke dream? There is an American dream often discussed, although a great many Americans struggle to locate it these days. The French might argue for a dream centered on the preservation, savoring, and endless perfecting of a certain kind of life. For South Africans, perhaps it is the dream of making unitary light of their racial rainbow. Most places, of course, are too small, humble, or stuck in the grind to worry about the nature of their national dream. I have met some Cambodians, for instance, and none spoke a word about the Cambodian dream.

Is there an Indian dream? If so, what is it? Is it, like the street-hawked books at Haji Ali in Mumbai, a pirated dream—a crude cut-and-paste job from some other place's dream? Or is something rich and particular to India surfacing in this era of churn?

There are those who see the Indian dream in civilizational terms: India as a uniquely open-source republic, with a long history of multiplicity and toleration, whose highest purpose now is giving proof that kaleidoscopic pluralism, even if burdened by poverty and illiteracy and disease, can thrive under democracy. One hears a neo-Gandhian version of the dream, in which India returns to the villages, but those villages are reinvented for new realities; a Hindu chauvinist version of the dream, in which pride and the resurrection of a trampled culture are the focus; a

Anand Giridharadas writes the "Currents" column for the New York Times *and is the author of* India Calling: An Intimate Portrait of a Nation's Remaking.

geopolitical version of the dream, in which India, the only nation to get its name on an ocean, superintends the region around it.

But in the time I have spent in India, traversing its cities and villages and market towns, collecting people's tales one gem at a time, a rather different vision of the dream has come to me. It is the dream of self-invention: of having the freedom and the means of authoring yourself into being. Your caste, your class, your native place, your religion, your parents' occupation, your family dietary habits—all these things be damned. It is the dream of becoming yourself, free of history and judgment and guilt.

The dream, presented this way, may seem too small to some. Is there no bigger thing that can be said about a great people than that they desire to become themselves? To which I would answer: The desire to do so rarely feels small to people who cannot.

Let others talk of "bigger" things. The Indian dream, as I've witnessed it again and again, in Jallowal and Bangalore, Mysore and Umred, Verla and Manchar, Mumbai and Kanchipuram, is modest and focused and fiery. It is a million acts of private daring.

The daring happens every time a young woman in a Delhi slum finally says, no, she will not marry that man, no matter how much sense it makes to all these people who won't be there night after night to endure his rum breath and slaps. It happens every time a young man in Pune gets his first cell phone and senses that, for the first time in his life, he has something akin to his own bedroom—a sphere of privacy and individual identity never known before. It happens every time they have one of those personality contests in Umred, and the young contestants, unaccustomed to being asked by adults what they think, walk onstage with a mandate, perhaps for the first time in their lives, to stand out rather than sublimate and blend.

The Indian dream is a million acts of private daring.

It happens, in short, every time someone questions: the authority of elders, the dictates of caste, the way things always were. We tend to think of revolutions as waged against faraway, unknowable powers—feudal lords, gilded kings, bunker-dwelling tyrants. The Indian case belies this imagery. Here the revolution is within—within the skulls of those who resolve, against the odds, to make themselves new; within the family, an institution more guilty of suffocating Indian potential than most people are willing to admit; within the larger clan, which faces new challenges from people desiring—heaven forfend!—to think for themselves.

But there is more to the Indian dream than this centrifugal impulse, this longing for selfhood. Were the dream just this, it would indeed feel like a crude derivation. But the dream is buffeted, as it ought to be, by countervailing currents.

A significant difference between India's period of modernization today and analogous periods in the history of the West is that Indians can see how their forerunners have fared. The West walked blindly into the revolution of selfhood. There was no way to anticipate what it would bring. Today's Indian, by contrast, can look at the changes around her and feel great excitement, but she also can sense how these changes, without careful rethinking, will play out. The afflictions of the West are, after all, no secret.

She may seek more freedom for Indians to love whom they wish and escape bad unions; but she fears her society's going so far as to replicate the West's divorce rates. She may cheer every time an Indian child flouts his parents' commands and pursues the vocation of his choosing; but she worries that the country will lose something if parents come to be ignored and discarded as readily as it appears in the West. She may celebrate a new meritocracy in which it no longer takes the effort of a whole family to push a child into success; but she looks at Western families, which often function like federations of independent contractors, and hesitates to destroy the habit of intergenerational sacrifice and investment. She welcomes more space for solitude in India, more time and freedom to think for oneself; but she considers the atomized, lonely lives she has seen in the West to be equally, oppositely maddening. She embraces the new power of money culture and consumption to challenge India's old hierarchies; but she looks at the West and reflects on how sad it would be if buying stuff became India's principal boulevard to meaning.

I have heard these fears again and again from Indians, in every corner of the country, at all levels of the society. The anxiety arises in a place almost as soon as the revolution is felt, because the saturation of Western popular culture leaves no doubt about where the revolution, undisturbed, will lead. When you stand on an early stretch on the arc of selfhood, more self is almost invariably better. But the examples of the societies at the far end of that arc suggest that more is better only up to a point. And so the question becomes: Where on that arc might the Indian dream lie?

Here we can only wonder, for the negotiations that will answer the question are in their earliest stages, taking place in one living room, one factory, one school at a time. But there does appear to be an emerging Indian synthesis between the longing, on one hand,

> What many Indians seemed to seek was a society that nourishes selfhood without tempting selfishness.

for greater selfhood, and the fear, on the other, of the erosion of family and community connection. After many years living in India, I realized that I was encountering new ways of thinking about the self and the individual neither typically Western nor traditionally Indian. What many Indians seemed to seek was a society that nourishes selfhood without tempting selfishness, and individuality without individualism. These may sound like rather strange distinctions, but they can be meaningful.

Think about the idea of selfhood or individuality as having to do with the opportunity to become the fullest possible expression of oneself; to have voice; to construct oneself through the imagination, without coercion from others or history. This opportunity matters profoundly to the rising generation of Indians, especially in the towns and cities, as it has to similar cohorts all throughout history. Now think of the second idea, of selfishness or individualism, as taking it a step farther: No longer are we talking about the right to become yourself; we're speaking of the right not to factor other people into your plans, to get on in the world by severing yourself from others as needed. It is this latter idea that I have found less meaningful to Indians—and may remain so.

Perhaps this points toward a bespoke Indian dream: a right to invent oneself poised against an enduring sense of duty to others. Perhaps it is already here. Just ask the young woman surfing for her second husband on SecondShaadi.com, while her parents stand behind her and help to edit her sales pitch. Or the young man who refuses to suffer his parents' vegetarianism but also refuses to desert them in their old age. He hires one of India's ever more popular kitchenette builders to construct one for him and his wife in their bedroom, just above Mummy-Papa's. Mummy doesn't want the smell of cooking meat in the house, but she wants her son in the house. They have negotiated a way: He can order non-veg from the outside and reheat it in the microwave if necessary. The dream, at least for now, is that he can walk his own path and still live no more than a mother's summons away.

———

making the next leap
Mukesh Ambani

As he transformed our small spice-trading business into what would eventually become India's largest private enterprise, my father, Dhirubhai Ambani, went to great lengths to instruct his children on the importance of creating opportunity for others and our duty to contribute to India's development. He held a deep and abiding faith in India's greatness. He saw India as a land where wealth had always been created by the hard work of an enterprising people; a land that once accounted for a major share of the world economy but was robbed of that productive power by colonization; a land of vast, unfulfilled potential that would surely rise again. It's a vision that has always inspired me, and one I have sought to help fulfill.

When I reflect on India's phenomenal progress over the past two decades, and consider what will be required for similar advances in decades to come, I often think back on what India was like in 1980, when I returned to Mumbai from Stanford University. Our company, built from nothing, was about to embark on a major undertaking—our first big polyester-manufacturing facility, to be built in Patalganga near Mumbai.

India's license raj was in full force back then. Companies had to get dispensation from the government for almost any decision of consequence. Public monopolies dominated many sectors; even when the government opened up certain industries to private firms like ours, it held power over our investment policy, production levels, prices, and financing. These sanctions created immense difficulties; they created an

Mukesh Ambani is chairman and CEO of Reliance Industries Limited.

artificial scarcity for everything a business needed to succeed. My colleagues needed vehicles to travel to and from the site, which was about sixty-five miles from Mumbai. The journey was arduous; at the time, there were no good roads to Patalganga. But the waiting period, even for a scooter, was ten years. Telephone line installation, too, routinely took years. Small wonder that we struggled to recruit international experts who could help set up the plant. Most of the foreign executives we approached let us know in a hurry that they didn't regard coming to India as the sort of experience that was likely to enhance their careers. Nor was it any surprise that India's economy was so sluggish in those days, and its industries so uncompetitive, given the pervasiveness of so many highly protected state enterprises with little incentive to meet global standards.

However, the license raj was in its final decade. As my father was privileged to have witnessed in 1947 the independence of India from Britain, I was privileged to have seen in 1991 India embracing economic reforms that liberated our country's entrepreneurial energies. These two transitions set India on the path of development and had a profound impact on the world in both political and economic terms. The reforms were compelled by a financial crisis, but nevertheless they were visionary and bold; the government scrapped its requirements for businesses to obtain licenses for private investment (except in eighteen key industries), reduced many of the high tariffs, and narrowed the list of imports subject to quotas and other restrictions. The performance of Reliance shows an amazing trend when mapped against time. The inflection point was 1991. We grew exponentially, eventually becoming India's biggest private enterprise, on the basis of the freedom to compete against the best in the world.

> As my father was privileged to have witnessed the independence of India from Britain, I was privileged to have seen India [liberate] our entrepreneurial energies.

In the mid-1990s, when my father entrusted me with the responsibility of building another large plant, this time a huge petrochemical refinery, the experience was markedly different from that in Patalganga a decade before. This time, we approached the project with confidence. If there were no roads, power stations, or ports, we would build them. I am proud to say that in addition to the world's largest refinery, thousands of acres of mango orchards are now flourishing in that once-barren area of Jamnagar, on the coast of Gujarat. There is also a sizable town and several villages with schools, hospitals, and clean drinking water—a classic example of how freeing the private sector to earn profits can dramatically improve the lives of people who previously faced daunting struggles to enjoy even the basic necessities of life.

Of course, we were hardly alone; the end of the license raj unleashed a wave of growth that exceeded all expectations. In nearly every field of human endeavor, Indian achievements since 1991 have been remarkable. Today Indian pharmaceutical companies sell lifesaving drugs and vaccines in Africa at one-tenth the price set by their bigger competitors in the West. Bollywood is vying with Hollywood for eyeballs across the globe. Aadhaar, an initiative of the Unique Identification Authority of India, will soon support the world's largest online platform to deliver government welfare services directly to the poor.

I believe India today is potentially poised for another, even more stupendous leap on its upward trajectory. India's relative weight in the global economy, and in world affairs in general, is bound to grow for many reasons. By 2030, India is projected to overtake China as the most populous country in the world, with the third-largest economy in U.S. dollar terms. Furthermore, India is a very young nation, with nearly two-thirds of its people below the age of thirty-five. Already, the Indian middle class exceeds four hundred million, and by 2040, it could conceivably top one billion—which would create a wave of new demand with the power to inspire all manner of innovative new products and services. Well before one billion people reach middle-income levels, roughly that many will be connected by mobile phones, a phenomenon that has the power to change the game for any industry—banking, education, entertainment, health care, retail. The possibilities are truly breathtaking.

The most exciting prospect of all is the impetus that could come from tapping the surging aspirations of the seven hundred to eight hundred million Indians who remain excluded from India's success story. If we manage to bring this segment of the population into the economic mainstream, the result will be an enormous enhancement in India's economic and noneconomic power, as we generate equality in access despite inequality in income.

Equally important is the dividend India can reap from its youthful demographic profile; young Indians are scripting the most dynamic transformations under way in our society. Generating the twenty million jobs a year needed to absorb the youth entering the labor force over the next ten years gives the country a chance to leapfrog into the future faster than ever before.

But doing all this will require a single-minded and concerted effort. Economic empowerment for the hundreds of millions of excluded Indians, and jobs for our youth, can be achieved only through the concerted action of all—citizens, businesses, and government working together. That is one of the great lessons of the past two decades, when the economy expanded at a rapid pace only after the government loosened its regulatory shackles.

Consider education. Reduced government control and centralization—especially in higher education—could make a major difference in providing excellent education for all Indians. While the public sector has an indispensable role in education, the private sector is uniquely equipped to contribute. Each year, over one hundred thousand Indian students pursue higher education in foreign universities; imagine the potential impact if we could reverse this trend by offering more attractive educational opportunities in India.

Agriculture, too, offers many opportunities to unleash the creativity of India's people. No grassroots or economic progress can be made without addressing this sector, given the huge swath of the population it employs. India has about 13 percent of the world's arable land, but Indian agriculture is still languishing at the low end of the agronomy value chain. I refuse to accept that Indian farmers are deficient in any way compared to those from other economies. But they face severe problems in getting their produce to market at decent prices, thanks in part to a complex and antiquated system of middlemen. Although the government has launched a host of ambitious programs meant to help our farmers, there are many hurdles to successful implementation. One of the biggest challenges farmers face is access to credit. There's a huge unmet need for crop insurance to protect farmers from the ravages of India's notoriously variable climate. We must streamline the regulatory requirements for public-private partnerships in agriculture.

> No progress can be made in India without addressing the needs of the agricultural sector.

Much more can be done to encourage broader dissemination of information about market conditions and new farming methods. Not least, we need much greater investment in basic agricultural infrastructure such as irrigation systems and cold chains. India's private sector has a wealth of knowledge and experience in all these sectors.

These are just two examples, but they give an idea of the direction India should go—not timidly, not in a small-bore way, but in a sweeping and comprehensive manner. As the old India gives way more completely to the new India, a certain amount of flux will be generated. However, the good developments will far outnumber others. My father, who fervently believed in India's promise, understood that better than anyone else I know. Most of the things he told me are indeed coming true!

what i learned in the war (on polio)
Bill Gates

I first began traveling to India in the 1980s, drawn by a fascination with this ancient country that cherishes its history, has a deep reverence for learning, and harbors great ambitions for the future. My interest in India was professional as well as personal. Microsoft was expanding, our need for talent was growing, and as a CEO I was attracted to the vitality and ingenuity I saw in the Indian people. I was really pleased when we opened Microsoft's Indian headquarters in Hyderabad in 1990.

A few years later, several colleagues and I were flying into Bangalore. As we made our final approach, I looked out the window and saw an area of densely packed, tiny, dilapidated homes stretching out for miles. At that moment, one of my Indian traveling companions declared proudly, "We have no slums in Bangalore."

Whether out of denial, embarrassment, or innocence, my colleague didn't see the "other" India. I don't mean to single him out. It can be easy to turn our eyes away from the poor. But if we do, we miss seeing a society's full potential.

I knew at the time that I was very fortunate to be collaborating with the most privileged people of India—highly educated citizens of great intelligence, diligence, and imagination. But when Melinda and I started our foundation's work in India, we began to meet people from the areas we'd been flying over. They had little education and poor health, and lived in slums or poor rural areas—the kind of people many experts had

Bill Gates is the cofounder and chairman of Microsoft and the cochair of the Bill & Melinda Gates Foundation.

told us were holding India back. Yet our experience in India suggests the opposite: that what some call a weakness can instead be a source of great strength.

Our foundation began working in India a decade ago with a number of grants to fight HIV/AIDS at a time many feared India would become a flashpoint for the disease. In the ten years since, the most marginalized groups in Indian society have proved indispensable in the fight against AIDS. Since 2003, the foundation has expanded into other areas, including vaccines; routine childhood immunizations; improving health outcomes for mothers, children, and newborns; family planning; agricultural development; and control of infectious disease. In each case, Melinda and I have seen many examples of India's poor making dramatic contributions for the good of the country. Nowhere have we seen the power of the poor demonstrated more clearly, however, than in the fight to end polio. Indeed, India's accomplishment in eradicating polio is the most impressive global health success I've ever seen.

> India's accomplishment in eradicating polio is the most impressive global health success I've ever seen.

That's a bold claim. Let me offer some history to back it up. In 1988, when the number of new polio cases was approximately 350,000 a year and the disease was crippling children in 125 countries, the World Health Assembly—representing all the world's countries—established the goal of eliminating polio worldwide. The Global Polio Eradication Initiative—which includes Rotary International, the World Health Organization, UNICEF, and the U.S. Centers for Disease Control and Prevention—was able to generate the political will and the funding for large-scale immunization campaigns. Progress came quickly. By 1994, the Americas were polio-free. Soon we saw the last case in China, the last case in the Pacific, the last case in Europe. By the year 2000, the number of polio cases had dropped by 99 percent. But the task of ending polio was not 99 percent done.

As the global map of polio shrank, and the remaining cases were concentrated in fewer countries, India was one of the last nations left. This was no surprise. India's urban centers are among the world's most densely populated. Its rural communities are dispersed across a vast and often inaccessible terrain. The country suffers from poor sanitation. Its 1.2 billion citizens are highly mobile, and give birth to 27 million new Indians every year. These challenges prompted experts to predict that polio would be eliminated in every other country before it was eliminated in India.

But India surprised them all: The country has now been polio-free for more than two years. As I see it, India's success offers a textbook script for winning some of the world's most difficult battles, not only in public health, but in most every area of human welfare, from business to agriculture to education. And the key has been the participation of the humblest, most vulnerable elements of the Indian population.

To be successful, any campaign this big has to include three elements: a clear goal, a comprehensive plan, and precise measurements—so you can see what is working and what is not and improve the plan as you go. India's polio program has benefited from all three. The goal is clear and ambitious: eliminate polio in India. The plan is massive and comprehensive, big enough to inspire the entire nation to action. The fact that India has fully funded its own antipolio plan is a ringing statement of Indian commitment and self-confidence. The measurements of vaccination coverage and the tracking of new cases allowed health officials to make midcourse corrections and refinements that proved decisive. In each of these three elements, India demonstrated its resilience, talent, and determination.

> That India fully funded its own antipolio plan is a ringing statement of commitment and self-confidence.

Above all, though, the campaign enlisted the support of the full sweep of Indian society, including health workers, ordinary citizens, and some of the poorest people in the most impoverished regions of the country. This program became their cause. It created a groundswell of enthusiasm and tapped the spirit of India.

The heart of the plan was a simple and inspiring mission: find the children.

To defeat polio, it's essential to achieve up to 95 percent vaccination coverage in afflicted areas. There is no way to measure whether you're meeting that mark unless you know how many children there are, where they are, and whether they've been vaccinated. That's a daunting challenge in a nation where millions of the most vulnerable people live in poor and remote regions.

India responded to this challenge with an army of more than two million vaccinators, who canvassed every village, hamlet, and slum, paying particular attention to the most polio-afflicted areas marked by the worst poverty. Vaccinators took the best maps they had and made them better. They walked miles every day and worked late into the night to find every child.

They found children in the poorest areas of Uttar Pradesh. They found children in the remote Kosi River area of Bihar—an area with no electricity that is often flooded and unreachable by roads. They found the sons and daughters of migrant workers in bus stations and train stations, accompanying their families on their way to find work.

The thoroughness of India's vaccinators was astonishing. When Melinda and I visited India in March 2011, two months after the last case of polio was identified, we traveled to a brick kiln where we met with workers who labored long hours at low wages and lived in mud huts. Despite their toil, these are some of India's poorest people. We met a young mother, perhaps twenty-two years old, and asked if her children had been vaccinated. She ducked into the hut where she lived, retrieved a bag that held all her possessions, and rummaged around the bottom of it until she proudly produced an immunization card listing names of all her children and showing that each had received the polio vaccine—not just once, but several times. We were amazed. The vaccinators had not only reached this migrant woman and her children; they had done so often.

Wherever India's vaccinators have gone, they've had help from local residents. In one Kolkata slum, a group of schoolchildren who call themselves the Daredevils have been relentless in their efforts to get every child vaccinated; their work is now featured in a film called *The Rev-*

olutionary Optimists. The Daredevils looked on the Internet for a map of their community and found that the area where they lived had been left blank. So the children decided to make a map. The community had never had house numbers, so the children assigned house numbers. Using donated cell phones that could connect to global positioning satellites, they created a digital map for their neighborhood, marking every house where children hadn't been vaccinated. They used both high-tech and low-tech methods. The film shows the children going into the streets with their handmade megaphones, shouting: "Polio vaccinations at the club this Sunday! Please come and bring your children!"

The Daredevils helped double the vaccination rates in their community from 40 percent to 80 percent. They're now taking aim at 100 percent.

The fight to end polio is not over, not even in India. Vaccinators have to continue their work, and the country needs to stay vigilant. If the world can maintain its funding and its commitment, we can eradicate polio globally within six years. That would be a tremendous accomplishment, but it will be only one of many benefits to come from India's polio program. The effort to find and vaccinate every child has created the basis for a better public health system throughout the country.

In 2011, Melinda and I accompanied polio vaccinators as they went door to door in Bihar. When we met women who were pregnant, the vaccinators talked to them about the importance of receiving maternal and neonatal care, and urged them to visit the local clinic. They promised on their next visit to bring information about child health care and teach the women about breast-feeding. They reminded the women to be ready to get their newborns vaccinated for other diseases and made sure they knew the way to the clinic.

This is why the accomplishments of the vaccinators and the children and the scientists and the politicians will not end when polio ends. They will be applied to the next challenge. This is the legacy of polio in India. They have found the children. Now they can bring them and their families other vaccines, and clean water, and education, and advice on maternal and child health, and support for agriculture, and all the things that people need to live healthy and productive lives. India has miles to go in this quest, by any measure, but it has shown it has the will and means to realize its full potential.

Years ago, on that day we were landing in Bangalore, I didn't know nearly as much about India as I do now. I saw India's obvious talent and energy, but, like my colleague, I missed its hidden strength—the rich, the powerful, and the poor working together toward a common goal. The antipolio campaign's extraordinary push to find every child has awakened the power of India—not just for the children who were found but also for all those who worked find them and tell them, "Your life is important to us. We will protect you."

> The antipolio campaign's extraordinary push to find every child has awakened the power of India.

The campaign showed India at its best—the relentless spirit, the idealism, the teamwork, the scientific power, the business acumen, the manufacturing skill, the political imagination, and the vast human resources that can deploy more than two million people and spark the imagination of a billion. Yes, India faces challenges in many areas that are well documented in the media. But in its fight against polio, India has shown the world that when its people set an ambitious goal, mobilize the country, and measure the impact, India's promise is endless.

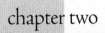

chapter two

politics & policy

rural india's iron ladies
Sonia Faleiro

The village of Jharki Bisalpur, deep inside a forest in Jharkhand, lies beyond three rivers. When the rains fall, the rivers swell, barricading the village from the outside world. Then Sheila Devi, the daughter of a farmer and a housewife, the first woman in her family to have a paying job, takes charge. She strides the length of the village in her mustard-yellow sari, urging residents to pen their cows, check their stores of grain, or cover the well. She devises a plan to send someone to the nearest town, five hours away on foot, to buy additional supplies. "This is the jungle," she says, from under a voluminous black umbrella. "But even the wild animals had the sense to move elsewhere."

Devi is the *sarpanch*, or village head, of Jharki Bisalpur, and she is an unusual choice of leader for this impoverished village. Still only in her thirties, she is making her first foray into local politics. Before becoming *sarpanch*, she worked for a nonprofit group. And yet women like her are no longer uncommon in rural India.

> "This is the jungle. . . . But even the wild animals had the sense to move elsewhere."

Devi's status is part of a trend running counter to the misogyny and patriarchy embedded in Indian society. Those forces exploded into public consciousness following the December 2012 rape and murder of a twenty-three-year-old woman in Delhi and the massive demonstrations that ensued. The long-overdue focus on pervasive sexual harassment and

Sonia Faleiro is a journalist. Her most recent book is Beautiful Thing: Inside the Secret World of Bombay's Dance Bars.

violence in India has spurred parliamentarians to toughen laws, while the police and judges—who have tended to treat rape casually, sometimes urging victims to marry their attackers—are scrambling to adopt more enlightened practices.

Whether those promises of change lead to fundamental improvement in Indian attitudes toward women remains to be seen. But as Devi's case shows, progress is possible, even in the most remote and tradition-bound parts of the country. For that to happen, action and reform by public policy makers is necessary—though it is hardly sufficient, given the myriad economic, social, and political complexities besetting life in places such as Jharki Bisalpur.

Devi is one beneficiary of a 1993 constitutional amendment aimed at confronting sexual discrimination by mandating that a third of all seats in the *panchayat*—the governing institution created to foster grassroots democracy—be reserved for women. Such "reservations," as this kind of quota is known, were the only way, supporters argue, for women to have a shot at leadership roles in local politics. Prior to this, social pressure kept village women in the home and, as a result, the *panchayats* were almost entirely male, with priorities that often excluded women's and children's issues such as day care and schooling.

> Progress on attitudes toward women is possible, even in the most remote and tradition-bound parts of the country.

The law may have required change, but the enthusiasm with which women grasped at the opportunity—with several candidates contesting each seat—showed readiness. According to the Ministry of Panchayati Raj, women comprise 1 million out of the 2.8 million elected members in the *panchayats*.

As *sarpanch*, Devi is less concerned with making a point than with doing her job. She is the only link between her voters and the state government—a vital link given the isolation and poverty of Jharki Bisalpur. Although Jharkhand is a mineral-rich state, and the forest was once mined for mica, it is no longer legal to do so. Still, with no other work available, every able-bodied man and boy, and women as well, dig for mica with whatever implements they can afford—hammers, knives, or even just their fingers. Families that don't have the manpower to dig deeply forage for mica debris. But at 3 rupees a kilogram, a family in Jharki Bisalpur often earns less than half the daily minimum wage of 120 rupees.

One of Devi's chief responsibilities is identifying development projects for the state to fund. Of these, there is no shortage. The village has no running water. All the adults have basic cell phones, but since there's no electricity, they must wait until they go into town to charge their phones and make calls. There's a school, but the teachers live outside the village, and the difficulties crossing the rough forest terrain cause them to miss work as often as three times a week. One reason why development has been so slow is that Jharkhand is newly carved out of Bihar and held its first *panchayat* elections only in 2011. Now Devi is almost entirely responsible for ushering her village into the modern world. Two things stand in her way—the first being the reluctance of the state government to release funds to develop land in the middle of nowhere.

Although the Forest Rights Act of 2006 grants traditional forest dwellers the right to live in the forest, the government would like nothing more than to get rid of them. By depriving the villagers of basic necessities of life, officials hope to hound them out and preserve the natural habitat for protected wildlife. But the villagers are tribals who know no other way than to live off the land. Before the forest was protected, private mining companies employed the villagers, building them brick huts and supplying them electricity. Once the mines closed down and the law was enforced, the villagers were warned against cutting wood or making further encroachments. Eking out a subsistence living does not secure their future. In her fight for change, Devi spends several days a week in town "running from one government office to another," her "head bowed and hands folded." "They are determined to be unhelpful," she says.

Devi's second challenge is overcoming the inherent patriarchy of Indian culture, which has manifested itself in the *panchayat* system through the rise of the *sarpanch pati*. The term, which means "husband of the *sarpanch*," refers to men who have their wives stand for election in reserved seats and then lead by proxy. It isn't clear whether these women are happy to cede power, or if they are made to do so under threat of violence or separation. Whatever it means, the prevalence of *sarpanch patis* recently led the Ministry of Panchayati Raj to recommend action against state officials who permit *panchayat* meetings to be conducted by the male relatives of women *sarpanches*. The taint has damaged the reputation of even those married women who lead independently. Devi often finds herself reminding people that her decisions are her own. Manoranjan Singh, an activist with the Bachpan Bachao Andolan, a nonprofit that works with mining communities in Jharkhand, agrees. "She's the boss," he says. "Not her husband."

Patriarchy isn't the only obstacle. Although urban India is largely divided on class lines, rural India—states like Jharkhand in particular—are deeply segregated by caste. Entire communities live, marry, and even choose their work on the basis of caste diktats. Lower-caste families have to live away from the upper castes; they can't use the same well, they are discouraged from applying for the same jobs, and inter-caste marriage is unthinkable. For decades, such villages have been dominated by upper-caste *sarpanches*, but reserving seats for women has changed this, making it possible for low-caste women to win elections. The change has sometimes had a brutal fallout—women find themselves threatened with physical violence, falsely accused of corruption or embezzlement, and even driven to suicide.

Although Devi exercises caution in her dealings with men, and upper-caste men in particular, she is independent and enthusiastic about her job—testament to the claim by the Ministry of Panchayati Raj that women *sarpanches* have fulfilled their promise. According to the ministry, women *sarpanches* have been especially effective in raising issues that the all-male *panchayats* tended to ignore, including child marriage, female feticide, and infanticide, as well as increased access to schooling and day care.

In fact, as a result of their exposure to the *panchayat*, rural Indian women may be more inspired than urban women to join political life.

Studies show such participation has important effects on village women's lives. As more women attend *panchayat* meetings, they access public spaces they would not have entered before. These interactions allow them to network, which leads to the formation of self-help groups and microcredit programs. Women are also more comfortable approaching female *panchayat* leaders for rights and services. These leaders are vested with real power, with access to funds. They may be able to have a road built or a fence erected, or press for more hand pumps—tangible changes that can transform living standards.

> Arguably, rural Indian women are more inspired to join political life than urban women.

Politics at a higher level is, inevitably, far more complicated and the bargaining required to achieve even small goals can be tedious and disillusioning. At the city or state level, politics appears distant and beyond the influence of ordinary voters. But Devi, like every other *sarpanch*, lives among her constituents. They know where she lives and can knock on her door almost anytime. Most urban women don't know the name of their legislator. If rural women are now starting to see local politics as a road to real change, urban women have exactly the opposite experience.

The success of the reservation has had a ripple effect. In 2011, it was increased from 33 percent to 50 percent, and several states have already implemented the measure. And this year, after much stalling, parliament is expected to take a vote on the Women's Reservation Bill, regarding the role of women at the state and national levels.

Like the constitutional amendment that helped Devi win the *panchayat* election, this bill seeks to reserve one-third of all seats for women in the democratically elected lower house of parliament and the state legislative assemblies. It also provides that one-third of seats reserved for Scheduled Castes and Scheduled Tribes be reserved for women of these groups.

The need for such a bill may seem surprising given the number of women who have occupied the highest ranks of Indian politics. But many of these women benefited from their proximity to great power: Former prime minister Indira Gandhi was the daughter of Jawaharlal Nehru, India's first prime minister. And Sonia Gandhi, the president of India's

India ranks 105th in the world in terms of women's participation in politics.

oldest party, is the widow of Indira Gandhi's son, Rajiv, himself a prime minister. Perhaps their success, despite the built-in advantages they enjoyed, does encourage other women to enter politics. But given India's tradition of dynastic politicians, and the widely held notion that without connections, money, or power a career in politics is a waste of time, those success stories merely confirm the stereotype that women get ahead by proximity to men, not on their merits.

In fact, India ranks a dismal 105th in the world in terms of women's participation in politics. Women account for only 11 percent of the lower house of parliament. In the upper house, which is determined by presidential nomination and the votes of state legislators, they comprise less than 10 percent.

Nonetheless, the reservations have had tremendous impact. Powerful women make it easier for other women to aspire to power. Successful women are able to convince voters that they can fight on their behalf. And the attacks against them have only justified the need for reservations. Both sets of actions have raised the question of whether familiarity with taking charge should be instilled at an even earlier age.

One upshot is the *Bal* (or Children's) *Panchayats*, which are mock *panchayats* conducted in rural schools. Members of the *Bal Panchayat*, both boys and girls, are elected by their schoolmates. They attend meetings of the (adult) *panchayat* and are encouraged to suggest development projects. At the least, the process familiarizes children with politics. At its best, it will create a generation of politically aware young women and men.

In 2012, I visited a *Bal Panchayat* in the northern state of Rajasthan. Here, far fewer women are literate and work professionally than men. In a small village outside Jaipur, where the villagers grow their own food on stamp-size parcels of lands, I met Pooja Gujjar, the eleven-year-old deputy *sarpanch* of her school's *Bal Panchayat*. Pooja and other members of the *Bal Panchayat* had successfully canvassed the adult *panchayat* for funds to build a kitchen for their school. Before that, their midday meal was cooked in the open, in fields sprayed liberally with pesticide. It wasn't unusual to find bugs in the dal and dirt in their rice. The kitchen, as it turned out, was only the beginning.

"We want more classrooms," Pooja told me firmly. "There are eight classes in this school, so we should have at least eight, not just two classrooms. And we need lights. And fans. It gets very hot in summer!"

something is working
Shekhar Gupta

It is easy—and for any Indian, quite natural—to argue with the very idea of reimagining India. To reimagine, you have to presume you have something that has already been imagined, a completed piece of work, philosophy, or idea. The trouble with that formulation is that, through the millennia, India, and the ideas upon which it is predicated, have evolved rather than been imagined.

At different junctures, many Indians have tried to mold India to fit their own imaginations: from Ashoka to Akbar, from Manu to Mayawati, from Gautama Buddha to Mahatma Gandhi, from Tughlaq to Jawaharlal Nehru, and from Kautilya to B. R. Ambedkar. And let's not forget the Sufi geniuses of the Middle Ages who scripted our syncretism; or the latter-day visionaries like Indira Gandhi, Atal Bihari Vajpayee, Manmohan Singh; or even Ram Manohar Lohia, V. P. Singh, and Lal Krishna Advani. What the collective imagination of all these thinkers has given us is, at best, a work in progress.

But that there has been progress is undeniable. We Indians are hard to please, particularly when we look at the state of our own nation and society. To be fair to ourselves, we have done reasonably well so far. The evolution of our nation, society, and economy—or reimagination, if you so choose to call it—is progressing.

To step back in history again, Emperor Ashoka was the first to imagine a peaceful, equal-opportunity state where the ruler was bound by *Rajdharma*, the duty of rulers, as much as his subjects were by laws made

Shekhar Gupta is the editor-in-chief of the Indian Express.

and enforced by him. Two millennia later, the Nehruvian idea of India emerged from that original thought. Ambedkar and his Constituent Assembly gave it a scripture—the liberal, federal, and secular Constitution, which endures. It is no surprise, then, that the most important symbols of our constitutional state, the three-lion emblem and the chakra wheel, are inherited from Ashoka.

In the sixties, it was almost impossible to imagine the India of today. The sixties, to borrow a phrase from renowned South Asian expert Selig Harrison, was India's "most dangerous decade." For me, that decade holds enduring fascination; no other period is as significant in our post-independence political and military history. India fought all of its crucial wars in the sixties: the 1961 liberation of Goa; the 1962 debacle against China in the high Himalayas; the indecisive but debilitating war of attrition against Pakistan in 1965; skirmishes in Kutch (against Pakistan, 1965) and Nathu La (in Sikkim, against China, 1967). The 1971 war that liberated Bangladesh also was an extension of conflicts originating in the sixties. The sixties was a time when tribal insurgencies held sway in two northeastern states, one briefly in Mizoram and another for much longer in Nagaland. These were the years of the distinctly separatist Akali and Dravida political movements in Punjab and Tamil Nadu, respectively. If, in the sixties, you were, like me, a young Indian schoolboy, you never would have dreamed that 1971 would see India's last major war; that insurgencies and separatist movements would be subsumed by this wondrous evolution of Indian constitutionalism; that famines, hand-to-mouth survival, and communal riots would all simply fade away—long before you yourself reached sixty.

And how did this remarkable transformation come about? It was hardly because this was a decade of towering political leaders. One of the greatest, Nehru, declined and passed away. Another, Shastri, lasted fewer than two years. And the third, Indira Gandhi, was still finding her feet. But hundreds of millions of Indians were meanwhile molding India to their own diverse ideas—ideas that, improbably, converged. I got this wisdom from an interview with one of the grand old men of Indian politics, M. Karunanidhi, patriarch of one of Tamil Nadu's dominant political parties, the Dravida Munnetra Kazhagam (Dravidian Progress Federation).

"Weren't you called a separatist in the sixties?" I asked him, with cameras rolling.

"No, no, I wasn't *called* a separatist," said the patriarch. "I *was* a separatist."

"Then what changed, and when?"

"When the wars with China and Pakistan took place, we realized that we could only have sovereignty if we were a part of a much larger republic, or outsiders would enslave us."

So here is a man who led one of the strongest and most popular ethnic separatist movements in India, who says he and his comrades gave up separatism when India was at its weakest, when it was fighting terrible wars and facing famine and political instability, and he could simply have walked out of the republic. Were people like him stupid? Or geniuses? Were they trying to reimagine their own concept of nationhood? Or did they, instead, decide to embrace what had already been imagined, and was emerging?

It is not my intention to review India's political history decade by decade; the sixties are a good metaphor, an instructive reference point for understanding how things change in India, and why. Careful study of those years also teaches us that there always is great continuity in change.

> We could describe the journey of the Indian voter as gratitude to grievance to aspiration.

At the risk of oversimplification, think of the following as the three major transformations currently in progress in India: (1) from grievance to aspiration, (2) from rebels to stakeholders, and (3) from preoccupation with domestic strength and political stability to ambition for "big-power" status.

The first transformation is evident in our election results in the past fifteen years. We could, in fact, describe the journey of the Indian voter as gratitude to grievance to aspiration. Gratitude, because for almost four decades after independence, the typical Indian voter supported the Congress and the Nehru-Gandhi family to thank them for winning our freedom, founding this liberal republic, and then holding it together—albeit often with brute force. As we Indians felt more secure, we became more questioning, and angry. This is when grievance overwhelmed us and we started to defeat incumbent rulers, challenging the one-party, one-family domination of four decades. Between 1989 and 1998, the voters tossed out more than 70 percent of all incumbent candidates. And then sentiment reversed again. Some leaders, even some we would have dismissed as casteist or sectarian in the past, started winning reelection. According to a detailed review recently published in India's *Economic & Political Weekly*, between 2004 and 2012, incumbents won 45 percent of elections—their best showing in three decades.

The economic reform of 1991 unleashed new forces that were economic as well as political, and both were virtuous. For a vast majority of Indians, so far the major concerns were of mere survival: *roti, kapda, aur makaan* (food, clothing, and shelter), that great metaphor dominating the entire subcontinent's politics. And then it faded away. It yielded to a new set of ideas—in fact, aspirations—that went beyond survival: *bijli, sadak, paani* (power, roads, water). And now, continuing on: *padhai, sehat, naukri* (education, health, a proper job).

The change from grievance to aspiration has brought new energies that drive today's India and redefine its politics, and it is hard to imagine where they will take us. Aspiration on such a scale, riding on a population where more than five hundred million citizens are below the age of twenty-five, comes with increasing impatience, providing a powerful impetus for faster change. The recent surge of urban activism—against corruption or, more recently, for gender rights in the capital—by disparate, ostensibly apolitical groups, is one manifestation of this new energy.

The other demon to have faded away is internal separatism. Even Kashmir is much more stable than in years past. And while Maoists fight on in resource-rich east-central India, their quest is not for a separate nation but for the same republic transformed to their vision, which they have neither the confidence nor the patience to try and achieve through the ballot. Chances are that over time they, too, will join the political mainstream like so many other rebels, armed or peaceful, who are now counted among the most formidable stakeholders in Indian society and power structure. Dalits, for centuries at the bottom of the awful caste pyramid, now have a leader of national stature in Mayawati. The middle castes—the so-called Other Backward Classes (OBCs)—have seen a revolutionary empowerment now represented by leaders ranging from Nitish Kumar and his rival Lalu Prasad Yadav in Bihar; Mulayam Singh Yadav and Kalyan Singh in Uttar Pradesh; Shivraj Singh Chauhan and Uma Bharati in Madhya Pradesh; and Narendra Modi in Gujarat. One of the most crucial markers in this strongly contested political terrain is these leaders' commitment to the security and prosperity of minorities, especially Muslims. We Indians often fret that we have a broken polity. But this broken polity has turned all these rebels into stakeholders. Whether you applaud or abhor the notion of dynastic rule, a polity composed of fifteen diverse and often competing dynasties is a far better proposition than a single dominant and all-consuming dynasty.

> We Indians often fret that we have a broken polity. But this broken polity has turned rebels into stakeholders.

The founding fathers were idealists who believed that India's democracy, its liberalism, its history, philosophy, and spirituality would all combine to give it a moral force that by itself would bring it the status of a globally respected nation, if not a major power in the conventional sense. But we live in a world that sets the bar much higher. It is only now, when India has subsumed its many rebellions and moved on from the politics of anger and grievance to the politics of hope and aspiration, that our nation is in a position to leverage its success as a liberal, diverse democracy—despite what many would see as its weakening center. Nuclear weaponization, the nuclear deal with the United States, the debate on the restructuring of the Security Council to acknowledge the rise of India, among others, are all indications, and a consequence, of this larger success.

Where India will be, one, two, or three decades from now is tough to predict. During the sixties, the grand preoccupation of all the writing, debates, and predictions was India's prospects for survival. Today, the primary topics are growth, competitiveness, and equity. So something has worked, is working, and will, hopefully, continue to work.

If there is one thing you can say with confidence, it is that India's founding fathers were wise in what they imagined for the nation. Millions of Indians, as themselves, and acting through their elected representatives, have taken their idea forward, noisily and chaotically but with tremendous success. I do not, therefore, see the need to reimagine or rethink. Maybe a better goal is to reenergize, reinforce, and renew to meet the challenges of the three transformations that define today's India.

The only quibble I have with the founding fathers is an editorial one. It's over a slogan they gave us: "Unity in diversity." I would prefer "Celebrate diversity." But you can't really call this reimagining India: More than a billion diverse and united Indians already are making it a reality. In so doing, they are scripting their own future.

federalism: promise and peril
Ashutosh Varshney

At its core, India's federalism is an answer to an enduring concern of modern Indian politics: How should the nation combine democracy and regional diversity?

The freedom movement led by Mahatma Gandhi wrestled with this question, as did the post-1947 polity led by Jawaharlal Nehru. Of the four major forms of social diversity in India—religion, caste, language, and tribe—the last two are territorially concentrated. Castes can be found virtually all over India and, with the partial exception of Sikhism, religions also are widely spread. In contrast, all languages of India are geographically concentrated, as are the tribal communities. History and political theory teach us that territorially based communities, if disaffected, can acquire separatist and secessionist impulses much more easily than geographically dispersed groups. Territorial concentration requires imaginative political handling.

The key issues always are twofold: How should these territorial communities be ruled? And how should they be made an integral part of the larger polity? India's federalism is an institutional device to deal with both questions. Almost all major linguistic and tribal communities of India have been given a state of their own in the Indian federation, with constitutionally assigned powers that Delhi can take away only under exceptional conditions, which are listed in the Constitution. All linguistic and tribal groups are, in principle, allowed to participate in the all-India

Ashutosh Varshney is professor of international studies and the social sciences at Brown University.

institutions as well: parliament, executive, judiciary, civil service, police, public media, public education, and others.

The execution of these federal principles has not been perfect, but in the scholarly literature, India's federalism is widely viewed as a substantial—and an unlikely—success. Indeed, the magnitude of success cannot be appreciated without understanding its improbability.

The story begins with the dominant conceptions of India more than a century ago. In the higher circles of British rule, India was viewed as a geographical or civilizational construct, much like Europe. It could not possibly be a nation, achieving political unity. A nation is often described by scholars as a political roof over one's cultural head; India had many cultural heads and no political roof.

> A nation is often described as a political roof over one's cultural head; India had many cultural heads and no political roof.

John Strachey, one of the most prominent official British voices in the late nineteenth century, reflected prevailing wisdom when he wrote in 1888, "That men of the Punjab, Bengal . . . and Madras, should ever feel that they belong to one Indian nation, is impossible. You might with as much reason and probability look forward to a time when a single nation will have taken the place of the various nations of Europe." By this logic, just as Europe had so many independent nations, the various units of India could conceivably become separate nations after the British left, but there could not be a single nation in India.

Nor was this conception confined to ruling British circles. After traveling in India in 1896, Mark Twain also concluded that Indian unity was impossible:

India had . . . the first civilization; she had the first accumulation of material wealth; she was populous with deep thinkers and subtle intellects; she had mines, and woods, and a fruitful soil. It would seem as if she should have kept the lead, and should be to-day not the meek dependent of an alien master, but mistress of the world, and delivering law and command to every tribe and nation in it. But, in truth, there was never any possibility of such supremacy for her. If there had been but one India and one language—but there were eighty of them! Where there are eighty nations and several hundred governments . . . unity of purpose and policy are impossible . . . patriotism can have no healthy growth.

Had they been alive, Strachey and Twain would have found post-1947 India utterly surprising. Today, fifteen languages of India are spoken by at least ten million people each, and yet all these linguistic groups are part of the Indian nation. Independent India has witnessed very few separatist movements. Even at the worst moment, 1989–1991, when insurgency in Punjab raged, separatist violence in Kashmir stirred, and northeastern discontent simmered, not more than 6 percent of India's total population was directly affected. At no point has India experienced a Sri Lanka–style insurgency affecting 18 to 20 percent of the population, let alone an East Pakistan–style separatism, circa 1970–1971, engulfing a majority of the country's population.

What explains this? The character of India's freedom movement played a pivotal role. Consciously breaking from the "one language, one nation" European principle, Mahatma Gandhi and his colleagues launched a new experience in human history. A larger all-India identity would be added to the existing linguistic/regional identity of Indians; linguistic diversity would not be erased. To use today's language, Indians would be hyphenated Indians, not undifferentiated Indians. The movement, reaching out to millions, created the sense that being a Tamil and an Indian, being a Gujarati and an Indian, being a Bengali and an Indian were simultaneously possible. Bengal, Gujarat, Tamil Nadu did not have to be separate nations. The Congress party, which led the freedom movement, was linguistically organized; it did not follow the provincial boundaries of British India. The movement lasted nearly three decades. An Indian nation was thus politically created where it did not readily exist.

Linguistic states after independence were a logical extension of this principle. Though Nehru, India's first prime minister (1947–1964), developed cold feet about linguistic states soon after independence, he eventually gave in, returning to the linguistic commitment of the freedom movement and presiding over the linguistic organization of Indian states.

A natural question follows: How could linguistically organized states and their residents communicate with those outside their boundaries? To facilitate nationwide communication, a three-language formula was also put in place in the late 1950s. The education system would teach three languages to Indians: the regional language, Hindi, and English. This is why educated Indians tend to be tri- or at least effectively bilingual.

> India allowed diversities to flourish, but it also nurtured commitment to the larger Indian political community.

In short, India engaged in a two-sided pursuit of nation making: It allowed diversities to flourish, but it also nurtured commitment to the larger Indian political community via politics, administration, and education. Nothing exemplifies this better than how the elite Indian Administrative Service (IAS) was conceptualized. The IAS is often lambasted for its red tape, and rightly so, but from a nation-building perspective, the story is more complex. IAS officers are part of both Delhi and states—they are selected by Delhi but allocated to a state cadre, going back and forth between Delhi and states during their careers. If India's civil service had been entirely state-based, or wholly Delhi-based, the problems of nation building would have been far greater.

Thus, Indian nation making, both before and after independence, sought to break the link between nation and language, which Europe first followed (Belgium and Switzerland being the only exceptions, and Spain partially one) and East Asia later did. To what extent has this departure from the historically given principles of nation building been a success? And to what extent has it been a failure?

Two pieces of survey research illustrate the success of Indian federalism. First, 85 to 90 percent of Indians say they are "proud" or "very proud" of India, a figure higher than in Germany, Switzerland, and Belgium;

and in the same range as in Canada, Spain, Argentina, and Brazil. Only the United States and Australia appear to rank higher. Second, roughly two-thirds of Indians say their identity is "only Indian," "more Indian than regional," and "equally regional and Indian." In contrast, only 20–22 percent of Indians say their identity is "only regional" or "more regional than Indian." The idea of India has thus gone very far. Trying to erase regional identities would have been a violent, and perhaps failed, enterprise. Accommodation of diversities has built a stronger, not weaker, Indian nationhood.

The failures of Indian federalism are most clearly manifested in the insurgencies in Punjab, Kashmir, Assam, Nagaland, and Mizoram. It should be noted, however, that other than Punjab, these were not parts of India that the freedom movement, with its organizations, deeply penetrated—either because British rules did not allow that, or because the areas in question were considered far from the principal theaters of political activity. Punjab in the 1980s was the greatest shock to the history of Indian federalism, but it is also clear that Delhi had badly handled the politics of the state. The failure in Punjab was an example not of the inadequacy of the basic federal principles but of the attempt by Delhi to centralize power. Indira Gandhi nurtured the argument that India's national unity required weaker states and a stronger center. She also practiced it by repeatedly suspending state governments run by political parties opposed to her. Suspension of state governments, according to the Constitution, was to be an exceptional, not a routine, occurrence.

What of the future? At this stage in the evolution of Indian polity, language as the basis for further state making has more or less exhausted its potential. All major language groups already have states of their own. The next round of state making is likely to be driven by the principle that smaller states are more governable, or they allow better developmental care of all parts of the state. Uttar Pradesh has close to two hundred million people. It would be the fifth-largest nation in the world by population if it were independent. Its breakup into four states is beginning to be discussed in political circles. Two other large states—Maharashtra and Andhra Pradesh—might also be split on grounds that some of their sub-

regions end up getting neglected in decision-making and they economically suffer as a result. Governance and lack of development are more
likely to be the principles of state making in the future.

It is sometimes suggested that the rise of a new middle class will
allow India to transcend its various diversities—caste, language, and
religion—and create a genuinely Pan-Indian consciousness. The recent
protests against corruption and gender violence can be viewed as examples of this new consciousness. One might also cite the unifying influence
of one of the most potent forces in India's popular culture: the sport of
cricket—or perhaps more precisely, cricket as played in the Indian Premier League. Consider Chennai, a southeastern city historically famous
for its proud regional culture, where the Chennai Super Kings have since
their inception been led by M. S. Dhoni, a cricketer from Jharkhand in
the north, who has no knowledge of the Tamil language. Such a phenomenon would have been inconceivable as recently as the 1960s.

As India's economy continues to grow and prosperity spreads, the
number of those who believe their identity is "only Indian" may multiply.
But the relationship between material prosperity and national identity
is complex. In many parts of the world, rising prosperity has led to a
continued assertion of regional identity. Think of Catalonia in Spain and
Quebec in Canada. In India, Mumbai, the richest city for decades, has a
long-established sons-of-the-soil movement led by the Shiv Sena, which
was first opposed to south Indian migrants in the city, then to Muslims
and, of late, to north Indians. A great deal of comparative scholarship
suggests modernization has a two-headed character: Both greater uni-
formity and greater consciousness of diversity can be expected to rise.

What can be said is that regional diversity no longer poses an existential threat to India. The primary objective of India's federal design
was to weave a nation out of its many diverse parts and protect national
integrity. In that, India's federalism has largely succeeded.

Whether federalism, in turn, hurts or aids India's economic development is an oft-debated question. Federalism's defenders may point to
recent history: India's rapid growth since the early 1990s has coincided
with a more federal polity, a time when the power of the states has un-

doubtedly gone up. Moreover, under this more federal system, successful state-level policy experiments have been studied and widely adopted. India's rural employment guarantee program was born in Maharashtra in the 1970s, and the midday meal program in Tamil Nadu in the 1980s. In recent times, too, a great deal of attention has been paid to some state-level developments: Gujarat's progrowth policies, often associated with its Chinese-style economic performance; Bihar's remarkable success in combating its perennial law-and-order problems. In a diverse polity, policy experiments can be a source of learning.

India's polity seems certain to remain diverse for the foreseeable future. Its own experience so far does not support the argument that greater diversity leads to lesser development.

The experiences of other Asian countries underscore the wisdom of India's decision to embrace diversity. In Indonesia, the third-largest Asian country, decentralization of governmental authority was extensively discussed after the fall of Suharto in 1998. But the anxiety that powerful provinces could pave the way for secession triumphed. On the whole, districts have been given a great deal of resources and effective power, not the provinces. It is perhaps too early to judge whether this was a good move, but there are many reasons for doubt.

Sri Lanka and Pakistan took approaches to nationhood that differed significantly from India's—in each case with disastrous consequences.

In South Asia, Sri Lanka and Pakistan's approaches to nationhood differed significantly from India's—in each case with disastrous consequences. In Sri Lanka, Tamils essentially wanted a federal polity, with a province of their own, right until the mid-1970s. When Colombo did not concede, the result was a bloody civil war that dragged on for a quarter century. In contrast, India's Tamil Nadu, in great ferment against Delhi till the late 1960s, increasingly became an integral part of Indian polity, as its diversity was recognized and the state became a major political player at the federal center.

Pakistan's attempt to impose Urdu on a Bengali-speaking East Pakistan, among other things, led to secession in 1971–1972 and contributed to the creation of Bangladesh. Post-1972, Pakistan has fluctuated between a regionally sensitive polity and a Punjab-dominated polity. No clear conception about how to embrace diversities has emerged.

On the whole, it will be hard to argue in the twenty-first century that erasure of diversity is a way to build national strength or unity. Norms about respecting diversity have changed, and violence against minorities is also watched more closely in the international system. Both on normative and pragmatic grounds, how to accommodate diversities has become an important political project. India was lucky to have had leaders who saw this more clearly than in most postcolonial countries.

parsing the grammar of anarchy
Patrick French

India was the first country to give large numbers of illiterate people the vote. The chief election commissioner at the general election of 1952, Sukumar Sen, thought it was "the biggest experiment in democracy in human history." Many commentators at the time, from different parts of the political spectrum, believed it to be a grave mistake. If voters were unable to read and write, could they not easily be duped by false information? Would it not be safer to have a tough and autocratic leader who could introduce democracy when India was ready?

The author of the Constitution, Dr. B. R. Ambedkar, had no doubt that the mass consent of the governed was essential if India was to progress. At the same time, if democracy was to function, it was vital to abandon the Gandhian methods that had given voice to millions in the freedom movement—"civil disobedience, non-cooperation and satyagraha [soul force]. . . . These methods are nothing but the Grammar of Anarchy and the sooner they are abandoned, the better for us." Only if they had the right to vote and to change the government, he believed, would the most disadvantaged Indians stand a chance of destroying the caste system and altering their fixed social position.

Anyone who has witnessed an Indian election at ground level knows that illiteracy is no bar to understanding what a candidate is offering. In fact, it sometimes seems that those who lack education are especially

Patrick French is the author of India: A Portrait *and* The World Is What It Is, *the National Book Critics Circle award-winning biography of author V. S. Naipaul.*

able to grasp the potential advantages on offer. If a candidate for the state legislative assembly offers to build a road to your village, or to double the amount of time each day that electricity is supplied, the trade-off is very clear: You vote, and you gain a benefit.

Indian electors also have shown an extraordinary knack for ejecting incumbent politicians who do not deliver on their promises. Voter turnout in many districts is often as high as 80–90 percent, whereas in U.S. presi-

> Anyone who has witnessed an Indian election knows that illiteracy is no bar to understanding what a candidate is offering.

dential elections, for example, it rarely rises much above 50 percent. Any conceptual study of democracy as a system of creating a nation's government must look at the Indian example, which through the later twentieth century influenced other Asian and African countries that were shifting out of the colonial mode. Today, the administration of elections in India is, for the most part, unexpectedly efficient.

Democracy has brought India numerous intangible benefits. It has a vociferous free press, a sense of national self-belief, and a degree of intellectual freedom that is missing in most of its neighbors. Many Indians believe, rightly or wrongly, that they have a stake in how their country should be governed, and they have no hesitation in expressing their opinions.

The problem in Indian politics is not that the leaders are unelected: It is that once they are elected, they are unaccountable until the next cycle of voting. Democracy functions, but governance does not.

Increasingly, representative democracy has failed to solve the ever more vociferous popular demand for good administration. As people's economic fortunes have improved, their expectations have risen. Anger over the way the system locks out the overwhelming majority of Indians from parliament and the institutions of national politics is growing. It has shown itself in the anticorruption movement started by the elderly ascetic Anna Hazare, in the intense interest in his former lieutenant Arvind Kejriwal's new Aam Aadmi (Common Man) Party, in the probably forlorn belief that a "strong" new national leader like Gujarat's chief minister Narendra Modi might somehow upend the ossified system. That anger also is reflected in the Maoist uprising in parts of eastern and central India. Both phenomena manifest a loss of faith in the alternatives to what Ambedkar called "the Grammar of Anarchy."

Even while cherishing the right to vote and to speak freely, Indians feel betrayed by their political system. In many circumstances, the rule of law does not apply to politicians, and citizens know that if, for instance, they go to the police to file a complaint against a public figure, they may well face further harassment. In short, there is in India a lack of demonstrable fairness and justice: Although some prominent politicians recently have been arrested and prosecuted, crimes by the powerful and the well connected can quite blatantly go unpunished. In some states, politicians enter politics in the first place in order to protect themselves and their interests, despite having criminal convictions; they calculate that they can operate outside the law.

Until now, no major political party has been willing to challenge this anomaly, which started in earnest in the 1970s. Most Indian parliamentary constituencies have more than a million voters, and an election is inevitably costly. In the decades before and after independence, political parties, and in particular the Indian National Congress, were funded by businesses and industrial companies. In April 1969, Prime Minister Indira Gandhi banned companies from making corporate donations in a plainly partisan move designed to limit the expansion of the promarket Swatantra (Independent) Party. Since the state offers candidates no funding, "black money" from businesspeople hoping for a favor in the future is the only way candidates can finance their campaigns.

Although this system has been slightly updated, it remains impossible to run an election campaign without illicit funds. During the 2009 general election, a candidate seeking to win a parliamentary constituency was estimated to need $2 million to $3 million to have a fair chance of success; officially, each candidate was permitted to spend only $55,000. Some of this money would be needed to run the cam-

It remains impossible to run an election campaign without illicit funds.

paign, but most would be given to local leaders who promised to deliver the votes of a particular caste or religious group that they claimed to be able to mobilize on election day. The rise of criminalization in some states, and of rich power brokers in others, has resulted in intraparty democracy largely disappearing. The well-entrenched political families who sit in parliament are served by this system; the handful of ambitious or idealistic individuals among them who attempt to alter it have little room to maneuver.

At a national level, that means politics has become ever more elitist and unrepresentative. The lower house of parliament, the Lok Sabha, has 545 members. Those who come from an established political dynasty already are, on average, nearly five times richer than those who have no nepotistic background in politics. MPs who come from hyperconnected political families—for example, those with a mother-in-law, an uncle, and a sibling in national or regional politics—are on average even richer than MPs who have entered parliament after a successful career in business. At present, two-thirds of India's sitting MPs under the age of forty already have a near relative in politics. This was not the case a generation ago. Politics has become a family business, because that is the easiest way to make it work. As in so many spheres of Indian life, an amorphous and opaque "family" of relatives, associates, and employees controls each local political operation.

In other democracies, the children of a president or a prime minister often seek to join the political rat race, but the parties themselves are not controlled by individual families. The leadership of the Labour Party in Britain would be unlikely to appeal publicly and plaintively for Tony Blair's offspring to take the reins of power for the good of the nation. In India, in Pakistan, and indeed in the Philippines, this is what happens. Benigno Aquino III, who became president in 2010, is the fourth successive generation of his family to hold paramount political power. In succession to his grandfather and his mother, the wealthy Bilawal Bhutto Zardari became cochairman of the Pakistan People's Party after his mother's assassination in 2007 (although at twenty-four he was too young to stand in the 2013 parliamentary elections). In India, Rahul

Gandhi is the most prominent national scion of dynastic politics, but his position is replicated right through the Congress and other parties.

The Bharatiya Janata Party and the leftist parties remain comparatively meritocratic, but a stunning nine out of ten Congress party MPs under the age of forty are hereditary, effectively having inherited a parliamentary seat, usually from a parent. Wealth and heredity correlate closely. Since few lawmakers declare the full extent of their wealth, it is hard to build a complete picture. But the election commission is increasingly organized and assertive, and the affidavits of assets that candidates are required to file along with their nomination papers make interesting reading. Taking the officially declared wealth of MPs as a starting point, fifteen out of the twenty richest MPs in the current Lok Sabha are hereditary, and ten of these belong to the Congress party.

Meaningful democracy and free elections depend not only on people being allowed to turn out to vote but also on a degree of merit-based accountability within the parties themselves. In most political parties, internal democracy barely exists.

The demands of creating an organization that can win elections in each large constituency are substantial. Except in rare circumstances, such as when a disadvantaged local community comes together in an upsurge of popular enthusiasm, it depends primarily on cash. Politicians need money in order to be reelected, and businesspeople need proximity to power if they are to get things done in a country where the administrative and legal systems are often dysfunctional.

As Raghuram Rajan, formerly the Indian government's chief economic adviser and now the governor of the Reserve Bank of India, pointed out in a speech at the Bombay Chamber of Commerce in 2008, few Indian billionaires made their wealth from innovative businesses such as IT. "Three factors—land, natural resources and government contracts—are the predominant sources of the wealth of our billionaires. And all of these factors come from the government." The rich need the politicians, and the politicians need the rich, and in some cases the rich and the politicians are the same people. It is a symbiotic relationship from which both sides benefit—only the nation loses.

To push forward and really make things change, India needs to mandate internal democracy in political parties and prevent them from operating as family fiefdoms; party finances should become more transparent, and some form of state funding has to be considered; candidates who have been convicted of a serious crime, or have charges pending against them and are playing the court system, should be blocked from running for office.

India's problem is not the individual politicians or even democracy itself—it is a system of governance and administration that has reached a state of chronic dysfunction. The system is paralyzed, and no new leader will be able to reform it without well-intentioned cross-party cooperation in a larger national interest, similar to the grand and historic deal that was put together in 1947.

overtaking the dragon
Yasheng Huang

Over the years, in my visits to India and my conversations with Indian scholars and journalists, I have heard a common refrain about Indian growth. Ask why India's economy performed badly in the 1960s and 1970s, and the answer—usually issued with a deep sigh—is "democracy." Ask about India's failure to build sufficient infrastructure or attract foreign direct investment, and the answer is the same. Ask about India's poor educational and health achievements—democracy again.

But if I ask about the rise of India's IT and software industry, suddenly the discussion becomes more lively and specific. Typically, the explanation for India's economic successes is that reforms introduced in 1991 opened India to international trade and competition, allowed partial privatization of the financial system and thus increased the amount of credit available to the private sector, and did away with a host of anti-growth regulations across many different sectors.

Notice a subtle shift in attributions of India's failures and its successes in this narrative. Its failures are blamed on politics—democracy. Its successes are credited to changes in the economic system. The logic of this narrative shapes how many members of India's chattering class—and many non-Indian thinkers as well—view China and India. The received wisdom holds that China has an economic advantage over India because it can implement reforms without bearing the burden of India's messy and lumbering democracy. No wonder, many Indians reason, China's

Yasheng Huang is professor of international management at the MIT Sloan School of Management.

economy has boomed and outperforms India's in the delivery of key so-cial services such as health care and education.

This view is widely accepted—and utterly false. The Indian economy's historic underperformance and its recent successes have both political and economic roots. The Indian economist Raj Krishna famously described the long stagnation that afflicted India before the 1991 reforms as the "Hindu rate of growth." But as Arun Shourie, a former Indian politician, observed, India stagnated because of the socialist policies adopted by the Congress party during the Nehru-Gandhi era, not because of anything intrinsic to Hindu religion or culture. India's economy posted anemic growth rates in the three decades after independence because policy makers in those years embraced the same import substitution and commanding heights, statist economic policies that depressed growth in other developing economies, most notably in the military regimes of Latin America.

> India stagnated because of socialist policies, not because of anything intrinsic to Hindu religion or culture.

In India, unlike the Latin regimes, the military never seized political control. But it is worth noting that the leisurely Hindu rate coincided with India's slide in an authoritarian direction under Indira Gandhi, who led India from 1966 to 1984. In those years, the Congress party had a lock on political power and governed like a feudal fiefdom. Consider this trenchant indictment of the Congress party rule in that era: "Millions of ordinary Congress workers are handicapped, for on their backs ride the brokers of power and influence, who dispense patronage to convert a mass movement into a feudal oligarchy. . . . Corruption is not only tolerated but even regarded as a hallmark of leadership."

The critic was none other than Rajiv Gandhi, the biological and political heir of Indira Gandhi herself. During the Indira Gandhi years, the famous Clintonian rule, "It's the economy, stupid," did not apply. Patronage and cronyism insulated Indian politicians from the normal electoral consequences of poor economic performance. The electoral successes of the Congress party in 1967, 1971, and then in 1980 were all preceded by a decline of per capita GDP. In 1974, the year before the scheduled election that Gandhi suspended, per capita GDP dropped by 3.11 percent.

Indira Gandhi's rule was anything but democratic. She stifled nominating and electoral procedures within her own party, nullified election results at the state level many times by invoking her "emergency" powers, and in 1975 attempted to dispense with democracy altogether by declaring a nationwide state of emergency. The Hindu rate of growth could be as easily blamed on her authoritarian rule as on India's unruly democracy.

Cronyism insulated Indian politicians from the normal electoral consequences of poor performance.

India's burst of rapid growth after 1991 occurred during a period when the political system became more open and more democratic. The government privatized TV broadcasting, and the Constitution was amended to allow more village self-rule. Indian citizens now enjoy greater access to information controlled by the state. A common critique of democracy is that it galvanizes opposition to painful reforms. But in India, nearly all important legislative reforms have been carried out by coalitions of multiple parties rather than by a single majority ruling party. This is true of the Congress party in the early 1990s, the Bharatiya Janata Party between 1998 and 2004, and the Congress party today. Indeed, the Congress party, in its majoritarian moment under Indira Gandhi, succeeded only in straitjacketing the economy and depressing growth, not in liberalizing the economy and encouraging growth.

Even so, critics of Indian democracy abound. In a recent *New York Times* online essay, for example, Steven Rattner, a prominent American private equity investor, declared that "India is losing the race" against China. China, he noted, is twice as rich as India; it has sixteen subway systems compared with India's five; GDP growth was 7.7 percent in 2012 compared with India's 5.3 percent; it invests 48 percent of its GDP compared with India's 36 percent.

Rattner stressed that he was "hardly advocating totalitarian government." But he sounded the familiar refrain about the perils of democracy: "We need to recognize that success for developing countries is about more than free elections."

But do developing countries that allow free elections do so always and everywhere at the expense of prosperity? Did China really grow faster than India because of its one-party system? Compare two Asian countries—let's call them Country A and Country B—using GDP data from the World Bank. In 1990, Country A had a per capita GDP of $1,209 (in 2005 dollars adjusted for purchasing power parity) while Country B had per capita GDP of $1,620. By 2011, their positions had reversed: Country A had $3,203 while Country B had $2,423. Which country is India? The answer is Country A, which appears to be the superior performer in this comparison because Country B is Pakistan. A comparison of authoritarian China and democratic India suggests a democratic disadvantage. But a comparison between democratic India and episodically authoritarian Pakistan suggests the exact opposite.

Proponents of the idea that authoritarian regimes enjoy economic advantages over democratic competitors often cite as evidence the success of the East Asian economies, particularly South Korea and Taiwan. But their conclusions are predicated on a deeply flawed reading of the data. The fable that wise government planners, unencumbered by democratic bickering, engineered an "East Asian miracle" can be told only by cherry-picking cases. The reality is that for each East Asian authoritarian success story, there is an East Asian authoritarian failure. Taiwan grew rich but authoritarian Maoist China didn't. South Korea developed rapidly but North Korea stagnated. Strong one-man rule in Singapore succeeded, but so did laissez-faire Hong Kong. In its totality, the East Asian experience precisely mirrors what social scientists have long understood about the relationship between political systems and economic outcomes: It is ambiguous and indeterminate. Authoritarian regimes are no more successful economically than democratic regimes.

But, one may argue, even if the authoritarian edge is not a general proposition, surely it must be true in the cases of China and India. The conclusion seems so obvious: China is authoritarian and it has grown faster; India is democratic and it has grown more slowly. But for reasons that have much to do with the vagaries of Chinese economic data, the comparison between China and India is far more complicated than it appears.

Consider Rattner's claim that China's per capita GDP is now more than twice that of India. That's true if one accepts the World Bank data, which show that China overtook India in per capita GDP in the early 1990s. The trouble, though, is that we do not know the real size of China's GDP before the country embarked on its reform program in 1978. To name just one of the technical discrepancies: Under central planning, the Chinese national income was calculated on the basis of "net material product"; national income accounting omitted the entire service sector. In 1986, the Harvard economist Dwight Perkins estimated China's GDP per capita in 1985 to be around $500 (in terms of exchange rate conversion). In the same year, India's GDP per capita was $301. Another study shows that China's nutritional levels and consumption of durable goods as of the early 1990s were broadly similar to Taiwan's of the early 1970s. The economists Ross Garnaut and Guonan Ma concluded that GDP per capita for China in 1990 ought to be valued at around $1,000. India's GDP per capita in that same year was only $370.

It is possible, in other words, that China has always been richer than India for reasons that have nothing to do with politics or, for that matter, economics. Perhaps the crucial difference is geography and thus climate: China is temperate whereas India is tropical. Or maybe it is that China's population is far more ethnically homogeneous than India's—a factor many studies have found to be an economic plus. The point is that there are multiple alternative explanations for why China is richer than India. We should not seize upon the authoritarian edge theory in the absence of empirical evidence strong enough to support serious policy implications.

Democracy does no harm to growth, and this is reason enough to favor democracy over its alternatives. Those clamoring for the Chinese political system might do well to reflect on the gruesome statistics marshaled by Steven Pinker in his recent book, *The Better Angels of Our Nature*: In the twentieth century, totalitarian regimes killed 138 million of their own people and authoritarian regimes were responsible for the deaths of an additional 28 million. Even today, China's vaunted authoritarian system is fouling the air and water in ways that jeopardize the health of hundreds of millions of its citizens and doing irreparable damage to China's economy.

Democracies have their failings—some severe enough to have led to unnatural deaths of their citizens. America's inability to control guns and the shocking revelations about the indifference of Indian police and court toward rape victims are cases in point. But all else being equal, it is far more likely that China will move closer to the political system represented by India than the other way around. In the early 1960s, about 20 percent of the world was democratic; today the figure is around 65 percent. The world is trending the Indian way, not the Chinese. Indians should continue to seek solutions to their problems within a democratic framework and ignore both fellow citizens and well-meaning outsiders seduced by overly simplistic notions about the ability of authoritarian governments to conjure rapid economic growth.

> It is far more likely that China will move closer to the political system represented by India than the other way around.

india rebooted
Azim Premji

For thousands of years, stretching back to the time of the great cities of the Indus Valley, India was never imagined as a single entity—nor even as one people with a shared destiny. There were brief periods in which the vision came close: the imperial ambitions of great leaders such as Ashoka (in the third century BCE) and Akbar (sixteenth century CE), for example, or in the ideas of some of our syncretic socioreligious thinkers. But it took the great intellectual ferment of the mid-twentieth century, energized by the struggle for independence from colonial rule and shaped by new notions of modernity, to finally crystallize our loose collective history and shared culture into the idea of India as one nation.

At the heart of this new imagination of India were three radical notions: that the subcontinent's huge and diverse population could come together as a unified people; that together they could realize a shared vision of a democratic, equitable, and humane society; and that creation of inclusive institutions and processes could overcome the obstacles created by our recent history of sectarian violence, internal division, prejudice, and poverty. Citizens of the new nation gave form and substance to those ideals through India's 1950 Constitution.

India's bold experiment has succeeded in many ways. The most important triumph of the idea of India is that the dreams of 1947 still have force and value. The institutions established by the Constitution have retained their core purpose of nurturing democracy and inclusiveness.

Azim Premji is chairman of Wipro Ltd.

Democracy has taken deep and abiding root in our country, empowering the disadvantaged and marginalized. And yet we remain far from achieving the many goals we set for ourselves in those first years of independence. Particularly when it comes to integrating the economic and social aspects of development, our young nation cannot claim great success.

Economic development was—and continues to be—integral to the idea of India. Early on in our journey, we realized that while there can be economic progress without social development, it is almost impossible to achieve social development without economic growth. So we subordinated our economic goals to a broader social vision. In the first five-year plan, we gave great emphasis to economic growth. However, government "guidance" of economic growth—which was necessary given the nascent stage of industrialization at the time and the need to allocate scarce resources in an optimal manner—quickly morphed into the license raj, with all its attendant problems. The result was forty years of economic stagnation.

The most important triumph of the idea of India is that the dreams of 1947 still have force and value.

The reforms initiated in 1991 unleashed genuine economic dynamism. For a few years in the 1990s and 2000s, India's economy accelerated at a rapid rate, leading to a mistaken belief that high growth in India was "inevitable" and the new natural state of affairs. In recent years we have learned otherwise, as the combination of a global slump and our own failure to push forward with fundamental economic reforms ushered in the current period of lackluster growth. Moreover, we are beginning to realize that, even in the high-growth years, the benefits of rapid expansion were not equally shared. The bottom line is that, after six decades, India has yet to fulfill the basic needs and desires of hundreds of millions of its citizens for access to quality education, opportunities to work, or even clean water.

What's needed now is a new burst of imagination—not of the basic idea of India but of the way we integrate our social and economic visions and put political institutions formed in our first sixty-five years to work in the service of our ideals. Let me highlight four areas in urgent need of reimagining.

First, we must increase our public social sector spending while cutting wasteful expenditures. We spend a mere 4 percent on education, 1 percent on basic health care, and less than 1 percent on social security against the OECD average of 5, 7, and 22 percent, respectively. For a country with our generally poor levels of educational attainment, health, and social security, these spending levels are inadequate. At the same time we spend billions on economically misguided and socially counterproductive activities such as subsidies for power and fuel and inefficient public sector enterprises, not to mention the enormous sums lost through inefficiency and graft.

> The land alone can no longer support all those who depend on it.

Second, we must find sustainable solutions for the seven hundred to eight hundred million Indians who still live off the land and the one hundred to two hundred million marginalized urban poor. Given the current state of Indian agricultural productivity, the land alone can no longer support all those who depend on it. The time has come for a new burst of investment and innovation in Indian agriculture aimed at dramatic productivity gains. We must address complex issues such as land degradation and excess water consumption, and strengthen the links between farms and markets. India's tangled regulatory web in agriculture and forestry has ensnared the disadvantaged; we must strip away these restrictions to unleash the entrepreneurialism of the nation's poor farmers.

Third, we must find new ways to satisfy our growing appetite for energy. While India ranks low compared to other nations in per capita energy consumption, we face the prospect of severe energy shortages in the future. If we are to continue growing, our economy will need more energy. We remain heavily dependent on imported oil, and our domestic energy projects will not generate enough supply to keep pace with rising demand. At the same time, we must minimize the ecological costs of developing new energy resources. The solution to our energy dilemma will require an unprecedented combination of conservation and disruptive innovation.

Finally, and perhaps most important, we must reimagine our approach to education. Over the years, the Azim Premji Foundation has worked with the public education systems of multiple states which, in total, administer more than 350,000 schools. My experience working with those schools has convinced me we need a new focus on equitable access to quality education. Over the past two decades, India has made considerable progress in ensuring that children have access to and are enrolled in schools. But the actual process of education at those schools is woefully inadequate. Unfortunately, there are no quick fixes for this problem. No one has a magic wand that can instantly improve the quality of how we teach our children. This will require increasing public expenditure and sustained, painstaking effort on the front lines.

One place to start is our teacher education system. We must overhaul the curriculum for new teachers and rethink its duration, institutional structure, and regulatory environment. We should also develop a cadre of education professionals and generate knowledge through research. To achieve that goal, I believe we should establish thirty to fifty high-quality education schools within our leading universities. At the same time, we must find better methods for enhancing the capacities of our 6.5 million existing teachers. What's needed is nothing short of a cultural revolution to clear away the current mechanical management practices and empower our teachers and our schools. In my view, it may require twenty-five years of sustained work for us to make our education system robust, vibrant, and a genuine integrator of our social and economic vision. But this integration is critical for India to fulfill its potential and its dreams.

These issues are complex and interlinked. Solutions will require political courage—and not just from career politicians. Too often in India we abdicate responsibility for such complex socioeconomic issues to the political class. If we are to truly reimagine our nation, every one of us—and certainly those of us in the business sector—must play a proactive, progressive role.

In sum, we must reaffirm the idea of India as articulated in our Constitution and reimagine a new India with an integrated social and economic vision. Only then can we realize the just, equitable, and humane society to which we all aspire.

a tale of two democracies
Edward Luce

Indians often point to America's robber baron period in the late nineteenth century as proof that freedom and rampant corruption can flourish side by side. At a time of entrenched kleptocracy in large parts of India and slowing GDP growth, many Indians find reassuring parallels in U.S. history; the alternative is to despair over the fraying health of their own democracy. Thankfully, India is in little danger of considering any other system. Yet as the twenty-first century progresses, India's quality of government is increasingly on trial. And so, ironically, is that of the United States.

Having lived and worked continuously in Delhi and Washington since 1999, I feel entitled to at least an honorary PhD in misgovernance. The capitals of strikingly different and complex countries are home to the world's largest and richest democracies. The names of both capitals have become national bywords for dysfunction and inertia. Both have turned paralysis into the chief default option. It is fair to assume that the recent performances of Delhi and Washington have prompted little or any soul-searching in Beijing.

As India's growth slows, the human price tag of inaction rises.

Of these two great democracies, India's predicament is the more acute. Sixty-five years after independence, the task of governing India from the center gets more difficult by the year. The country's forty-year-

Edward Luce is Washington columnist for the Financial Times *and author of* In Spite of the Gods: The Strange Rise of Modern India.

long process of party fragmentation has yet to run its course; fashioning coherent governing coalitions is likely to become more difficult, not less, in the coming years. Political scientists say the 2014 general election may prove the first in India's history in which the two main parties, Congress and the Bharatiya Janata Party (BJP), achieve less than half the national vote between them—a worryingly low threshold for stable government.

Until recently, the transition from the single-party Congress rule of India's early decades to the multi-party coalitions of today was assumed to have been a success. Coalition governments of up to twenty-four parties were considered stable as long as they had a strong anchor—either Congress or the BJP. But the anchors keep getting lighter. Increasingly, India's government seems to have come completely unmoored. Manmohan Singh's Congress-led United Progressive Alliance (UPA) offers a case study of the damage fragmented politics can do.

The UPA was born amid great optimism in 2004 with Sonia Gandhi's well-staged act of renouncing India's prime ministership. Singh's admirers expected him to continue with the gradual economic reforms of Atal Bihari Vajpayee's BJP-led predecessor, the National Democratic Alliance, while dropping its menacing communal edge. The latter was certainly borne out. India's last really big communal flare-up was more than a decade ago. Singh also has proved adept at lowering the temperature in India-Pakistan relations. But on almost all else, the UPA has been a bitter disappointment. Time and again, reforms have been stillborn. As India's growth slows, the human price tag of inaction rises.

The UPA has suffered from three disabling problems. The first is its peculiar separation of political from executive power within the Congress party—the so-called dyarchy between Sonia Gandhi's dynastic center at 10 Janpath Road and Singh's formal residence on Race Course Road. Power without responsibility and responsibility without power is a terrible formula for good government. Reformers in Singh's government have been stymied by a kind of intraparty shadow cabinet of

> True power in India rests with the Gandhi family; the formal government largely has assumed the role of eunuch.

Gandhians, leftists, and dynastic courtiers, all currying favor with Sonia Gandhi. The most frequent result of the tug-of-war between cabinet and shadow cabinet is deadlock. True power rests with the Gandhi family; India's formal government has largely assumed the role of eunuch.

The UPA's second problem is the growing leverage of narrow caste, language, and regional parties—groups with one key trait in common: the absence of any national agenda. Most, such as Mamata Banerjee's Trinamool (Grassroots) Congress in West Bengal, or Jayalalitha's All India Anna Dravida Munnetra Kazhagam in Tamil Nadu, view Delhi chiefly as a source of spoils. They tend to oppose privatization and attempts to slim down large state bureaucracies, such as Indian Railways, since this would deprive them of their most lucrative satrapies. In their own somewhat dyarchic way, regional parties see no contradiction between pursuing reform in their states, as many chief ministers have done, while wrecking it at the national level. Singh has spent much of his second term trying to prevent the UPA from falling apart. Since coalitions move at the pace of their most reluctant member, this has helped stall active government in Delhi.

Regional parties see no contradiction between pursuing reform in their states while wrecking it at the national level.

The UPA's third problem is the continued degradation in India's government machinery. In 2004, Singh promised to make reform of the bureaucracy one of his chief priorities. With the exception of the 2004 Right to Information Act, which opened up much of Indian government to public scrutiny, Singh has been blocked by the bureaucracy he has sought to reform. His increasingly ineffectual efforts tapered off long before the end of the UPA's first term in 2009. Singh's government has been almost continually mired since then in corruption scandals from the 2010 Commonwealth Games through rigged telecoms spectrum auctions to coal block misallocations, bribery by defense helicopter manufacturers, insider government land sales, and so on. The sense of spreading graft is tangible. Delhi's senior civil service was once seen as the steel frame of an unruly democracy. But the elite Indian Administrative Service is losing its reputation for probity. Almost everyone, it seems, has his or her price nowadays—not just the politicians.

If fragmentation is sapping Delhi, in Washington it is polarization. The United States has only two parties compared to almost two hundred in India. But America's deepening gridlock is producing similar results. A few months before he died, Steve Jobs, the legendary founder of Apple, met President Barack Obama at a dinner in Silicon Valley. They did not see eye to eye. "The president is very smart," Jobs told his biographer, Walter Isaacson. "But he kept explaining to us reasons why things can't get done. It infuriates me." To be fair, the U.S. president was only describing reality.

There have been two distinct phases to Obama's presidency. During the first, which ended in November 2010, Obama had a Democratic majority in both chambers of Congress. He was able to push through an $832 billion stimulus package, the Dodd-Frank bill reregulating Wall Street, and his controversial plan for health-care reform. During the second, which has yet to come to an end, Republicans took control of the House of Representatives and Obama's legislative agenda came juddering to a halt. Obama's priority between now and the midterm elections in November 2014 will be to win back the House and restore the conditions that he enjoyed for his first two years. Even then, he would have only a year or so to act before his term was over.

In earlier eras of U.S. history—such as during Ronald Reagan's administration in the 1980s, which coexisted productively with a Democratic Congress, or Lyndon Johnson's in the 1960s, when the Democratic chief executive needed the support of Republican legislators to push through the civil rights reforms—cross-party fluidity was common. Opposition legislators often voted with the president on a case-by-case basis. Today, such promiscuity is no longer tolerated, particularly among Republicans. America's separation of powers has morphed into a semipermanent handcuff on government. Far from returning the United States to its roots, as some constitutional fundamentalists argue, such paralysis is new. It is hard to see what will bring it to an end.

What can the United States and India learn from each other? Leo

Tolstoy, one of Mohandas Gandhi's heroes, said that each unhappy family was unhappy in its own way. Much the same could be said about dysfunctional systems. There is nothing as stubborn as a country's political culture. In my observations of India and the United States, I continually run into one trait they share: Both tend to see unique faults in their own political setup. Both also imagine the grass is greener elsewhere. Americans are increasingly suffering from "parliamentary envy"—the promise of decisive Westminster-style government. And more and more Indians are nowadays musing on the benefits of the presidential system. I am often struck by this irony.

There are many words to describe what the two are suffering: "entropy," "atrophy," and "stasis" spring to mind. Or perhaps we should coin a new word: "vetocracy." But neither India nor the United States is likely to change its system in the foreseeable future: Democracies rarely overhaul themselves unless forced to do so. Rather, both seem likely to remain mired in a self-fulfilling culture of declining trust in public institutions. In the United States, the electorate's faith in Congress has fluctuated between 8 and 13 percent since 2010—a historic low. But perhaps this isn't surprising given that the U.S. Congress has failed to pass a budget since 2009. In India, the share of elected politicians with criminal backgrounds continues to rise (lawmakers cannot be prosecuted). And what few pieces of legislation achieve consensus in today's barely functioning Lok Sabha, the lower house of India's parliament, should rarely be confused with policy making.

In India, the share of elected politicians with criminal backgrounds continues to rise.

In his recent book, *The End of Power*, the Washington-based economist Moisés Naím notes that governments everywhere have found it harder and harder to exercise power as they once did. This applies to wealthy countries like the United States and poor countries like India—and even extends to autocracies such as China. It also applies to companies, armies, newspapers, and many other traditional sources of authority. Everywhere, power is becoming easier to acquire, harder to wield, and easier to lose. The rise of material aspirations and the spread of technological autonomy are making politics (and much else) more volatile and less predictable. Indians and Americans tend to curse the unique failings of their own political classes. Few grasp how typical they are.

In pondering their governance woes, and in observing, for that matter, those of countries like Italy and Britain, it is hard to escape the thought that each would be better off if it had more effective defenses against the rolling caprice of the twenty-four-hour news cycle. If you break down public trust polling in the United States and India, unelected and independent bodies, such as the U.S. Federal Reserve and the Indian Election Commission, consistently top the rankings. Both institutions are shielded from day-to-day political interference, although they are ultimately accountable to elected officials. Neither pays much attention to ratings. Sometimes, perhaps, less democracy can mean more.

To propose detailed remedies for the political maladies of India and the United States is beyond my competence. But it would be hard to exaggerate the importance of that renewal—or how difficult it will be.

The Yale political scientist Jacob Hacker has written, "The Catch-22 of American politics is that the only viable and defensible route to fixing our broken political system lies through our broken system." Hacker's observation is no less true of India—indeed, it applies with all the more force and urgency to India given the country's relative poverty and the high proportion of Indians who are young and male. These youthful multitudes, often celebrated as India's "demographic dividend," will need jobs. And if sufficient formal sector jobs cannot be created, they will still need income. It is not impossible to imagine India's demographic dividend turning into a nightmare. America can afford to drift along for another decade or two. India cannot.

the precocious experiment
Arvind Subramanian

"Precocious" is a word seldom used in describing India, a country whose ancient civilization spawned the Sanskrit hymns of the Rig Veda, the epic poems of the Mahabharata and Ramayana, and three of the world's great religions—Hinduism, Buddhism, and Jainism—five centuries before the birth of Christ.

And yet modern India can be described as precocious in two fundamental senses: economic and political. Indeed, India can be deemed the critical test of the viability of a unique experiment I call the Precocious Development Model.

For a host of reasons stemming from its statist policies of the 1950s and '60s, India has embraced an economic model that relies for growth on a limited pool of skilled labor rather than its abundant supply of cheap, unskilled, and semiliterate labor. This strategy has meant that India specializes in services rather than in manufacturing and manifests traits found in much more advanced economies. Direct investment abroad by Indians is a prominent example; never before has such an underdeveloped country invested so heavily in much richer countries. The anomaly of Indian businesses running Corus Steel and Jaguar Land Rover offers vivid evidence of the Indian economic model's precociousness.

With the experiences of Imperial Britain, Pax Americana, and more recently China clearly in mind, Lee Kuan Yew famously noted that no country in history became a great economic power without first becom-

Arvind Subramanian is a senior fellow at the Peterson Institute for International Economics and at the Center for Global Development.

ing an industrial power. India's challenge is thus to defy the Sage of Singapore and find a trajectory to economic greatness that does not involve heavy reliance on manufacturing and cheap labor.

Politically, too, India's precocity is remarkable, as witnessed by the democracy it has sustained at unusually low levels of income, education, industrialization, and urbanization. The Indian democracy exception is a staple of political science debates. But very few countries, especially large ones, have sustained economic growth as continuous democracies. In the postwar global economy, the dominant experience has been for some form of politically centralized authority (the military in Korea, the party in China, strongmen in Chile) to initiate and maintain rapid economic development.

The peril and potential of India's economic future can be understood only in the context of these two types of precociousness. The interaction between India's imperfect democracy and the limits of its skill-reliant economic model will shape the arc of the country's development.

Let's examine the latter factor first. After thirty years of robust economic growth—6 percent for two decades and nearly 9 percent in the last decade—the Indian economy is decelerating. India's development model itself may be responsible for this slowdown. How so? Consider some key factors of production that determine growth.

Skilled labor has been India's primary source of comparative advantage. But two decades of double-digit growth in remuneration of skilled labor are signaling that demand is running ahead of the ability of India's shambolic higher-education system to turn out capable knowledge workers. Skilled labor has become a scarce resource—a stark manifestation being the well-known penchant of recently minted university graduates to hop from one job to the next.

As for unskilled labor, India's abundance of it contributes little to growth because a panoply of regulations—a legacy of state-led development—stifles the expansion of labor-intensive industries such as apparel, furniture, and metal fabrication. At least a million low-skilled workers will enter the job market every month for the next several decades, but it is unlikely that they all will find employment given the country's development model.

And eroding the gains generated by the private sector is the continued heavy hand of government and associated rent seeking—that is, the siphoning off of wealth, both legal and otherwise, by public officials and government agencies. Once an import-quota-license raj, in which massive bureaucracies held power of approval over minor business operating decisions and purchases from abroad, India has become a resource-rents raj, with new forms of rent seeking and corruption impairing the supply capacity of the economy. Rent seeking in land acquisition has affected the provision of infrastructure and impeded the development of large-scale manufacturing. Rent seeking in coal has affected power generation capacity. Rent seeking in allocation of frequency spectrum for mobile phones erupted into a scandal that nearly paralyzed the process of government itself.

At the same time, thanks in large part to the compulsions and flaws of its democracy, India's macroeconomy is now one of the most vulnerable in the emerging market world. Stubbornly persistent double-digit inflation and widening current account deficits are reminiscent of Latin America in its dark era of debt crises. The underlying source of this looming instability is high and rising fiscal deficits that are now close to 10 percent of GDP. Over the last decade, both at the central and state levels, expenditures per capita—mostly on social programs—have doubled, the result of fiscal populism that in turn derives directly from the nature of the political system.

> On most measures of market friendliness, India lags behind Latin America and even sub-Saharan Africa.

What, then, is the hope for India? The glib answer is: strong leaders who will deliver good governance and reforms, such as Gujarat Chief Minister Narendra Modi. But there may be deeper reasons to maintain faith in India's economic possibilities.

The advantage of backwardness. With living standards about one-tenth those of the richest countries, India is still so poor that considerable scope for growth remains via catching up to the frontier of economic advancement. Further, demography may not be destiny, but India's demographic dividend will surely impart dynamism—the burgeoning number of young people means more entrepreneurship, more savings, more ideas. And as long as they can be provided reasonable opportunities, growth can be lifted.

Growth begets growth. India's rate of economic expansion should arguably be much more modest—4 to 5 percent a year, not the 8 percent-plus of recent years—given its aforementioned impediments to market forces. On most measures of market friendliness, India lags behind Latin America and even sub-Saharan Africa. Conventional explanations of its puzzlingly rapid progress focus on elite education and a dynamic information technology sector. These have played important roles in kick-starting growth but are too small in size and too narrow in the benefits they generate to sustain momentum in such a large economy. The real explanation may be that, although policy makers have done the minimum to start growth, growth itself is now the driver of change and is begetting more.

This dynamic works through different channels. First, a three-decade-long growth spurt has fostered entrepreneurship. India, in the words of the political scientist Devesh Kapur, is now a nation of hustlers, constantly searching for economic opportunities—including ingenious ways of circumventing onerous rules—that, in turn, keep the economic engine purring. As the protagonist in Aravind Adiga's *The White Tiger* says, "The Indian entrepreneur has to be straight and crooked, mocking and believing, sly and sincere, at the same time."

Second, rising demand allows the private to supplant the public sector. In education, for example, where the government's failures to provide good schools are well known, growth has changed the picture dramatically, largely because it has increased the returns from education—and hence the demand for it. Evidence is provided by the work of the economists Karthik Muralidharan and Michael Kremer, who show that private schools are mushrooming in rural India (many prominently advertising "English medium") because of teacher absenteeism in public schools. And companies are creating training centers to build skills in the cities (such as the Infosys Leadership Institute in Mysore) because institutions of higher education are notoriously inadequate.

Competition between states. The weakness of the central government reflects a considerable shift in power to the states. Indeed, most issues that critically concern investors—land, infrastructure, human capital, law and order—are largely under state domain. So, hard as it may be to envision the federal government getting its act together, what happens in the states will increasingly determine India's economic fortunes.

It is not that leadership in the states is better on average than at the center, but in a decentralized India, a few visibly successful experiments can have powerful economic repercussions. Capital and labor can and will flow from the laggard states to the performing ones, and laggards will have fewer excuses for nonperformance if the experience of a neighboring state is better. In the past, the southern states were the pacesetters. This is no longer the case today. There are encouraging improvements across India—in the north (Haryana), west (Gujarat), east (Bihar), and central India (Madhya Pradesh).

> Private schools are mushrooming in rural India because of teacher absenteeism in public schools.

An example was the experience of the Nano, an iconic attempt to produce a reasonably priced car for India's mass market. Overregulation discouraged its manufacturer, the Tata Group, from starting a factory in West Bengal. In the India of old, this would have killed the project. But now the better-governed state of Gujarat has taken the project instead.

Decentralization is not without risks. High-performing states tend to be run by "authoritarian democrats," leaders who, once elected, face few checks and balances. Moreover, states have been very reluctant to extend the advantages of decentralization all the way to the local government level, the result being a pernicious effect on urbanization. Cities in India do not have autonomy to raise resources, nor are their leaders directly accountable to citizens, resulting in crumbling infrastructure even in a city such as Mumbai.

Changing democratic politics. The competition between states cannot generate lasting benefits unless voters reward good governance. Until recently, India's political system was characterized by anti-incumbency, with identity politics trumping other criteria for choosing a candidate. As a result, politicians had little incentive to deliver essential services and enact lasting reforms. Recently, though, Indian voters have reelected many incumbents who improved economic outcomes; meanwhile, some poor performers—as exemplified by the Communist Party in West Bengal—have been ousted.

Democracies and crises. In India there is a strong consensus for weak reforms, as Planning Commission deputy chairman Montek Singh Ahluwalia has wryly observed. But to be fair, the enactment of strong reforms in the absence of crisis is rare in almost any country. Indeed, the recent experience of the United States and Europe, as well as other major democracies, suggests that crises are the unavoidable, even necessary, midwives of reforms. India is hardly unique in this regard. After the global crisis of 2008, India's growth appeared to be cruising at about 8 percent, so the government did not feel obliged to undertake growth-enhancing reforms. Nor was there any serious attempt to squeeze double-digit inflation out of the system—for fear that growth, which voters had come to take for granted, would suffer.

But when growth recently began to fall below 5 to 6 percent and, critically, when this deceleration began to seem more permanent, panic galvanized policy makers into action. Strengthening their resolve was the threat of downgrading by the rating agencies, which would have further undermined investor confidence and growth. In other words, India fulfills the minimal requirement, common to most democracies, of reforming to avert crises. The difference is that in the West crises are characterized by zero or negative growth, while in India that threshold now is about 5 percent. From collective acquiescence at the "Hindu growth rate" of 3 percent to restiveness even at 5 percent is a measure of how far India has come.

At the end of the day, for all the positive developments noted above, there are at least as many dispiriting ones. The writ of the Indian state, for example, covers only about 80 percent of the country, with the tribal belt essentially contested by Maoist insurgents. The Indian state is increasingly unable to provide a range of basic services—health, education, physical security, rule of law, water, sanitation—which disproportionately affects the poor. This is captured in the deep despair of a girl in the slums of Mumbai described in Katherine Boo's recent book, *Behind the Beautiful Forevers*: "We try so many things, but the world doesn't seem to move in our favor." The private sector can overcome some of these deficiencies but never completely, and because it cannot, the outcome can be chaotic, unregulated growth.

Moreover, talent is fleeing the public sector, reflected in the dramatic increase in unfilled vacancies in India's police, military, administrative services, and even the elite institutes of higher education. In the long run, growth is determined by effective state capacity—and that is India's weakness compared with China.

India's democratic politics has provided the space to minimize the risks from some of the country's numerous social cleavages such as language and caste, but others—such as religion, region, and skill levels—may be less easy to manage. And then, in addition to rampant corruption, are the other growth-sapping features of the political system: coalition politics that favors the status quo and stymies change, deterioration in the quality of politics and politicians, and the obliteration of boundaries between private and public interests. There is a race between rot and regeneration of public institutions, and perhaps neither will triumph but just coexist as India muddles along.

A decade or two from now, a simple metric may be sufficient to assess whether India will have risen to the economic challenge: economic growth of no less than 8 percent per year. That pace will be necessary to provide employment opportunities to the massive additions to the labor force and to meet the rising aspirations of ordinary Indians. And there is another reason to use that metric: China—India's partner, neighbor, model, competitor, and sometimes aggressor—posted 10½ percent growth for thirty years.

Can India make it? Is India not at least three-quarters as efficient and capable as China? Because India is attempting a historically unique experiment—the Precocious Development Model—the statistical odds are against it. The objective analyst that I aspire to be would have to say the odds India will make it are no better than forty in favor and sixty against. But the visceral nationalist in me nudges the odds up to, in the comedian Keshto Mukherjee's memorable and stock phrase, "phipty-phipty."

demographic dividend—or disaster?
Victor Mallet

You don't have to visit India to understand that the world's population, already exceeding seven billion, continues to grow at an alarming rate. But it certainly helps. Better still, come to the banks of the River Ganges during a Kumbh Mela—a Hindu religious festival that takes place every three years and last occurred in early 2013—and watch the crowds surging into the holy if somewhat polluted waters to wash away their sins.

A precise head count is impossible, but Indian police and officials say eighty to one hundred million pilgrims came to Allahabad during the two months of the 2013 Mela, a particularly auspicious celebration of a religious cycle completed once every 144 years. They estimate that twenty to thirty million people bathed in the Ganges on February 10 alone. Managing such enormous crowds on the river's sandy banks is an extraordinary challenge (rule #1: Keep them moving). Despite authorities' best efforts, thirty-six people died that day in a stampede at the Allahabad railway station.

The millions of Indians gathered in the shallows and in the Kumbh Mela's collection of tents and temporary temples—described by Harvard researchers as a "pop-up megacity"—are believed to have constituted the largest gathering of humans on earth.

India is crowded at the best of times. It was in Delhi that Paul Ehrlich, the neo-Malthusian author of *The Population Bomb*, experienced his hellish epiphany about overpopulation: "People eating, people washing, people sleeping. People visiting, arguing, and screaming. People thrust-

Victor Mallet is the South Asia bureau chief for the Financial Times.

ing their hands through the taxi window, begging. People defecating and urinating. People clinging to buses. People herding animals. People, people, people, people."

And that was forty-five years ago, when India's population of just over 500 million was less than half what it is today. With more than 1.2 billion inhabitants, India is on track to overtake China as the world's most populous nation by 2025. At its likely peak four decades from now, India's population will exceed 1.7 billion.

Such projections sound fantastical, but among population experts, they are not in dispute. Such is the ineluctable arithmetic of "demographic momentum." Even when a fast-growing country's fertility rate falls toward replacement levels, the population keeps increasing for decades because of the large cohorts of young women reaching childbearing age.

What is in dispute is whether the increase in the number of inhabitants—bearing in mind that India will add some five hundred million people, equivalent to the entire population of the European Union—will help or harm India's economy and society, and whether the country's institutions will be able to cope. A review of India's record to date of investment in the "soft" and "hard" infrastructure vital for development—education and health care, as well as school buildings, hospitals, roads, and power stations—is hardly reassuring.

Indian politicians and international economists are easily seduced by the notion of a "demographic dividend"; many speak as if any nation with a rising population can count on a great boon, automatically conferred by providence. Optimistic about the commercial prospects for emerging markets, these "population boosters" note that a greater number of inhabitants results in a higher gross domestic product and a bigger workforce, while a fast-growing population produces a period when the dependency ratio falls—that is, when there are more workers relative to children and old people and therefore higher savings and investment to increase per capita income.

An easy prop for such arguments is to mock the famously incorrect predictions of Thomas Malthus, the snobbish economist who foresaw famine and disaster in his 1798 treatise, *An Essay on the Principle of Population*, because he failed to predict improved farm productivity as a result of mechanization and other scientific advances. Malthus, however, was right about many things, and population size has in fact been cited at least as a contributory factor in various famines, including the eighteenth-century Irish potato famine and the Ethiopian disaster of 1984. He was right about population pressures being a cause of war, particularly when aggressive pastoralists attack settled farmers: Think Darfur in Sudan. Intriguingly, he also predicted two hundred years before the event that densely populated China would become a powerful exporter of manufactured goods.

Attacking Malthus, however, is easy because he was wrong—at the time, at least—in his central prediction. But the mistakes of Malthus two centuries ago should not excuse the loose talk by everyone from the Indian politician and cabinet minister Kamal Nath to the UBS economist Andrew Cates about the supposedly beneficial economic consequences of population growth. A shrinking population, or declining population growth, is almost always defined in speeches and investment bank research papers as "unfavorable," while a fast-growing population is inevitably "positive." The "losers" in this fantasy world are Japan, Russia, and Europe. The "winners" are Bangladesh, Pakistan, Egypt, Mexico, Nigeria—and India.

Yet no one who knows Pakistan or Bangladesh, say, would conclude that these are future winners in anything other than a strictly demographic sense, or that they need more people of working age to boost their economies.

Indian policy makers, because their country is adding so many people in absolute terms to its population, would be wise to ignore blithe assurances that they have only to sit back, relax, and wait for their demographic dividend to roll in. Instead, they should be frantically scrambling to defuse a potential demographic time bomb.

> Policy makers should be frantically scrambling to defuse a potential demographic time bomb.

There are several flaws in the arguments of the anti-Malthusian population boosters. First, although the absolute size of the economy, like the absolute size of the population, may provide a measure of global influence, it does not confer happiness on a country's inhabitants. Look at Australia or Norway or Costa Rica. For prosperity, at least, what matters is income growth per capita. Pakistan's economy has been growing, but only a little faster than its population, which is why Pakistanis on average are not becoming much richer.

Second, in an era of globalization and digital hyperconnectivity, nations can no longer accept on faith the old anti-Malthusian promise that a low dependency ratio (that is, a large number of working-age people relative to children and elderly dependents) outweighs the perils of rapid population growth. In the industrial age, nations with low dependent-to-worker ratios enjoyed obvious economic advantages. China, for example, owes much of its industrial success to the millions of young migrants who have poured into factories in the nation's coastal cities.

But the world is changing. One of India's largest carmakers recently boasted that it was selling more vehicles than ever, especially to China, and that it was hiring an extra eight hundred workers for its factory. But the plant employing those workers belongs to the Jaguar Land Rover subsidiary of Tata Motors and is in the English Midlands, not in job-hungry India. It is true that the lack of manufacturing jobs is in one way a particularly Indian problem and could therefore be reversed by a change of policy; the difficulty of acquiring land, restrictive labor laws, and bureaucratic obstacles have long discouraged both local and foreign investors and pushed them to invest in capital equipment rather than labor. Only about ten million Indians are currently employed in private sector companies with ten or more workers, although an estimated twelve million young people are joining the labor force every year.

The shortage of well-paid manufacturing jobs, however, is not a peculiarly Indian problem but an incipient global phenomenon. In the six months before this essay was written, U.S. manufacturing added no net new jobs, but productivity and output rose sharply. U.S. employers are paying for new robots, not new workers. That has disturbing implications for the American middle class and the potential middle class of India. Indian investors, too, are automating their factories.

That leaves the service sector, long hailed as the potential savior of the Indian economy. Unfortunately, employers in information technology and business process outsourcing face intense international competition and regularly complain about India's generally poor standards of education. There simply are not enough jobs for India's low-skilled workers, and not enough high-skilled Indians for the few million new jobs that might be available in high-end services. This is not a new conundrum (Rajat Nag, the managing director general of the Asian Development Bank, warned three years ago that "the demographic dividend can easily become a demographic curse" and foment social unrest if people are not properly provided with skills), but Indian policy makers have been slow to grasp its significance.

The third and final flaw in the case of the population boosters is that their position is framed in the wrong terms. These anti-Malthusians ask whether it is feasible for the world, and for countries such as India, to host a much larger population, and they then come up with a positive answer. They dismiss Ehrlich as a prophet of doom who did not foresee the green revolution in agriculture that saved hundreds of millions from starvation, any more than Malthus himself foresaw earlier advances in agriculture. But this is the wrong question. They should be asking not whether it is possible but whether it is desirable for the world greatly to increase its population beyond the level of nine to ten billion or so it is already almost certain to reach. The answer is no, for all the obvious reasons arising from overuse of natural resources, environmental damage, and the unpleasant consequences of overcrowding.

Luckily for India, its fertility rate (the number of children per woman in her lifetime) and its population growth rate have been declining steadily, with the southern states in particular leading the way. But population momentum creates daunting challenges in the future, especially in the densely populated north. The annual increase in absolute numbers has only just started to decline—India's population grew by 181 million in the decade to 2011—and a rise of nearly 50 percent in the total number of inhabitants is unavoidable.

So the immediate task is not to control the size of the population but to mitigate and manage the impact of the vast numbers of extra inhabitants already on the way. It is hard to maintain that India has done a good job so far. Good schooling, electricity, fresh water, and even basic sanitation—six hundred million Indians defecate in the open—are in short supply.

> A rise of nearly 50 percent in the total number of inhabitants is unavoidable.

Instead of bragging about the uncertain economic benefits of India's purported demographic dividend, policy makers should be working out how to grow the food, provide the water, build and staff the schools, and construct the roads and power stations that the country's existing inhabitants, as well as its future ones, so desperately need. It will not be an easy task.

five ideas for inclusive growth
Rajat Gupta, Anu Madgavkar, and Shirish Sankhe

Ballu Bhuiyan's village in Bihar has no roads, no running water, no doctor, no nurse. Last year, Mr. Bhuiyan found work as a farm laborer for only six months; his family of five sometimes subsisted on a single meal per day. When his three-year-old daughter got typhoid two years ago, probably from unclean water, all Mr. Bhuiyan could afford was to take her to an untrained local health worker. She died. There are 110 million Indians like Ballu who are considered "excluded," because they lack the basic necessities of life—enough to eat, a decent hut, and a minimum amount of energy.

Life is marginally better for Suman Devi, who lives in Behata, a village of about twenty-six hundred people in Uttar Pradesh. Her husband tills less than an acre of land, and she has two cows. Together, the couple makes just enough to feed their family of six. She walks almost a kilometer a day to collect water because the local well has dried up. Less than one-fifth of the homes in their village have a toilet, and diarrhea is rampant. More than 250 million Indians like Suman Devi are considered "deprived"—below the official poverty line, but better off than the "excluded."

Bivaji Jadhav migrated to the city of Pune, where he became a chauffeur. He earns enough to support his wife, children, and parents back in his home village. His family does not worry about food, and their home

Rajat Gupta is a full-time director and Shirish Sankhe is a senior partner in McKinsey's Mumbai office. Anu Madgavkar is a senior fellow at the McKinsey Global Institute.

even has a small color TV. Bivaji's children are in school. In his village, Bivaji is considered a success. Still, it is a harsh kind of success. He had to borrow from a moneylender at usurious interest rates to secure the rights to his sixteen-square-meter shanty. His wife waits forty-five minutes each morning to buy water from a tanker. Life and health insurance are out of reach. Bivaji Jadhav and his family are considered "vulnerable" to poverty, because one shock to the system—an illness in the family, an accident, or a job loss when the employer moves—can push the family back into poverty. There are 450 million Bivajis in India.

The families described above are composites, based on people and places we know. But they are typical of the 800 million–plus Indians who can be classified as "excluded," "deprived," or "vulnerable." To put it another way, more than half of India's 1.2 billion people lead lives of quiet desperation. The goal of inclusive growth is to fill the gap between what they have and what they need—basic services that ensure a decent standard of living and a modest sense of security. Our early estimates are that a basic package of essential services (food, drinking water, sanitation, health care, schooling, energy, and housing) can be delivered to the poor for about 6,100 rupees ($130) per household per month. A poor household today consumes just two-thirds of this, and the average "excluded" household less than half.

> More than half of India's 1.2 billion people lead lives of quiet desperation.

India already spends a substantial amount of money to bridge the gap between what these households need and what they consume. Subsidies and social spending have grown 2.2 times over the last five years to the equivalent of $103 billion a year. The government spends half this amount on education, a third on food, fuel, and employment subsidies, and the rest on health, drinking water, and sanitation. Hypothetically, were this money simply paid out to needy households, it would be sufficient to eliminate the gap for the "deprived" and "excluded."

In fact, however, due to poor governance and mismanagement, not much actually reaches the poor. Access to basic services is spotty or, as in Ballu Bhuiyan's village, nonexistent. Based on government surveys, only about 20 percent of food subsidies, for instance, reach people below the poverty line. Even where services have been made available, the quality is often poor. Take rural primary education. While school construction has surged and net enrollment has apparently soared (to 96 percent, according to official statistics), there is a one-in-four chance that the teacher is absent, and most fifth-year students cannot read at even second-grade level.

> Only about 20 percent of food subsidies reach people below the poverty line.

Here are five ideas that will facilitate inclusive growth for India and make a substantial dent in reducing India's poverty. There are two threads that tie these ideas together. One is improved governance, without which none of these ideas can work. The other is on improving access to regular employment and helping the poor to become more productive—the most "inclusive" economic strategy of all.

1. *Build one hundred industry clusters to create up to twenty million new jobs.*

The best way to improve the incomes of the poor is to create jobs that help people like Suman Devi and her husband move off the farm. This has been the path that some of India's Asian neighbors have taken, but India has barely started it. While South Korea's farm employment fell by 3.9 percent each year from 1975 to 1995, and China's has shrunk 2.4 percent a year over the last decade, India's actually grew over the same period (up 0.7 percent a year). We estimate that India needs 135 million new nonfarm jobs in the next decade, in labor-intensive sectors such as manufacturing, construction, and retail. Doing so could bring forty-five million Indians off the farms and raise the incomes of the bottom third above the official poverty line.

Building industry clusters—geographic concentrations of businesses in specific manufacturing fields, such as textiles or electronics—can play a critical role in stimulating job growth. Admittedly, this idea is hardly new. India first tried to create such clusters (called special economic zones, SEZs) beginning in 1965, about fifteen years before China took up the idea. But the effort had limited success because the government did little, in the form of infrastructure or logistics, to support it. India's industry clusters today directly account for a tiny percentage of employment.

The experience across China, Dubai, Singapore, Egypt, Malaysia, and many other nations, however, shows that done right, SEZs can help attract foreign investment and create jobs. The key is to put the essentials in place, such as infrastructure, rational taxation, and minimal bureaucracy, and to provide the prerequisites for competitiveness. For example, a food-processing cluster will require cold chains and efficient transport linkages. A chemicals cluster will require the right tax structure for feedstock and products, along with efficient ports and reliable power. In India, where the politics of land is complicated and intense, models that help landowners participate in development will also be required.

One project to watch closely is the proposed Delhi–Mumbai Industrial Corridor, a plan to create infrastructure for twenty-four industrial cities in the relatively well-developed western region. This is still very much a work in progress and faces many obstacles. In principle, though, India needs to complete these kinds of projects and do so rapidly and at scale—to create one hundred such cities, for example—and to focus on poorer states as well as richer ones. Possible result: up to twenty million new jobs.

2. Provide skills training for poor workers.

Like Bivaji Jadhav, 43 percent of India's poor who have exited agriculture are engaged in low-skill informal services—vegetable sellers, food handlers, handcart pullers, shop clerks, maids, and drivers. These jobs just about pay the bills, but little more. Skills building could be a powerful way to improve incomes for these people.

India's growing urban middle and affluent class is demanding more skilled urban services (such as trained child care, cooks, nursing aides, hairdressers, shop assistants, plumbers, and electricians). An unskilled house cleaner might make 1,500 rupees ($28) a month. As a trained cook, child minder, or elder-care giver, she could make five times as much. The problem is that poor workers have few avenues to build such skills.

Short training courses (from a week to three months) and certification systems could help workers improve their skills and, thus, their incomes. There are proven ways to do this; these should be identified and scaled up. An Andhra Pradesh–based NGO has trained more than fifty thousand young people for the retail and hospitality industries in three-month programs. An NGO in western India uses mobile vans to offer fifteen-day programs in skilled trades like plumbing to some one hundred thousand rural students. Assessment of these and similar programs are encouraging.

Public funding of five hundred social-sector and private enterprises could offer earn-as-you-learn skill-building programs to poor workers, training some fifteen million people over a decade. The money for such courses could be given as grants to trainers once workers are certified, or workers could get vouchers that allow them to choose among providers. Some programs could evolve into marketplaces that link certified trainees with employers willing to pay for quality. Working with many such programs, the government could make this a major national mission.

3. *Unleash private and social innovation in service provision.*
India's social and private entrepreneurs are demonstrating affordable, effective ways to provide high-quality education, health care, water, and sanitation. A Pan-Indian foundation builds water purification plants to provide clean drinking water at less than half what Bivaji Jadhav's wife pays for untreated water. A social enterprise in Odisha helps build community-shared piped water and sanitation with a tap and toilet in each home—at a fifth of the cost of conventional systems. The group has achieved an 85 percent reduction in waterborne diseases; it is the kind of service that might have saved Ballu Bhuiyan's young daughter. A Punjab-based for-profit social enterprise provides underserved rural communities with videoconferenced medical advice, at a price of just 20 rupees (37¢) per consultation. Technology-enabled education has shown

> At a fifth of the cost of conventional systems, one NGO has achieved an 85 percent reduction in waterborne diseases.

it is possible to deliver high-quality outcomes at one-fourth the cost of current spending.

Considering the manifest failures of public delivery, the government should seek to speedily scale up such innovations. It could outsource basic service provision to nongovernment agencies, and ensure cost and quality outcomes through selection, monitoring, and oversight rather than direct delivery. Government can also help to expand proven delivery models by providing venture capital, grants, tax and land incentives, and flexibility in licensing and accreditation.

4. Transfer benefits directly to the poor.

There will always be a certain number of people who need social transfers; the problem is that a large percentage gets lost in transmission. If food subsidies went straight to recipients, in the form of cash or vouchers, rather than distributed through "fair-price" shops, half the current outlay would feed India's poor. Suman Devi, then, could simply buy what she needs at any store and not rely on the government shops for subsidized rice and cooking oil, where mismanagement (and worse) means these are often out of stock. Giving benefits directly to people could cut the leakage and corruption characteristic of all too many of India's antipoverty programs.

The government is moving in this direction, enabled by Aadhaar, the digital identification system that is assigning a number to each citizen; the goal is to cover everyone by 2014. Income benefits will be sent directly to an Aadhaar-enabled bank account. The benefits could be immense, as Brazil and Mexico's successful cash-transfer programs have proved. In both countries, households are required to demonstrate at least 80 percent school attendance and regular health checkups to get benefits. Compliance is tracked through technology; in both cases, outcomes improved. Administrative costs are less than 10 percent, much lower than leakages in India.

5. Name twenty to thirty people to lead important missions.

Misgovernance is part of the reason India does a poor job of helping the poor; improving governance therefore has to be part of the answer. Just as more jobs, skills, innovation, and direct transfers empower the poor, India needs to empower leaders charged with executing these ideas.

Consider two of India's most successful public initiatives: the rollout of Aadhaar and the building of the Delhi metro. In each case, the government appointed a leader (Nandan Nilekani, founder of Infosys, for Aadhaar, and Elattuvalapil Sreedharan, a senior engineer with the Indian Railways, for the metro); gave him authority and a budget; backed him up; and monitored his progress. Both missions have succeeded.

India should identify twenty to thirty Nilekanis and Sreedharans and name them to lead designated national priorities. A group of leaders, each entrusted with implementing a single national project from beginning to end—building manufacturing clusters, say, or delivering clean water or building skills partnerships—could change the fabric of India. Individual states could do the same. The leaders would be appointed by the highest government authority and be accountable for outcomes. Success would breed higher expectations from citizens, encouraging the rest of government (and politicians) to raise their game.

mind the gaps

India is not short of ideas. Nor is it short of resources. The real gap is in governance and execution. Our five ideas would put India on the right track and build momentum toward creating the kind of country its people deserve. We acknowledge that entrenched interests and weak government capacity make it difficult to implement good ideas rapidly, and in a big way. But there are enough examples of things that work well, at reasonable cost, that make us believe that these ideas are not impossible, either.

There are at least 800 million reasons why India must do better.

business & technology

"we're not in kansas anymore"
Howard Schultz

Since the establishment of our first coffee shop in Seattle's Pike Place Market back in 1971, Starbucks has opened a lot of new stores—more than eighteen thousand of them, in fact, across sixty-two different international markets. Each store is special in its own way. But in all my years at Starbucks, we've never had an opening like the October 2012 launch of our India flagship store in Mumbai.

The Mumbai store's location, on the ground floor of the historic Elphinstone Building in south Mumbai, is ideal. Customers pass under the building's glorious Venetian Gothic arches into a five-hundred-square-meter space that is a shrine to great coffee and India's rich heritage. The store interior was designed by local craftsmen and artists. We furnished it with Indian teakwood, vintage trunks, leather-bound books, hand-carved wooden screens, and old-fashioned milk cans like the ones used by Mumbai milkmen. It's elegant but also comfortable and homey. I think it's our most beautiful store.

The opening of the Mumbai store was the most successful launch we've ever had. That first night we hosted a celebratory reception with the Tata Group, our Indian business partner. It felt almost like the Oscars. Tata's then chairman, Ratan Tata, one of India's most revered business leaders, invited what looked to me like the entire who's

> The opening in Mumbai was the most successful Starbucks has ever had.

Howard Schultz is the chairman, president, and chief executive officer of Starbucks.

who of India. There must have been a hundred reporters and photographers, with flashbulbs popping everywhere. They had to close the whole block. As we listened to Ratan tell the crowd of his enthusiasm for our partnership, my wife leaned over and whispered to me that old line from the *Wizard of Oz*: "Howard, I don't think we're in Kansas anymore."

We've since opened more stores in India—five more in Mumbai, and five in New Delhi. Eventually, we hope to have thousands of stores in India. I look forward to a day in the not-too-distant future when India takes its place alongside China as one of our two largest markets outside North America.

Of course, getting there won't be easy. And our successful beginning in India has not been without hurdles; on the contrary, it has been a complicated six-year journey. Along the way, though, we've discovered a lot about India and ourselves.

We'd watched the Indian market develop for many years. We could see that all the important prerequisites for success were falling into place: the emergence of a growing middle class with strong aspirations and an enthusiasm for Western culture and brands, the gradual development of the nation's infrastructure, and what seemed to be healthy changes in the regulatory framework for foreign investment. Lately India's coffee market has been growing at a rate of 15 percent a year. We tried a number of times to enter India, but we kept running into obstacles. Finally, in October 2010, I came to India to narrow our list of potential business partners.

Naturally, the Tata Group was a leading candidate. But before our meeting with Ratan Tata, his people asked if I would pay a visit to Karnataka, where Tata has its coffee farms. I didn't know what we were going to see. We drove for hours. It turned out that our destination was a school for children with special needs. We toured the school, met the headmaster, met the teachers. And we met the kids, many of whose parents were migrant laborers working on the coffee farms. The kids put on a play for us. It was very emotional.

I was impressed. The Tata name didn't appear anywhere on that school. They weren't running it for public recognition. They were doing it for the kids. They were doing it because those are Tata's values; that's who they are. And it struck me that building a school was exactly the kind of thing that we would do at Starbucks—and that feeling of a responsibility to give back was what I'd want a new business partner to understand about us before committing to a joint venture. I think I knew, right then, that Tata was the right partner for us.

We've developed an incredible relationship with the Tata organization. We have learned about their culture of benevolence and seen how they communicate to employees in all the Tata companies a sense that the group has responsibilities beyond just making a profit. We spent a lot of time with Ratan Tata and R. K. Krishna Kumar, vice chairman of Tata Global Beverages. I could sit and listen to Ratan for days on end. He has so much wisdom and insight, not only about India but about the world.

We announced our joint venture with Tata in January 2012. Ten months later the government loosened restrictions on foreign investment in the retail industry. From a legal standpoint, we could have tried to set up shop in India on our own. But I can't imagine bringing Starbucks to India without the assistance we've received from Tata.

> I can't imagine bringing Starbucks to India without the help we've had from Tata.

They helped us find great locations for our stores (the Elphinstone Building, for example, is one of Tata's). They helped us with store design and in getting the food menu right (*tandoori paneer* rolls and cardamom-flavored croissants!). They helped us overcome the many logistical and infrastructure obstacles to make sure everything on our India menu is fresh.

They also helped with recruiting. At job fairs to hire staff for our first stores, the response was astonishing. Thousands of people applied to work for us as baristas. The lines snaked out the door. Attracting great people is crucial for us; as we keep getting larger and larger, we also have to figure out how to stay small—how to maintain a sense of intimacy with our own people and our customers. That's the essence of Starbucks: to make that human connection—one person, one cup, one neighborhood at a time.

The other unique aspect of our alliance with Tata is the ability to source and roast coffee beans locally in India. India is the only major market in the world where we can do that, and it's only because of our relationship with Tata, which is the largest coffee estate owner in all of Asia. They not only own farms but also operate their own roasting facilities. So we were able to work with them to develop an India-only espresso roast, designed specifically for India and every bit as good as the espresso we serve all over the world.

Of course, developing an Indian espresso required us to do some things differently. At Starbucks, the people in our coffee department, who source coffee beans and oversee the roasting process, are respected and enthroned like royalty. Within the company, they have enormous influence. So when I sat down with them and asked their support for doing something a little bit special in India, they weren't exactly thrilled. They were more skeptical when I said, "We want to create a different blend of coffee for India." And when I told them that the India blend was not going to be roasted by our team, they just looked at me incredulously. "Are you suggesting that we do something we haven't done in the forty-two-year history of Starbucks? How can we guarantee quality?" It was a tense conversation.

> Developing an Indian espresso required us to do some things differently.

I promised them they would have full decision rights on what the blend would be. But it was a real test of our trust in our new partner. To get the blend we wanted for India, we'd have to share with Tata some of the family jewels—roasting secrets we've perfected over four decades and guarded very closely.

Our coffee team from our support center in Seattle made a half dozen trips to India. There must have been at least one hundred tastings. And the result was well worth it. Our Indian Espresso Roast, sourced from and roasted by Tata, is a fantastic blend.

Teaming with Tata to come up with an Indian roast was a huge step for us. And we learned a lot about ourselves in that process: that not everything needs to be invented in Seattle and that we can collaborate and coauthor, as long as there is a foundation of trust.

People always ask me to compare our prospects in India and China. In a way, that's an unfair question. We have a big head start in China. We've been there for fourteen years and have more than eight hundred stores on the mainland. But I believe China and India offer Starbucks one of the greatest opportunities for growth. Our plan over time is that the number of our stores in India will rival the size and scale of what we have planned for China—thousands of stores. Our relationship with Tata makes that possible.

At the celebratory dinner the night of the Mumbai opening, Ratan Tata offered a toast that really moved me. He said in his dry, understated way, "You know, the Tata Group has done a few things over the years, and we've had a bit of success. We have partnered with some good global companies. But I've never had the kind of recognition I've received from this relationship with Starbucks. People I've never met stop me on the street just to congratulate me. And what I have learned from this relationship is that Starbucks is far more than just a company that sells coffee."

It was perfect—and so heartfelt. This is a man with so much grace. A few weeks after returning from the opening of our Mumbai store, we held one of our big open forum meetings where we get the entire company together. And as I tried to describe that moment for everyone, something came over me. I started to cry. It just hit me emotionally. In India, we'd had a chance to do something extraordinary, something truly world class. And I'm excited that we have a chance to grow and give back in a land where so much opportunity lies ahead and to contribute to making it a little better place than the one we found.

innovation: india inc.'s next challenge
Nitin Nohria

I graduated from the Indian Institute of Technology Bombay in 1984 and left immediately for the United States. More than two-thirds of my fellow graduates did the same; three decades later, most of us still live and work in America. Why? Because America was where the brightest researchers studied, where the boldest innovations were discovered, where the greatest companies were built. In America, if you had talent and were willing to work hard, anything was possible. To me and my classmates, *Time* publisher Henry Luce's sweeping declaration that the twentieth century was the "American Century" seemed neither boastful nor profound— merely obvious.

When I started teaching at the Harvard Business School in 1988, America dominated the curriculum. Nine of every ten case studies focused on U.S. companies. I don't recall a case about an Indian firm, nor do I remember thinking that unusual. Students came to Harvard from all over the world to learn from the best, about the best.

A quarter century later students still flock to HBS for the same reason. But more than half of the 250 cases we produced last year examined non-American companies. No one thinks that unusual either. HBS students now expect to learn about innovative companies from all over the world. We, in turn, expect them to graduate with a thorough understanding of companies, ways of working, and business opportunities everywhere from India to Brazil, Turkey to Nigeria.

If the twentieth century was an American Century, the twenty-first

Nitin Nohria is dean of the Harvard Business School.

century will be the Global Century—an era in which businesses and executives from many countries and regions shape the growth of the world economy.

As someone born in India more than a half century ago, I have been particularly gratified to watch Indian companies develop into global competitors. To understand how Indian firms emerged—and how they can sustain their competitiveness—one must first recognize how businesses in this new Global Century create value. Those who have done so most successfully have excelled at what my HBS colleagues Sumantra Ghoshal and Christopher Bartlett and I believe are the three keys to value creation in this new world: efficiency, local responsiveness, and innovation. Indian firms have demonstrated their ability to master the first two of these areas. If they can figure out the third, students all over the world may clamor to learn more about India just as eagerly as we once studied the United States.

> In the early 1990s, Indian companies were terrified of global competition.

Japanese companies first demonstrated the opportunity to create value through steady improvements in efficiency in the early 1970s and 1980s. Sony and Toyota shocked American competitors by introducing low-priced, high-quality consumer electronics and automobiles. Inspired by Japan's success, businesses in Taiwan and South Korea soon emerged to challenge the dominance of American manufacturers. U.S. firms eventually responded to that challenge. Many embraced Japanese manufacturing methods. A free-trade pact with Mexico enabled many American firms to lower their labor costs by moving production to Mexico. That shift, in turn, helped manufacturers in other Latin American countries learn to become more efficient by cutting labor costs.

India entered the fray in the 1990s, shortly after China did. Economic reforms set in motion by Deng Xiaoping quickly transformed China into the dominant global force in low-cost manufacturing. India backed into similar reforms only after a 1991 balance of payments crisis forced the country to beg for help from the International Monetary Fund. Not surprisingly, Indian companies were initially terrified of the prospects of global competition. Many Indians worried their economy would be re-colonized by foreign multinationals. But Indian firms soon found their footing—starting with IT services—and thereafter discovered that integration into the global economy also brought new opportunities

Wipro is a classic case. Founded in Mumbai by Mohamed Hasham Premji in 1945, the company, originally called Western India Vegetable Products Limited, began as a manufacturer of vegetable oils. After the founder's death in 1966, his twenty-one-year-old son, Azim, newly graduated from Stanford, returned to India to run the business. In the 1980s, the younger Premji made a bold decision to diversify into computers and information technologies. In the 1990s, as the effects of economic reforms in India gathered momentum, companies around the world were belatedly discovering that they would need armies of new programmers to prevent their IT systems from crashing in the transition to the new millennium—the dreaded "Y2K bug." Safeguarding their systems from the Y2K threat was a vital but unglamorous task—the sort of work big companies were glad to outsource. Y2K enabled Wipro and other Indian IT services companies to build capacity and prove their skills. Now Wipro, alongside India's two other large IT players, Infosys and TCS, deliver sophisticated high-value software services to clients around the world. By now the success of India's IT service providers is well known. Other companies, like Sundram Fasteners, have shown that, in the new Global Century, Indian firms in some manufacturing sectors can also hold their own.

Yet the one thing we know about global competition is that to maintain their lead in the efficiency race, companies must run ever faster. Already, new competitors to China and India have emerged in Vietnam and Cambodia. The hundreds of millions of new workers who will enter the global labor force in the next three decades can be trained to produce commodity products and services ever more efficiently. Keeping pace with this constantly moving "efficiency frontier" will be the great challenge for twenty-first-century global managers, including those from India. The important lesson for Indian managers is that competing on the efficiency dimension requires relentless discipline: To succeed, their companies must achieve continuous productivity improvements and ascend ceaselessly into activities that add greater value for their customers.

Companies like Tata Motors have demonstrated that Indian firms can capture global opportunities in a second way: by developing products uniquely suited to local markets. In 2001, after posting a $125 million loss, Tata moved aggressively to cut costs and raise quality. Most important, Tata Motors executives also introduced a barrage of new products, including a smaller and sturdier commercial truck called the Tata Ace. The vehicle satisfied a huge need in India's growing economy for trucks that could carry goods the "last mile" in the supply chain—off the highways and into towns and villages. The Ace boasted a short turning radius and was able to maneuver through tight lanes. At $5,500, the truck cost half as much as other four-wheel commercial vehicles in India and was significantly cheaper than the pickup trucks with smaller payloads found in international markets. Tata had in fact created an entirely new product category: Until 2005, when the truck was introduced, overloaded three-wheel rickshaws and bullock carts had dominated the "last mile." In 2011–2012, more than two hundred thousand Aces were sold, bringing the total to over one million.

Products like the Tata Ace exploit what my HBS colleagues Tarun Khanna and Krishna Palepu call "institutional voids." This refers to the fact that emerging markets often lack institutions—credit, or transportation infrastructure, or a well-functioning legal system—that are taken for granted in developed markets. Businesses able to exploit these voids can generate enormous opportunity. One would expect domestic companies to have the inside track in exploiting institutional voids. But the success of South Korea's LG in developing white goods tailored to the needs of Indian consumers, and Vodafone in devising customized cellular services, show that even "outsiders" can realize big gains from responding to local needs.

In the modern global economy, growth increasingly is driven by consumers in emerging markets. Indian firms may be especially well

> Businesses able to exploit "institutional voids" can generate enormous opportunity.

suited to responding to these needs. Much like American firms did in the twentieth century, Indian firms stand to benefit from the vast scale of their home market and are in position to leverage those gains in expanding into other emerging markets. Companies like Bharti Airtel, which is now successfully venturing into markets in Africa, provide a great example of this opportunity.

The third and most powerful way to create value in the Global Century is through innovation. Innovation was the key to the dominance of American firms in the twentieth century, and will play an even more decisive—and unpredictable—role in our current hyperconnected age. Today breakthrough change can come from anywhere. That's fortunate for consumers, because we desperately need big breakthroughs to cope with the challenges of energy and environmental sustainability, health care and quality of life, and a constantly expanding digital landscape. Indian companies have as much chance as competitors from anywhere else in achieving these breakthroughs and emerging as Global Century winners. Their high levels of intellectual capital and ingenuity may even give them an edge in competing along the innovation dimension.

Innovations can come in two forms: those that create genuinely new products and services for global consumers, and those that enable the world to meet existing needs with radically fewer resources and at dramatically lower prices than current alternatives. So far, with the exception of Sony's Walkman or Matsushita's VHS VCR, few global products and services have originated in Asia. That may change: Samsung, for instance, now ranks among the top ten companies in global patents awarded annually. In India, too, Piramal Life Sciences and Biocon have set their sights on bringing new patented drugs to the global market. If they succeed, they could transform the way the world sees India's capacity for innovation, just as the success of firms like Wipro reshaped perceptions of India's ability to compete on the basis of greater efficiency.

Innovations of the second type, which can be described as "frugal innovations," can meet the needs of the billions who live below the poverty line and are desperate to enter the circle of prosperity that others have so long enjoyed. The most celebrated example of such an innovation is microfinance, pioneered by the Grameen Bank in Bangladesh. In India, Narayana Hrudayalaya Hospital has shown that heart surgeries can be performed at scale and at order of magnitude lower prices with equally successful outcomes. Products like the Tata Nano or GE's new cardiac monitor developed in India also suggest the potential for frugal innovations to transform the global economy.

The Indian capacity for *jugaad* (creative improvisation), which is highlighted in the book *The India Way*, may well give Indian firms a leg up when it comes to frugal innovations.

In the last two decades, India has emerged as one of the Global Century's most promising players. Indian firms have shown that they can create value by exploiting opportunities that arise from efficiency, local responsiveness, and innovation. A decade ago, few students left Harvard Business School fully prepared to compete in the Global Century. Now, each year, we graduate nine hundred MBAs and nine thousand executives who, we hope, see global opportunities far more clearly. The Global Century has only begun. Indian firms and their leaders can and should aspire to be leading contenders in this new Global Century. Vast opportunities await, in India and throughout the world.

> The Indian capacity for *jugaad* may well give its firms a leg up when it comes to frugal innovation.

the promise of connected growth
Sunil Bharti Mittal

Technology has always been a game changer for modern India. The 1960s saw the advent of heavy manufacturing, changing the face of industry. The 1970s saw the Green Revolution in agriculture, transforming the country from import dependency to near self-sufficiency. More recently, vibrant telecommunications and information technology industries have bolstered the country's confidence and ambitions to vault into the ranks of economically advanced nations.

We stand today on the threshold of a new era of technological innovation. In this decade, the convergence of mobile telephony and new digital technologies will open extraordinary new vistas and transcend traditional developmental challenges.

The Government of India's Unique Identification initiative offers a real-time case study of the transformation under way and hints at the possibilities in store. Recognized as one of the world's most ambitious national identity programs, the project is now taking its next logical step with the introduction of direct benefit transfers, enabling the government to send cash electronically to recipients of various public subsidies. By routing transfers through the UID payment system, the government can curtail transaction costs to a fraction of the previous level and almost eliminate the massive leakages that have plagued such disbursements in the past. This new payment method is currently available in fifty-one districts; the rest of the country will be getting it in a phased manner.

The Direct Benefit Transfer is just one example of what is possible as

Sunil Bharti Mittal is chairman and group CEO of Bharti Enterprises.

technology integrates with everyday life—and the greatest promise lies in bringing geographically remote and low-income groups into the economic mainstream. We have already moved some way on this path and are reaping tangible benefits as a result. Thanks to e-Governance—the government's plan to make many public services available via electronic media—people no longer must travel to district and state headquarters to update their land records or check the status of their job applications. I am convinced that we are only scratching the surface in applying these technologies to public services.

In our age of rapid technological change, government is no longer the sole agent of public welfare. Today, entrepreneurial zeal provides an equally important force propelling technology closer to people and enhancing their newfound capacity to absorb and make the best use of it in improving quality of life. Most heartening is the fact that this can evidently take place in a low-literacy (not just low-tech literacy) environment.

> In our age of rapid technological change, government is no longer the sole agent of public welfare.

Dwarfing the technology-induced changes in public services are the parallel efforts by manufacturers and service providers to experiment with new technologies, spurred by an across-the-board increase in employment opportunities, rising disposable incomes, and greater affordability of mobile devices. Today, even a low-income vegetable vendor can benefit from a $20 water purifier to provide clean drinking water for his children. Similarly, the mobile phone has become indispensable to those whose professions are "mobile" in nature, such as salespeople and those in the construction industry. And even for those who don't work in such fields, the Internet's benefits are no farther away than their fingertips. Mobile-banking applications have eliminated the distance between the customer and the bank. M-commerce applications have done the same to the marketplace. Forget about smartphones; many feature phones are capable of delivering a majority of these services despite being just a step up from basic phones good only for calling and texting.

India's hinterland has become one of the most powerful arenas for empowerment through technology. Farmers are getting real-time information on weather, commodity prices, and fertilizer availability in the local market—all for free. The potential for inclusive growth of these initiatives far outweighs the initial investments that have gone into them in a country where 60 percent of the population still depends on agriculture. Rural artisans and small entrepreneurs no longer have to travel to urban markets to vend their products; they can do it over their mobile phones.

The next great frontiers are health care and education—two critical sectors that stand to gain immensely from technological leapfrogging. Lack of brick-and-mortar models in these sectors remains a significant constraint, compounded by limited public investment. M-health services are already starting to help overcome the 1:1,700 doctor-patient ratio in the country; private firms are offering medical consultations and diagnostic services via mobile phone and text messaging, and plans are afoot to deploy devices such as the "m-steth" (mobile stethoscope) for transmitting heart data of cardiac patients. M-education has also made a beginning. Both sectors stand to gain tremendously in India from what McKinsey has estimated will be the largest addition of Internet users of any country in the world, reaching 330–370 million people by 2015, more than in the United States and second only to China. The fact that an estimated three-quarters of the new users will be accessing the Internet solely through mobile handsets or tablets opens boundless new possibilities in education and health.

How, then, can India realize the full promise of mobile broadband? As we move to the "Internet of things," in which not only people but also everyday objects like cars, appliances, and even consumer products can be linked together in digital networks, we need to remove disparities, not only in access but in speed and functionality as well. To create the perfect tango, a host of forces must move in tandem, including communication technology standards (3G, 4G, and future generations), network speed and reach, handset capability and proliferation, application development, and manpower training. But this broadband revolution requires a nurturing regulatory landscape, in which government regulators seek out global best practices in policy making. That will mean balancing the revenue the government reaps from the telecommunications sector against the improvements in public welfare that will stem from the industry's development. It will also mean ensuring sufficient availability of quality spectrum without technological or service restrictions, managing data traffic with transparent rules, safeguarding competition, and fostering the development of a national broadband network.

With a population of more than 1.2 billion, which is well on course to be the largest in the world by 2030, inclusive growth is not a choice. It is a necessity for India.

As technology helps raise living standards among those previously excluded from the economic mainstream, I strongly believe the business opportunity at the bottom of the pyramid is not only going to be enduring but also will constitute the pivotal base of India's future growth story. Entrepreneurs perforce will be eager to go the extra yard to calibrate their business models to cash in on these new prospects.

As Victor Hugo said, you cannot resist an idea whose time has come. We are at the dawn of a data-driven civilization. How we as a society choose to leverage this opportunity will be our legacy.

thinking outside the bottle
Muhtar Kent

I moved to India with my family as a young boy. My father, a career diplomat, was dispatched to New Delhi to serve as the Republic of Turkey's ambassador to India. We lived in New Delhi for two magical years. I don't remember anything from those days about India's politics or economics. What I do remember are the vibrant colors of clothing and flowers and shops that lined the streets, and the natural beauty of the Indian countryside, from the mountains to the north, to the plains of the Ganges basin to the south. I remember the mysterious music, the aromas of spicy curries and chutneys that friends of my parents would prepare for us. And of course I remember the people: friendly, bright-eyed, ambitious, and sometimes very poor. Everywhere, crowds of people.

India was unlike any of the other places my family had lived—Sweden, Iran, Poland, Thailand, and the United States. From the moment I arrived, India captured my imagination.

Today, as a businessman, I see global companies drawn to India in much the same way I was as a boy. They are dazzled by the promise of adventure and extraordinary opportunity. They are intoxicated, even overwhelmed.

> If you come to India with some master plan, prepare to be distracted, deterred, even demoralized.

But as I learned, even as a young a boy, in India, appearances can be deceiving. For outsiders, there is always a hint of mystery. Even

Muhtar Kent is chairman and CEO of The Coca-Cola Company.

if you live and work there, you can never be entirely sure you understand. It is best to assume that you do not. If you come to India with some grand, predetermined strategy or master plan, prepare to be distracted, deterred, and even demoralized.

That's something I keep in mind as I think of The Coca-Cola Company's experiences in India. Coca-Cola launched operations in India in 1950 shortly after independence. Our business grew steadily. But in 1977, we exited (along with other multinational companies) after a new law diluted ownership of our assets and operations.

We returned to rebuild our business in 1993 as economic reforms unleashed a period of robust growth. It was harder going than we'd imagined. We struggled at first to find and keep talented employees. We learned that although Indian consumers were eager to embrace global brands, they resented any hint of global corporate dominance. It took us time to understand that small stores, many operated by families out of the front of their homes, were an unappreciated source of economic opportunity.

Today our India business is thriving. I am happy to report that India now ranks among our top ten markets in unit case sales. Our growth in recent years has been particularly dynamic. I still see enormous potential in India—which is why last summer I went to New Delhi to announce that The Coca-Cola Company and its global bottling partners will invest $5 billion in our India operations between 2012 and 2020. By the end of that period, we think India could be one of our top five global markets.

The key to this success has been learning to see the Indian market as it is, not as we wished it to be.

Our first challenge was building the right team. For many years after our return to India, turnover among Coca-Cola workers was too high; as recently as a decade ago, our Indian attrition rates were 34 percent. That was a key weakness, not least because it prevented us from building relations with suppliers and consumers. So we focused on

> The key to Coke's success has been learning to see the market as it is, not as we wished it to be.

training and talent recruitment. We recruited a lot of young professionals with deep experience in India's retailing culture and provided them additional training in customer relationship management, sales, service, and conflict resolution. These changes helped lower attrition by two-thirds.

At the same time, we worked hard to source more products from within India and deepen our ties to the Indian market. For example, we began growing mangoes and invested in citrus farms that supplied our business. Those efforts helped send an important message: All over India, people knew we were there not just to sell to them but to buy from them and invest in them as well.

> People knew Coke was in India not just to sell to them but to buy from them and invest in them as well.

And we made it a point to understand our customers. India's people still cherished long-held goals of self-sufficiency and sustainability—and those ideals were essential to our continued growth. Through careful study of how Indian consumers live—people all over the nation, not just those in cities—we learned that most are more likely to buy our products at a small family store than a big supermarket.

At the same time, we saw how a rising generation of young Indians, most of them raised without landline telecommunications infrastructure, has embraced wireless technologies and, in many ways, is leading the global revolution in mobile commerce.

Recognizing that small stores play a huge role in the lives of our customers has required us to do many things differently in India than we do in developed markets. We figured out, for example, that it wasn't enough to provide small stores with Coke signs and teach them to display our products. Often, these stores had more basic concerns. Many couldn't keep our drinks cold because they weren't connected to the electrical grid. More critically, small stores in India often are run by women, who have more difficulty than men in exercising economic rights like getting access to credit. We found we could help store owners address those and similar problems in ways that helped them, helped their communities, and also helped Coke.

For instance, when our bottlers help supply nearby villages with access to running water, the women in those villages are spared the considerable time and trouble of walking to a well, drawing water, and bringing it home. When we help bring electric power to village stores, that helps us sell our products cold—but it also means electricity for the whole village, boosting literacy rates by making it easier for kids to study after dark. When we help a woman secure property rights for her store, that makes it easier for us to sell Coke products and also enables her to build a business and employ other residents. We recently launched our "5by20" initiative, which seeks to bring additional business training, finance opportunities, and mentoring to five million women entrepreneurs across our global value chain by 2020. Indian women make up a significant focus of this program.

One of my favorite examples of how we're trying to come up with solutions tailored for the Indian market is eKOCool, a solar-powered mobile cooler we developed for use in the tens of thousands of rural Indian villages that lack electricity. The eKOCool looks a little like an ordinary pushcart, but it's actually a sophisticated marriage of technology and local market savvy. Stores using our eKOCool solar coolers can stay open later and generate enough extra power to do double duty recharging mobile phones or electric lanterns. We hope to distribute more than one thousand eKOCool carts to rural store owners in India by the end of 2013—and we have begun testing them in dozens of other countries.

Back when my father was stationed in India, the country was only a few years removed from colonialism. Indians had had a long and painful experience with foreign businesses exploiting their market without contributing to the well-being of the local economy. What we now understand intimately—and what other companies who want to sell in India must recognize—is that our future is tied to the communities where we operate. A thriving and sustainable India creates thriving and sustainable business opportunities for us.

For The Coca-Cola Company in India, the rewards from being in the market will materialize only if we see our investment in broad terms: not just capital investment in bottling plants and trucks but also human investment in schools and training, social investment in women entrepreneurs, and technological investment in innovations like solar carts that can power a cooler, a mobile phone, or a lantern by which a young boy or girl can study. That's an expression of our commitment to India—and our commitment to succeed on India's terms.

finding the right remedy
Miles White

In business, sometimes you find the most valuable insights in places you'd least expect them. In my case, it was a crowded Mumbai alley full of "chemist" shops where I went to buy some medicine. That brief visit helped me understand why, after imagining India for a long while, my company had to become an integral part of it.

It was 2009. I had embarked on what might be called an immersion course in India—in particular its health-care system. I was well aware, of course, of the remarkable rise of India's economy. But for a country so large, dynamic, and diverse, there clearly was no substitute for firsthand observation. So I went to India myself. I toured its hospitals and other health-care facilities, at all levels of service. I visited private homes across a broad spectrum of socioeconomic levels. I tried to understand as well as I could what it was like to be an Indian citizen during this extraordinary moment in the country's history and what it was like to provide and receive health care there.

As it happened, in the course of investigating India's health-care system, I came to need a little care myself. That's how I found myself in the lanes surrounding Bombay Hospital, where about thirty chemist shops, each with a storefront perhaps three to five meters wide, serve the hospital's many patients. I knew of course that modern, American-style pharmacies were the exception in India. Still, the scene I encountered was eye-opening.

Clerks clamored for my attention as I walked past. Indian pharma-

Miles White is chairman and CEO of Abbott Laboratories.

cies function as informal doctors as well as medicine purveyors, but the people manning these shops were unexpectedly young and could have been selling any commodity. Once I chose a shop, the young man at the counter asked numerous questions about the malady I wanted to treat. After a loud discussion between him and someone in the back—during which passersby could easily overhear details of my symptoms—I received a small bag of generic medicines. The drugs prescribed were just what I needed, and I was stunned by how little they cost—a fraction of the price I would have paid for them in the United States or almost any other developed country.

In a way that no spreadsheet or PowerPoint ever could, this experience drove home to me how crucial it was for us at Abbott to be part of India's health-care solution—and in a big way. India is famously challenging for foreign companies, given the regulatory regime and the vestiges of *swadeshi* (self-reliance) that inspired its independence movement. But we saw that India's robust economic growth, combined with the readiness of its health-care system for significant improvement and expansion, created a unique and compelling opportunity.

The medicines I bought that day were what are known as "branded generics," and their prevalence in India underscores the essence of the country's health-care system. At the tip of the iceberg is outstanding, advanced care for the relatively few who can afford it. But the overwhelming majority of people receive a very different level of care, if any. For this majority, branded generics are appealing because, although their patent protection has expired, they offer the quality of manufacture

India's intellectual property rights regime affords a relatively low level of legal protection to patented drugs.

and trustworthiness of consistency that comes with the imprimatur of a major pharmaceutical firm, at a much more accessible price than newer, patent-protected drugs.

India is a powerhouse for generic drugs, due to its wealth of scientific and managerial talent and its low production costs. An arguable disadvantage of India for pharmaceutical makers is the country's intellectual property rights laws, which afford a relatively low level of protection to proprietary, patented drugs. But by focusing on branded generics, which have no patents to protect, we avoided this pitfall.

We concluded that securing a major foothold in India would provide Abbott an ideal base from which to sell not only to the 1.2 billion people there but also to fast-growing markets throughout the developing world. And so we resolved to become a major *Indian* company.

A little history is in order here. More than a century ago, Abbott first initiated business outside the United States. Of the three countries chosen, two—the United Kingdom and Canada—involved culturally simple moves; the third was India. We have no record of why Dr. Wallace Abbott decided that his young enterprise should undertake such a far-flung effort, but I suspect that it was essentially the same prospect that attracted me and my team—the sheer size of the population, the need for care, and the chance to make a powerful impact.

Although our motivation may have been consistent with our predecessors', our methods have been radically different. When Abbott first entered the Indian market, in 1910, it was in a way appropriate to a young company in a less-connected world, with local agents representing our products. History, politics, and economics kept Abbott's presence in India steady but relatively small. Until recently, we were seventh in the Indian pharmaceutical market, and our nutrition products business was very small; our total annual revenues from India stayed below $100 million.

That's in stark contrast with our current effort to make India a major part of our growth strategy. When I began my immersion in India, I feared we might already be too late, that the time for capturing opportunities there had passed. What I found was the opposite. When economies emerge, improving health is among people's top priorities. In India I saw a health-care system and market still in formation—with strata ranging from high to early development. India currently spends less than 2.5 percent of its GDP on health care (the comparable figure for the United States is 18 percent); over the next twenty years, that percentage will grow exponentially. Already the Indian market is one of the world's largest in terms of volume for pharmaceuticals, and we think it will grow at a 15 percent pace for the next two decades.

This tide was strong enough to lift any boat, so we decided to build big. Our goal was to be the country's number-one company in pharmaceuticals and nutrition within five years. We knew we couldn't achieve that through organic growth alone; that kind of presence would require acquisition or partnership.

But buying a company in India isn't simple. Even large Indian enterprises often are family owned or controlled, with the first- and second-generation owners still active. Getting to know them takes time; it took eighteen months of meetings to finally do the deal that would make us the country's pharmaceutical leader.

> Buying a company in India isn't simple. Even large enterprises often are family owned or controlled.

We made a series of key transactions in 2010, acquiring the pharmaceutical business of Belgium-based Solvay, which had an Indian operation larger than our own, and forming a partnership with a major Indian pharmaceutical maker to market drugs in emerging economies outside India. Then came the deal that was fundamental to our vision: our $3.7 billion acquisition of Piramal Healthcare Solutions (PHS), a part of the Piramal Group, one of India's largest companies.

Naysayers said the price was excessive, but we felt that to realize our goal of becoming a truly Indian company, we needed to establish roots, not merely sell products. PHS brought us both manufacturing and research operations in-country, as well as a portfolio of hundreds of valuable medications, and a sales and distribution system that ran throughout the breadth of the country—even into rural areas with relatively little health-care infrastructure.

These actions made us one of the largest players in the health-care system of the second most populous nation on earth. In just four years, we've achieved our goal of attaining a number-one position in India's pharmaceutical sector, where we have about 7 percent of the market.

India now represents more than 4 percent of our total sales and almost 5 percent of profits—percentages that will surely grow.

As important as India is for Abbott, investments like ours are equally important and beneficial to India. We have not just a commercial presence in India today but also a scientific presence and a manufacturing presence. We're creating jobs, collaborating with universities. We are helping to bring health care to more people than live in all of the traditionally developed economies put together—advanced care for millions, and effective care to hundreds of millions more who previously had little or no access. That our company has a 125-year record of not only providing high-quality medical products but also of continually advancing the standard of care matters.

So it is my hope that India will continue welcoming foreign investors—and that other multinationals will seize the chance. Our experience so far suggests that India itself is evolving no less dynamically than our operations there. We've come a long way since I bought that medicine in Mumbai, and I believe that the benefits, both corporate and societal, are as large as the country itself, and that they'll keep accruing for years to come.

bricks and clicks
Philip Clarke

In markets the world over, consumers are embracing new technologies and radically changing the way they shop. Whether they reside in Manchester, Manhattan, or Mumbai, customers are increasingly making purchases online, logging on to social media to discuss and choose products, and using smartphone apps to find the best deals. Global e-commerce topped $1 trillion in 2012; it grew 33 percent in the Asia Pacific region, which could soon surpass North America as the number one region for online sales. The changes sweeping the Asia Pacific are now gathering momentum in India.

As it expands and builds in strength, this extraordinary transformation is improving the living standards of hundreds of millions of people. The spread of digital technologies has unleashed powerful and sometimes disruptive changes in retailing all around the globe. India, too, will benefit from—and be buffeted by—those forces.

Change in retailing has been the subject of intense controversy in India in recent years, mainly because of concerns about the effects of investment by foreign retail chains in the Indian market. It's no secret that as the world's third-largest retail company, we at Tesco are advocates of the benefits foreign direct investment in retail can bring to consumers, suppliers, and communities. We've welcomed the debate about foreign investment. But we also believe the conversation should evolve and widen, to consider where India's vast consumer market is heading in the next decade or two.

Philip Clarke is CEO of Tesco PLC.

My view is that over the next ten years, new technologies will have a profound and lasting impact on the way Indians shop, altering consumers' lives far more meaningfully than the size or glitziness of their towns' shopping malls. Technology was once simply a way to improve operations in-store or enhance a supply chain. But now, in India as in the rest of the world, the balance has shifted. With digital devices at their fingertips, consumers are the ones driving the change.

> New technologies will have a profound impact on the way Indians shop, altering consumers' lives far more meaningfully than the size or glitziness of their towns' shopping malls.

India bears all the hallmarks of a country where digital technology will bring enormous benefits. Already India has 120 million Internet users, making it the third-largest base of users in the world. The rate at which Indians are adopting the Internet is much faster than advanced economies and many developing economies. In 2011, Google predicted India would add two hundred million Internet users by the end of 2013. A survey conducted by the Internet and Mobile Association of India suggests the number of Internet users in rural parts of the country reached forty-five million by the end of 2012.

But in many ways, India's digital commerce revolution will be unique. In India, people who access the Internet only through a mobile or a tablet device are expected to account for 75 percent of new users and 55 percent of all users by 2015. Inevitably that will mean greater demand for content designed for the small screen. As Internet penetration increases and this new multichannel world expands, Indian consumers will enjoy unparalleled choice: not just more information and a greater variety of goods and services to buy but also a choice of ways to shop at whatever time they like. Taking full advantage of the multiplicity of channels, they can bargain-hunt online, then browse in-store, order online, and pick up their purchase at the store. And they will exercise far more clout than before thanks to social media, which creates fashions in seconds, making or destroying brands within a day. The explosion of information also has given customers the power to force companies to become more transparent and accountable to those they serve.

Here's a recent example of how new technologies have helped us at Tesco engage with our customers and learn from them: In the UK, we asked customers on Facebook to think of a new ice cream flavor. We got more than a thousand entries. The winning flavor—Amaretto, cherry, and almond—is currently being developed and should be available later this year.

Indian retailers, too, can grasp such opportunities. India's retailing path will differ from that of the West, where organized retail progressed from market stall to physical stores and national chains. The combination of the nation's diversity and scale with digital technology suggests India could leapfrog from traditional retailing, focused on physical stores, straight into the multichannel world of "bricks and clicks." Although starting from a lower base than other large markets, such as China, India's e-commerce sales are set to rise faster—from $1.6 billion in 2012 to $8.8 billion in 2016, according to Forrester Research.

> India could leapfrog from traditional retailing, focused on physical stores, straight into the multichannel world.

Whether you are a large, small, or even a narrow niche retailer in India, there will be no physical constraints on your ability to reach customers. For larger retailers, it will be easier to manage challenges such as expensive real estate, parking, and transport links. Niche retailers can operate from smaller spaces yet reach more customers across the country.

To capitalize more fully on these new opportunities, Indian retailers must work with suppliers to drive growth and efficiencies in the supply chain and distribution networks. Developing partnerships with suppliers will help improve products' quality, freshness, and flavor.

At Tesco, we're using blogs, discussion forums, and customer data to make our operations more transparent and accessible to our suppliers. With social media causing consumers' tastes to change ever more quickly, the challenge now is to keep up with the change by analyzing data rapidly and sharing it throughout the supply chain, so manufacturers, farmers—and anyone involved in shaping the product—can help maximize its appeal.

With that aim in mind, a new dedicated Tesco online community for our international producers, farmers, and growers—including India—is forging more productive relationships among Tesco and other producers across the globe, down the supply chain. By tapping into this knowledge through an Internet forum, individual suppliers can learn from our buyers what customers want, exchange ideas with their peers across the world, and also let us know how we can be a better partner to them.

To drive modern retail fully forward, India needs to develop its own skills and experience. That is happening at our Hindustan Service Centre in Bangalore, where a staff of over sixty-five hundred has built a core expertise in applying technology to modern supply chain and retailing in the West, working on everything from store layouts to app developments to the mathematics of the supply chain. One of the teams, which focuses on transport planning, receives store orders daily from Thailand and provides optimized transport plans for our distribution centers there. They plan eight hundred to one thousand trips per day, covering five major distribution centers, five regional hubs, and over one thousand stores.

This kind of experience is already creating the thinkers, entrepreneurs, and innovators who will help India make the leap into modern retail—one that is right for the Indian customer. In the midst of change, retailers should not get carried away by new technology but remain focused on the customer. Technology is always changing, while consumers' instincts and values remain constant. They will always want value, choice, and convenience, delivered by a retailer that truly understands their needs and can anticipate their wishes. And they will always want a retailer that goes the extra mile for them to win and retain their loyalty.

In this ever-changing world, in any country, that loyalty remains the key to a successful retailer. India is no different—though the opportunities and rewards for success are immense. Exploiting technology adeptly will be critical to winning the competitive battle. But the most important consequence of all will be the gains reaped by the Indian people.

decoding digital india
Vikash Daga and Vivek Pandit

Over the next three to five years, India will be one of the fastest-growing and most vibrant digital markets in the world. More important, the rise and expansion of digital technologies will challenge economic, political, and social orthodoxies at an unsettling pace. Digital technologies represent a major business opportunity; we believe that they will also transform how Indians connect with their society.

Digital India is on the cusp of major change for three mutually re-inforcing reasons: (1) the billions being invested into technologies like 3G/4G, including the government's national broadband plan to expand digital access to 160 million more users; (2) the evolution of low-cost smart devices and India's well-established local content and service eco-system; and (3) a strong desire to replace decrepit and restrictive structures in favor of political accountability and enhanced social mobility. Considering that half of India's 1.2 billion citizens are below the age of twenty-five, the momentum is irreversible—and the consequences will be momentous.

In economic terms, the Internet contributes about 1.6 percent of India's GDP, or $30 billion, and accounts for six million jobs (directly and indirectly). According to McKinsey research,[1] that could double by

---

[1] *Online and Upcoming: The Internet's Impact on India,* December 2012, www.mckinsey.com/locations/india/mckinseyonindia/pdf/Executive_Summary_Online_and_upcoming_The_Internet_impact_on_India.pdf.

Vikash Daga is a partner in McKinsey's Delhi office. Vivek Pandit is a senior partner in McKinsey's Mumbai office.

2015—if India makes the right investments. This is not just a matter of profits. Already, India has found that better connectivity can bring unexpected but welcome benefits. For example, one study found that infant mortality was lower in areas where Internet kiosks provided information on pre- and postnatal care. And enterprises like Drishtee, whose franchisees have created profitable e-businesses (chiefly related to education and banking) in rural Assam, Bihar, and Uttar Pradesh, prove that the digital economy can succeed in diverse conditions. Digital technologies and access have made doing well while doing good easier than ever.

The government's relative secrecy about its inner workings and its claims about India's progress no longer go unchallenged.

Politically, digital literacy is testing several pillars of the state. For example, the government's relative secrecy about its inner workings and its claims about India's progress no longer go unchallenged. That brings a wider cross section of society into the debate. Citizens are creating their own measures to evaluate government performance.

Socially, online communities are redefining identity and allowing individuals the freedom to shape their destinies. Assigned identities based on caste, religion, ethnicity, and other politically convenient divisions have long shackled the aspirations of too many youths. In a country where an estimated 85 percent of marriages are arranged, for example, there is now a multibillion-dollar industry of more than thirty million online matrimonial profiles. Of these, only 40 percent are managed by parents. Such digital domains profoundly accelerate freedom of choice and will play a pivotal role in India's social evolution.

India is still at the beginning of its digital journey and needs to do more to reach its potential. In March 2013, the *Economist* concluded, "The original emerging-market tech pioneer has fallen behind in the Internet era." We think it is going to catch up: The infrastructure is building, the economics are changing for the better, and the desire is there. Digital technologies represent a major business opportunity; we believe that they will also change the consumer and, in important ways, transform how Indians connect with their society.

the business opportunity

India has 124 million Internet users, third in the world after China and the United States. That is an enormous figure in absolute terms, but it also means that Internet access has reached only 10 percent of the population, a low percentage even compared to other developing countries (e.g., 30 percent in Nigeria and 35 percent in Indonesia). In the next three years, however, we expect that, based on actions already taken, the number of Internet users in India will triple (to about 350 million people, translating into a 28 percent penetration rate). Then it will keep growing.

What's interesting, though, and distinctive, is *how* Indians will access and use the Internet.[2] India is the only country among those we surveyed where users spend more online time on mobile devices (90 minutes a day) than on PCs (64 minutes). Unlike other countries, then, India's Internet growth story will be led by mobile devices, with up to two hundred million mobile-only Internet users by 2015, compared to about forty-five million in 2012.

The mobile sector has filled the gap because PCs are expensive and India's fixed-line network is inadequate. In an example of textbook capitalism, fierce competition, from domestic vendors in particular, has driven mobile prices down and usage way up. Mobile devices now have a penetration rate of more than 55 percent (compared to less than 10 percent for PCs). In short, Indians are voting with their wallets for small screens, in the form of phones and (to a lesser extent) tablets. And again, there is a generational dimension to consider. Younger Indians (age fifteen to twenty-four) are more than twice as likely as older ones (thirty-five and up) to use small screens. The increasing availability of 3G, and the introduction of 4G services in some cities, such as Bangalore and Kolkata, is another boost to the mobile Internet. In effect, India will by-

---

[2] Since 2008, McKinsey has done wide-ranging surveys aimed at understanding changing consumer digital behavior. We have looked at six emerging Asian markets (China, India, Indonesia, Malaysia, the Philippines, and Vietnam). This data forms the basis of much of the analysis. In India, we interviewed more than five thousand people in twenty different cities.

pass the personal computer (not to mention the country's poor fixed-line telephone network) and proceed directly toward the mobile Internet.

Not surprisingly, then, smartphones, which barely existed in India in 2008, have a robust future. Mobile-phone penetration is already high—half of rural households have one, and three-quarters of urban ones—and consumers in all pockets of the country are used to them. The next natural step is to migrate to the mobile Internet. Some companies are already seeing 100 percent year-on-year growth.

More than half of mobile-phone owners want to upgrade to a smart-phone, and the marketplace is responding. There are already smart-phones that cost less than $50, making them available to a wide swath of society. No other emerging market is nearly as mobile dominant as India. By 2015, Internet-enabled smart devices will account for about three-quarters of all new users.

Smartphones will also make India a more lucrative market for tele-coms and service providers. Smartphone users spend more time doing everything from making calls and using Internet services to getting cricket updates. And that translates directly into spending: Smartphone owners spend 482 rupees ($8.90) a month on services, compared to 390 rupees ($7.20) for all mobile-phone owners. One interesting, and proven, phenomenon is that those who first access the Internet on mobile devices are willing to pay more for services than those who begin on a personal computer.

changing the consumer sector

The relatively high cost of broadband has discouraged Indian businesses from offering online services, even compared to other developing countries. This carries enormous opportunity costs. Small- and medium-size businesses that use the Internet report higher sales, lower costs, brisker growth, and improved productivity. But watch out: The Internet is going to change Indian consumers, too.

There are two areas of particular promise. One is media. It's hardly surprising that the land of Bollywood loves entertainment, but in fact Indians are relatively starved for it. According to the recent census, two hundred million Indians do not even have a radio, and two-thirds of rural households do not have a TV. The Internet is already proving a useful alternative. Indian Internet users spent more than five hours a day consuming media of all kinds. Between 2010 and 2012, though, how they did so changed markedly, with traditional media (print, TV, radio) all declining, and digital forms rising sharply. With nearly nine hundred million mobile connections (six hundred million mobile-phone owners, plus three hundred million more mobile connections via SIM cards) and more than four hundred million active data subscribers, access exists as never before.

The land of Bollywood loves entertainment, but in fact Indians are relatively starved for it.

The Indian media has noticed—and is responding. Traditional players are increasingly using digital formats to stimulate online video usage. Star Plus, MTV India, and Sony all distribute free mobile-ready online content; many broadcasters are increasing their reach by adding YouTube channels. Zee TV offers live television that can be accessed on a variety of devices, including mobile ones, and downloaded via apps. In 2011, Bollywood marketed *Zindagi Na Milegi Dobara*, a coming-of-age movie, online—getting fifty-five million hits in two days. In 2012, tens of millions viewed cricket's Indian Premier League online.

In business terms, a major problem is that Indian consumers have grown accustomed to free media. Therefore, determining how to make money from content is still a matter of experimentation. In some cases, people can get movies for free but pay for connectivity. YouTube doesn't charge for videos, but it has lots of ads. There will be a shakeout, and it's premature to pick winners. What can be said is that the direction is clear: more varieties of experience from more providers. And because media is distributed wirelessly, there are comparatively few barriers to dissemination. There is considerable room for foreign players (such as ABC, Hulu, and Netflix) to enter the Indian market and bring their own ideas for innovation and monetization.

The same dynamics hold true for another great opportunity—e-commerce. The experience of going online to order things is still nascent; we estimate that only 2 percent of Indian Internet users have done so. By far the most popular purchases are low-risk virtual items—rail bookings, movie tickets, airline tickets, hotel bookings, games, music, and the like. Credit cards are not widely used in India, and the digital sector needs to develop online payment options that people trust; compared to Africa, the use of mobile money is still limited.

But Indians are experimenting with online shopping, and venture capital is still investing, even though a large proportion of early bets have gone bust. We expect e-commerce to grow faster than any other category in the next few years, in part because it is so small now (less than 10 percent of China's revenues, for example), and in part because of the spread of the mobile Internet. If e-commerce participation rises to half of all Internet users—and that is still well short of U.S. levels—by 2015, it could have ninety-five million customers and $44 billion in total sales (compared to seventeen million and $9 billion in 2012).

> Consumers consider going online the second most important way they make major buying decisions (after word of mouth).

More important than any single sector, however, is the way the Internet is changing how companies and consumers interact. Already, consumers with access to the Internet consider going online the second most important way they make major buying decisions (after word of mouth). And companies are investing more and more in connecting digitally.

the social opportunity

Indians are not just consumers; they are also citizens and parents and students with desires more profound than downloading the latest Bollywood extravaganza. And it is in this regard that digital India will find its broadest impact. Indians, particularly in rural areas, will begin to find health, education, and financial services available to them in a way they never have been before.

Consider the possibilities for mobile health care. Seventy percent of India's rural citizens do not have access to modern health facilities. Remote health solutions, such as smart-device-based monitoring of health conditions, can significantly widen the reach of medical care. Doctors can diagnose certain conditions remotely and then prescribe medications via mobile applications to local providers.

Banking is another area where digital technologies could make a huge difference. Forty percent of India's urban residents, and more than half of those in rural areas, do not have a bank account. Mobile-phone-based money deposit and transfer solutions could help to fill the gap. Airtel Money, launched in 2012, allows customers to use their mobile phone to pay bills, transfer money, and shop online. This improves reliability and cuts transaction costs.

Perhaps the best-developed mobile solutions relate to agriculture, which accounts for the majority of the Indian workforce. Using Tata's mKRISHI platform, for example, farmers can use their mobile phones to call a number and get advice or information, in local languages, on subjects like pest control, crop insurance, travel schedules, government policies, and fertilizer use. They can even send photos for analysis.

The digital infrastructure, as we have argued, is going to be there to allow all this to happen. The bigger problem is figuring out how to monetize these services. The business case for them is still unsettled, although major players, both domestic and foreign, are trying. At some point, they will succeed. Eventually, the demand for such services will create the supply. Success will ripple outward. India has proved in many sectors that it excels at low-cost innovation. There could be significant export markets for this expertise, notably in Africa, where Internet penetration is higher than in India, but technical capabilities are not as deep.

the perils of potential

As is so often the case in India, the potential is enormous—and so are the problems associated with reaching that potential.

A report from the McKinsey Global Institute concluded in late 2012, "While India scores well on the availability of human and financial capital, it rates poorly on Internet infrastructure, Internet engagement, the e-commerce platform, the ease of Internet entrepreneurship, and the impact of e-governance." The MGI research noted that India has only about 6 percent as many secure Internet servers as South Africa (on a per capita basis). India also scores poorly on government-related e-services.

There are issues not directly about the Internet that nonetheless inhibit its development. The unreliability of the country's electricity supply is one such difficulty and is particularly acute in rural areas. There also is the voluminous red tape associated with entrepreneurship. Logistics is another problem; at least one of every five packages mailed does not make it to the intended destination.

All this is true—yet none of it is going to stop digital progress. Along every dimension, the pressure for more, better, and cheaper digital services is intense and cumulative. For business, that makes India a compelling market. And for India, taking advantage of these digital opportunities could be the single most important thing the country does to improve the lives of its people.

the way of the *antevasin*
Nisaba Godrej

Antevasin is Sanskrit for someone who lives at the border. In ancient times it referred to someone who had left the worldly life to live at the edge of the forest where the spiritual masters dwelled—on the border between the material and spiritual worlds. As Elizabeth Gilbert notes in her book *Eat, Pray, Love*, "In the modern age . . . [the] image of an unexplored forest would have to be figurative. But you can still live there . . . on that shimmering line between your old thinking and your new understanding, always in a state of learning."

I've found this modern interpretation of the *antevasin* to be a useful notion as I try to reimagine the role of a modern corporation like the Godrej Group, a 117-year-old diversified conglomerate whose products and services are used by half a billion Indians each day. We have one foot planted firmly in the past, but as our firm gets older, India grows younger, and the world becomes more interconnected and complex. To understand the aspirations of young Indians and to respond to new challenges facing our ancient land, Godrej must, like an *antevasin*, live on the border between our company's storied past and an exciting if uncertain future. Here are four initiatives that reflect our efforts to do that.

different by design

The most obvious way we try to straddle borders between old and new is our approach to product design and marketing. Darshan Gandhi,

*Nisaba Godrej is president for human capital and innovation
at Godrej Industries.*

an alumnus of the prestigious National Institute of Design, heads our "design thinking" team, which brings together the best and most creative minds from our R&D labs and our marketing and design divisions. By adopting an *antevasin* mentality at every stage in the product process, from conception to marketing, we've had some big breakthroughs. For example, our new line of hair-coloring crèmes, Godrej Expert Rich Crème, introduced last year, has been a big success.

Godrej has long been India's market leader for hair-coloring products, and we dominate the market for coloring powder, the product used by 90 percent of Indian consumers who color their hair. But we wanted a product that would broaden the appeal of hair-coloring crème, which traditionally has been viewed as an aspirational product and priced as high as 170 rupees (about $4)—far beyond the reach of ordinary consumers. Our team developed a new crème that in blind product tests scored higher than the leading brand.

Taking inspiration from the way India's shampoo market exploded after the introduction of individual sachets, our design team devised a method of packaging Godrej Expert in two easy-to-use, premeasured sachets that could be mixed and applied with a low-cost hair-coloring kit and priced at only 30 rupees (about $1). We made the packaging gender and age neutral, another innovation (traditionally, packaging for hair coloring crème in India has featured women, even though the biggest consumers of hair-coloring products are men), and rolled out the new product with an ad campaign built around the phrase *Jawani Janeman* (literally, "youthful beloved"), drawn from the lyrics of an iconic Bollywood song. The market response has been staggering. We captured 2 percent of the market with our new crème in fewer than six months, the fastest share gain of any new launch in the hair color category. By challenging old assumptions, we introduced an affordable, convenient product that meets the aspirations of millions of Indian consumers—and is also a winner for Godrej.

moving outside corporate boundaries

Mark Kahn joined Godrej Agrovet, our agribusiness company, in 2007, as part of a turnaround team. In late 2010, Mark proposed that we launch India's first agricultural technology, or agtech, venture fund with Godrej the anchor investor. Mark named the fund Omnivore Partners, after Michael Pollan's 2006 bestseller on food policy, *The Omnivore's Dilemma*.

Agriculture accounts for 14 percent of India's GDP but employs 53 percent of the nation's labor force. As those disparate ratios suggest, India lags far behind global averages and emerging market competitors in agricultural productivity. Mark argued the best way to address India's agricultural challenges was by funding young Indian entrepreneurs seeking to create products and solutions to revolutionize agriculture. By supporting agricultural start-ups, Omnivore Partners aims to catalyze the development of a nationwide agtech entrepreneurial ecosystem.

Thus far, Omnivore has raised $50 million and is currently supporting five entrepreneurs and start-ups working on agtech products and services across India. Godrej has more than just a financial stake in Omnivore; we also provide significant advisory support to the fund. The Omnivore team is backing start-ups in areas such as weather forecasting, agricultural mechanization, farm automation, agribusiness IT, and livestock processing. Our portfolio thus far includes businesses headquartered in Rajkot, Guwahati, Mangalore, Delhi, and Bangalore.

> Our team is backing start-ups in areas such as weather forecasting, agricultural mechanization, farm automation, agribusiness IT, and livestock processing.

Omnivore forced us to confront whether Godrej should support entrepreneurship beyond our corporate boundaries. Ultimately, we decided that it did not matter where disruptive innovation took place, as long as Godrej could play a part in it.

blurring the boundaries of culture, academia, and business

Sometimes a modern *antevasin* must straddle more than one boundary. The Godrej India Culture Lab is an experimental space started on our corporate campus two years ago to cross-pollinate the best minds in

India with leading global thinkers. The Culture Lab is the brainchild of an *antevasin* in his own right: Parmesh Shahani, an MIT-educated TED fellow who had worked as a technology entrepreneur, a venture capitalist, and a fashion magazine editor.

The Culture Lab connects academia, the corporate world, creative industries, nongovernmental organizations, and the public sector. It hosts activities under different formats, including conferences on themes such as urbanization, lectures featuring visiting global academics such as the Japanese designer Kenya Hara of Muji and the world-renowned architect Tadao Ando, as well as plays, music performances, and even a one-day pop-up museum.

Through initiatives like the Culture Lab, we're trying to reimagine the role of a company in society. We recognize that modern global corporations have broad responsibilities that extend beyond the interests of shareholders or a handful of charitable causes and philanthropic actions. Godrej's multifaceted relations with the cultural, intellectual, and corporate worlds are part of our efforts to create a modern successful but also socially and culturally relevant company.

finding our next *antevasins*

To find and hire the experienced, multitalented, creative people needed to reinvent a modern company, we're reimagining the way we look for the next generation of *antevasins*. The good news is that today's young Indians have begun to look at life holistically, moving beyond the singular career focus that drove their parents and older siblings. We decided to incorporate this trend into our campus talent recruitment process, with Godrej LOUD.

LOUD threw out the rule book for hiring summer interns, replacing it with a single criterion—how compelling the deepest desire or goal of the candidate was. LOUD stands for "Live Out Ur Dreams" (forgive the SMS lingo), and it was launched as an online contest across eight Indian business schools. Winning entries

> Young Indians have begun to look at life holistically, moving beyond the singular career focus that drove their parents.

received funding from Godrej to make their dreams into reality and were invited to join the Godrej Group's summer internship program.

Godrej LOUD received thousands of "likes" on Facebook and substantial press coverage. Fifteen finalists were short-listed from 422 applications, and ultimately seven dreams were selected for funding, including a painting holiday in Spain and the digging of a well in a small Indian village. By blurring the lines between employer and benefactor, Godrej is gaining recognition as a place that values young talented people not just for the work they do for Godrej but also for their creativity, their ability to dream and find ways to transform those dreams into real achievements.

looking into the future

These are four of many ways Godrej is seeking to straddle the border between old and new. We have embraced the idea that to succeed in an ever younger, ever more globalized country like India, we must always be ready to undertake radical experiments and innovations that transcend the boundaries we all accepted only a decade ago.

the next five hundred million
Eric Schmidt

In spite of its well-deserved reputation as one of the world's leading information technology and software development hubs, India is far from being the connected society many foreigners imagine. In 2004, when Google set up its first R&D center outside the United States in Bangalore, we were surprised to discover that one of our biggest challenges was Internet connectivity. Our ability to transmit data between India and our facilities around the world was extremely limited, an obstacle that, given the nature of our business, we had to surmount quickly.

Much of the connectivity developed in India over the past twenty years is the result of large domestic and international companies doing just what we did—figuring out how to develop their own private networks to work with subsidiaries and clients. So far, though, those efforts have yielded relatively few connectivity benefits for the Indian population as a whole.

Today India, with a population of 1.2 billion people, has more than 600 million mobile-phone users but only about 150 million people who regularly connect to the Internet. In 2011, India's Internet penetration rate (the percentage of the population using the Internet) was 11 percent, according to the International Telecommunication Union. That's far below that of developed nations, where penetration rates average 70 percent, and less than a third of China's

> By any reasonable definition, India is an Internet laggard.

Eric Schmidt is executive chairman of Google and coauthor of The New Digital Age: Reshaping the Future of People, Nations and Business.

penetration ratio of 38 percent. It's also less than half penetration rates for all developing countries, which average 24 percent. The number of India's broadband users, twenty million, is even smaller. By any reasonable definition, India is an Internet laggard. To me, the Internet in India today feels a little like where it was in America in about 1994—four years before Google was even born.

The good news is that there's tremendous potential for increased Internet penetration to have a positive impact on India's economy and society. India is on the cusp of a connectivity revolution. I believe India has the chance to leapfrog its current connectivity challenges, bring Internet access to a majority of its citizens—and even raise its penetration ratio to 60 or 70 percent within the next five to ten years. Connecting its next five hundred million will make India the largest open-access Internet market in the world. In ten years' time, I predict it will be almost impossible for any child in India to imagine what life was like before the Internet. But to realize that promise, India must make the right technology choices.

> In ten years, it will be almost impossible to describe to any child in India what life was like before the Internet.

One key choice will be how and how quickly India builds out the fixed-line networks in its cities and towns. Fiber-optic cables are, by far, the best way to promote higher connectivity. You want to bury them underground in every place you can: every road, every path, every ditch, every piece of land. Fiber-optic cables with optical amplifiers will last thirty, even forty years and will scale to almost infinite bandwidth. Each fiber-optic cable will carry all the data that's around us in the air today and much more with some fairly straightforward techniques involving wavelengths. For cities and towns, fiber-optic cable extends Internet coverage much faster and at a much lower cost than trying to provide connectivity to everyone the old-fashioned way by cable or phone line.

A second area to get right is cellular technology. India should make the transition from 2G and 3G to 4G technology as quickly as possible because 4G makes far more efficient use of the spectrum and users can get so much more bandwidth out of it. It may take time for India to achieve these two goals because its telecommunications industry is undercapitalized and has a lot of debt. But I am confident that eventually the transformation will happen.

Investing in a bigger, faster telecommunications network will have a big payoff for India as that network combines with one of the most radically life-altering developments of the last decade: the emergence of moderately priced mobile devices. These days, it's common for people in developing countries who don't have televisions, refrigerators, or even indoor plumbing to have mobile phones. And even those who don't own a phone themselves almost always know someone in their village who does. Now imagine what the world will be like when not only phones with voice and text capability are cheap and ubiquitous, but so are mobile devices that can connect to and navigate around the Internet. There's every reason to believe in the next five years, we'll see the emergence of smartphones with a moderately powerful screen at a cost well below $50—a huge breakthrough. True, Internet access speeds for those phones will be modest compared to more expensive devices in places like the United States. But as has been demonstrated repeatedly around the world, as cell-phone usage spreads, access to advanced information technology can be life changing. Suddenly, all kinds of new things are possible.

In India, this phenomenon is sure to unleash a customer-driven revolution on a scale we've never seen before—in education, financial services, health care, entertainment, and almost every conceivable aspect of life. In education alone, the possibilities are staggering: Parents who believe their children are not getting proper instruction in local schools will be able to use mobile phones or tablets to help fulfill their kids' educational needs. Great teachers can connect to children in remote villages. Indian students can watch Ivy League professors on YouTube or share knowledge and ideas by video chat with experts or other students thousands of kilometers away.

Similar changes are in store for banking and financial services. India has a huge number of people whose banking needs are underserved.

The government's Unique Identification project, led by my friend Nandan Nilekani, is creating enormous new possibilities for e-commerce. Already, we're seeing the emergence of many new start-ups created to help middle- and lower-income consumers move money around, and because of the sheer scale of the market in India, these new businesses are likely to be highly profitable.

I see the creative potential of India's people all around me in Silicon Valley, where India-born entrepreneurs account for 40 percent of start-ups. Just think what will happen when India's entrepreneurial innovators are able to create great global companies without leaving their country. They'll change the world.

Hundreds of large firms focused on the Internet will be founded and will succeed by focusing purely on Indian consumers, Indian taste, Indian style, Indian sports. Can one of those companies ultimately become the next Google? Of course. That may not happen for quite a few years. But if India plays its cards right, we'll soon see Indian engineers and small businesses tackling Indian problems first, then exporting the solutions that work best.

The other potentially game-changing impact of the democratizing Internet access is on governance. It's no secret that India is plagued by corruption, which impedes the country's economic progress, frustrates ordinary people's efforts to advance themselves, and seriously infringes on individuals' rights to fair treatment by the authorities. One of the Internet's great virtues is that it empowers individuals and groups to expose the excesses and abuses of those in positions of power. It can shine a light on human behavior to allow—or force—society to curb the abuses, especially against those least able to defend themselves. As the Internet penetrates India, we'll see dramatic improvement in, for example, the status of women, access to education, and the transparency in public life necessary to improve governance and attack corruption. All of those are necessary preconditions to the economic and commercial success that India's remarkably talented people deserve.

Because India's next five hundred million Internet users aren't connected yet, we don't hear much from them now; we don't know who they are, what they want, or what they'll want to say. What we do know is that they will be a very different group from the first one hundred million connected Indians. We know they'll be far more diverse, in income, lifestyle, education levels, and their languages (which I see as a big opportunity for Google Translate). And we know we're about to hear from them in a very big way.

India's ambivalence about Internet freedom often surprises those who don't live, travel, or do business there.

All of that potential, however, hinges on an even more fundamental choice: Will India embrace an open network or a closed one? The political impulse to try to shield people from inflammatory, obscene, or defamatory commentary and images in a country as diverse and often fractious as India is understandable but misplaced. At Google we believe that, in fact, the freer a country's Internet, the better chance that country has of exposing deep-rooted problems and confronting them honestly.

India's ambivalence about Internet freedom often surprises those who don't live, travel, or do business there. Other countries, like China, are far more famous for exerting command and control over cyberspace. India, on the other hand, is known for its freewheeling democracy and boisterous political debate. But a Google search of "India Internet censorship" generates thousands of hits documenting episodes in recent years of government authorities, both at the national and state levels, demanding the closure of websites or dispatching law enforcement officials to intimidate people for posted material deemed to be objectionable.

These actions often are well-intentioned, especially when they are aimed at suppressing ethnic violence. In general, though, such policies are misguided and inimical to India's broader national interests. Internet freedom will produce information and images that are displeasing, even appalling to many segments of society. False accusations and hateful commentary are inevitable, if unfortunate, components of the Internet mix. But trying to control what people say is a losing proposition. It's much better to let good speech overwhelm bad speech, using the kinds of principles that have worked reasonably well on the free and open Internet we enjoy in the United States and other developed countries.

Having witnessed India's progress over the past decade, it is hard not to be optimistic about the next ten years. Global success and a vast improvement in living conditions for hundreds of millions of its citizens are within the country's grasp, but only if India's leaders invest in the right infrastructure and embrace the transparency and openness of the Internet.

solving india's most pressing challenge
Louis R. Chênevert

The Raj Bhavan in Kolkata, now the official residence of the governor of West Bengal, houses an Otis elevator installed in 1892. Known by locals as the "bird cage lift" and still in operation, its longevity is a testimony to both the underlying technology developed in the United States and the technical skills and attention to detail of the Indian staff who have operated and maintained the lift for more than 120 years. That symbiosis of skill and conscientiousness lives on in UTC's current operations in India, including our aerospace systems factory in Bangalore and the strategic partnership between our Sikorsky business and Tata Advanced Systems Limited to manufacture aerospace components and helicopter cabins.

To fulfill the aspirations of its people, Indians will need to match the very best of their own skills and creativity with the right technologies, whether developed at home or adapted from abroad. The scale of the economic and societal transformation required is staggering: India's middle class is expected to double to 575 million by 2025, with a similar number of Indians living in cities by then. Those city dwellers, with an average age of under thirty, will be educated, ambitious, and mobile—providing India with the prerequisites for a thriving consumption-driven economy. But these newly empowered twenty-first-century Indians deserve—and are sure to demand—a modern and sustainable infrastructure.

Can India meet the challenge? The answer to that question remains to be seen. The average infrastructure investment in countries across Southeast Asia is about 12 percent of GDP. India's current infrastructure

Louis R. Chênevert is chairman and CEO of United Technologies Corporation.

expenditures amount to less than 8 percent. India's government wants to push this figure above 10 percent, which, if done right, would present unique opportunities for accelerating growth, creating jobs in the short term, and making India more competitive and comfortable in the long term. Still, given its fiscal limitations, India will need creative solutions to make optimal use of resources and invest for future development.

India's most pressing challenge is energy. On current trends, India's energy consumption is likely to double by 2030. Given India's lack of indigenous energy sources and local concerns about the social and environmental impact of exploiting those resources, the most promising solution over the short term is greater energy efficiency. On the demand side, promoting and implementing efficient energy practices is low-hanging fruit—an endeavor that can yield significant tangible returns for individual consumers and the nation as a whole for many years to come. We have observed that Indian households will invest more capital up front if they can be assured that products such as automobiles, air conditioners, and other household appliances will generate economic benefits throughout that product's life cycle. More important, investments in energy efficiency pay for themselves over time and need not depend on government or other subsidies as is the case with investments in renewable energy.

> Given India's lack of indigenous energy sources and local concerns about the ... impact of exploiting those resources, the most promising solution ... is greater energy efficiency.

Innovations in supply-side areas like microgrids and renewable energy must also play a major role in India's energy future. The changes may be small: an elevator that produces electricity as it descends under gravity, for example. But in a nation as large and populous as India, even small measures can have enormous impact if implemented across the entire country. Energy efficiency offers a vast and low-cost energy resource for the Indian economy, but only if the nation can craft a comprehensive approach to unlock it.

In the medium to long term, India must focus on ensuring that the places where people live, work, and socialize are not only safe and affordable but also smart and sustainable. Technologies that integrate build-

INTRODUCING INDIA

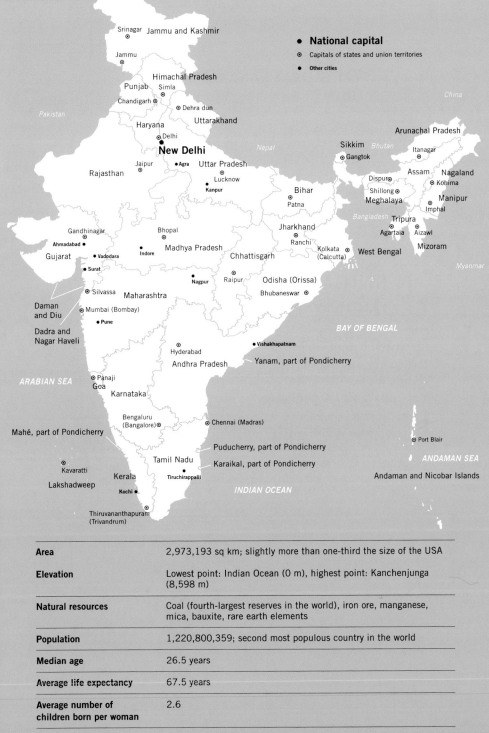

Area	2,973,193 sq km; slightly more than one-third the size of the USA
Elevation	Lowest point: Indian Ocean (0 m), highest point: Kanchenjunga (8,598 m)
Natural resources	Coal (fourth-largest reserves in the world), iron ore, manganese, mica, bauxite, rare earth elements
Population	1,220,800,359; second most populous country in the world
Median age	26.5 years
Average life expectancy	67.5 years
Average number of children born per woman	2.6

Sources: Survey of India, CIA World Factbook

A REMARKABLE RISE

1991 GLOBAL RANKING
BY PPP-ADJUSTED GDP ($ BILLION)

8	UK	937
9	Brazil	822
10	India	787
11	Mexico	661
12	Spain	585

When India started reforms in 1991, the size of its economy was comparable to those of much smaller countries.

AN ENIGMATIC ECONOMY

The rise of India's information technology and outsourcing sectors is a familiar story. But while India is a technology titan, it's also an agrarian country where wealth comes from energy and natural resources.

AGRICULTURE

SHARE OF TOTAL EMPLOYMENT: 53%

Agriculture is still what the vast majority of Indians do for a living, but it also counts for a shrinking share of the country's economic activity. Indian farmers must become more productive to feed a growing population and compete in export markets.

SHARE OF GDP

1990	2012
29%	**18%**

787

1991

Since economic liberalization began in 1991, India has experienced strong growth on the way to becoming one of the world's largest economies.

2013 GLOBAL RANKING
BY PPP-ADJUSTED GDP ($ BILLION)

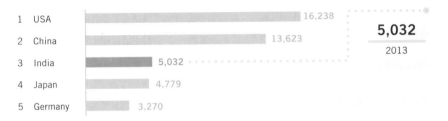

1	USA	16,238
2	China	13,623
3	India	5,032
4	Japan	4,779
5	Germany	3,270

5,032
2013

SERVICES

SHARE OF TOTAL EMPLOYMENT: 21%

The technology sector is a symbol of India's economic progress. But the combined workforces of the ten biggest IT firms total less than half the number of jobs at government-owned Indian Railways, the country's largest employer.

INDUSTRY

SHARE OF TOTAL EMPLOYMENT: 19%

Manufacturers rank among India's most profitable companies and industry has the potential to create great wealth and new jobs, but India hasn't yet realized its potential as a place that makes things.

SHARE OF GDP

1990 **44%**   2012 **56%**   1990 **26%**   2012 **27%**

SHARE OF GDP

Sources: International Monetary Fund, World Economic Outlook Database, October 2012

PROSPERITY AND INEQUALITY

Indians and foreigners alike often presume that the country's cultural fault line is between the impoverished, struggling north and the rapidly developing south. But economic and population data shows that levels of development vary widely across the country and within regions.

In the past decade, the population of India's north and east has grown faster than that of the south and west. Typically, slowing population growth goes hand-in-hand with rising levels of income and urbanization.

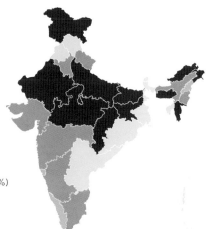

POPULATION GROWTH RATE, 2001–11 (%)

- 20.1–25
- 16–20
- 11–15
- 0–10

National average: 17.6

The economic differences between the regions are reflected in the everyday lives of India's citizens.

ADULT LITERACY RATES, 2011 (%)

- 61–70
- 71–80
- 81–90
- 91–100

National average: 74

HOUSEHOLDS WITH TOILETS, 2011 (%)

- < 50
- > 50

MOVE TO THE CITY

Besides being crowded, India's cities also lack adequate services, housing, and amenities. Here's how far Indian cities fall short of the levels of services that they need to provide.

■ Current level
□ Basic level of adequate service

SEWAGE AND SEPTIC TANK COVERAGE
% of population

100
63

PIPED WATER COVERAGE
% of population

100
74

PARKS AND OPEN SPACE

Square meters per capita

9.0
2.7

SOLID WASTE COLLECTED

% of total waste generated

100
72

WATER SUPPLY QUANTITY

Liters per capita per day

150
105

City residents' representation in parliament has been rising steadily, offering hope for the future.

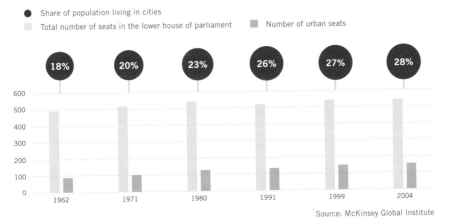

● Share of population living in cities
□ Total number of seats in the lower house of parliament
■ Number of urban seats

18% 20% 23% 26% 27% 28%

600
500
400
300
200
100
0

1962   1971   1980   1991   1999   2004

Source: McKinsey Global Institute

Mahatma Gandhi famously said that India lives in its villages. He and other leaders saw their country's heartland in its thousands of rural communities. In the future, though, many more people will be living in cities, as they move off the land in search of opportunity.

But while India is primarily rural, its cities are among the most densely populated places on earth.

POPULATION PER SQUARE KILOMETER, 2011

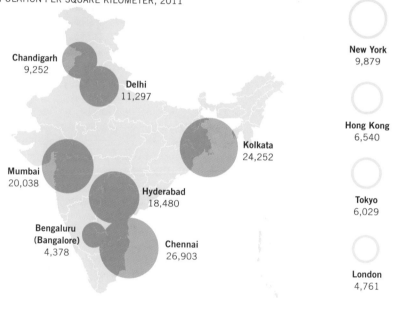

Chandigarh
9,252

Delhi
11,297

Kolkata
24,252

Mumbai
20,038

Hyderabad
18,480

Bengaluru
(Bangalore)
4,378

Chennai
26,903

New York
9,879

Hong Kong
6,540

Tokyo
6,029

London
4,761

Their growth rates will also slow less than those of many other megacities in the future.

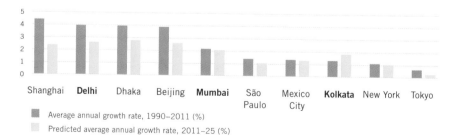

Shanghai   **Delhi**   Dhaka   Beijing   **Mumbai**   São Paulo   Mexico City   **Kolkata**   New York   Tokyo

■ Average annual growth rate, 1990–2011 (%)
□ Predicted average annual growth rate, 2011–25 (%)

Sources: United Nations Department of Economic and Social Affairs/Population Division, Indian and other national censuses

In 1962, India was about 20% urban; now the figure is over 30%. Still, the country is under-urbanized compared to both the developed world and other emerging markets.

SHARE OF POPULATION LIVING IN URBAN AREAS, 2011 (%)

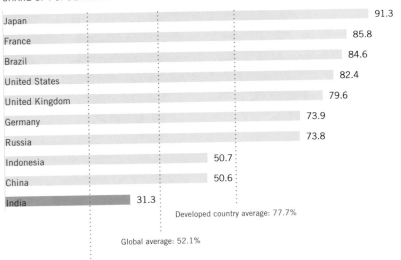

Japan	91.3
France	85.8
Brazil	84.6
United States	82.4
United Kingdom	79.6
Germany	73.9
Russia	73.8
Indonesia	50.7
China	50.6
India	31.3

Developed country average: 77.7%

Global average: 52.1%

Least-developed country average: 28.5%

India's leading cities are among the world's biggest, and getting bigger.

POPULATIONS OF WORLD'S LARGEST URBAN AGGLOMERATIONS, 2011 (MILLIONS)

Tokyo	Delhi	New York	Mexico City	Shanghai
37.2	**22.7**	20.4	20.4	20.2

São Paulo	Mumbai	Beijing	Dhaka	Kolkata
19.9	**19.7**	15.6	15.4	**15.4**

Meanwhile, foreign investment has gone almost entirely to the western and southern states. That's helped produce a clear divide between a wealthier west and south and a poorer north and east. At its most extreme, that divide means that the average income for a resident of the eastern state of Bihar is only 12% of that of a resident of Delhi.

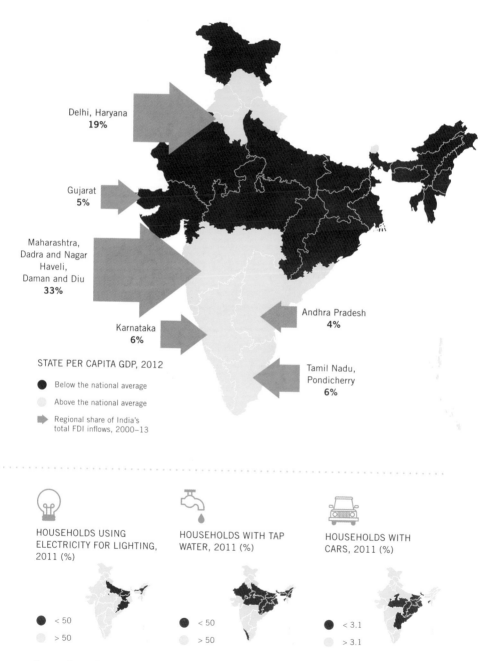

Delhi, Haryana
19%

Gujarat
5%

Maharashtra, Dadra and Nagar Haveli, Daman and Diu
33%

Karnataka
6%

Andhra Pradesh
4%

Tamil Nadu, Pondicherry
6%

STATE PER CAPITA GDP, 2012

● Below the national average

○ Above the national average

➡ Regional share of India's total FDI inflows, 2000–13

HOUSEHOLDS USING ELECTRICITY FOR LIGHTING, 2011 (%)

● < 50
○ > 50

HOUSEHOLDS WITH TAP WATER, 2011 (%)

● < 50
○ > 50

HOUSEHOLDS WITH CARS, 2011 (%)

● < 3.1
○ > 3.1

Sources: Reserve Bank of India, Census of India

ing automation with other functions like air-conditioning, security, fire alarms, and lighting will become the norm, offering customers a high degree of convenience and customization en route to energy savings. In this case, the fact that India's economy remains at an early stage of development can be an advantage. Building sustainability into a new structure is less expensive than retrofitting an old one, and only about a third of the buildings that India will need by 2030 exist today. Buildings are responsible for 40 percent of the world's energy consumption, and technologies—particularly for air-conditioning

In a nation as large and populous as India, even small measures can have enormous impact if implemented across the entire country.

and lighting—already exist to reduce building energy consumption by as much as 70 percent. Early indications suggest India is embracing this trend. Indian policy makers should lend their support by creating and enforcing strict whole-building energy efficiency codes, labeling standards, and regularly scheduled energy audits, hardly any of which exist today.

Beyond these individual initiatives, India must adopt a more holistic approach to energy efficiency if it is to achieve sustainable growth and find more opportunities for coordination between the public and private sectors. In Gujarat, United Technologies has partnered with six other global businesses and the World Business Council for Sustainable Development to publish *A Solutions Landscape for Gujarat Cities.* This study, based on extensive research and dialogue with city officials, offers recommendations on how the four largest cities in Gujarat can be supported in their urban planning, energy efficiency, and wastewater management efforts.

The people of India should look to the future with confidence and pride. The technologies already exist to build the world-class infrastructure the country requires. Indian companies and their foreign partners have demonstrated the ability to deliver advanced solutions, and the marketplace, with appropriate government regulation and subsidies, seems set to provide the necessary financial incentives. The results will be continued economic growth, greater investment in India's economy and its people, and quality-of-life improvements for all.

betting big on bio
Kiran Mazumdar-Shaw

When I set out to create a biotechnology business in 1978, the environment in India for such start-ups was hostile at best. Venture-capital funding was nonexistent, bank credit carried usurious interest rates, and the license raj was unparalleled in its ability to throw up obstacles to entrepreneurial innovators. The business initiatives that did find favor focused on reengineered low-cost technologies often under license. Those companies viewed R&D as little more than a tax break to pad earnings, whereas I saw it as integral to my strategy. More than three decades later, Biocon, the company I created, is a globally recognized maker of affordable products that have changed the lives of millions—from patented enzymes to generic statins, and from biosimilar insulin and biologics to patented novel molecules.

> Although the bureaucracy is less obstructionist, it shows no inclination to nurture the sort of start-ups that could be game changers.

Today the license raj is largely just a painful memory. Indian entrepreneurs have become famous around the world for their remarkable success in the most advanced markets, particularly Silicon Valley. Unfortunately, my youthful counterparts, the entrepreneurial innovators of 2013, face many of the same obstacles here in India of that bygone era. Investors are far more interested in stable returns than in backing high-risk but potentially high-reward start-ups. Although the bureaucracy is

Kiran Mazumdar-Shaw is chairman and managing director of Biocon Limited.

less obstructionist these days, it shows no inclination to nurture the sort of start-ups that could be game changers, particularly in the biotechnology field.

Such innovation is essential if the Indian economy is to overcome the challenges facing it. Industrial output is down, exports are declining, inflation is high, and the fiscal deficit has reached worrying proportions. India's biotech sector, with annual revenues today of $7.5 billion, has the potential to promote socioeconomic progress by transforming energy, health care, the environment, and agriculture. The effect would be to create a new "bioeconomy," based on India's rise as a leading biotechnology hub. Start-ups and existing firms have launched potentially transformative technological solutions in a piecemeal fashion in pilot projects, but for this sector to reach its full potential, India must do more than incrementally remove the hurdles that face start-ups. We must now plot a strategic road map for biotech that enables these innovators to replicate and scale up across India.

Biofuels. India's dependence on imported energy, particularly transportation fuels, is exploding to keep pace with economic growth. Biofuels could replace significant amounts of conventional liquid fuels and are a renewable source of energy that offers the option of clean power generation. Indian firms have already begun to harness the energy found in the microalgae and seaweed that grow abundantly along India's coastline using novel enzyme technologies for fuel alcohol. Biotechnology has the potential to make India energy independent, just as Brazil has done with its bioethanol production from sugarcane bagasse. But just as the Brazilian government supported the creation of that industry, India must institute fiscal policies that provide grants and tax credits in order to build specialized skills as well as scale that enhance investments in developing new manufacturing technologies and capacity building in biofuels.

Health care. India is already one of the world's leading manufacturers of generic drugs and vaccines at the lowest cost. A "made in India" vaccine immunizes a third of the world's children just as one in three generic drugs is of Indian origin. India can position itself as a laboratory and pharmacy for the world by offering cost-effective research capabilities to develop affordable drugs, vaccines, and diagnostics for use globally. One area of particular concern is the increase in mosquito-borne diseases. Every year, more than twenty million Indians contract malaria and millions more get dengue fever. Research to develop both conventional and DNA-based vaccines to combat these communicable diseases is well under way, giving India the opportunity to have a first mover advantage to provide such vaccines for the world.

> A "made in India" vaccine immunizes a third of the world's children.

Public sanitation. About half of Indians do not have access to proper toilets. The illnesses, lost productivity, and other effects of this inadequate sanitation cut India's GDP by 6.4 percent in 2006, according to a World Bank study. Biotoilets, which use bacteria that digest waste and turn it into biogas and odorless compost, can change all that. At about $100 each, these biotoilets are not only economical to set up but also eliminate the need to build sewers and sanitation treatment plants, and they cut water use. The Biocon Foundation has partnered with the government of Karnataka in building both community and individual household toilets as a means to offer safe sanitation to several villages.

Agriculture. Although more than half of India's labor force works on the farm, agriculture accounts for less than a fifth of our GDP. Biotechnology can usher in a second green revolution by providing scientific techniques that optimize the use of available resources without placing additional demands on land or water to boost yields. These solutions can easily be scaled across the country while improving the quality of the produce with disease-free and nutritionally enhanced varieties of crops. The early benefits of biotechnology already are being reaped by Indian farmers as they increasingly opt for genetically modified Bt cotton seeds to improve productivity, converting India from a net importer to a net exporter of cotton, further supporting India's job-generating textile industry.

Apart from genetically modified crops, agricultural biotechnology is leveraging molecular markers in crop breeding for the selective propagation of genes that improve yields and resist disease. Beyond cultivation, biopesticides and biofertilizers have the potential to help farmers move up the value chain. The government needs to put in place a clearly articulated policy on agribiotechnology that provides checks and balances to ensure safety instead of making ad hoc decisions under political compulsions.

Biotechnology is a powerful enabler for transformational economic reform. We must embrace an innovation-led path ahead that combines new technologies, new methods, and new knowledge. India acutely needs new economic policies that go beyond removing barriers to innovative entrepreneurs and actively supports them. Only through this approach can we reimagine an inclusive and enlightened economy that ensures a better quality of life for all of India.

why virtual infrastructure is a real problem
Frank D'Souza and Malcolm Frank

At Cognizant, we have had a problem—one that is welcome but daunting. A surge in demand for our services has obliged us to hire more than twenty thousand people per year on average over the past half decade, two-thirds of them in India. In fact, some years we have hired more than twenty people every business hour to meet client requirements for the information technology, consulting, and business process services we provide. Fortunately, we have been able to bring these recruits on board while also increasing client and employee satisfaction. That is a testament to the strength and vitality of India's technology sector, which exported $40 billion worth of IT services and $16 billion in business process services in 2012.

Rapid and healthy as this growth has been, India's technology industry could be poised for even greater expansion, with a more transformative impact on the country's economy and society than it has to date. But that will depend on the nation's infrastructure.

By infrastructure, we're not using the term in its traditional old-industry sense of roads, ports, and energy grids. India's rickety, overburdened transport and energy network has received plenty of attention, and deservedly so. The massive blackout of July 2012 drove home that point with a vengeance.

While enhancing India's physical infrastructure is clearly necessary, it is equally if not more important to develop an upgraded national in-

Frank D'Souza is CEO and Malcolm Frank is executive vice president of Cognizant.

formation infrastructure—one that brings seamless digital connectivity to every town, village, and hamlet. Just as railroads and superhighways helped propel England and the United States to industrial leadership and societal development in the 1800s and 1900s, a similar outcome could result from India's full development of the networks, on-ramps, and connectivity that form the backbone of technology-driven industries and an information-based society. Among the most crucial benefits to be reaped from such an investment is improvements in education, with children using mobile devices to get much of the instruction the traditional school system doesn't adequately provide. This is hardly a novel idea, but its implementation has lagged for years. The time to kick it into high gear is now.

So far, India's IT industry has benefited enormously from an educational, financial, and cultural "ecosystem" that has furnished thousands of firms with the talent, financing, and entrepreneurial spark needed for supercharged growth. The results are manifest in the attainments of the top five IT and business services firms (TCS, Cognizant, Infosys, Wipro, and HCL), which employ more than eight hundred thousand people.

However, the salutary effects of the industry's boom have been concentrated mainly in cities with technology clusters, such as Mumbai, Bangalore, Pune, Chennai, and Hyderabad, leaving the lives of hundreds of millions of Indians relatively untouched. For the industry to extend its leadership in technology services, and flourish in a way that can serve as a much more powerful social and economic catalyst, the information infrastructure must connect every corner of India with the rest of the world.

India has made a start in building out its information infrastructure, and at least in absolute terms the numbers are impressive. More than 600 million mobile phones are in use in the country, and about 150 million customers log on regularly to the Internet. However, in today's global economy, this is far from adequate in terms of percentage of the population. Internet connections and users need to increase by an order of magnitude, and they need to extend much farther into the hinterland. This will obviously entail government subsidization, because serving rural areas requires high capital costs, while revenues from low-density areas with low-income residents are insufficient to provide adequate returns.

The government has shown commendable awareness of this problem, which afflicts both Internet and mobile-telephone connectivity, by establishing the Universal Service Obligation Fund (USOF). Based on similar approaches used in other countries, the USOF assesses levies on the gross revenue of companies in the industry, with the funds used to provide incentives for laying fiber-optic cable, erecting transmission towers, and creating other infrastructure, so that service providers can lease bandwidth at reasonable usage fees to provide access directly to customers.

Unfortunately, progress has been severely plagued by delays in execution. The fund, first approved by the cabinet in 1999, wasn't fully established until 2003, and since then it has spent only about half of its nearly $8 billion in levies. A study issued in April 2013 by GSMA, the association representing mobile operators worldwide, noted that many of the fund's initiatives "appear to be either frozen at the conceptual stage or still in a pilot trial mode." Even in cases where projects were completed, "the completion dates seem to be long after the initial target date and, in some cases, the service coverage and completion targets have been reduced."

We are keenly aware of the need to ensure that fair competition and transparency prevail at every step of this process—as witnessed by the scandals concerning mobile-phone spectrum allocation that erupted in recent years. But much greater urgency is in order.

At Cognizant, we have gained a deep appreciation for the benefits of ubiquitous connectivity. Our company's network combines the powers of broadband, mobile devices, social media, and telepresence—the ability to conduct high-definition videoconferences and virtual work with our 150,000+ associates around the globe from one's office, home, or even the road using a tablet computer. A typical workday for us at Cognizant may include two "face-to-face" morning virtual meetings in Chennai, followed by another in Hyderabad. Paris and London will follow, and later in the day it's on to New York and California. Although travel is still a necessity for us on the executive team, on any typical day 25 percent of our meetings are in person; the remaining 75 percent are virtual. Moreover, we use a social computing platform for handling many of our most complex client projects so that we can exploit the skills of employees spread across vast distances. That way, instead of fifteen people working in the same room at the same time to solve a problem, a project team can be distributed across geography and time while working together in a coordinated fashion.

Specialized and technically demanding as such activities are, many of the capabilities we utilize at the company level have similar applications broadly in Indian society—education being the most exciting. Addressing India's educational needs (and its inherent chasms between the village and city, geographies, and cultures) through traditional methods alone will simply take too long and will prove too costly. By making effective use of the information infrastructure, and deploying e-learning methods whose benefits are well documented, these chasms can be crossed. Not only will students become facile with new technologies; more important, they can gain instant access to high-quality and individualized instruction. A virtual extension to India's bricks-and-mortar educational system can provide the foundation for widening the base of India's educational pyramid.

> Addressing India's educational needs through traditional methods alone will take too long and prove too costly.

The gains would not be confined to education; job growth is another area ripe for improvement. Over the past two decades, talented Indians have dispersed across the globe to find employment. With proper virtual work platforms, instead of the individual going to the work, the work can come to the individual. The positive implications for social stability could also be enormous. Indians today are confronting the question of whether they must sacrifice cherished traditions to fully embrace a modern economy. A highly developed information infrastructure doesn't force one to ignore or reject social traditions; it enables citizens to remain in their communities and with their families.

Yet many of the issues that have constrained India's physical infrastructure don't apply when it comes to information infrastructure. Many Indians regard the superhighways, strip malls, and concrete jungles of developed nations with great ambivalence. An information infrastructure, by contrast, is inherently "green" in many respects, not least of which is the substantial reduction in the need for daily work commutes. All the more reason, then, to give its implementation much higher priority than it is getting today.

> Many Indians regard the superhighways, strip malls, and concrete jungles of developed nations with ambivalence. An information infrastructure, by contrast, is inherently "green."

India's technology and business services industry has captured the public's imagination, motivating today's managers to protect what has been built and inspiring tomorrow's leaders to think big. If an information infrastructure becomes a truly national reality, not only will our industry reach new heights but so shall the nation as a whole.

how to win at leapfrog
Vinod Khosla

There's a general tendency in life to want to do what others have done. It's an understandable impulse but shortsighted. One of the great things about being a relatively poor, trailing, but rising power like India is that you have the opportunity to see what you want to imitate—and, more important, what you want to skip.

Here's an example. In 2000, I chaired a three-day telecommunications seminar for McKinsey & Company in New Delhi. I talked to everybody about skipping the landline. I said, "If I were India, I wouldn't worry about adding ten million more copper lines. I would go straight to voice over Internet and mobile." I didn't have it exactly right; I missed how big mobile could become and how quickly. But my argument was that the giant traditional telecom equipment and system providers were offering the wrong system for the twenty-first century. Happily for India, despite its plans to the contrary and its focus on "traditional technology" landlines, the right thing (mobile) has happened. And India is not alone in this path—Africa has taken a similar evolution toward mobile telephony.

Was this a one-time phenomenon? No. There are many areas where a developing country can apply this kind of "leapfrog" mentality and find a different path to a better future: education, health care, energy, even infrastructure. But the key, which leapfrog advocates often miss, is *how* you go about creating this alternative path.

It's not enough to say, "Let's look beyond today and plan for 2025."

Vinod Khosla is founding partner of Khosla Ventures.

Most emerging market countries do that. Such plans are usually far too prescriptive: Let's build forty new universities by a certain date, add eighty thousand doctors, build eight thousand kilometers of new highway, or install ten million solar panels. Usually they are based on a regressed estimate of today's baseline. Rushing to do specific things is a big mistake. Technology advances in ways that are quirky and unpredictable. It's unwise to rely on plans that presume to see the future too clearly; strategic planning and consultant forecasts almost invariably mislead.

So rather than trying to predict the future, India's leaders should be trying to fit into the future as it happens. Instead of setting out ten concrete goals, they should encourage one broad direction and adopt an evolutionary mind-set. That way, as the world changes, as the price of oil shifts or a breakthrough technology comes along, India can adapt.

> Rather than trying to predict the future, India's leaders should be trying to fit into the future as it happens.

Take transportation, a pressing future need for India. In a linear model, you might presume that if there are eighty cars per one hundred people in the United States, then that's where India will end up and begin to plan for that. But if I were building the system, I would look for ways to anticipate and skip what exists today (my rule #1), while trying to lean in the right direction (rule #2). I would consider the possibility that, for the world in 2025, self-driving cars, like the ones Google is well on the way to successfully developing, will be widespread. And then I would ask: What are some of the implications of that assumption?

The first implication is we'll need a different type of transportation infrastructure. With a system of self-driving cars at scale in the United States, you might end up with one-fifth the current number of cars sold annually. Instead of owning cars individually, perhaps drivers of the future will think of cars more the way we do taxis and limos now, or like fractional jet ownership of the sort that NetJets pioneered—as fleets you could tap into for different occasions and with a lower total cost of ownership. With the fleet approach, the quality of service could improve because customers wouldn't be tied to the cars they bought. For a night on the town, you might get a BMW; for everyday use, a Prius; for hauling stuff over the weekend, a Suburban. And all ordered on your smartphone.

A second implication of the spread of self-driving cars and adoption of a fleet approach to car ownership is that cities can set aside less space for parking. Think what phone companies do in dense urban spaces. They don't add a phone line for every person in a building. They multiplex: If there are one hundred people in a building, they run twenty-five to thirty lines. With self-driving vehicles, we could multiplex cars the same way.

A shift toward a multiplexed fleet of auto-navigating vehicles would enable India to cut resource usage in a major way, lessening the need for capital investment, reducing expenditure for steel. Electric cars would become more affordable; the usage factor would be much higher, so the payback time would be much shorter. Even with today's batteries, you could justify paying a higher price for electric cars. Instead of being driven 6,500 kilometers a year, electric cars would be driven 160,000 kilometers a year, like a taxi. That, in turn, would lower oil consumption.

Such a distributed system would be much more adaptive than making a massive investment in a new electric rail network. Loads would dynamically balance to fit demand. A distributed approach to transportation doesn't require betting on a single $10 billion project. In effect, the transportation network can be built out one $20,000 car at a time.

If these assumptions are correct, the future of India's transportation system will look very different from the one the government is planning for. That's what happened to India accidentally in communications. Why not learn from the telecommunications experience and apply the lesson to cars? The precise outcome doesn't matter (my assumption may be wrong). The main thing is to create a regulatory and investment climate to support the right broad policy goals (access to transportation) rather than lock everyone into specific technologies. In a nutshell, we don't know what the future winners are—and it would be foolish of government to attempt to determine it. But we can try to set the groundwork.

This isn't just about waiting for technology to advance. Governments with an evolutionary mind-set—those that seek to encourage rather than prescribe—can use incentives, taxes, and standards to push in broad directions without trying to force specific solutions. With self-driving cars, I'd offer a huge tax advantage to the first million cars deployed. I'd also lay out standards—whether for refrigerator efficiency, lighting efficiency, or car and truck efficiency. The right way to do that is to make those standards self-modifying and dynamic, so that they change in step with technology.

For example, why not set a tax of 10 percent on the 25 percent of vehicles with lowest energy efficiency and offer a subsidy worth the same dollar amount for the top 25 percent of cars with the highest energy efficiency? That way, the companies at both the top and bottom have an incentive to keep pushing, and as technology advances, the standard ratchets up. That's much better than the U.S. approach of saying, "Let's set fifty-four miles per gallon efficiency standards for 2025 even though we don't know what technology will be available."

More broadly, India has a major opportunity, thanks to its massive domestic market, to change the rules of its future development. For example, R&D tax credits encourage more R&D; a fat depreciation tax credit encourages very large capital-intensive facilities. The first favors distributed development and a more level playing field. The latter is more rigid and centralized and favors fewer, bigger players. Every policy contains some kind of bias in one direction or another. The question is: What do you want to bias your system toward?

If the environment is changing rapidly, then you want to bias your system toward change, flexibility, and adaptability. You want to foster what I call "innovation capitalism" versus "incumbency capitalism." Incumbency capitalism relies on generous depreciation rules that favor big established players, those who have the most capital and can pay for $400 million plants. Innovation capitalism offers generous R&D tax credits that favor start-ups, people with ideas who are willing to experiment and create.

India needs more innovation capitalism. Take education. In Kenya,

Khosla Ventures has funded a start-up called Bridge International Academies, which is operating hundreds of schools that break even at $5 per child per month, a price even the poorest can afford. We're opening one or two new facilities a week. The model combines physical schools that can take up to three hundred kids, but instead of using textbooks, the pedagogy runs off mobile phones. We compete head-to-head with public education provided for free by the Kenyan government and are winning—both in outcomes and in the minds of low-income parents who willingly choose the Bridge option over others.

The shift to online education is slashing costs and transforming traditional approaches to teaching. Instead of a prescriptive system that specifies a strict time (four years of high school) and variable results in terms of learning, we're moving to a world of fixed learning (the set of things you master and skills you acquire) and variable time. The increasing sophistication of online assessment tools allows each student to advance at his or her own pace.

So when India plans for education in 2025, it may still want to build many more Indian Institutes of Technology. But it also needs to think about how it can leverage the technology revolution to reshape education at all levels and rethink its physical infrastructure. It needs to be sure it is creating policies that encourage these trends and funding lots of experiments.

One thing we've learned with Internet start-ups is that everything needs to be iterated continuously. A successful venture like Pinterest went through three hundred evolutions before it caught on. With online education, it will be the same. Like any biological system, it won't be perfect at first, but it will keep on getting much better.

The same principles apply to health care. Today, if you compare the doctor-to-population ratio in the United States and India, India's is ten times lower. The resource-intensive answer is to say we need to build ten times the number of medical schools we currently have. A better alternative is to accelerate the adoption of new computer diagnostic systems, delivered via cell phones and cheap tablets. I believe such systems can eventually replace 80 percent of doctor visits and deliver results with better and more consistent quality of care.

Happily, India, despite its painful shortages in physical infrastructure, is well on its way to creating a massive adaptive advantage by building out the foundations of a twenty-first-century electronic infrastructure through its Aadhaar program and its growing success in establishing universal digital identification. Having these fundamentals in place enables far more than simply authenticating that a person requires a government service from the National Payments Corporation of India, which in turn avoids the need for a physical visit to fill out forms in triplicate. With the right authentication system and new regulations to spur things like electronic contracts, you can build out a new digital reputation system. Just as an eBay seller has a reputation and people always migrate to the person with the most stars, every one of a billion people can have a reputation tied to his or her digital ID. That will fundamentally increase trust in the system, which in turn reduces risk and transaction costs (both major burdens in doing business in India today). In this way, India is establishing a framework that the private sector can build upon in myriad ways.

I'm not arguing India doesn't need more and better physical infrastructure—roads, ports, power plants, and the like. I'm saying that the size of that future increase can be reduced through scaling out an alternative electronic infrastructure, which is also cheaper to build.

Despite India's well-known problems, I am optimistic about its prospects. Its enormous young English-speaking population is a huge advantage. Its democracy, despite its messiness, adds resilience and stability to the system and gives it an advantage over planned-and-directed economies like China, despite China's reputation for "getting things done." The overseas Indian community is increasingly emerging as a great resource for seeding—not only capital but also a desire to experiment and try something different. And frankly, new ideas are more important than capital.

The critical missing link is to marry that leapfrogging mind-set to a better policy framework that sparks innovation and experimentation—one that reimagines the future by encouraging instead of prescribing.

power switch
Jean-Pascal Tricoire

Venture into one of India's remote villages, where paved roads and power lines have yet to reach, and in the evening you may find people using one of our company's products, called the In-Diya. Launched three years ago, the In-Diya is a home lighting appliance, powered by solar energy plus rechargeable batteries, with some models including mobile-phone-charging capacity and small fans. We have high hopes for it, considering that the main alternative for many low-income villagers is kerosene lamps—with all the attendant pollution, danger, dimness, and inconvenience involved in keeping them filled—or just settling down in the darkness.

If we are to reimagine India, products like In-Diya are going to have to be a lot more pervasive than they are now. Even if In-Diya doesn't take off—and we recognize that it still has a long way to go—India needs technologically ingenious solutions to provide on-site, widely distributed renewable energy generation at the end-user point. The country's continued development and prosperity depend on it.

The world learned in late July 2012 that India has a serious energy problem, when the largest power outage in history—affecting more than six hundred million people—struck in twenty-two of the country's states, spawning chaos on roads and trains, and shutting down hospitals and even water supplies for millions who rely on wells with electric pumps. Shocking as the blackout's extent was, Indians themselves already considered unreliable electricity a fact of life; outages occur almost daily, if

Jean-Pascal Tricoire is chairman and CEO of Schneider Electric.

only for brief periods, even in well-to-do areas. And for us at Schneider Electric, the outage provided dramatic (if regrettable) reinforcement that our company—with its broad lines of business focused on making energy safe, reliable, efficient, productive, and green from plant to plug—has important work to do in India.

The real issue is not what happened in July 2012—that kind of accident in the grid could conceivably occur in almost any country—but much more deep-rooted worries about whether India can close the gap between its surging demand for power and its lagging supply of reasonably clean, dependable energy sources and power-generating capacity.

India has less than 1 percent of the world's proven oil and gas reserves, so it depends on overseas sources for most of its petroleum, which weighs heavily on the trade balance. Despite having the fourth-largest coal reserves in the world, the country has not yet been able to exploit this resource to good effect, and in any case, using more coal would generate significant additional carbon emissions. That is a problem India cannot possibly ignore; it is more vulnerable than almost any other country on earth to the consequences of climate disorder, in the form of droughts, floods, and typhoons. Although there is plenty of wind and solar energy potential, and some progress has been made over the last decade in the renewable-energy-generation sector, a combination of factors prevents such renewables from extensive development. These include the current electricity costs for these sources, the small installed base of renewable-generating capacity, and political difficulties that often complicate the acquisition of land needed for the development of wind farms and other infrastructure.

Moreover, an appalling amount of the electricity that India generates goes to waste because of what we in the industry call T&D losses—transmission and distribution problems that cause power to leak, or be diverted, somewhere between generation and the intended end user. India's 25 percent rate of T&D loss is three to five times the rate in China, the United States, and Britain. One major reason is the issue of governance and the inability of public distribution companies to collect money owed and clamp down on illegal connections. This fact, coupled with the Indian government's propensity to distribute free power, leads to massive cross subsidies and financial distress for public sector distribution companies—a huge dampener on the economy. Poor infrastructure is another important contributor to higher losses in power transmission and distribution.

> India is more vulnerable than almost any other country to the consequences of climate disorder.

Around three hundred million Indians have no access to electricity in their homes, and another four hundred million or so have access only four to six hours per day. (To put those figures in perspective, the number of people in India with fewer than four to six hours a day is well over the entire population of the European Union.) For those who do have access—both consumers and businesses—prices are among the highest in the world, in terms of purchasing power parity.

Add to those issues the imperative of ensuring that India's leading industries, information technology in particular, get the quality and reliability of energy supplies that they need to thrive. Mission-critical facilities such as data centers cannot serve global customers cost-effectively on an uncertain and unreliable grid or with very expensive power backup based on pollution-spewing diesel generators.

Here's the grim result once all the numbers are totted up: To keep pace with burgeoning demand and prevent its economic growth from being derailed, India needs to add almost six hundred gigawatts of power-generation capacity to its current installed capacity of around two hundred gigawatts. That is equivalent to bringing one six-hundred-megawatt power plant online every week for the next twenty years. Along with the transmission and distribution infrastructure upgrades required, this translates into a cumulative investment of approximately $1 trillion—more than half of the nation's annual GDP at current levels—over the next twenty years.

Daunting as this arithmetic is, reasons for hope abound. Most important, being a late mover may bestow enormous advantages on India.

The country will be making its major investment in energy at a time when energy and power-generation and -transmission technologies are

Being a late mover may bestow enormous advantages on India. changing more than they did in the past century. The use of the Internet and digitization to enhance energy efficiency, the exploitation of distributed and renewable energy technologies at affordable prices, plus smart grid, smart city, and smart storage technologies, are transforming the world of energy as we know it.

Marrying India's strength in IT to its energy sector could result in these technological changes providing substantial benefits much more rapidly than elsewhere. Of course, the country will also need to make large investments in power plants and transmission lines. But conceivably, India can address many of its energy challenges in a very different and innovative manner, without incurring all the costs and collateral damage of the traditional model.

A first priority must thus be to increase efficiency at the point of end use. Commercial buildings offer one of the best examples. Studies have shown that typical office buildings in India consume approximately 250 kilowatt-hours per square meter per year, even as some IT companies are cost-effectively constructing and occupying new buildings that operate at around 75 kilowatt-hours per square meter per year. Consider too that air-conditioning of typical office buildings in India has been found to cool fifteen to eighteen square meters per ton of refrigeration, whereas state-of-the-shelf technology coupled with thoughtful design approaches, available at competitive costs, can easily reach air-conditioning utilization of fifty square meters per ton of refrigeration. In both cases, cost-effective approaches offer savings potential of as much as 70 percent; similar potential is likely there for the taking in the residential, industrial, and agricultural sectors. Capturing energy savings downstream offers three to four times the benefit in terms of generation capacity upstream, thanks in part to the savings that can be achieved along the entire transmission and distribution infrastructure.

A second priority is to make India's national power grid much "smarter"—that is, with as much interactivity as possible between the point of generation and point of end use, so that the amount of electricity generated closely matches demand. This is an especially challenging prospect for India, but it is badly needed, because of the state governments' penchant for maximizing power consumption within their own borders and the difficulty faced by power producers and load dispatchers who do not have effective tools to halt illegal power draw. India also currently lacks utilities that can impose the widespread use of smart meters to capture information. To be realistic, it is difficult to harbor much optimism about the likelihood that India will progress far in the smart-grid direction anytime soon. But overcoming those obstacles could provide big payoffs; smart grid technologies make it possible to do much more with less.

A third priority—and most important in terms of reaching people at the bottom of the economic and social pyramid—is self-sufficiency and distributed generation using renewables, of which In-Diya is just one example. Making the most of these kinds of technologies could significantly reduce the need for elephantine projects and disruptive infrastructure, while helping the hundreds of millions still mired in rural poverty to obtain the energy needed for decent living standards.

I do not want to overstate the ease of making progress in this area. A brief account of In-Diya's development provides some idea of the difficulties. It started as an outgrowth of our corporate social responsibility program, and although we hoped to make it a self-sustaining, profitable business line, we had to subsidize it at its inception with funds from our company foundation, because there was no other way of bringing the full costs down far enough to make it financially attractive to poor villagers.

The In-Diya uses a light-emitting-diode-based lamp, which provides excellent illumination; we take immense satisfaction in hearing that it enables village children to study at night. An LED also lasts many more years than other types of lighting, and when grid power isn't available, the unit relies on a battery that can be charged with solar panels. The basic package costs around 4,000 rupees ($80), which spread over a number of years offers significant savings on a per-day basis compared with the alternatives, including kerosene. But Indians in rural villages, in addition to having low incomes, are squeezed for liquidity and credit; they are extremely resistant and in many cases unable to make large up-front payments.

We finally settled on a business model in which specially trained village-based entrepreneurs would rent the units to households in their villages, and assess a small daily fee for the service involved in picking up, charging, and returning the batteries. But then a new constraint emerged—the inability of the local entrepreneurs to buy, or finance the purchase of, a number of units. Bank loans for such undertakings are either unavailable or too costly, even from microcredit institutions. So in a pilot program, our foundation had to donate the start-up costs for the entrepreneurs. Proud as we are of what we've accomplished so far, we are still experimenting with how to make this model commercially viable.

Whatever the fate of the In-Diya, I hope India will seize its golden opportunity to create a distributed and intelligent electrical grid that relies on more end-use efficiency and renewables. This is a moral imperative—especially considering the potentially dire consequences of continuing on the current path of inadequate supply and lack of access for hundreds of millions. By integrating energy with its skill in IT, India could even become a world leader in energy, banishing for good the scourge of energy poverty and insecurity.

smart cities, sustainable cities
John Chambers

In a fast-urbanizing world, India is setting the pace. Over the next ten years, more than one hundred million Indians will move from villages to cities, seeking schools for their children, health care for their families, and jobs for themselves. With more than 833 million people still living in the country's 640,000 villages, this unprecedented exodus will only accelerate.

"Mass urbanization" is an abstract concept, but one piece of data may help illustrate the enormity of changes ahead: India today has only 20 percent of the total floor space it will need by 2030 to accommodate the millions expected to migrate to its cities. Put another way, India must build a staggering 900 million square meters of new urban residential space in less than twenty years. Without radical innovation, expansion on such scale will place an unsustainable strain on the environment.

I visit India regularly and always return with deep admiration for its people's optimism and work ethic. In the world's largest democracy, change often happens slowly, and it can seem messy and chaotic. But I have no doubt change will come to India. Its people will face up to their problems and get the solutions right.

As India devises those solutions, however, it would do well to embrace some basic principles of successful development. The first is open standards. Imagine the savings in energy costs, carbon emissions, and water that could be realized by adopting global open standards such as Leadership in Energy and Environmental Design (LEED). At our offices

John Chambers is chairman and CEO of Cisco Systems.

in India, we've already implemented LEED standards at their highest levels, dramatically reducing energy usage compared to our buildings in the United States.

Another challenge is traffic. By 2020, motor vehicle traffic in India is expected to increase fivefold—and yet, over that same period, the nation's highway network is projected to grow by only 4 percent per year. At Cisco we like to say, "Don't commute to compute." We have launched a number of initiatives around the world to make it easier for people to get work done without having to move around and consume energy resources. South Korea, for example, has adopted a plan to create 450 "smart work centers" by 2015. Based on open platforms, these centers will result in $1.3 billion savings in transit expenses with a reduction of 1.1 million tons in carbon emissions. Telecommuting can save money and reduce traffic, but only if the digital and energy infrastructure is reliable.

> By 2020, motor vehicle traffic in India is expected to increase fivefold—and yet, over that same period, the nation's highway network is projected to grow by only 4 percent per year.

As the country develops, it must employ smart planning techniques and make targeted investments in its cities. To date, in postindependence India, the only major cities created are the capital cities of Chandigarh and Gandhinagar. Indian planners are looking to change the economic face of the nation through the Delhi–Mumbai Industrial Corridor (DMIC). As part of this $90 billion undertaking, the world's largest infrastructure project, India will build twenty-four new cities across fifteen hundred kilometers, improving the living standards of 180 million people. When completed, DMIC will create a center of global manufacturing and trade supported by world-class infrastructure. Cisco is working with DMIC to provide master planning and information and communications technology, as well as offering citizen services including education, transportation, and public safety and security, all while creating and supplying a new digital urban infrastructure from the ground up.

DMIC will reduce the time it takes to ship goods between Delhi and

Mumbai from fourteen days to a single day, allowing the government to work toward its goal of increasing the share of India's GDP created through manufacturing from 15 percent to 25 percent by 2022. DMIC, which aims to generate one hundred million new manufacturing jobs, is a powerful example of how visionary leadership can transform communities and cities. India needs more such examples.

Unfortunately, technology is often an afterthought for city planners and real estate developers. When cities were built in the United States, gas and water were cheaply available and cities were designed mainly for cars, not people. Today, it is possible to create smart cities with intelligent networks that manage basic citizen services and replace sprawling concrete jungles fit only for cars with spaces that are walkable, bikeable, and livable. By embracing smart regulation, India can leapfrog less productive traditional stages of development and benefit from best practices employed all over the world. Smart regulation, exemplified by the potential of India's Unique Identification project, can accelerate how technology at scale enables sustainable growth.

Public-private partnerships should also play a critical role in providing the talent to build and run these new cities—and they are not as complex as many think. At Cisco, we call our Networking Academy program "the world's largest classroom" because we have trained more than 4.25 million students worldwide. In India alone, we have 197 academies that provide training and certifications to thousands of students.

More is needed. In 2010, India had 500,000 civil engineers and 45,000 architects. That sounds like a lot until you measure it against what's needed to match projected growth: 4 million civil engineers and 366,000 architects. Millions of young Indians must be trained and jobs created to address this skill shortage. Although India has a National Skill Development Fund to help train workers over the next decade, the gap cannot be closed unless industry, academia, and the government work together. India's IT industry offers grounds for optimism, having addressed its own challenges by training its workforce in creative ways and completely changing the labor ecosystem.

Urbanization will drive India's return to the center of the world stage.

But to realize that potential, its cities cannot grow in the unplanned way they traditionally have. Instead, India must foster urban spaces that are sustainable economically, socially, and environmentally. The essential building blocks are visionary leadership buttressed by global open standards, smart regulation, and public private partnerships—all underpinned by technology. As it creates these new cities, India has a chance to be the model for twenty-first-century civilization. I couldn't be more excited about what the future holds.

> Urbanization will drive India's return to the center of the world stage.

jump-starting india's start-ups
Naveen Tewari

Seven years ago, three friends and I were living in a small apartment in Mumbai, where every morning we would roll up our mattresses, flip open our laptops, and start working—right there in our living quarters, which doubled as our "office." I had moved back to India from the United States to pursue what I admit was a rather unfocused vision of building a big, successful business. Along the way, we tore up numerous business plans (in one case just a couple of days after receiving some seed money), we maxed out fourteen credit cards to keep afloat, and we endured anguished questions from our parents, who were understandably curious about what the hell we thought we were doing and how we were going to pay our next month's rent.

Our folks aren't quite as anxious about us now. We finally figured out a business plan that made great sense—using technology to place advertisements on smartphones, tablets, and other mobile devices. Even though we heard plenty of warnings that nobody would want to use the Internet, much less look at ads, and on such small screens, we were convinced that we could exploit a lucrative niche serving as middlemen between advertisers and publishers (i.e., companies hosting websites and providing content that rapidly growing multitudes of consumers use their mobile devices for). By 2009, InMobi had established operations in most of South and Southeast Asia; by the middle of 2010, our business had spread to Africa, Europe, and North America—and by the end of

Naveen Tewari is founder and CEO of InMobi, an India-based mobile advertising network.

2012, we reached about 578 million consumers spread across 165 countries, through 93 billion impressions (our industry's jargon for ad views) every month.

India needs a lot more people like me and my partners. Please don't think me immodest for saying so; I hardly mean to suggest that we're uniquely gifted. The country is loaded with world-class technical talent, including people who (like quite a few of us at InMobi) returned home after spending time in Silicon Valley. And there are plenty of people here with both the drive and competence to create businesses; the Startup Genome report, which surveyed fifty thousand start-ups globally, rates entrepreneurial caliber in India as equal to that found in Silicon Valley.

> The Startup Genome report rates entrepreneurial caliber in India as equal to that found in Silicon Valley.

The point is that start-ups like InMobi are probably India's best hope for generating the job growth the country must have in decades to come. Don't take my word for it—ask the government's Planning Commission's own blue-ribbon panel. In a report issued in June 2012 titled "Creating a Vibrant Entrepreneurial Ecosystem in India," this group of experts observed that large Indian businesses "have not generated significant employment in the past few decades and are unlikely to do so in the coming decade or two." The same goes for agriculture, where nearly half the country's people work. The report cited persistent stagnation in the numbers employed in this sector and, echoing widespread predictions, said that the figure "is likely to decline . . . due to improvements in productivity."

Of course, the information technology services and business process outsourcing industry that sprang up in the past twenty years directly employs 2.8 million people and indirectly provides work for nearly 10 million more. But that's far from sufficient, given the hordes of young Indians reaching employment age over the next decade, for whom ten to fifteen million new jobs will be needed *each year.* India stands a chance of satisfying that demand for employment, according to the Planning Commission panel, if ten thousand start-ups are launched, and if about one-quarter of those evolve into sizable businesses.

Could that happen? In important ways, the signs are increasingly propitious for the sprouting of firms like ours. Indian society has become more accepting of risk taking and entrepreneurial experiments. Rather than stick to the safe route of providing services for multinational giants based abroad, more Indian companies are taking bigger chances by building businesses around their own innovative products and technologies. By some estimates, the number of product-based Indian companies has been growing at 30 to 40 percent per annum for the last half decade. Last year, more than 90 percent of the most promising companies spotlighted by NASSCOM, India's tech industry association, were banking on their own intellectual-property-led business models rather than the provision of low-cost transaction-oriented services to foreign clients.

> Indian society has become more accepting of risk-taking and entrepreneurial experiments.

Furthermore, Indian venture capitalists are gradually becoming more open to backing early-stage start-ups. In the first eleven months of 2012, Indian investors pumped nearly $400 million into 149 early-stage deals. That represented 50 more deals and $60 million more in funding than had been on the table in 2010, according to Venture Intelligence, India's largest information bank on business deals.

Still, for a country the size of India, the number of start-ups remains vanishingly small. Around five hundred companies are incubated in India annually, compared with about eight thousand in China, according to the Planning Commission's report. And the domestic support system for even so few enterprises is grossly inadequate. In the Startup Genome report, whereas Silicon Valley unsurprisingly ranks first in terms of the ecosystem necessary for start-ups to thrive, Bangalore ranks nineteenth, below Tel Aviv, São Paulo, and Moscow.

Consider, for example, the number and amount of "angel" investments—that is, those made by high-net-worth individuals, who operate either individually or in groups, to provide fledgling firms with capital and sometimes mentoring and networking help. In 2011, Indian angels invested only about $20 million in around fifty deals, compared to $390 million invested by angels in Canada (a country with less than 3 percent of India's population), according to the report;

meanwhile, in the United States, angels funded a whopping sixty thousand deals. The report shows how poorly India also fares in comparisons of venture capital—that is, institutional investors that pool funds from wealthy individuals for management by professionals with experience in nurturing entrepreneurs. The amount invested annually by such firms in the United States is about twenty-five times the amount invested by their Indian counterparts. Likewise, India lacks a sufficient number of incubators, which provide entrepreneurs with infrastructure (e.g., office space) and services such as mentoring. Only 159 such institutions currently exist in the country; many times that many are needed.

To be sure, determined and worldly Indian entrepreneurs can find financing overseas if it's unavailable at home. At InMobi, we benefited from an initial investment of $500,000 from the Mumbai Angels, a network of wealthy Mumbai-based Indians, but when we took our most ambitious plans to Indian venture-capital firms in 2007, we were shown the door everywhere we went. It was shocking—only one potential angel even agreed to a second meeting. Thanks to familiarity with Silicon Valley, I hopped a plane for the U.S. West Coast, and we were able to raise about $7 million from marquee investors—which was followed later by a much bigger investment from Japan's SoftBank. But not all Indian businesspeople with a vision will be able to tap foreign funders—and they shouldn't have to.

There are plenty of sensible recommendations in most government and industry reports of what the Indian government, universities, and other institutions should do to foster more entrepreneurship. But perhaps the most exciting development I see on the horizon is the emergence of new technologies that will enable Indian entrepreneurs to think big—and think global.

The wide adoption of technology frameworks like cloud computing has made many more markets immediately accessible around the world. Tiny start-ups can now service and support customers in remote geographical locations at much lower costs than ever before.

It was the chance to build a truly global business that gave InMobi its commercial viability. By the time we took the business to market, mobile devices had become ubiquitous around the world, and businesses had begun to experiment with mobile ads. Our potential customer base was thus much bigger than the population of Internet-enabled cell-phone users in India in 2007. We concluded, too, that we shouldn't target the established markets of the West; instead, we would focus on the developing world, where mobile penetration was skyrocketing. Indeed, that was why we based ourselves in Bangalore—it provided better access to the emerging markets we wanted to serve as well as the high-quality talent we wanted to hire.

> Not all Indian businesspeople with a vision will be able to tap foreign funders—and they shouldn't have to.

Of course, start-ups in other countries can take advantage of cloud computing and the other new connectivity-enhancing technologies. But given India's reservoir of technological expertise—and the relatively low cost of tapping it—I believe the number of companies like InMobi could burgeon in the years to come. If a systematic effort is made to strengthen the ecosystem supporting entrepreneurship, India could become the world's next start-up nation.

chapter four

challenges

a technology solution for india's identity crisis
Nandan Nilekani

In rich countries, the emergence of powerful new digital technologies combined with new capacities for creating, organizing, and analyzing vast quantities of data have aroused widespread concerns about privacy and the right of individuals to preserve their anonymity. But for most of the 1.2 billion people who live in India, those are curious preoccupations. Hundreds of millions of Indians born in poverty or outside the nation's large metropolitan centers have exactly the opposite problem: They cannot prove their formal identity. No official records hold their names, and therefore they can't prove who they are. Their existence may be a physical reality, but the fact that it has not been translated into ones and zeros and recorded in any officially recognized database effectively strips them of their access to government benefits and services.

Imagine you are a twenty-year-old man who has migrated to Delhi from a distant village in Assam in the hopes of eking out a living as a street sweeper or construction worker. You were born at home without a birth certificate. Your parents have given you your name but have not registered it with any government office. You know the name of your village and have your memories of your family and neighbors there. You may have a card issued by a local government for some particular purpose such as food rations or receiving a pension. But beyond that, your formal identity as recognized by the state is tenuous. You hold no nation-

Nandan Nilekani is chairman of the Unique Identification Authority of India and cofounder and former CEO of Infosys.

ally valid portable or reliable proof of who you are. You aren't even sure you're really twenty.

This ambiguity hardly mattered to previous generations of rural Indians, who lived their entire lives in the same village surrounded by people who knew them and could vouch for them. But in the rapidly urbanizing India of today, lack of proper identification bars millions of Indians from gaining access to health care, education, and basic government services, and may preclude them from claiming benefit payments to which they are entitled. Lack of an ID may even prevent them from opening a bank account or renting a mobile phone.

Fortunately, technology offers India the opportunity to dismantle many of these oppressive obstacles. Our nation has embarked on one of the world's great social experiments, aimed at giving every resident of India who wants one a nationally accepted, unique identity number that public agencies, banks, and private companies can use with ease and confidence. In the process, we are relying on the latest technology—chiefly fingerprint and iris-recognition technologies. This is a far more secure and portable system than the use of physical cards, because a person's fingerprints and irises are readily amenable to online verification, and the technology, if carefully administered, is all but impervious to fake and duplicate identities. And people don't have to worry about losing the card or forgetting to bring it with them.

That is the promise of the Aadhaar project (*aadhaar* means "foundation" in Hindi), also known as UID (for Unique Identification), which the prime minister launched in 2010. As the person heading the organization entrusted with implementing this project, I am all too aware that the journey has just begun, and that concerted effort, coordination, and hard-nosed implementation will be required over the next few years. Aadhaar is using biometric technology for the purpose of development, inclusiveness, and poverty alleviation. Success is imperative. There is much hope that this innovative use of technology for development will prove a game changer—transforming the prospects of India's least fortunate residents and, indeed, the nation as a whole

Aadhaar is progressing at a rate that has surprised skeptics, with more than 380 million Indians enrolled and 320 million unique twelve-digit numbers issued as of spring 2013. It is already beginning to show results, as some enrollees have opened their first bank accounts, acquired mobile-phone connections, and obtained more of the services they rightly expect from public agencies. As word of Aadhaar's advantages spreads, hundreds of millions more will become eager to participate. We are on track to enroll six hundred million—half the population—by 2014, and hope to enroll the rest of the country in the years that follow.

> We are on track to enroll six hundred million—half the population—by 2014, and hope to enroll the rest of the country in the years that follow.

This is a very complex undertaking, requiring an extensive infrastructure. At thousands of enrollment centers around the country, people are lining up to have specially trained personnel take their photos, fingerprints, and eye images, which go to central servers for digital checking to make sure nobody gets more than one ID. The potential for mistakes and falsification is not completely absent, and we use the latest data analytics tools to constantly review evident errors. The system must be capable of handling high throughput (one million Aadhaars per day), at near-perfect levels of accuracy (detecting duplicates at better than a 99.9 percent rate) and a very large scale (a database potentially of 1.2 billion people). Based on the analyses conducted so far, we are confident that the enrollment system is proving to be reliable, accurate, and scalable.

The Indian government spends about $60 billion a year on subsidy programs involving products such as food, fertilizer, and petroleum. In theory, the poor are able to obtain inexpensive food at nearly half a million Fair Price Shops around the country. But studies show that these programs often have leakages, thus leading to anomalies in benefits reaching the intended beneficiaries. India's own Planning Commission found in 2008 that more than one-third of subsidized grain supposedly destined for the poor went to better-off households instead, due in large part to fraud and corruption. Errors in delivery and identification resulted in even greater losses of subsidized grain. The failure of benefits to reach intended beneficiaries has hindered full implementation of the National Rural Employment Guarantee, a program aimed at providing each poor household in rural areas with a certain amount of work.

The Planning Commission found in 2008 that more than one-third of subsidized grain supposedly destined for the poor went to better-off households instead, due in large part to fraud and corruption.

Such siphoning off of public funds will become much more difficult once the identities of both public employees and eligible recipients become traceable at each step of the subsidy-dispensing process. Of course, those who are unjustly enriching themselves under the current system will lose out. But the genuinely poor will gain much more by getting the benefits and subsidies they deserve under the law.

Aadhaar can thus revolutionize the way public services are delivered as well as dramatically enhance the inclusiveness of Indian society. One of the most important features of the program is that it will enable people to confirm that they have received the services they are supposed to get, or prove that they have not, and give them multiple ways of accessing the public service system—including the filing of grievances. If a poor person can obtain subsidized food only from a designated ration shop, or purchase subsidized fuel only from a designated petroleum dealer, the potential for being cheated or extorted is high, because bargaining power lies mainly with the supplier. But through the use of technology, modern supply chain management, and electronic payments, any registered dealer could sell food and fuel in ways that would ensure the fair and proper processing of subsidized purchases. This provision of choice will empower consumers rather than suppliers, which will go a long way toward eliminating petty corruption.

With the aim of further reducing the amount of "leakage" in the system, the government is moving toward direct transfer of benefits to individuals, sending subsidies or entitlement payments directly to Aadhaar-enabled bank accounts. Suppose, for example, that the market price of propane gas is 900 rupees per canister and the subsidized price is 400 rupees. Instead of providing the gas at the subsidized price, the government can directly deposit the 500-rupee difference into the account of a purchaser who qualifies for the subsidy.

The expansion of opportunity for the use of private services may be equally valuable to many Indians. Having a bank account linked to one's Aadhaar number enables the transfer of money in an electronic, auditable, and convenient way. With the Indian workforce being increasingly migrant, people need a payment infrastructure that provides access to financial services and resources anytime, anywhere in the country. An estimated one million Aadhaar-enabled micro-ATMs—handheld devices with fingerprint recognition pads and mobile connectivity—are in the process of being added to the existing set of one hundred thousand bank branches and ATMs; of course, those with Aadhaar IDs will also be able to make use of self-service through the Internet and mobile devices. They will also be able to top up their mobiles—that is, increase their calling and messaging capacity—at any location in the country.

More applications will no doubt materialize as the number of enrollees grows. Intriguing possibilities arise in online education, for instance. Students who have "attended" online classes and studied digital course material will want to obtain certification that they have passed examinations—and they may be able to do that online, too, by using their unique ID number and biometric data to prove their identity at exam time.

The Aadhaar project is not a panacea. But it can provide a powerful impetus for making governance more transparent, efficient, and accountable in a country that has suffered from the other kind of governance for far too long. And the choice and convenience average middle-class Indians enjoy will be available to poor migrants from the villages. Why should the quality of service be less efficient or convenient for the marginalized? Why shouldn't they benefit from new systems to ensure they get the government support that is lawfully theirs? Technology can be a great leveler of Indian society. And it will be, if Indians continue to welcome Aadhaar in the spirit with which it is intended.

stepping back from the precipice
Vikram Singh Mehta

For the last thirty years I have maintained a home in the middle of the Binsar forest sanctuary in the Himalayan foothills. The house sits at the edge of a promontory twenty-five hundred meters high and boasts a panoramic view of the valley below. In some ways the area hasn't changed at all in three decades. Once night falls, darkness blankets the valley. The few pinpricks of light one sees come from kerosene lamps—the fuel more likely than not acquired on the black market—and wood fires. There is no evidence of electric power. LPG (liquefied petroleum gas, i.e., propane) cylinders are scarcely available, and solar is an expensive and unfamiliar alternative. An abandoned windmill, built years ago but no longer operating, blots the skyline.

Much else about the place has changed greatly, though. Mud tracks have been tarred, thatched roofs have been replaced by solid beams, guesthouses and restaurants have proliferated, cars and motorcycles have crowded out bicyclists, and everyone now carries a cell phone. Though locals still lack access to secure, reliable, and clean energy, their demand for the appurtenances of modern life continues to grow. The results are obvious to the naked eye: The forest cover has been denuded, streams have been reduced to a trickle, and the scent of pines can be difficult to discern amid the exhaust fumes. In this Himalayan retreat one can witness all the aspects of the crisis that plagues India's energy sector: Demand is surging, supply is struggling to keep pace, and the environment is getting squeezed between the two.

Vikram Singh Mehta is chairman of Brookings India and former chairman of the Shell Group of Companies in India.

When I first bought the forest bungalow, India imported 30 percent of its oil requirements and a small quantity of high-quality coal. Domestic production was rising after the discovery of the giant Mumbai High offshore oil and gas reservoir. Analysts expressed cautious optimism that Oil and Natural Gas Corporation (ONGC) and Oil India Limited (OIL)—the two state-owned exploration and production companies—would soon replicate this success elsewhere and that the gap between demand and supply would narrow even further.

Today the import ratios have flipped, and the optimism has evaporated. India now imports more than 80 percent of its fossil fuel requirements, and hopes of energy independence are fading fast. There are many reasons for this reversal, but the most important have to do with prosperity, policy, and geology.

Demand for energy has risen in lockstep with economic development. Two decades of relatively high growth have pushed India onto an energy-intensive trajectory. Industry and services now account for around 80 percent of GDP, whereas agriculture, which requires far less energy, contributes less than 20 percent. Prosperity has also reshaped consumption patterns. A growing middle class has sought to trade up from bicycles to motorcycles, cars, and trucks. Electric appliances like washing machines, cookers, and TVs are now essentials, and conspicuous materialism has become a badge of individual success. The government's populist policy of artificially holding down the cost of transportation and cooking fuels including diesel, kerosene, and LPG has further encouraged consumption.

Domestic supply has struggled to keep pace with the surge in demand. India is not endowed with huge hydrocarbon resources. And what reserves do exist tend to be trapped in complex geology, inhospitable terrain, and often both. It's not easy to find these resources or, once found, to develop them on a sustainably commercial basis. India does have large coal deposits, but the quality is generally poor.

The government has worsened these natural constraints with policies that discourage and delay investment in the energy sector. Exploration licenses are mired in bureaucracy. Land is never easy to acquire.

Delhi is often at loggerheads with state governments and in recent years has taken to unilaterally changing commercial and fiscal terms of deals—hardly the kind of behavior to inspire investors.

To make matters worse, the distribution and transport infrastructure is inadequate. There are, for instance, only two interstate gas pipelines in the entire country, and none that link gas production to south India. Poor road and rail connections mean that coal often doesn't get to utilities in time, resulting in frequent power outages.

The government has worsened natural constraints with policies that discourage and delay investment in the energy sector.

The environmental consequences of this imbalance between demand and supply have been severe. More than half of the population has no access to commercial fuels and must resort to burning wood or cow dung to meet their cooking, lighting, and heating needs. This has led to widespread deforestation, the depletion of water tables, and air pollution. Indian cities now rank among the most polluted in the world.

The hard truth is that India's energy sector is standing at the edge of a cliff. It can pull back, but only if the state rethinks its energy policies and the institutions set up to implement it.

In fact, the first thing India needs is a true, unified energy policy—one that provides an integrated and holistic picture. Instead we have a host of disconnected policies promoted by a variety of decision makers. There are today, for instance, six different cabinet ministers engaged with energy. These include ministers for petroleum and natural gas, coal, power, atomic energy, renewables, and the Planning Commission. Each has a defined constituency and looks at energy through a narrow lens. They get together formally around the cabinet table, but cabinet meetings are hardly the venue for rigorous discussion.

This fragmented structure misallocates resources and inflates costs. Prices of a fuel are often set without reference to the price of a substitute because the latter falls within the domain of a different ministry. Infrastructure investments get duplicated, and governance and accountability are diffused and compromised. The first thing the government needs to do is create an overarching authority with executive responsibility and accountability to develop and implement an integrated energy policy.

A key tenet of the economic reforms of the early 1990s was to simplify the nature and system of bureaucratic controls—to end the so-called license raj. Unfortunately, these reforms did not percolate through to the energy sector. Procedural and regulatory red tape continues to hobble efficiency and competitiveness. The state-owned energy giants lag behind their international competitors in the adoption of cutting-edge technology. With bureaucrats constantly breathing over their shoulders, managers have more incentive to stay on a path they know is headed in the wrong direction than face a possible inquisition for shifting strategies.

The opportunity cost of these governmental shackles has been and continues to be enormous. The recovery rate of oil from producing fields in India is currently only 28 percent, compared to around 40 percent for fields of similar geology internationally. This is because ONGC and OIL do not have the autonomy to freely adopt new oil recovery technologies. The cost of petroleum subsidies has also eaten into their cash flow, forcing them to slash their R&D budgets.

This has not only slowed innovation but also led to an exodus of skilled talent. My experiences as chairman of Shell in India convinced me that India could quite easily stand on the forefront of energy technology and innovation. In 2006 we set up a technology center in Bangalore. Its goal was to provide high-end technology support across the oil and gas value chain to Shell subsidiaries across the world, as well as to do primary research. The center employs approximately one thousand engineers and scientists—more than 90 percent of whom are Indians and many of whom had started their careers with OIL or ONGC. The quality of the support pro-

> My experiences as chairman of Shell in India convinced me that India could stand on the forefront of energy technology and innovation.

vided by this center has been so outstanding that Shell has announced it will close all but three of its several technology centers around the world.

Clearly the state companies could achieve the same level of excellence if they were unshackled from intrusive bureaucracy and overweening regulation, and if they were allowed to promote an environment that encouraged creativity and innovation. The added value for the country in terms of increased recovery rates of oil and gas, operational excellence, and the development of talent would be enormous.

Lifting such institutional and regulatory constraints might pull the energy sector back from the edge of the cliff. But the only way to reverse its current direction is to contain demand. This half of the energy equation must now be assigned higher priority on the policy agenda.

The government has made some positive moves. It has tightened building standards and provided fiscal incentives to encourage energy efficiency. A number of major cities are investing substantially to improve public transport. But much more needs to be done. More resources need to be allocated to promote energy efficiency, and public messaging has to focus much more strongly on the need for conservation.

Ultimately the only way to ensure sustainability is to move away from fossil fuels. This will take decades. In the short to medium term, therefore, the focus should be on "greening" the existing energy basket. Above all that means investing more in the infrastructure to import and distribute natural gas—a much cleaner fuel than oil or coal.

Looking ahead, we also need to start laying the foundations for a future based on renewable energy. It's worth remembering that although Edison illuminated lower Manhattan in 1882, American factories had not been designed to use this revolutionary new technology. They did not finish converting from steam to electric power until 1935. Our focus now should be on encouraging cost-competitive alternatives to fossil fuels and on developing the "smart" and "clean" infrastructure we'll eventually need to scale up the supply, distribution, and usage of these resources.

There is no panacea for India's energy problems. A number of initiatives—some focused on the immediate task of improving supply, others on managing demand, still others on preserving the environment—will have to be taken simultaneously. The challenge is to make these initiatives work in harmony, keeping the ultimate goal in mind: to weaken the link between economic growth, energy demand, and environmental degradation. I am optimistic that in another thirty years, the glow of lightbulbs, not kerosene fires, will illuminate the valley of Binsar, and the air will smell once again of sweet pines.

health care for all
K. Srinath Reddy

From all over the world, people needing hip replacements, cardiac by-passes, or even bone marrow transplants are increasingly flocking to India for treatment. Top-flight hospitals in Chennai, Mumbai, Delhi, and elsewhere are performing sophisticated procedures on hundreds of thousands of "medical tourists" each year thanks to the renowned skill of Indian doctors and the comparatively low cost of a hospital stay.

Considering how successful our health-care system has become at delivering effective and affordable treatment for foreigners, the prospect of decent care for all Indians might seem to be within our grasp. Unfortunately, that dream remains as distant as ever.

Take infant mortality: At forty-four per one thousand live births, the rate in India is three times higher than in China, four times higher than in Sri Lanka and Thailand, and even higher than in Bangladesh and Nepal. Equally discouraging are the inequities that exist within our country. An infant born in Madhya Pradesh is six times more likely than her peer born in Kerala to die before her first birthday.

Indeed, by a host of indicators we lag behind other major emerging nations, our South Asian neighbors, and even some countries in sub-Saharan Africa. Forty-two percent of Indian children under five years suffer from undernutrition—"a national shame," according to our

K. Srinath Reddy is president of the Public Health Foundation of India.

prime minister (the corresponding rates are 7 percent in China, 7 percent in Thailand, and 14 percent in Ghana). Coverage with DPT immunization is 72 percent in India, while it is 99 percent in Sri Lanka, 96 percent in Botswana and Bangladesh, and 82 percent in Nepal. India accounts for a third of the world's measles deaths and a third of TB cases. And within India, vast inequities are apparent on all these indicators across states, and within states, across urban-rural, education, income, gender, and caste divides.

I therefore propose a new metric by which to measure India's progress in the coming two decades: the healthy life expectancy of a tribal girl born in Madhya Pradesh.

As imperative as it is for moral reasons to advance toward that goal, the potential benefits to society provide another powerful incentive, because poor health is exacting a rising toll on the Indian economy. In addition to being afflicted with disorders of underdevelopment, India is rapidly racing to the pole position in cardiovascular diseases and diabetes, with cancers, respiratory diseases, mental illness, and injuries also impairing productivity. Due to a high proportion of cardiovascular deaths occurring in the age band of thirty-five to sixty-four years, India is estimated to have lost 9.2 million potentially productive years of life in 2000 and is projected to lose 17.9 million years in 2030 (570 percent and 900 percent more, respectively, than the comparable losses in the United States). The cost of treating these diseases is also staggering, estimated at 254 billion rupees (about $5 billion) in 2004 and projected to rise rapidly over the next two decades.

> Due to a high proportion of cardiovascular deaths . . . India is estimated to have lost 9.2 million potentially productive years of life in 2000 and is projected to lose 17.9 million years in 2030.

Multiple handicaps burden India's health system as it faces these challenges. Public financing of health, at 1.04 percent of gross domestic product, is among the lowest in the world, especially when measured in per capita terms. As a result, the average Indian consumer pays 70 percent of his or her health care costs out-of-pocket—again a mark of dubious distinction at the global level. About sixty million Indians are estimated to sink below the poverty line each year, due to unaffordable health-care expenditure, while one out of five Indians cannot afford even to seek medical treatment.

The health workforce is also deficient in numbers and maldistributed in favor of cities. There are shortages across the board of specialist and basic doctors, nurses, allied health professionals (such as technicians and paramedics), and community health workers. Public health expertise is not available for policy development or program design, delivery, and evaluation, since India neglected to establish schools of public health until very recently. Managerial expertise is sparse in the health sector. At 0.9 hospital bed per 1,000 population, India is well below the global norm of 3 per 1,000.

Yet positive trends abound, in addition to the international acclaim accorded Indian doctors. The state of Tamil Nadu offers a rare example of a well-run health system, with effective primary health-care services and free medication. The launch of the National Rural Health Mission (NRHM) in 2005 has improved access to maternal and child health services in many states with an increase in institutional deliveries and accelerated decline in infant and maternal deaths. Janani Suraksha Yojana (JSY), a central-government-sponsored program that offers cash incentives to encourage pregnant women below the poverty line to give birth in medical facilities rather than at home with an unlicensed midwife, has proved particularly effective. JSY, the world's largest conditional cash transfer program, has unleashed the energy of nearly a million village women who act as social mobilizers (accredited social health activists) for stimulating health-care-seeking behaviors, especially for institutional deliveries and immunizations. Rashtriya Swasthya Bima Yojana, a national health insurance program that subsidizes hospital care for unorganized workers and other vulnerable groups, now has more than three hundred million beneficiaries.

Such developments offer at least a faint ray of hope for the firm commitment to universal health coverage expressed in India's five-year plan for the years 2012 to 2017. The plan proposes to make the National Health Mission (with an urban component now added to NRHM) the principal vehicle for its implementation. The plan also envisions increasing the level of public financing for health to 1.87 percent of GDP by 2017, though the recent fall in India's economic growth rate is beginning to cast a cloud on that prospect. It is likely that the government will soon commence its efforts to reduce out-of-pocket expenditure by providing essential drugs free of cost at public facilities.

Though the Indian health system was originally designed to deliver most of the services through the public sector, resource constraints progressively weakened its capacity to do so. The private sector consistently grew in strength from the 1980s and has now become the major provider, by default. However, the care offered ranges from the unqualified solo rural practitioner to the large urban corporate hospital. The weak regulatory systems do not ensure quality or cost control. If universal health coverage is to be carried out in such a mixed health system, it is necessary to ensure that both public and private sectors work in tandem, within a well-designed and adequately regulated framework that ensures equity, access, quality, and affordability.

The need to overcome current financial and human constraints and rapidly advance the outreach and effectiveness of health services, especially in primary care, has become a stimulus for innovation. Widely cited in public health and business schools, for example, is the Aravind Eye Care model, which is based on the principle that clinics can subsidize care for the poor with funds charged to patients who can afford to pay. The success of low-cost, high-volume surgery, even in complex fields such as cardiac surgery, has won admiration in high-income countries that are burdened by escalating health-care costs. India's strength in information technology and the ubiquitous use of mobile phones are the sources of several innovations in health service delivery and monitoring, which are now under evaluation for impact and scalability. The organization I head, for example, has undertaken an initiative to promote the use of a tablet device called the Swasthya Slate (*swasthya* is the Hindi word for "health"), which enables users to perform various diagnostic tests including ECG, blood sugar, blood pressure, and heart rate. Rural clinics and community health centers can transmit data for individual patients to central servers once an Internet connection is established; doctors can then dispense care remotely.

All these favorable signs may come to naught, however, unless policy makers take far-reaching action on the social determinants of health, ranging from water and sanitation to nutrition and environment. From agricultural policies to urban development and from gender equity to energy policies that reduce indoor air pollution by replacing biofuels, action in other sectors can have a major impact on health. Substantial gains in health will accrue only by an effort throughout all of society that addresses the factors influencing health rather than just disease management.

Can India assure good health to every citizen at all stages of life, with every state matching Tamil Nadu for efficiency and Kerala for social determinants? Of course it can, but doing so will entail an enormous collective effort, dedicated to addressing the needs of that baby girl from Madhya Pradesh.

the ed-tech revolution
Salman Khan and Shantanu Sinha

As the children of South Asian immigrants growing up in New Orleans, we benefited from parents who cared deeply about education, even though our public high schools were not exactly world class. When we met as sophomores on a national math team, however, that's when things really got interesting. Suddenly each of us had someone who could challenge the other to see just how far he could go. At MIT, where we were freshman roommates, we competed to see how many courses we could take—and between us ended up getting seven degrees. We pulled each other up.

Now imagine a world where everyone is able to pull himself or herself up through online education. In such a world, a self-taught genius like the famous southern Indian mathematician Srinivasa Ramanujan, who died nearly one hundred years ago at age thirty-two, wouldn't have to scribble his groundbreaking insights into number theory in a private notebook, isolated and uncomprehended by family and neighbors. He'd be able to connect, ask questions, and swap answers with teachers and peers, whether they lived in Tamil Nadu, California, or São Paulo. Instead of reinventing basic theorems, he'd have access to the entire sum of human knowledge, literally at his fingertips, and a community of global learners with whom to explore it.

That world, of course, already exists, and it's benefiting not just a few geniuses but millions of ordinary people, including many in India.

Salman Khan is founder of the Khan Academy, a free online education platform. Shantanu Sinha is president of Khan Academy.

Society is hitting another "printing press moment." When the printing press came along, it broke the elite's grip on the essentials of literacy and education, and made content available to a broadly dispersed population. Today the game is changing once again, thanks to the ongoing ed-tech revolution. Replicating for hundreds of millions of aspiring learners what a few thousand previously experienced in the lecture halls at Harvard, Massachusetts Institute of Technology, or Stanford through traditional teacher training and textbooks would require an absurdly large investment. But we no longer need to do that, now that all this information is available to anyone with a cheap laptop and an Internet connection.

> Replicating for hundreds of millions of aspiring learners what a few thousand previously experienced in the lecture halls at Harvard, MIT, or Stanford would require an absurdly large investment. But now that information is available to anyone with a cheap laptop and an Internet connection.

True, universal access remains a challenge, especially in a country like India, where hundreds of millions lack even basic access to electricity. But Moore's Law is on our side. We already have fairly sophisticated tablets that cost less than $100, and the cost of these devices is going to plummet over the next few years. Given this opportunity, at Khan Academy we're continuing to make a huge effort to ensure that the right content is available, by creating freely licensed open-source education resources that can move out to the parts of the world that so desperately need them.

What's really driving the advance of online education, however, isn't simply broader access to great content but also the ability to combine that with intense personalization and real-time assessment. That's when deep learning takes place. Think of it as ed-tech meets big data.

At Khan Academy, just as important as our growing library of four thousand–plus videos teaching math, science, and art history is the fact that we recently passed the one billion mark in terms of the number of math problems students have solved on our platform. We can track how long it takes them on each problem, where people tend to get stuck, where they're pausing and rewinding videos. Not only does this enable us to reengineer and continuously improve our broad approaches—by adding new hints, say, or by tinkering with our sequences—it also allows us to understand what *you* as an individual need and where *you* specifically are going wrong.

At Khan Academy, we recently passed the one billion mark in terms of the number of math problems students have solved on our platform.

For example, maybe in algebra your big hang-up is that you never quite nailed fractions. With good assessment, we can get the prerequisites right, give you problems in the correct sequence, and also recommend, just as Amazon and Netflix do, the best possible additional readings and resources to help you learn quickly—and, most important, to retain what you learn.

But to complete the coming education revolution—to get to a world where individualized learning replaces one-size-fits-all lectures and where the goal is not simply to pass a "course" and get a "degree" but to develop mastery of a broad set of specific skills that you can continuously build upon—we need to do two more things: develop the right blended model of delivery and revise our antiquated system of credentialing.

No matter how good online systems get, they're never going to entirely replace the need to combine innovative technology with some kind of active in-person interaction between students and instructors. That's especially true for K–12 education. And to move away from thinking that the four years of college, plus graduate school, are the only time where advanced learning takes place to a world where you are constantly upgrading specific skills throughout your life, we need to agree upon a new system in which microcredentials, continuously updated, become what really matter.

And it's here, in modeling these big societal shifts, where India should play an important role. First, it needs to continue accelerating access to the required technology, especially in its villages and rural areas. But even when that's done, a billion-dollar challenge will remain: creating enough mentors and teachers to really support these students, especially in English, which is the language you need to connect to a global community of learners. That won't be easy. Scaling this human infrastructure will require a massive common effort on the part of governments, nonprofits, and businesses. But the good news is India does not have to build a thousand new Indian Institutes of Technology or turn millions of local instructors into deep-content experts. The skill building and assessment can come through online. What's needed is a vast cadre of people sophisticated enough in an Internet world to help connect students to the resources they need and reinforce them as they connect the dots for themselves. For a country like India, this is a much easier model to scale up and a far more efficient way to reach the goal—an education system capable of more rapidly lifting the broad population versus just a top tier.

India's other big opportunity is to show the way in addressing our antiquated system of credentialing. For more than a century we've used the degree as a kind of basic signal: If you attended an Ivy League college or one of IIT's, a prospective employer assumes that you must be smart, so you will probably be a high-quality employee. But there's always been a disconnect between the skills companies are actually looking for and what the education system delivers. This is a huge and growing global problem. Studying French literature may have been a great experience and made you a well-rounded individual, but you need different skills to join a call center or become a programmer. In general, traditional education is a terribly inefficient way to train a broad population and match those efforts against the skills employers truly need.

> Traditional education is a terribly inefficient way to train a broad population and match those efforts against the skills employers truly need.

In India that problem is especially pronounced, in part because of the economy's rapid growth over the past fifteen years and in part because of the shortcomings of its education system. Any Indian graduate who has even a vaguely technical degree is valued tremendously. Employers take them in, work with local universities to try to teach relevant additional courses, train them for six months, and then, because it's such an unbelievably competitive market, lose them six months later. In a country with more than one billion people, such a persistent shortage of trained talent suggests a daunting supply-side problem.

The answer is to rethink the process of credentialing and signaling to better match supply with demand. Again, agreeing on what microcredentials could replace a traditional degree is no easy task. In many countries, the education establishment will resist in order to protect vested interests. But trying to creatively solve this challenge is hugely relevant for India, because there, as in the broad IT space, it's already clear many employers don't really value the four years spent in college and the diploma that goes with it. What they value are the skills an employee has and the portfolio of work he or she has created.

This trend is already clear in Silicon Valley, an economy based on attracting the top talent from around the world. But today if you go to any start-up, they'll tell you that at the end of the day, a high GPA is a pretty poor signal of how good a programmer someone is going to be. What matters more is one's portfolio on GitHub, the open-source online code sharing that is fast becoming the place where programmers the world over collaborate. What projects has he or she completed? How has he or she taken initiative and shown creativity? All of that can increasingly be assessed and reassessed online, independent of the traditional education system. We see it at Khan Academy, where some of our programmers, who did not do well in school or dropped out, are running circles around everybody else once they're actually in the workplace.

Here is where India's employers have a real opportunity to get together and drive the credentialing process in a major way. They offer the jobs that India's striving middle class wants to secure. So if they went out and took a stab at laying down what matters to *them*, it would change the market enormously. We should probably expect a host of experiments, varying by sector, before any big push to reach a broad consensus. What's certain is this: If the big Indian IT companies insisted, say, that if you score in the top 4–5 percent in specific introduction to computer science courses, they'll give you an interview—that's a signal that matters.

How fast can India expand access to online education at scale, address the tutor supply challenge, and solve the critical issue of microcredentialing? Sitting where we are in Silicon Valley, we don't want to sound arrogant. These are massive challenges and we know we don't have all the detailed answers.

But we have seen firsthand how effectively the blended model we envision is already working at R. N. Podar, a private school in Mumbai that's using Khan Academy math modules to deliver more personalized instruction across multiple grade levels. We've seen similar promising examples at the American School of Bombay and at Akanksha, a teacher-training organization that identifies and accelerates mastery for teachers who are drawn from local communities. We've watched the dissemination of our courses in more rural areas. Some fourteen hundred of our videos have been translated into Bengali and another one thousand into Hindi-Urdu.

Most of all we know full well how highly education is valued by Indian culture and the passion that Indians have for pursuing it as the surest path to a better life. Nothing captures that combination of aspiration and investment more than the huge percentage of the population that isn't elite but is middle class, learning English and willing to spend a sizable portion of its own limited resources on private education.

Throughout recorded history, the world, like India, has been struggling forward using less than 10 percent of its human potential—basically the lucky few who are able to secure a spot at a top university. But over the next two decades we expect to witness a fundamental shift in that paradigm, a shift to what we call the digital "one world schoolhouse." It's a world where hundreds of millions—the fat part of the bell curve, not the thin end—will be able to draw upon the best lectures and instruction, learn at their own pace, and collaborate across distances to pull one another up. Imagine the human potential that this change is going to unleash. We believe India can and will be part of this accelerating education revolution.

who needs classrooms?
Madhav Chavan

Education in India is woefully deficient, both quantitatively and qual-itatively. That is hardly a novel observation. Indeed, it is the reason Pratham, the organization I head, was founded in 1994, with the motto, "Every child in school and learning well." During my years of working in this field, India has made efforts to improve the status of education, but these repeated reform efforts haven't delivered what is needed because they are aimed at merely expanding and enhancing the existing struc-ture and systems. The futility of these measures has led inexorably to the conclusion that the system is not only inadequate and incapable of meet-ing the demands of a changing India, it is fundamentally bankrupt. The traditional model of the Indian school has never served the vast swath of the student population from socioeconomically disadvantaged families, because it is designed to push out those who cannot survive the cram-ming grind to reach the tertiary level.

So impervious is the system to genuine improvement that for the past couple of years I have been asking my colleagues whether Pratham should perhaps change its motto to, "Every child *not* in school *but* learn-ing well." As shall be seen from the admittedly radical vision I propose below, I am only half joking.

Since 2005, we have been facilitating the Annual Status of Education Report (ASER), which is based on data collected by volunteers in close to fifteen thousand villages around the country. Year after year, the re-

Madhav Chavan is cofounder and CEO of Pratham, a nonprofit organization dedicated to providing quality education to India's underprivileged children.

ports show that although very high percentages of children are enrolled in schools at the elementary level, the amount of learning they experience is appallingly low. In 2012, the overall enrollment of children up to age ten stood at 96 percent. However, less than half of those in fifth grade can read even a second-grade text, and three out of four have difficulty solving a simple division problem. Barely 30 percent of children make it to secondary school and fewer still beyond, as barriers of gender, distance, costs, and simple inadequacy of infrastructure and qualified teachers make it impossible to pursue learning. The quality of learning among those who do make it past eighth grade is so poor that two Indian states participating in the Program for International Student Assessment (PISA) survey for fifteen-year-olds still in school stood seventy-second and seventy-third among seventy-four global participants. What is worse, their modal scores in reading and math literacy were at the lowest possible level just because PISA did not allow an even lower grade.

The focus on "completing the curriculum" and imparting knowledge rather than learning skills is at the root of the problem. Most children start lagging behind from the primary stage as the teacher rushes through textbooks in front of a multigrade class or one that is full of students at vastly different levels of skill attainment. The front of the class is "taught," while the rest simply loses interest. Predictably, by the time they reach secondary school, children in the back of the class have neither skills nor knowledge and often find themselves unprepared to advance even to vocational training, let alone tertiary education. They start manual work and somehow learn on the job what the system failed to teach them.

The system reflects Industrial Revolution–type thinking of a factory assembly line, wholly unsuited for modern times. Classes are regimented, with the goal of passing mass examinations. We focus on language and grammar rather than communication; we focus on cramming laws of science while ignoring the understanding of technology—a linear process that kills initiative and curiosity. Children are neither learning the basics required in the past century, nor are they being prepared with life skills required to navigate a much more challenging future.

Thus the Right to Education (RTE) Act, enacted in 2009, is proving to be a "right to schooling" act with very poor correlation between years of schooling and the actual learning/education acquired. Unfortunately, RTE followed previous (unsuccessful) efforts to set things right. The Sarva Shiksha Abhiyan (educational for all mission) was aimed at enrolling all children age six to fourteen by guaranteeing that primary schools would be located within one kilometer of all homes and would provide students with a proper midday meal as an incentive for continued attendance. Although enrollment levels have been high, and over 87 percent of schools provide hot cooked midday meals, attendance in many states is between 50 and 80 percent, indicating that the enticement of food is not adequate to spur participation in a dysfunctional academic system. Before that was the National Policy on Education of 1986 that supposedly made primary education a national priority, including the allocation of substantial new resources. The Constitution of India itself directed the state in 1950 to provide free and compulsory education to all children up to the age of fourteen within ten years. At the center of all these initiatives was the "school," which was to take charge of children's education.

Although we acknowledge the African proverb "It takes a village to raise a child," our schools and colleges are isolated from society. Barring a small percentage of exceptional individuals, those appointed to teach at any level have neither the knowledge nor the skills to educate; meanwhile, the human resources of skilled and knowledgeable people in other occupations have no role to play in transferring their competencies to the next generation. This is purely because the process of certification is monopolistically controlled by boards, universities, and government institutions that are hidebound and barely changing.

The National Policy on Education of 1986 said in its very first paragraphs that linear approaches will not suffice to meet the challenges of the future. Open universities and open schools have arisen, but they are the system's stepchildren. Even though they have opened doors to those who cannot enter mainstream institutions, they are burdened by all the features of traditional universities except for the distance-learning materials they provide.

All the above raises a question, the mere asking of which may strike some as bizarre: Why are schools and colleges needed at all?

Their job ostensibly is to transfer knowledge. But they also serve two other functions—not terribly well, but better than their provision of instruction. First, they provide day care for young children, keeping them safe and out of trouble as parents go about their work. Second, they provide an environment in which to learn social skills. These are important functions that need to be taken seriously and developed systematically with significant contribution from human resources in the surrounding community, while reorganizing the learning process from early childhood to adolescence.

Fortunately, the development of new information technologies offers significant opportunity to change the organization of the overall learning process. By creating new pathways for children to learn in nonlinear ways, with interactions and access to the wider world that current schooling doesn't provide, technology helps to enable a rethink of the whole system.

Here, then, is what I propose.

First, we should move away from the age-grade system that is now formalized in the RTE act. Instead we need an age-stage system that allows children to meet learning goals in both the social and academic spheres when they are ready, transitioning to each stage at their own pace.

I envision three main stages. The first stage, for children up to the age of eight or ten, would be to learn to socialize and attain basic learning skills including elementary reading, writing, and math along with speaking, expressing, and thinking. Such "schools" would have many features of day-care centers, with parents and/or older siblings taking turns participating in the classroom. This would be as much for the sake of the children's learning as for improving the ability of mothers and fathers to deal with children and help them learn at home. The role of parents in bringing up and educating children deserves much greater emphasis. Just as maternity leave is now recognized as a necessity, allowing time for parents to participate in their children's learning—with compensation for daily wage workers if need be—should be possible. After all, we have a Mahatma Gandhi National Rural Employment Guarantee Act. Why couldn't parents be compensated for this work of national importance? Teaching basic learning skills is not rocket science. I would expect older children to deal with texts and problems at a simple level more or less independently and be able to use computers or tablets to retrieve and enter information. I see this neighborhood day care–cum–school catering to no more than one hundred children, which is about the average size of an Indian primary school.

At the second stage, for children as young as nine to as old as sixteen, the "school" would really be a social hub or a children's club. It would cater to about five hundred children from different communities, with community spokes that are learning centers with digital learning equipment and a couple of facilitators supervising about one hundred children in batches. Half the children would be playing, painting, or engaging in other enjoyable activities at the club while the other half would be working at the learning centers. Local artists, craftspeople, and athletic coaches would engage children at these clubs while counselors would help with issues of growing up. Online assistance and audiovisual material created by expert communicator-teachers in different subjects would be available so that children could plan their studies with the help of mentors. There would be no need to learn an entire curriculum at any particular age; rather, students would navigate studies in one subject or skill at a time and get certified in phases by varied authorities whenever they are ready for examinations, which could be taken multiple times in a year.

In tertiary education, for children sixteen and above, online courses accompanied by availability of licensed tutors would become the norm. The tutors would be compensated with vouchers, either given free by the government or by donors, or purchased depending on the students' family circumstances. For example, a student might choose to learn accounting online and hire a tutor locally or online to help out. If the student is learning sciences, a facility with laboratory equipment should be accessible.

And why should a student in rural Odisha not have access to the best teachers of Delhi, especially if those teachers are government paid? Elite institutions have created artificial barriers to admission while their teachers draw salaries from public funds. Lectures, notes, and assignments of any teacher paid by the government should be online. Teachers who are found to be unqualified should all become tutors or assistants in courses given by the masters.

> Why should a student in rural Odisha not have access to the best teachers of Delhi, especially if those teachers are government paid? Lectures, notes, and assignments of any teacher paid by the government should be online.

Presumably the reason for my reconsideration of Pratham's motto is now clear. Remember, this is the land of Ekalavya—a hero of the epic Mahabharata—who because of his caste is denied access to the knowledge of Dronacharya, the great teacher of Pandav and Kaurav princes. When it turns out that Ekalavya has taught himself to become a superbly skilled archer, he is not only denied certification but also forced to cut off his right thumb to prevent him from using his "illegally acquired" knowledge.

It is time for the Ekalavyas who have been denied access to the masters and high-quality content to be given the chance to compete for high-level certification. What I propose may appear anarchic and impractical. But there are elements of what is possible tomorrow in the reality of today. India should seize the opportunity to reinvent its education process.

the creaky wheels of indian justice
Zia Mody

Shortly after I returned from five years of practicing law in New York to start afresh in the Bombay High Court, a woman approached me about her nephew. She had allowed him into her home, but he later physically assaulted her and even threatened to seize ownership of her apartment. I told her that since he could not be called a forcible trespasser, we would have to file a suit that could take seven years to resolve. She did not return. I bumped into her sometime later and inquired about the case. In a soft voice she told me, "I sorted it out." In short, she had resorted to extrajudicial means to get the justice the court could not deliver to her in a timely manner.

Her experience is all too common in India today. India's judicial process is effectively a defendant's court, in which the accused can drag out proceedings almost indefinitely. If justice delayed is justice denied, then for millions of Indians, their judicial system regularly fails them. In India, a civil case can take anywhere from a few years to a few decades to conclude—a situation that presents a formidable challenge to the country's development. India's legal system is founded on the bedrock of Commonwealth jurisprudence as adjudicated by some of the world's finest justices. As such, it ensures that legal outcomes are consistent and

NOTE: The author wishes to thank Stanford Law School research fellow Abhinav Chandrachud for his contributions to this essay.

Zia Mody is managing partner of AZB & Partners, one of India's largest law firms.

that India operates under the rule of law and not fiat or political whim. But in the Indian system, the wheels of justice grind too slowly.

Two recently concluded criminal cases highlight India's judicial torpor. The first was the trial of Ajmal Kasab, the lone surviving gunman in the 2008 Mumbai terror attacks. The case was given highest priority. Kasab, a member of the Lashkar-e-Taiba (Army of God) militant group, was found guilty of eighty offenses, including murder, waging war against India, and illegal possession of explosives. He was sentenced to death by the Bombay High Court in February 2011, a sentence that was upheld by the Supreme Court in August 2012. Kasab was executed the following November. That his case took "only" four years was celebrated as a great triumph for India's judicial system.

The second high-profile case involved Sanjay Dutt, one of Bollywood's most popular actors. Dutt was arrested in 1993 under India's Terrorist and Disruptive Activities Act on charges of illegal possession of a 9mm pistol and an AK-56 assault rifle, and implicated in the March 1993 "Black Friday" bombings that killed more than 250 people in Mumbai. A special court was set up to exclusively hear all cases relating to the 1993 bombings. Even so, Dutt's case dragged on for twenty years. In 2007, he was cleared of terrorism charges but sentenced to six years' imprisonment on the weapons charge. The Supreme Court upheld that decision in March 2013, although it shortened his prison sentence to five years. As his trial ground on, Dutt starred in one blockbuster after another, sometimes as a mobster, sometimes as a cop chasing down terrorists, and flirted with a career in politics.

The sheer volume of legal actions accounts for most of the delay in India's judicial system. According to data published by the Supreme Court of India,[1] a staggering 31.2 million cases were pending in India at the end of March 2012. More than 80 percent of them were in the lower courts. The

India has just 1.2 judges for every 100,000 people.

---

[1] *Court News* 7, issue 2 (April–June 2012), http://supremecourtofindia.nic.in/court news/2012_issue_2.pdf.

INDIA EMERGES

India has been home to a thriving civilization since the Bronze Age. From 1000 BC to 1800 AD, India accounted for roughly 25% of the world's GDP. But the present-day nation is a creation of the 20th century and is becoming a power in the 21st.

● Political transitions　　● Conflicts and challenges　　● Milestones

1947 August 15: The former British colony is split into two independent countries, India and Pakistan. Hundreds of thousands later die in violence related to the partition.

1948 Political and spiritual leader Mahatma Gandhi is assassinated by Hindu extremists. War breaks out with Pakistan over Kashmir territory.

1951–52 The Congress party led by Jawaharlal Nehru wins the first general elections.

1962 India fights a border war with China.

1965 India fights a second war with Pakistan over Kashmir.

1966 Nehru's daughter Indira Gandhi becomes prime minister.

1971 India supports the breakaway region of East Pakistan in a war that creates the independent nation of Bangladesh.

1974 India successfully tests a nuclear weapon.

1975 Indira Gandhi declares a state of emergency, restricts civil liberties, and jails political opponents.

1977 Indira Gandhi's Congress party loses the election. She returns to power in 1980.

1984 Indira Gandhi is assassinated. Riots following her death kill 3,000 people. Her son Rajiv becomes prime minister.

1991 P.V. Narasimha Rao becomes prime minister in a coalition government. Finance Minister Manmohan Singh (*pictured*) sets out to revive the economy by reducing regulation and introducing market-oriented reforms.

1992 Riots erupt after Hindu fundamentalists demolish a mosque in Ayodhya. Retaliatory bombings kill more than 250 in Mumbai several months later.

1998 A coalition led by the Hindu nationalist Bharatiya Janata Party takes power.

1999 India and Pakistan fight over the Kargil region of Kashmir.

2000 The one billionth Indian citizen is born.

2002 India tests its first nuclear-capable ballistic missile. Pakistan does likewise. Hindu-Muslim riots in Gujarat kill more than 1,000 people.

2004 The Congress party returns to power and India applies for permanent membership on the United Nations Security Council.

2006 India signs a nuclear cooperation agreement with the United States.

2007 India's first commercial space rocket enters service. A year later, India sends a probe to the moon.

2008 Terrorist attacks kill 166 people in southern Mumbai.

2009 Prime minister Manmohan Singh's Congress-led alliance wins a landslide victory in elections.

2012 The worst power failure in history affects 670 million people across India.

2013 GDP growth slumps below 5%. The prospect of higher United States interest rates triggers a sharp sell-off in the rupee.

INCREDIBLE INDIA

22	Number of languages given official status in the Indian constitution.
356	Number of indigenous languages spoken in India.
343 MILLION	Number of Indians who speak more than one language.
10%	Share of Indians who speak English.
2025	Year when India is forecast to overtake China as the world's most populous country.
17.4%	Share of Indian households that are located in slums.
35.7%	Share of households in Andhra Pradesh that are located in slums, the highest level of any Indian state.
40%	Share of India's urban residents who do not have bank accounts.
70%	Share of Indians who are below the age of 36.
2	Rank of India among the world's countries in number of new engineering graduates annually. China is first.
4.4	Average number of years of formal education received by Indian adults.
46,306	Number of registered trade unions.
45%	Share of the new jobs created in cities over the past decade that are in the information technology sector.

43% — Share of children under age five who are underweight, the second-highest figure in the world, after East Timor. Twenty years ago, 60 percent of India's children were underweight.

8 — Number of Olympic gold medals won by Indian field hockey teams 1928–1980. 0: Number won since 1980.

6 — Number of medals won by Indian athletes in shooting, badminton, boxing, and wrestling at the 2012 London Olympics.

1.5 MILLION — Salary in dollars paid to cricket star Mahendra Singh Dhoni for the 6-week 2012 season of the Indian Premier League. He earned an additional $23 million from endorsements.

80 MILLION — Estimated number of pilgrims attending the 2013 Maha Kumbh Mela festival during which they bathe in the Ganges River.

4–5 MILLION — Estimated number of *sadhus* or ascetic holy men living in India

1,255 — Number of feature films produced in India in 2011.

206 — Number that were Hindi-language Bollywood productions.

0.38 — India's Gini coefficient, a measure of inequality, in 2012. In 1990, India had a Gini score of 0.33. A higher Gini coefficient indicates greater inequality.

6 — Number of major religions in India.

828 MILLION — Number of Indian Hindus.

138 MILLION — Number of Indian Muslims, the third-largest Muslim population in the world behind Indonesia and Pakistan.

2.3% — Share of Indians who are Christians. 1.9% of Indians are Sikhs, 0.8% are Buddhists, 0.4% are Jains, and 0.6% practice other religions.

Source: Census, UNDP, McKinsey & Company, RBI, Statistical Yearbook of India, UNICEF, Forbes, IOC, Government of Allahabad, *Sadhus: India's Mystic Holy Men* by Dolf Hartsuiker, UNESCO, ADB, Press reports, OECD, Census of India, Central Board of Film Certification

INDIA AND THE WORLD

TRADE

Despite maintaining protective tariffs and other restrictions on commerce and foreign investment, India is a major player in world trade.

VALUE OF WORLD TRADE, 2011 ($ MILLION)

◢ Rank among countries in trade

	Exports		Imports	
Goods	302,905	19	464,463	12
Services	137,085	8	123,749	7

TRADING PARTNERS (% OF TOTAL TRADE)

TOP EXPORT DESTINATIONS, 2011

1. European Union   18.1
2. United Arab Emirates   12.4
3. USA   10.9

TOP SOURCES OF IMPORTS, 2011

1. China   12.0
2. European Union   11.9
3. UAE   7.7

FOREIGN POLICY AND THE MILITARY

India has tended to avoid conflicts and alliances beyond its region, but it faces both ongoing tensions with Pakistan and China's growing influence in South Asia. As a result, India maintains one of the world's largest armies and is also the world's top arms importer. The government plans to raise military spending and weapons production over the next decade.

ACTIVE-DUTY MILITARY PERSONNEL (THOUSANDS)

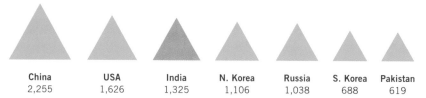

China	USA	India	N. Korea	Russia	S. Korea	Pakistan
2,255	1,626	1,325	1,106	1,038	688	619

Rising nations often seek to assert their influence through aggressive diplomatic and military posturing. After independence, though, India emphasized self-reliance and development at home and wary non-alignment abroad. But as India's importance to the world economy increases, its relations with other countries matter more, too.

FOREIGN INVESTMENT

India retains some protectionist policies, but its economic reforms have brought plenty of investment from other countries. Since 2000, $284 billion in foreign direct investment has flowed into India.

TOP SOURCES OF FOREIGN DIRECT INVESTMENT

SHARE OF TOTAL FDI, 2000–12 (%)

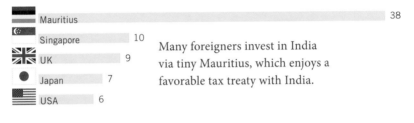

Mauritius 38
Singapore 10
UK 9
Japan 7
USA 6

Many foreigners invest in India via tiny Mauritius, which enjoys a favorable tax treaty with India.

FOREIGN INSTITUTIONAL INVESTMENT FLOWS ($ BILLION)

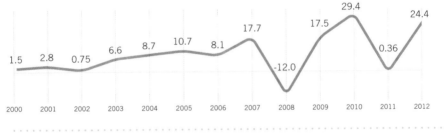

1.5 2.8 0.75 6.6 8.7 10.7 8.1 17.7 -12.0 17.5 29.4 0.36 24.4

2000 2001 2002 2003 2004 2005 2006 2007 2008 2009 2010 2011 2012

NUMBER OF INDIANS RESIDING IN EACH COUNTRY, 2012 (MILLIONS)

THE DIASPORA

The more than 21 million Indians living outside the country are key links between India and the world. Most "overseas Indians" left for economic reasons and their work ranges from professional occupations in developed countries to unskilled labor in the Persian Gulf region.

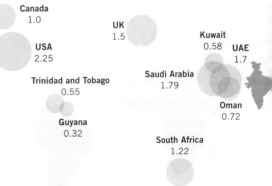

Canada 1.0
UK 1.5
Kuwait 0.58
UAE 1.7
USA 2.25
Trinidad and Tobago 0.55
Saudi Arabia 1.79
Oman 0.72
Guyana 0.32
South Africa 1.22

Sources: WTO, RBI, Ministry of Overseas Indian Affairs, Global Security

INDIA'S FUTURE: PROMISE AND PROBLEMS

India is on track to overtake China as the world's most populous country in fewer than twenty years.

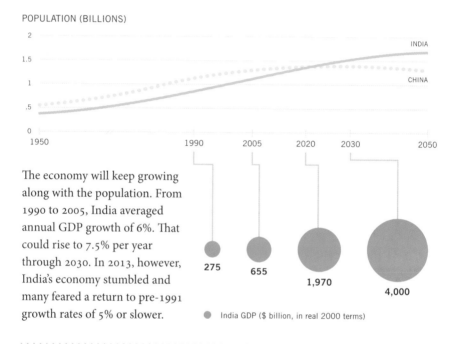

POPULATION (BILLIONS)

INDIA

CHINA

The economy will keep growing along with the population. From 1990 to 2005, India averaged annual GDP growth of 6%. That could rise to 7.5% per year through 2030. In 2013, however, India's economy stumbled and many feared a return to pre-1991 growth rates of 5% or slower.

275   655   1,970   4,000

● India GDP ($ billion, in real 2000 terms)

In the 40 years from 1971 to 2011, the urban population rose by 230 million. It will take only half that time to add the next 250 million urban Indians. Midsized cities such as Bangalore, center of the technology industry, and Pune, an automotive and pharmaceutical hub, are likely to grow faster than megacities such as Mumbai and Delhi.

POPULATION (BILLIONS)

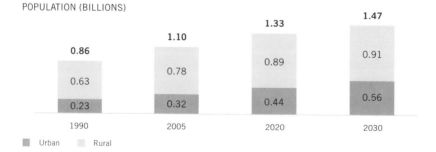

■ Urban   ■ Rural

India will soon become the most populous country in the world and will continue to get wealthier and more urban. Some of India's troubles will get bigger, too.

Growth will help transform a country where many struggle to meet basic needs into one with a middle class* of 583 million people.

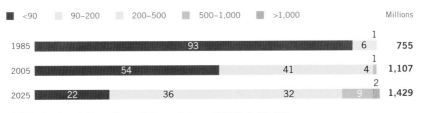

% OF POPULATION IN EACH ANNUAL INCOME BRACKET (THOUSAND RUPEES)

■ <90	░ 90–200	░ 200–500	▨ 500–1,000	▨ >1,000	Millions

1985	93			6	1	755
2005	54		41	4	1	1,107
2025	22	36	32	9	2	1,429

* Middle class households are those with income between 200,000–1,000,000 rupees per year.

Prosperity will improve millions of lives. But as demand increases for houses, cars, and electricity, the impact on the environment also grows.

TOTAL FLOOR SPACE
Billions of square meters

4   8   22   41
1990   2005   2020   2030

VEHICLE FLEET
Millions

21   51   222   377
1990   2005   2020   2030

TOTAL POWER DEMAND
Terawatt hours (TWh)

350   700   1,870   3,870
1990   2005   2020   2030

Even if economic growth is slower than expected, India's emission of heat-trapping gasses into the atmosphere will increase dramatically.

If average yearly GDP growth through 2030 is...

...average annual carbon emissions (in billions of tons) would be:

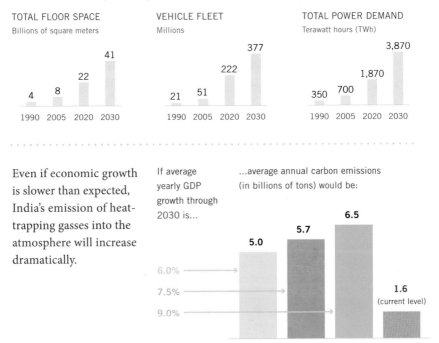

6.0% → 5.0
7.5% → 5.7
9.0% → 6.5

1.6 (current level)

Sources: United Nations Department of Economic and Social Affairs/Population Division, McKinsey Global Institute

INDIA'S FUTURE: PROMISE AND PROBLEMS

The effects of higher carbon emissions from India will be felt worldwide. They may hit hardest in places that are already most at risk from climate change–related calamities.

UNITED NATIONS RANKING OF LARGEST CITIES AT HIGHEST RISKS OF NATURAL DISASTERS

DROUGHTS

1. Kolkata
2. Karachi
3. Los Angeles
4. Chennai
5. Lahore
6. Ahmadabad
7. Santiago
8. Belo Horizonte

FLOODS

1. Tokyo
2. Delhi
3. Mexico City
4. New York
5. Shanghai
6. São Paulo
7. Dhaka
8. Kolkata

Even if efforts to reduce the growth of carbon emissions succeed, India's environment will strain to meet the demands of growth.

WATER SUPPLY AND DEMAND, 2030 (BILLIONS OF CUBIC METERS)

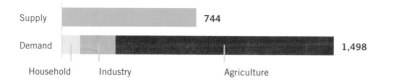

Supply — 744

Demand — 1,498

Household   Industry   Agriculture

A more crowded landscape will also further pressure Indian wildlife, such as the endangered tigers who have already lost most of their habitat. Greater wealth, though, makes it more likely that India will be able to support wildlife programs such as one that seeks to double the global tiger population by 2020.

● Present-day tiger reserves

Sources: United Nations Department of Economic and Social Affairs/Population Division, McKinsey Global Institute, National Tiger Conservation Authority

High Courts of India—comparable to circuit courts in the United States, though India has a unitary court system with no separate state and federal courts—had more than four million. The Allahabad High Court takes the prize for the most backlogged docket, with over one million cases pending. India's Supreme Court had over fifty-nine thousand cases pending. The good news is that lower court dockets have been shrinking since 2010. The ominous news is that since appeals are relatively easy and cheap to file, the backlog of cases before India's higher courts will continue to grow.

The roots of this judicial gridlock are many, but a leading cause is India's surprisingly low number of judges per capita. Data compiled by J. Mark Ramseyer and Eric Rasmusen[2] suggest that for every 100,000 people, the United States has 10.8 judges, Canada and Australia between 3 and 4. India has just 1.2 judges for every 100,000 people.[3] Judges' pay is linked to government pay scales of bureaucrats. The need to delink is obvious but not considered a priority. Yet first-year associates at some law firms in India draw higher salaries than Supreme Court judges, whose monthly pay plus perquisites is approximately 200,000 rupees ($3,100). Prestige and a passion to mete out justice must be the defining characteristics that drive the higher Indian judiciary.

First-year associates at some law firms in India draw higher salaries than Supreme Court judges.

Reforms to improve standards, salaries, and continuing judicial education in the lower judiciary would go a long way in addressing some of these underlying issues. More courts need to be set up and more judges

---

[2] J. Mark Ramseyer and Eric B. Rasmusen, *Comparative Litigation Rates,* Discussion Paper No. 681, John M. Olin Center for Law, Economics, and Business, Harvard Law School, November 20, 2010.

[3] The Supreme Court, High Courts, and district and subordinate courts of India together had a working strength of 14,797 judges in 2012, according to data published by the Supreme Court. *Court News* 7, issue 2 (April–June 2012). This figure presumably does not include judges who served on tribunals during that time. Then again, the backlog data published by the Supreme Court also presumably does not include cases pending before tribunals.

appointed, but that requires a greater allocation of state resources. Judicial reform is largely not a high-priority item for the government, as it yields few political dividends in the short run.

India's legal system also suffers from a systemic leadership crisis. The chief justice of India—the most important judge in the country and the only person capable of reforming the judicial system—serves in office for little over a year, on average.[4] As a result, no chief justice is able to make long-term changes and see them implemented. India's legal culture is partially to blame as well, as it lays far too much emphasis on the courtroom as the crucible of justice. This dates back to the colonial era, when judges considered it inappropriate even to read case papers at home, for fear that they might bias themselves before hearing the arguments in court. Today, although most judges read case papers in advance, far too much court time is wasted on arguments. Cases are frequently adjourned and poorly managed.

> The chief justice of India—the most important judge in the country and the only person capable of reforming the judicial system—serves in office for little over a year, on average.

The political system has at least begun to address some of the procedural problems that beset India's legal system, starting more than a decade ago with a series of far-reaching amendments to the colonial era Code of Civil Procedure of 1908. Now, affidavits, typically drafted in advance by lawyers, have replaced direct witness testimonies. Witnesses can still be cross-examined, but this process can take place before a "commissioner" out of court. Another amendment makes it mandatory for courts to send a case for alternative dispute resolution if "elements" of a settlement appear to exist. Cases that would ordinarily have taken years to get started have now commenced thanks to the evidence collection amendments.

The change is especially perceptible in the Delhi High Court, where suits that once took ten years or so to be decided now take two to three

---

[4] Abhinav Chandrachud, "The Informal Constitution: Unwritten Criteria in Selecting Judges for the Supreme Court of India," JSM thesis, Stanford Law School, May 2012.

years. E-filing has also become more prevalent in the Delhi High Court—a few of its courtrooms are entirely paperless, and it is mandatory in some cases to submit both electronic and paper versions of filings. Apart from some formal procedural amendments, several steps have been taken to address the backlog. In Mumbai, the Bombay High Court transferred most of its original jurisdiction to subordinate civil courts in the city. Fast-track courts have been set up in some parts of the country to decide criminal cases, especially in the wake of the recent brutal gang-rape of a girl in Delhi. Further, the rate at which a judge disposes of his or her cases is now taken into account in determining promotion.

India's judicial system provides swift outcomes for some litigants. Clever litigators have developed strategies to circumvent judicial delays. Though it takes several years for a case to reach final judgment, some litigants in commercial cases in just a few months can obtain from a court "interim relief" in the form of temporary orders issued before the case is decided. This tactic often forces the losing party to negotiate in earnest to avoid years of delay and the risk of an adverse final decree. Although problematic, such approaches provide an avenue for the sophisticated litigant to avoid the law's delay.

Despite its shortcomings, India's judicial system remains the country's bastion of the rule of law, standing above the clamor of party politics and ensuring that justice is done, even if often too slowly. Time and again, courts have risen to address political crises, to hold officials accountable, and not only to keep fundamental human rights alive but also to give those rights meaning. Judges are overworked and underpaid, but the vast majority of them are respected as men and women of the highest integrity. India may not have the well-oiled judicial system to optimize the legal transactions needed by a rapidly modernizing and globalizing country, but it does have a judiciary that should be the envy of many other societies. And the reforms introduced both nationally and in some of the High Courts demonstrate that speeding the judicial process and bringing it into the twenty-first century requires only that India's political leaders come to understand the benefits to society of modest investments in the legal system.

india's infrastruggles
Rajiv Lall

In India, journeys often involve travel through time as well as across space, as today's India spans multiple historical time zones—from the ancient to the ultramodern. A recent trip began in the soaring departure lobby of the new Terminal 3 at Delhi's Indira Gandhi International Airport, a cathedral of glass, steel, and duty-free shopping, built to accommodate sixty million passengers a year. I flew to Varanasi, a city of 3.5 million, famed as the spiritual capital of India's Hindu and Buddhist communities, but for those of us who live in the material world, it lacks a functioning system for solid-waste disposal, and driving across town can take hours. When I finally reached National Highway 2, a splendid new six-lane toll road, I covered the 130 kilometers to the outskirts of Allahabad in less than ninety minutes.

At Allahabad, I took the last exit to a rocky hilltop that offers an awe-inspiring view of the Sangam, the confluence of the Ganges and Yamuna Rivers and the site of the Kumbh Mela, a religious festival held every three years, said to be the world's largest gathering of humanity. As dusk descended, I gazed down upon an enormous tent city connected by 156 kilometers of temporary roads and illuminated by twenty-two thousand streetlamps, all provided by the government of Uttar Pradesh. On February 10, 2013, thirty million faithful, under the direction of multiple religious orders, bathed at the Sangam, an area of about twenty square kilometers, largely without incident. How are Indians capable of such

Rajiv Lall is the executive chairman of the Infrastructure Development Finance Company.

discipline and organization unable to clear the garbage that litters the streets of Varanasi a few kilometers downriver? How can we make telecommunications affordable to the millions carrying cell phones at the Kumbh but not give them access to clean drinking water or toilets at home? This is the great conundrum of infrastructure in India.

india's infrastruggles

In the twentieth century, the quality of public infrastructure—roads, water, sanitation, electricity, and telecommunications—became the sine qua non of economic development. In most countries, the public sector built and maintained the vast bulk of those essential services. Private participation emerged only about thirty years ago, when chronic budget deficits obliged many governments to seek new sources of capital.

In India, however, our fiscal stresses emerged long before the government had a chance to build public infrastructure to minimum global standards. Populist electoral politics have pushed a rising share of government spending into wages, interest payments on public debt, and nonproductive subsidies such as for fertilizer and fossil fuel. What little remains for public investments goes first to education and health care, where the government must be the service provider of last resort.

India has had to turn to the private sector for help in building and maintaining crucial public infrastructure. Over the past decade, government spending on infrastructure increased modestly from 3.5 to 4.4 percent of GDP while private investment in infrastructure, all but nonexistent in 2003, expanded to nearly 3 percent of GDP in 2011. But India lags far behind China, where infrastructure investment has remained constant at approximately 9 percent of GDP for the past two decades, and trails the 7.3 percent for developing Asian countries in 1992–2010. The McKinsey Global Institute has estimated the value of all Indian infrastructure at about 60 percent of GDP, well below the ratio in China or most developed countries, where infrastructure is typically valued at more than 75 percent of GDP.

Private sector investment in Indian infrastructure would seem a win-win for both the public and the private investors who provide the capital and expertise. Citizens generally understand that some level of private profit is essential to attract investment, but the topic has not been fully discussed, and politicians have done little to prepare the electorate for the inevitable controversies. India's leaders also failed to recognize that this rapid intrusion of the private sector into the public space required an upgraded administrative and regulatory infrastructure. These political and administrative inadequacies have combined to produce a particularly toxic concoction, what I call India's infrastruggle cocktail.

India's power sector provides a painful illustration of that cocktail's hangover. My firm, the Infrastructure Development Finance Company (IDFC), was set up by the government to channel private funds into infrastructure and is now a listed company with ownership dispersed across a broad range of private shareholders. IDFC has played a leading role in providing capital to meet the skyrocketing demand for electricity by financing private sector projects. Over the past five years, we've invested $5.5 billion just in energy infrastructure and helped raise another $10 billion from other private sector investors.

IDFC played an important part in the development of India's private power sector, in which nearly half of total capacity was added in the last five years. Unfortunately, many of these new plants will not operate at optimal capacity because Coal India, a government-owned monopoly, cannot deliver the fuel it has promised, blaming onerous environmental regulations and protests from civil society activists. The higher price of imported coal would have to be passed along to consumers, but state electricity boards are prevented by their political masters from raising electricity rates and thus upsetting voters. The result is gridlock.

the way ahead

Skill constraints and the increasingly fragmented nature of coalition and federal politics have impaired government execution and decision-making capabilities. Our judicial system is overburdened and inefficient. Two decades after reforms began to lift the stifling controls of the old license raj, India still sits at 182 out of 185 countries in the World Bank's ranking of ease of obtaining construction permits. A reimagined

India with an infrastructure befitting a modern, globalized nation requires addressing three primary challenges.

A modern regulatory system. When the public sector builds and maintains infrastructure, regulatory oversight can be minimal, since disputes are adjudicated within the government. India's rapid growth of private sector involvement found governmental bodies unprepared. This has made the conflicts between public and private sectors, which would occur in any country, even more acrimonious and intractable. Finding the right balance between the public interest and that of service providers is an art, not a science. It requires arbiters to be empowered, independent, and objective, and to have deep sectoral expertise in and knowledge of public policy, law, business, and finance. Building a cadre of qualified regulators requires that the government pay reasonable salaries to attract and retain them, and it must also foster the development of the academic disciplines to provide the required training.

> Two decades after reforms began . . . India still sits at 182 out of 185 countries in the World Bank's ranking of ease of obtaining construction permits.

The government must also bolster the technical capacity and speed of our judicial system. One possible solution is the creation of specialist courts devoted solely to handling these often contentious regulatory issues.

Transparency. Inefficient administration and outright corruption combine to form a central, poisonous ingredient in India's infrastruggle cocktail. The most effective antidote to these ills is transparency. As an important first step, the Right to Information Act of 2005 set out the public's right to access government information and has provided a huge impetus to openness.

The next legislative step will be passage of the proposed Right of Citizens for Time Bound Delivery of Goods and Services and Redressal of Their Grievances Bill. The legislation would, through a citizens' charter, require government authorities to establish a time frame within which they agree to provide goods and services and a grievance mechanism to hold them accountable for timely delivery. The agency responsible for overseeing the construction of a section of a highway, for example, would have to provide firm estimates of cost and completion dates with regular progress updates. The legislation would initially apply only at the national level, but it would play a major role in activating the sort of informed public oversight and expectations essential to efficient government operations.

Public engagement. The governance of our country will improve only when politicians run on platforms based on how well they deliver public services rather than relying on the vocabulary of identity—caste, language, and religion. Increased transparency will give citizens the tools they need to hold their political leaders accountable for their promises, and it is to be hoped that the rising aspirations and growing political maturity of India's youth will serve to make performance the key electoral criterion over the next decade. After all, at the next national elections in 2014, one hundred million young Indians will be eligible to vote for the first time.

> The governance of our country will improve only when politicians run on platforms based on how well they deliver public services rather than relying on the vocabulary of identity—caste, language, and religion.

In fact, we can already see the elements of a transition from identity-based to performance-based electoral politics. In Gujarat, the Bharatiya Janata Party, which began as a Hindu nationalist party, has increasingly campaigned and won on the basis of its ability to deliver public services and consistent economic growth. BJP candidates sought voter support by actually delivering on services promised and stood by their record at election time. The result was that support for BJP candidates transcended old boundary lines of caste, religion, and geography. Exit polls showed the party was rewarded for making good its promise of economic development. A similar scenario played out in Bihar, long regarded as India's most lawless and corrupt state, and may repeat itself in several other states in 2014.

For India to unleash its economic potential, it will require a twenty-first-century infrastructure that its public purse simply cannot finance on its own. Private sector involvement will continue to be crucial, but for it to succeed the public must feel that the services they receive are worth their own contributions (taxes) as well as the profits reaped by the investors. The Indian public and its elected officials will have to invest the time and effort to build a stable political infrastructure of administrative, regulatory, and judicial bodies that can provide predictability for investors and a sense that the public's rights and the country's wealth are of equal value.

making sense of census towns
Sukumar Ranganathan

In an area of Tamil Nadu state once famous for its jasmine farms, where the main source of employment used to be the cultivation of fragrant blossoms, a fast-growing but unlovely settlement of small businesses and houses called Padappai bestrides one of the national roads. Many of its jasmine fields have been sold for housing or else lie fallow in anticipation of rising real estate prices. Open drains and swaths of rubbish belie Padappai's recent rural past, as do the demands of the customers at local shops for products they see on television, such as hair conditioners, air fresheners, fizzy drinks, processed cheese, chips, and cosmetics.

The stereotype is that Indians live in places very different from Padappai—either sleepy villages or teeming cities. In the India depicted in mass media and pop culture, hundreds of millions of people continue to reside in pastoral backwaters raising crops and tending livestock, while the rest of the population throngs metropolises with glittery high-rises and sprawling slums. The reality, however, is that India's booming economy of the past two decades is giving rise to many places like Padappai, where large numbers of Indians already live, and the country's urbanized future is rapidly unfolding in haphazard fashion.

Padappai is a "census town," the Census Department's term for a village no longer dependent on farming. The number of such towns has

NOTE: The author wishes to thank *Mint* deputy managing editor Anil Padmanhan and *Mint* staff writer Cordelia Jenkins for their contributions to this essay.

Sukumar Ranganathan is editor of Mint, *the Indian business newspaper, and* LiveMint, *its online counterpart.*

almost tripled since 2001, to about four thousand, according to the 2011 census. Their proliferation is bound to continue, perhaps even accelerate, as more and more farmers abandon the shrinking plots of land inherited from their forebears.

Therein lies a potential wellspring of prosperity, because large companies operating in India—both domestic and foreign—increasingly favor rural areas over cities for their factories and other labor-intensive facilities. But the governance problems of census towns pose an enormous challenge; having no formal status as municipalities, they often are unable to provide modern infrastructure and good educational systems that both their residents and major corporate investors need. And powerful interests prefer keeping the loosely organized, low-tax governance arrangements of census towns in place.

Technically, census towns are part of rural India, which according to government figures still encompasses nearly 69 percent of the population. But they are much more urban than their official classification would suggest. To become a census town, a village must have a population of at least five thousand, a density of four hundred people per square kilometer, and a male working population that is at least 75 percent engaged in nonagricultural pursuits. Although census towns exist in many parts of the country, they are not evenly spread, with two out of every three being concentrated in just six states—West Bengal, Kerala, Tamil Nadu, Maharashtra, Uttar Pradesh, and Andhra Pradesh, in that order. Kanhu Charan Pradhan, a researcher at New Delhi's Centre for Policy Research, used Google Maps to plot the locations of the twenty-five hundred or so census towns that have emerged since 2001; his data shows dark clusters radiating from a number of industrial cities.

Several factors are driving the growth of census towns. One is the spread of India's road network, which has served as not only an economic multiplier but also an urbanizing influence that increases movement of goods and people between villages, surrounding towns, and large cities. The total length of national highways in India more than doubled, to twelve thousand kilometers, between 2005 and 2012, according to the National Highways Authority.

The expansion of electrification and mobile-phone connectivity are also important spurs to the development of census towns and other semiurbanized villages, because people perceive economic opportunity in places where they can hook up appliances, generate light in the evening, and use mobiles to conduct business. The national electricity grid added more than 107,000 villages between 2005 and 2012, according to the Rural Electrification Corporation, and teledensity has risen exponentially, from 6.5 million mobile-phone connections in March 2002 to 920 million in March 2012.

The expanding reach of television, too, plays a key role in luring people from tiny hamlets to more urbanized settings such as census towns. Whereas census estimates put the number of Indian households with TVs at about 60 million in 2001, that number has risen to nearly 150 million households, according to TAM Media Research, and the vast majority of those have access to the radically more diverse content (movies, soap operas, talent contests, sports, and spiritual discourse) currently available on hundreds of cable and satellite channels that have emerged in recent years. As a result, rural Indians have learned a lot about how the other half lives, and their aspirations have soared along with their purchasing power.

D. Sudha, a drugstore owner in Padappai, sees the trend among the women shopping at her outlet, who are no longer satisfied with run-of-the-mill products when it comes to important considerations such as lightening their skin. "They watch television and come back with all these queries," Sudha says. "Now they ask for Pond's White Beauty, which I need to stock." Thanks to higher demand, she rarely has to collect her supplies from dealers in person as she did previously; most of them deliver to her door.

> Large companies often find it too expensive or bureaucratically troublesome to acquire sizable plots of land in major cities.

The good news for places like this is that they are increasingly attractive magnets for the manufacturing plants India needs to gainfully employ its burgeoning youth population. Large companies often find it too expensive or bureaucratically troublesome to acquire sizable plots of land in major cities, given the sketchy land

and property titling procedures in many parts of the country, which have stymied countless investment projects. In rural areas, land acquisition is much cheaper and easier, if not entirely hassle-free.

Molachur, about forty kilometers from Chennai, is a census town that is benefiting from such corporate calculations. A decade ago, most of its inhabitants earned their livelihoods growing rice, lentils, and watermelons, or from embroidery. Today it is on the doorstep of factories built by Hyundai Motor India, Ford India, BMW India, Mitsubishi India, and Nokia India. That is a boon for people like Sakkayanmary, one of the few tenant farmers left, whose two younger children work at plants operated by the mobile-phone-component maker Foxconn Technology Group and the glassmaker Saint-Gobain. The siblings' combined earnings of 7,000 rupees (about $140) a month is a tidy sum for a family accustomed to village living standards. A new ecosystem of small businesses to service the factories and their workers also provides income for many residents.

Evidence for this phenomenon is more than anecdotal. Ejaz Ghani, an economic adviser for South Asia at the World Bank, coauthored a recent report for the Harvard Business School that concluded that while informal and unorganized small industries (such as Molachur's embroidery trade) were moving from rural areas into cities, the reverse was true of the formal industrial sector—the Hyundais and the Nokias. The trend "cuts across industries and states," according to Ghani. He cautions, however, that "new plants tended to open in places that had better infrastructure and better education facilities."

And there's the rub. Though they may feel semiurban, census towns are still run by *gram panchayats*, or village councils, which have limited financial resources because they do not tax their communities, and in most of rural India no one pays property taxes. As a result, public services in many census towns and urbanized villages are appallingly substandard. *Panchayats* do obtain some funding from central government development programs, but that flow of money would dry up if the towns became full-fledged municipalities. That dilemma, and the reluctance of some residents to pay local taxes, hinders change.

The tangle of conflicting interests is evident in Boisar, a large census town in Maharashtra state with a population of 150,000 (too many people for just one *panchayat*; Boisar has six of them). The town boasts a large supermarket, branches of private banks, and decent schools. But its roads are riddled with potholes and lined with garbage, and as for public transport, the only conveyance on offer is a fleet of exhaust-belching six-seat auto-rickshaws. For ten years, a body of residents called the Boisar Citizens' Forum has been pressing the Maharashtra government to upgrade the town's status to municipality—to no avail. The forum alleges that local politicians, loath to give up fiefdoms they control, are blocking progress. Another impediment is state governments, which often are unwilling to loosen their grip over certain types of patronage—the appointment of village teachers, for example.

At least Boisar has public education worthy of the name. In Chandpur, a census town bordering the city of Varanasi in Uttar Pradesh, there are no government schools, only four private ones—and though some of the private schools in the area are well run, their fees are far too steep for many of the village's original residents, while the cheaper alternatives offer dubious instructional value.

In Chandpur, too, some citizens agitate for municipal status. Upset over problems such as sporadic garbage collection, crumbling roads, and the rapidly depleting supply of groundwater, people like Sanjay Itankar, a retired railway worker, say they are impatient for Chandpur to shed its rural status and merge with Varanasi. "Of course we will pay taxes!" said Itankar. "If we get the facilities, we will be happy."

But a vocal group of dissenters is opposed—Ram Sharan Patel, a rotund, garrulous businessman is one of them. "The day they make this a town, I am going somewhere else," said Patel, who runs a successful weaving and dying factory in Chandpur. At fifty-four years old, he doesn't want to start paying municipal taxes, he explained, before admitting that his business probably also exceeds the city pollution limits.

Perhaps India will muster the resolve to overcome that kind of resistance, so that development of its hinterlands proceeds in a manner that will enhance the vast majority of lives among its rural populace. On the present trajectory, however, such an outcome does not appear likely to materialize.

it takes more than a village
Sonalde Desai

Nearly seventy years after Mahatma Gandhi declared, "India begins and ends in the villages," the statement still rings true. Only three out of ten Indians currently live in cities. The lives of the rest can seem scarcely changed from Gandhi's time. Any tourist driving through Rajasthan today will pass women in brightly colored saris, silver bangles clanking, trudging through the desert with jugs of water on their heads as they did in Mughal times. Golden fields of mustard in Uttar Pradesh and stretches of emerald coconut groves in Kerala look like advertisements for the serene, timeless India imagined by generations of Western travelers.

But look closer. In a prosperous Punjabi village one might see a batch of *lassi* being mixed up in a shiny washing machine. Instead of riding a bullock cart into the fields each morning, young men in Tamil Nadu hop onto motorcycle taxis to commute to their jobs in nearby towns. Even real Indians don't necessarily want to live in the "real India" any longer: Those Rajasthani women may look picturesque, but don't forget that they have to walk for miles just to get safe drinking water.

The fact is, Gandhi's India cannot and should not survive in today's world. When he said, "India lives in her . . . villages, and the cities live upon the villages," he may have been right: At independence, more than 50 percent of the Indian economy depended upon agriculture. Now, though, agricultural stagnation and shrinking plots have made living off

Sonalde Desai is a demographer and professor of sociology at the University of Maryland and a senior fellow at the National Council of Applied Economic Research.

the land nearly impossible for India's millions of small farmers. The only villages to survive in the future will be those with links to economically dynamic towns where jobs are available. Even if they don't live in cities, "real" Indians will ultimately have to work there.

> Even if they don't live in cities, "real" Indians will ultimately have to work there.

This trend is irreversible and has been developing for years. The size of the typical Indian farm shrank drastically between 1970 and 2005—from an average 2.28 hectares to 1.21 hectares. At the turn of the twentieth century, large farmers and *zamindars*, landlords who employed tenant farmers, dominated rural India. Since then, the *zamindari* system has virtually disappeared. Laws limiting the size of individual holdings, as well as the natural chopping up of plots to divide them between successive generations, have fragmented the landscape still further. More than 80 percent of Indian farms today are tiny, less than 2 hectares apiece. This shrinkage stands in direct contrast to the trend in Western countries, where farms are large, as well as in thriving Asian nations like Japan and Korea, where farms are tiny. In the United States, during this period, the size of the average farm rose to 180 acres, up from 150 acres, while in Japan farm size grew to 1.2 acres, up from 1 acre, and in Korea farm size grew to 1 acre, up from 0.9 acre.

Productivity on farms in India lags behind that on farms in many other developing nations. The average Chinese farm is half the size of an Indian one yet is nearly twice as productive. In India, small farms are more productive, on a per hectare basis, than large farms. Even so, India's lilliputian plots cannot provide a decent livelihood for their owners. Recent studies have shown that the average farming family in India earns barely $500–$600 per hectare annually. If Indian farmers had to subsist solely on agriculture, more than 60 percent would sink below the poverty line.

Fortunately, towns and cities have begun to offer a lifeline to the most well-connected villages. The key to economic well-being in rural India is access to sources of income other than farming. Three-quarters of the richest rural households now earn money from nonagricultural activities. In villages that are linked to urban areas by roads, buses, trains, banks, and telephones, the range of potential moneymaking activities expands greatly. Villagers might work construction jobs in nearby towns in between harvests, or might set up small businesses there. Within villages themselves, jobs for teachers, clerical workers, artisans, and shopkeepers become more viable.

In the countryside, one out of five adult males now holds multiple jobs, both agricultural and nonagricultural, throughout the year. Nearly half of all rural households derive at least some income from work unrelated to farming. Good infrastructure betters lives overall, too. The less isolated teachers and nurses feel, the more likely they are to live in the village where they work, which in turn raises the quality of education and health care. Nongovernmental organizations, too, are more likely to set up in villages where staff can remain connected to the outside world.

Understanding this reality should force us to reexamine how we approach the question of rural development. The focus should not be on preserving farming as a way of life; the picture-postcard version of the Indian village is no longer viable. Instead, we should strive to increase access to nonfarm work—to connect the disconnected.

> The focus should not be on preserving farming as a way of life. Instead, we should strive to increase access to nonfarm work—to connect the disconnected.

Simply funneling money to the poorest rural districts, as is done now, won't work. Villages near district headquarters tend to be relatively well developed already. Instead, aid strategies need to be much more targeted, focusing first on the states with the worst infrastructure, and then within those states on the most isolated villages. Otherwise the two-tier system that's already emerging—between villages with access to infrastructure and those without—will only become more entrenched.

We must be alert to another danger, too. One might think that as villagers' fortunes improved, old fault lines of caste and religion would gradually fade away. Instead, they appear to grow stronger. The worst inequities tend to follow an inverted U-shaped pattern: The old divisions matter least in the poorest villages (where everyone faces a similar struggle for existence) and the biggest cities (where ambition matters more than background). In between, though, in newly prosperous villages and small towns, the competition for well-paying salaried jobs is fierce. Children who come from traditionally better-off classes have a head start: Studies have suggested that while two-thirds of upper-caste kids can read, less than 45 percent of Muslim and Dalit (or untouchable) children can.

Even those who do manage to get college degrees often find themselves frustrated. With so many more graduates nowadays and so few white-collar jobs available, those youth with better social connections often snap up all the good positions. Thus privileged groups become more privileged, and marginalized groups more marginalized.

That's not an argument to slow rural development, of course. Instead, the task is twofold—not just to increase villagers' access to infrastructure but also to expand social and educational opportunities for the least-privileged communities. The village India Gandhi knew is going to disappear regardless. Our task is to make sure that a brighter future replaces it.

india's farms: harvesting the future
Barnik C. Maitra and Adil Zainulbhai

The image of upwardly mobile India is an urban one, of high-rises and well-educated young people working at their computers before going to the mall. That is true enough, but in an important way, not true to the reality of India. About 70 percent of Indians live in rural areas. And the fact is that living in rural India can be very difficult indeed.

Some three hundred million rural Indians live below the poverty line, literacy is only 46 percent, and only one in five has access to basic sanitation. Although more than two-thirds of Indians (833 million people) live in the countryside, agriculture accounts for only 14 percent of GDP. Forty-two percent of India's children under five are underweight, the second-highest figure in the world (only Timor-Leste ranks higher).

Can Indian agriculture help to plant a different kind of future, in which its rural citizens are more prosperous, its children more robust, and the national economy stronger?

Yes, it can.

We believe in a successful future, because we have seen success in the past. Despite poor infrastructure, policy barriers such as restrictions on procurement and marketing, and land laws that prevent land consolidation, India's farmers have proved admirably resilient. India has been self-sufficient in food grains since the mid-1990s, with production rising from 130 million tons in 1980 to 240 million in 2010. India is the world's third-largest agricultural producer ($260 billion a year, behind China and

Barnik C. Maitra is a partner in McKinsey's Mumbai office. Adil Zainulbhai is chairman of McKinsey India.

the United States), and is the global leader in producing bananas, mangoes, papayas, milk, buffalo meat, spices, castor oil, and sesame seeds.

Pockets of excellence demonstrate the potential that improved practices can deliver. For example, when farmers in Gujarat used better seeds and drip irrigation, they doubled their yields and quintupled their income. What we also see, unfortunately, are opportunities lost or never attempted. India exports only 10 percent of the value of its domestic production (the average for the top fifteen global producers is 39 percent). Part of the reason for the low export figures, of course, is India's need to feed its own people. But low productivity and the failure to meet global quality standards are also important factors. Another lost opportunity is in food processing; less than 10 percent of Indian output is processed within India, much less than in Brazil or Indonesia.

> Low-quality seeds are the most important single reason for India's relatively low crop yields.

Moreover, yields are often poor. The world's best wheat producers produce twelve tons per hectare; India produces three. Or consider the dairy sector. The Food and Agriculture Organization estimates that production per Indian animal (about one thousand kilograms a year) is half the world average.

India is on the cusp of change that will reward success. Per capita GDP is expected to increase by 320 percent over the next twenty years; as income rises, people's eating habits change, specifically away from cereals and legumes, and toward fruit, vegetables, seafood, and meat. With India's population growing, food consumption will grow 4 percent a year. At the same time, consumers in India will demand high-quality, safe, and healthy food.

Put it all together, and the conclusion is that this an important moment for Indian agriculture. If the country can imagine, and then make real, this opportunity, the result could be broader prosperity and higher health and living standards all across the nation.

- We imagine an India that is a global agricultural powerhouse, with exports approaching $164 billion a year by 2030 (compared to $30 billion in 2011).

- We imagine an India with agricultural output of $620 billion by 2030 (compared to $270 billion in 2011).
- We imagine an India with a food-processing GDP of $120 billion by 2030 (up from $24 billion in 2011).
- We imagine an India where the income of rural citizens rises sixfold and approaches that of those in the cities.
- We imagine an India that is a leader in agricultural research and innovation.

reimagining indian agriculture

That is the vision. What needs to be done to make it happen? Here is our to-do list.

1. Improve agricultural technology, including seeds and farming practices.

Low-quality seeds are the most important single reason for India's relatively low crop yields. Better seeds can boost the yield of potatoes by up to 40 percent, but India produces only 10 percent of the amount required. That adds up to at least $600 million in lost value. Across the country, India supplies less than 20 percent of the demand for quality seeds. To take just one example, despite being the world's largest producer of mangoes, India ranks sixtieth in terms of yield. In addition, poor postharvest management allows up to 20 percent of the crop to be wasted. We think India can increase yields by 40 percent and cut waste in half by doing no more than adopting proven practices. India should start a coordinated effort to create high-yield varieties of seeds suitable for different regional climates, educate farmers to adopt them, promote mechanization and modern irrigation, and disseminate best practices.

> We think India can increase yields by 40 percent and cut waste in half by doing no more than adopting proven practices.

2. Make soil and water sustainability a priority.

India has 18 percent of the world's population and just 3 percent of its water. The efficient use of water is essential for increasing agricultural production, but the subsidy system encourages the opposite. For example, because of generous subsidies for urea-based fertilizers, farmers rely on these alone rather than using them in conjunction with potassium phosphate ones, which is more effective. To start, India needs to create a better base of knowledge—a national map of soil type and water availability—and use geographic information systems (GIS) to monitor various land-use activities and watershed projects. India should emphasize research on cropping practices that use soil nutrients efficiently and decrease land degradation. New approaches need to be adopted to avoid overexploitation of resources, starting with farmer education and supported by incentives, planning, metering, and allocation of quotas in selected areas. As an example, mobile testing labs could be set up to provide farmers with "prescriptions" for their soil—a simple card that tells them how much fertilizer, pesticide, seed, and water to use.

3. Promote farmer-producer organizations (FPOs), farmer-producer companies (FPCs), and local aggregators.

In India, it is almost impossible to aggregate land to create larger farms, and for both social and political reasons, this is not going to change. But FPOs and FPCs can help to create the economies of scale and improve productivity by allowing small farmers to leverage their collective strength and increase their competitiveness by offering them easier access to credit and technology. These organizations can also reduce the costs of distribution and provide greater marketing power and negotiation capacity to farmers. The government needs to encourage more equity participation in FPOs/FPCs through focused grants. These companies, in addition to local aggregator companies, could then become the "connective tissue" of a globally competitive food and agriculture sector. For example, Jain Irrigation provides mango farmers in Chittoor with irrigation, technology, and extension support. Then Jain processes the produce, which is sold to Coca-Cola for use in its mango beverage (Maaza).

4. Deregulate the marketing of agricultural produce.

In several important agricultural states, including Punjab, Haryana, Maharashtra, Andhra Pradesh, Tamil Nadu, West Bengal, and Uttar Pradesh, processors and marketers are not allowed to buy directly from farmers; they must go through intermediaries (known as *arathiyas*). In some states, processors and marketers must obtain a permit in order to buy from the agricultural markets (known as *mandis*), a remnant of the license raj that is well past its expiration date. This system results in more wastage because the food has to go through additional hands before reaching the market; it also hurts farmers because they get less of the pass-through price. A better approach would be to allow farmers to sell their produce straight to the market. The adoption of technology solutions, such as mobile apps or online platforms, to access price information across *mandis* would help to prevent exploitation of farmers, who could then use this information to choose where and to whom to sell their produce.

5. Launch a public-private export initiative.

Florida has become strongly associated with oranges for good reason: It grows lots of them. But the state has also worked hard to identify itself closely with the fruit, and worked with the industry to promote demand. India could do the same with, say, bananas, of which it is the world's leading producer. By converting just 3 percent of its total banana area to dedicated export zones, India could match the export volume of the second-largest exporter, Costa Rica, at current yields. An export initiative would identify the most promising exports and markets, invest in market creation, and help producers meet international benchmarks. At the same time, India needs to create a national master plan that maps current and future agricultural flows, and then build sorting, harvesting, packaging, storage, and transportation (particularly cold chains) infrastructure linking producing regions to export hubs.

6. Promote private investment.

As a huge market with enormous value waiting to be extracted, India should be attractive to agribusiness. But only two of the top twenty-five global agriculture companies, and fifteen of the top twenty-five food companies, have a significant presence in India because of policies that limit foreign participation. As a result, the country is missing out on the global expertise that can help it to tap its potential in processing, packaging, and branding high-value crops; it is also unable to get access to the private capital that could give the sector a big boost. Specifically, the government should encourage investors with tax incentives, road shows, and capital-subsidy grants (linked to new technology deployment) to attract marquee food processors and marketers.

7. Scale up megahubs for processing.

The government recently allocated $11 million to develop "mega food parks"—business zones dedicated to agricultural produce marketing, storage, and processing. The goal: increase processing to 20 percent of output by 2015. India's established food parks have the required infrastructure, such as cold storage, quality grading, and testing, but they have not managed the necessary forward linkages (with marketing and distribution companies) and backward ones (with farms).

8. Upgrade extension services through private participation.

Extension services introduce and integrate science and technology into the farming system. These do exist in India, but they are inadequate to the country's needs. India has about one hundred thousand extension agents—one-tenth the number required, and it spends just 40¢ on research for every $100 in production, a third less than sub-Saharan Africa. Nor has the output of this work been impressive; the emphasis has been on primary production, not postharvest and marketing education, where the economic payoff for the farmer is higher. To do better, the government could encourage and enable industry to participate in extension services.

9. Establish world-class food and agricultural universities.

India cannot be a global powerhouse in agriculture if it is does not build its own distinctive research and technology expertise. Right now, it ranks poorly in terms of both quality and quantity. The Indian Institutes of Technology (IITs) have shown how transformational great education can be to a given sector. It is well past time for a network of Indian Institutes of Agriculture & Technology (IIATs) to try to do the same for the industry that employs more of India's citizens than any other. The task of the IIATs would be to create a generation of agriculture and food experts who focus on specific technologies and of entrepreneurs to commercialize them. At least one of these new IIATs should be in the east, an area that is underserved.

10. Finance agribusiness investment funds.
The agricultural sector needs entrepreneurs, and entrepreneurs need capital. Central and state governments should contribute 50 percent to an agribusiness investment fund, with private players supplying the rest. The fund, $100 million to start, should be professionally managed and support thirty to forty projects. Projects should be focused on the cultivation of high-value crops, new technologies, and commercialization of India-specific farm equipment.

This ten-point program is ambitious but not ridiculous. It is based on established strengths and does not propose anything revolutionary. India needs to recognize the business acumen of its farmers and then empower them to make the right choices. There is no dearth of talent, whether it's the Punjabi farmer who designed his own potato-harvesting machine or the Tamil Nadu exporter who set up a best-in-class banana cultivation ecosystem.

In a larger sense, we believe that India must consolidate its numerous programs and plans into a more systematic and mission-oriented approach. The Green Revolution of the twentieth century boosted yields through better techniques and technology; this "agricultural renewal revolution" can help India to take the next step toward a wider prosperity.

The real transformation needed is in our mind-set. In our imagination, we dream of a prosperous and peaceful India—and that dream lives in its villages.

a roadmap for energy security
Anil Agarwal

Kalahandi district in Odisha was once a proud part of the ancient Tel River civilization famed for its gemstones—including diamonds, rubies, sapphires, and topaz—and rich cultural life. Today it is known mostly for its extreme poverty, severe unemployment, malnutrition, and lack of basic health care. In the course of my travels in building Vedanta, I have encountered this paradox often. In district after district, I find that India's poorest, most marginalized inhabitants live atop our country's richest lands. The Kalahandi paradox is characteristic of India as a whole. Our nation has been blessed with enormous mineral wealth—and yet India runs a trade deficit of $200 billion year, much of it due to our imports of energy and minerals such as oil, coal, bauxite, gold, and rock phosphate.

> In district after district, I find that India's poorest, most marginalized inhabitants live atop our country's richest lands.

When I reimagine India, I see a nation that produces 50 percent of the oil it consumes, and 100 percent of many other minerals and raw materials, including liquefied natural gas (LNG), coal, rock phosphate, and gold. That vision is no fantasy; it is attainable within the next ten years through proper exploration and sustainable production. India's geology offers a remarkable resource bounty—comparable to that of Australia and South Africa and the nations of South America. Our bor-

Anil Agarwal is executive chairman of Vedanta Resources PLC.

ders encompass lands bearing twenty thousand known mineral deposits and recoverable resources of more than sixty minerals. Even with the very limited exploration that we have undertaken so far, India boasts the world's third-largest deposits of thermal coal, fourth-largest deposits of iron ore, and fifth-largest deposits of bauxite. My view is that we have discovered only a small fraction of our resource potential.

Why does so much natural wealth remain hidden? Consider the problems bedeviling the oil and gas sectors, where exploration has come to a halt over the last five years due to administrative and regulatory challenges. India has explored only 22 percent of known sedimentary areas, neglecting a huge opportunity to increase domestic energy production. Explorations by Cairn India in Rajasthan resulted in India's richest onshore discovery in twenty years. Today, Cairn India accounts for 20 percent of the country's total crude oil production. India has only a handful of oil and gas companies; we need fifteen to twenty to develop a proper exploration and production value chain.

For minerals, the problem is much the same. Australia has completed geophysical and geochemical mapping for nearly 100 percent of its landmass. For India, the figure is less than 4 percent. Resource-rich countries such as Australia, Canada, and Chile all experienced significant gains in mining and exploration reserves after adopting more progressive mining policies.

> Australia has completed geophysical and geochemical mapping for nearly 100 percent of its landmass. For India, the figure is less than 4 percent.

The first step toward increased resource production is more and better survey data. India must raise the percentage of land for which we have reliable geochemical and geophysical data from 4 percent to at least 30 percent, focusing on areas with obvious geological potential. Baseline data should be created and collected by the Geological Survey of India in collaboration with private companies; Australia undertook a similar effort successfully in the 1970s with active private sector involvement. If that data were made available to exploration companies, I believe we would see a tenfold increase in investment in exploration. The mining application process must be made more transparent, with strict limits on the length of time for government consideration of applications. In Chile, for example, every mining application is approved or rejected within 120 days of submission; if no action is taken, permission is deemed granted.

India must also improve mineral security. Coal blocks and gold mines should be auctioned in a transparent way that minimizes impact on existing employees. Both public and private sectors should be allowed to bid to ensure competition, a level playing field, and the best financial outcome.

A planned approach to exploration and mining could unlock potential in other areas of India's economy. If we can cut our import bill by $150 billion by 2020 compared to the business-as-usual scenario, we would free up capital for new investments. New oil and gas revenues could bring as much a $75 billion a year in new revenue for India's treasury—money that could be used to increase spending on essential social programs and eradicate poverty, ill health, malnutrition, and illiteracy.

It is imperative that we develop our resources in a way that protects both the environment and the communities that sit atop these minerals. I believe that can be done. The world is fast developing ways not just to protect but also to enhance the lands while they are mined. In Sanquelim, a town in northern Goa, Sesa Goa Ltd., a Vedanta company, has undertaken a mine reclamation project that is considered one of the best in the world. In this once-barren mine, we have developed a flourishing fruit orchard and a spice and cashew plantation. There is a medicinal and aromatic garden to improve the biodiversity of the area. All these plantations are irrigated with rainwater harvested in the exhausted mining pit, which itself has been converted into a flourishing aquaculture pond in collaboration with the National Institute of Oceanography.

There has to be fair distribution of costs and benefits of development among the local community, the government, and the private sector. A fair distribution would make a serious positive impact on the prosperity of communities. Creative solutions must be explored. Perhaps royalties that now go to the national treasury might be shared directly with the local communities.

In developing a sensible framework for resource exploration and extraction, India has a long way to go. But in the Kalahandi district, at least, I see signs of change. We made the first and only industrial investment in the region, setting up an alumina refinery in Lanjigarh, which now employs, directly or indirectly, more than seven thousand people. We partnered with the community to establish hospitals, the area's first English medium secondary school, health-care camps, midday meals, and child-care centers. These are small steps; much more must be done to restore Kalahandi to its rightful status as one of India's most developed areas. But they are a start.

I believe we can achieve energy and mineral security in India in a sustainable and equitable way. The opportunity is knocking. It is time to seize our moment.

day of the locust
Ramachandra Guha

In September 2012, the environmental community worldwide (but especially in the United States) marked the fiftieth anniversary of the publication of Rachel Carson's *Silent Spring.* It was the first book to highlight the threats to human health and natural systems posed by unregulated economic growth—and it did so in such a compelling way that it sparked a major popular movement across Europe and North America.

In March 2013, the environmental community worldwide (but especially in India) marked the thirty-ninth anniversary of the birth of the Chipko Andolan, a movement of Himalayan peasants against the clear-cutting of forests by timber contractors. Chipko was representative of a wide spectrum of natural resource conflicts in the 1970s and 1980s—conflicts over forests, fish, and pasture; conflicts about the siting of large dams; conflicts about the social and environmental effects of open-cast mining.

In the West, the environmental movement stemmed from a desire to protect endangered animal species and natural habitats. In India, however, it arose out of the imperative of human survival. This was an environmentalism of the poor, which sought to promote social justice with sustainability. It argued that present patterns of resource use hurt local communities *and* the natural environment. Thus peasants saw their forests being diverted by the state for commercial exploitation; pastoralists

258

saw their grazing grounds taken over by factories and engineering colleges; tribals lost their lands and homes to hydroelectric projects; artisanal fisherfolk were squeezed out by large trawlers.

Silent Spring was followed by such influential books as E. F. Schumacher's *Small Is Beautiful*; Chipko was followed by other articulations of the environmentalism of the poor, such as Chico Mendes's rubber tappers' movement in Brazil and Wangari Maathai's tree-planting campaigns in eastern Africa. These books and struggles spawned a wider debate on the meanings and dimensions of what was now being called "sustainable development."

In *Silent Spring*, Rachel Carson identified two reasons for the lack of attention to environmental abuse. "This is an era of specialists," she wrote, "each of whom sees his own problem and is unaware of or intolerant of the larger frame into which it fits. It is also an era dominated by industry, in which the right to make a dollar at whatever cost is seldom challenged." Carson (and Chipko) offered the integrative science of ecology as a corrective to specialized approaches, while outlining the costs to ordinary people of the state always privileging the demands of industry.

Back in the 1970s, when the state occupied the commanding heights of India's economy, and the nation was closely allied to the Soviet Union, critics dismissed the activists of Chipko and other such movements as agents of Western imperialism who wished to keep India backward. Slowly, however, the sheer persistence of these protests forced some concessions. In 1980, the central government established a Department of Environment, which became a full-fledged ministry a few years later. The state enacted laws to control pollution and to protect natural forests. There was even talk of restoring community systems of water and forest management.

Through hard, even heroic, work, the Indian environmental movement had brought about a (modest) greening of public policy. Pressures from popular agitations such as the Chipko Andolan had made the nation's forest policies more sensitive to local communities and to ecological diversity. A movement led by a professor-priest in Varanasi had committed the government to a Ganga Action Plan, which aimed to clean the polluted holy river as a prelude to the restoration of other water bodies. The scientific and social critiques of large hydroelectric power projects had compelled a closer look at decentralized and nondestructive alternatives for water management.

Meanwhile, the environmentalism of the poor began to enter school and college pedagogy. Textbooks now mentioned Chipko as well as the Narmada Bachao Andolan, the likewise nonviolent, Gandhi-inspired struggle against large dams in central India that were displacing hundreds of thousands of villagers and submerging massive tracts of superb natural forest. University departments ran courses on environmental sociology and environmental history. Elements of an environmental consciousness, finally, had begun to permeate the middle class.

In 1991 the Indian economy started to liberalize. The dismantling of state controls was in part welcome, for the license-permit-quota raj had stifled innovation and entrepreneurship. In June 1992, exactly a year after the economy began to open up, then finance minister Manmohan Singh gave a speech titled "Environment and the New Economic Policies." Singh urged "objective standards industry-wise for safeguarding the environment, asking industry to certify compliance with these standards, institution of an effective system of verification and industry audit, and heavy penalties for non-compliance with approved environmental standards and norms."

> Over the past two decades, India's lands, forests, rivers, and atmosphere have been subjected to a systematic assault.

Singh also expressed the hope that ending bureaucratic regulation of industry would "set free a substantial amount of scarce administrative resources which can then be deployed in nation-building activities like rural development, education, health and environmental protection." The finance minister ended his lecture by saying that "I for one am convinced that the new economic policies introduced since July 1991 will provide a powerful stimulus to an accelerated drive both for poverty reduction and the protection of our environment."

Singh's optimism has not been justified: Environmental sustainability has become the prime victim of economic liberalization. Over the past two decades, India's lands, forests, rivers, and atmosphere have been subjected to a systematic assault. Time and again, the state has granted clearances for new industries, mines, and townships without any thought for our long-term future as a country and a civilization.

In a densely populated country like India, environmental issues have both an ecological and a human dimension. Programs to clear-cut natural forests and replace them with exotic species deplete the soil even as they deprive peasants of access to fuel, fodder, and artisanal raw material. Mining projects, if not properly regulated or carried out with state-of-the-art technologies, ravage hillsides and pollute rivers used by villagers downstream. In this sense, in India environmental stewardship is not a luxury but the very basis of human (and national) survival.

This was the key insight of the Indian environmental movement of the 1970s and 1980s, which informed both scientific research and public policy. Since economic liberalization, however, environmental safeguards have been systematically dismantled. The Ministry of Environment and Forests has approved destructive projects with abandon. Penalties on errant industries are virtually never enforced. By law, every new project has to have an Environmental Impact Assessment. These, admitted then environment minister Jairam Ramesh in March 2011, are a "bit of a joke," since "under the system we have today, the person who is putting up the project prepares the report."

This undermining of India's natural life-support systems is ignored—indeed, at times encouraged—by both state and central governments. Consider the official hostility to the comprehensive, fact-filled, and carefully written report on the Western Ghats, a natural treasure more precious even than the Himalaya, whose forests, waters, and soils nourish the livelihoods of several hundred million Indians.

The report was submitted to the government in August 2011 by a team of experts led by the world-famous ecologist Madhav Gadgil, urging a judicious balance of development and conservation, whereby local communities as well as scientific experts would be consulted on mining, tourism, and energy generation projects. However, its recommendations do not sit easily with those who would auction our natural resources to the highest bidder or the entrepreneur with the best political connections. Chief ministers from many states have condemned the report without reading it. The union minister of the environment has refused to meet the distinguished authors of a report her own ministry commissioned.

Once, the mainstream media (in English and Indian languages) played a catalytic role in promoting environmental awareness. Through the 1970s and 1980s, journalists including Anil Agarwal, Bharat Dogra, Kalpana Sharma, Darryl D'Monte, Usha Rai, Shekhar Pathak, and Nagesh Hegde wrote extensively on issues such as deforestation, species loss, water abuse, and sustainable energy policies. But when economic growth began to accelerate in the 1990s, an antienvironmental backlash picked up. Influential columnists began to demonize people such as Medha Patkar, leader of the Narmada movement. They accused her of being an old-fashioned leftist who wished to keep India backward. Environmentalists were now portrayed as party poopers, as spoilers who did not want India to join the ranks of the Great Powers of the world. In a single generation, environmentalists had gone from being seen as capitalist cronies to being damned as Socialist stooges. Many newspapers now laid off their environment correspondents or perhaps sent them to cover the stock market instead.

Environmentalists were attacked because, with the dismantling of state controls, only they asked the hard questions: Where would new factories find the water or land they needed? What would be the consequences for air quality, the state of the forests, and the livelihood of the people if a new mine were built? Was the high (and seismically fragile) Himalaya the right place for large hydroelectric power projects? Was a system in which the Environmental Impact Assessment was written by the promoter himself something a democracy should tolerate? Was development under liberalization only going to intensify the disparities between city and countryside? These and other vital questions were brushed off almost as quickly as they were posed.

In 1928, forty-five years before the birth of the Chipko movement, Mahatma Gandhi wrote, "God forbid that India should ever take to industrialization after the manner of the West. The economic imperialism of a single tiny island kingdom [England] is today keeping the world in chains." If India blindly followed the Western model of development, warned Gandhi, it "would strip the world bare like locusts."

Two years earlier, Gandhi had remarked that to "make India like England and America is to find some other races and places of the earth for exploitation." Since the Western nations had already "divided all the known races outside Europe for exploitation and . . . there are no new worlds to discover," he pointedly asked, "what can be the fate of India trying to ape the West?"

The key phrase in Gandhi's remarks is "after the manner of the West." Gandhi did not glorify poverty; he knew the Indian masses needed decent education, dignified employment, secure housing, freedom from want and from disease. Likewise, the best Indian environmentalists— such as the founder of the Chipko movement, Chandi Prasad Bhatt—have been hardheaded realists. They do not ask for a return to the past, but for the nurturing of a society and an economy that meets the demands of the present without imperiling the needs of the future.

As their economies grow, will India and China indeed strip the world bare like locusts?

India, like China, is trying to ape the West, attempting to create a mass consumer society whose members can all drive their own cars, live in their own air-conditioned homes, eat in fancy restaurants, and travel to the ends of the earth for their family holidays. As their economies grow, will India and China indeed strip the world bare like locusts? This is a crucial, if rarely asked, question facing these countries and their peoples today.

There are three environmental challenges posed by the economic rise of India and China. First, at the global level, is the threat of rapid and irreversible climate change due to the accumulation of greenhouse gases. As the early industrializers, the nations of the West were the original culprits; that said, the two Asian giants are rapidly making up for lost time. Second, at the regional or continental level, the rise of India and China will have environmental (and social) impacts beyond their national borders. The West has for some time worked to relocate its dirty industries to the south, passing on the costs to the poor and the powerless. In the same manner, the externalities of Indian and Chinese consumers will be increasingly borne by the people of other lands.

The third challenge is that posed to the environments of these countries themselves. Chinese cities have the highest rates of air pollution in the world. Rivers such as the Ganga and the Yamuna are effectively dead. India and China have also witnessed, in recent years, the large-scale depletion of groundwater aquifers, the loss of biodiversity, the destruction of forests, and the decimation of fish stocks.

There are two standard responses to the environmental crisis in India. One is to hope, or pray, that in time and with greater prosperity we will have the money to clean up. The other is to see ecological degradation as symptomatic of the larger failure of modernity itself. The first response is characteristic of the consuming classes; the second, of the agrarian romantic, who believes that India must live only in its villages, that, indeed, the majority of Indians are happy enough to live there.

Both responses are deeply wrongheaded. Life for the peasantry can be nasty, brutish, and short. Most Indian villagers would cheerfully exchange a mud hut for a solid stone house, well water for clean piped water, kerosene lanterns for steady and bright tube lights, a bicycle for a motorcycle.

The living standards of the majority of Indians can and must be enhanced. At the same time, the living standards of the wealthiest Indians must be moderated. The demands placed on the earth by the poor and excluded are disproportionately low; the demands placed by those with cars and credit cards are excessively high. A rational long-range sustainable strategy of development has to find ways of enhancing the resource access of those at the bottom of the heap while checking the resource demands of those at the top. This strategy must then be broken down into specific sectors—for example, we can design suitable policies for transport, energy, housing, forests, pollution control, water management, and so on.

In the 1980s and 1990s, the finest minds in the environmental movement sought to marry science with sustainability. They worked to design and implement forest, energy, water, and transport policies that would improve economic productivity without causing environmental stress. They acted in the knowledge that, unlike the West, India did not have colonies whose resources it could draw upon in its own industrial revolution.

In the mid-1980s, the government of Karnataka began producing an excellent annual state of the environment report, assembled by the top-ranking biologist Cecil Saldanha and with contributions from leading economists, ecologists, energy scientists, and urban planners. These essays sought to direct the government's policies toward more sustainable channels. Such an effort is inconceivable now, and not just in Karnataka.

A wise and caring political class would have deepened the precocious, farseeing efforts of our environmental scientists. Instead, rational, fact-based scientific research is now treated with contempt by the political class. India's leading journal of opinion, *Economic & Political Weekly*, notes that the Union Environment Ministry has "buckled completely" to corporate and industrial interests. The situation in the states is even worse.

India today is an environmental basket case, marked by polluted skies, dead rivers, falling water tables, ever-increasing amounts of untreated wastes, disappearing forests. Meanwhile, tribal and peasant communities continue to be pushed off their lands through destructive and carelessly conceived projects.

A new Chipko movement is waiting to be born.

culture & soft power

bollywood: inside the dream machine
Jerry Pinto

For centuries, India treated performers with something close to contempt. Actors, singers, and musicians might be revered, even worshipped, but you didn't marry them, you didn't let your sons associate with them, and you certainly didn't let your daughters perform in public. The line between performer and audience was drawn in blood.

Which is why Bollywood was all wrong from the beginning. The Indian film industry as we know it now was brought into existence in the early years of the twentieth century by a Brahmin, a member of the priestly class, who ventured to Germany in 1909 to learn more about motion picture technology. For a Hindu in those days, crossing the seas that surrounded India meant a loss of all the buttresses of Hindu society— caste, kinship, friends, family, and food.

> The father of Indian cinema was inspired by a film on Jesus.

Dhundiraj Govind Phalke didn't seem to care. We know that Phalke, the man now hailed as the father of Indian cinema, was inspired by a film on Jesus; he wondered (perhaps a hangover from being a temple child) whether the new medium could be used to tell stories from Indian mythology. But what drew the young boy from the coast of Maharashtra to cinema is not clear. In that very different age, no one, least of all Maharashtra's Brahmins, saw cinema as an art form.

Perhaps Phalke was driven by the idea of using film to stir up oppo-

Jerry Pinto is a novelist, poet, and journalist whose recent works include Em and the big Hoom *and* Helen: The Life and Times of an H-Bomb.

sition to the British, who were harvesting souls and opium in India. Perhaps he was just fascinated by the technology; he loved getting his hands dirty, another no-no for elites of the time. Or maybe he was a storyteller who recognized the new medium's potential.

Whatever his urges, Phalke (or Dadasaheb, as he came to be known) was uninhibited by the culture of his time. He went abroad to learn how to film. He dirtied his priestly hands with not only technology but also money. So low was acting in the hierarchy of professions in India that when he sought female talent for his films, even the sex workers turned him down; to play the women's parts, Dadasaheb had to train a group of boys.

Phalke's first film, *Raja Harischandra*, recounted the story of a king from Ramayana legend who sacrificed his kingdom for honor. Shot and edited in Bombay and first shown to the public in May 1913 at that city's Coronation Cinema, the forty-minute reel is considered the first movie produced in India. It was an immediate box office smash.

So began what we know as Bollywood—but with an important difference. Today Bollywood means cinema in Hindi. The films Phalke made were silent and so could have any of the twenty-plus languages to which what the British called their Indian territories was heir. To change the language of the film, all one had to do was swap in new intertitles.

The advent of talkies changed all that. But there was no reason Hindi movies should have originated from Bombay. The city by the sea was home to three languages: Marathi, Gujarati, and English. As far back as the 1850s, signs for the city's monumental Victoria Terminus were created only in English and Gujarati. Those were the languages of commerce, and the men who spoke them were the ones who rode on trains.

But Bombay has always had a knack for keeping one eye on the West and the other on India's hinterland. One can imagine the Gujarati-speaking financiers, seeking a new industry to parlay profits earned in textiles and shipping, peering over a map of India, marking out a vast swath of land from the northern state of Kashmir through to the heartland of the Central Provinces. It would have been easier to make films in

Gujarati or Marathi, but either language would have limited the market to a single state. Shooting films in Hindi, on the other hand, opened a huge market sure to bring in the punters.

But an art form aspiring to be Pan-Indian would have to appeal to a daunting variety of people and cultures. It would need a fight for the young men, a romantic story for the women, a devotional song for the elderly. Films made for the entire Hindi-speaking market would have to be patriarchal, right wing, jingoistic, and patronizing in their attitudes to anything non-Indian and nonmajoritarian. The Bollywood formula all India has come to know and love—the three-hour, six-song-and-dance-routine extravaganzas that have dominated the Indian imagination since the 1950s—was crafted to please the great unwashed.

> The Bollywood formula all India has come to know and love . . . was crafted to please the great unwashed.

Producers saw no need to conceal their contempt for audiences. They happily boasted to English-language film journalists that they made cinema for "the masses." The great 1970s director Manmohan Desai liked to say that he made films for people who had to sell their blood to see them. (In those days, before hepatitis B and AIDS, the standard fee paid by blood banks in public hospitals matched the price of the cheapest cinema ticket.)

Today, as India emerges as a superpower, those of us who think of ourselves as part of India's middle class feel free to confess that we too have always loved Bollywood—the over-the-top sentimentality, the florid sets, the breast-jiggling dance routines. It makes us feel a little better that Richard Corliss, the *Time* film critic, shares our guilty pleasure. On his blog, Corliss quotes an American film preservationist who admits that "there is something almost intoxicating about movies that are so emotional and unashamed of it."

But an efficiency expert visiting the set of a Hindi film would marvel that anything gets done there. What Bismarck said about the law and sausages is true of Bollywood. On set within one of the cavernous studios our visiting expert will find all manner of glitter and beautiful people. But the light boys and "spot boys" (gofers) have no insurance and the extras get greasy lunches from fly-spotted vessels. The costumes come from a trunk, the toilets are backed up, and the wiring is a swarm of black, red, and yellow snakes. Nothing happens on time.

Even so, Bollywood sets exude self-satisfaction. Even the lowliest extra knows he is living the Indian dream. In the realm of Indian fantasy, only cricket players rank higher.

Popular art emerges from the space between gut and heart. In India, that relationship feels especially visceral. Folk performers at country fairs and religious festivals will repeat a line again and again, milking every last tear and laugh. Even classical musicians feel their way thorough a performance, encouraged by the audience's loudly expressed appreciation or hastened on by its silence. Indians carry these patterns over to film viewing. Spontaneous applause breaks out after a well-delivered line. Showers of small coins patter and tinkle during dance sequences. In smaller towns, audiences harangue the projectionist to show a certain reel again. He always obliges, even if it means skipping other reels to finish on time. In Hindi cinema, audience response often dictates how many minutes a film plays as well as how many days it remains in the theater.

Production can drag on for years, with costs mounting astronomically. Record keeping is spotty. Contracts are largely unheard of. Plagiarism is rampant from stories to storyboards to songs. And most films flop; only 10 percent recover their costs. And yet Bollywood continues to churn out new films year after year, providing jobs for six million people in defiance of economic logic.

The industry is not as large as one might think. Bollywood sells more tickets than Hollywood but it prints fewer films; where an average Hollywood film will have five thousand prints made, a top-line Hindi film will have five hundred to seven hundred and play them until they are almost completely worn out. The annual box office for Bollywood films made in Hindi is thought to be about $1 billion, barely a fifth that taken in by films made in Telugu, a South Indian dialect—though no one can be entirely certain; India's film industry has a history of underreporting income. By even the most conservative estimates, however, Hollywood's worldwide revenues are fifty times those of Bollywood's.

And yet, from a cultural standpoint, Bollywood rules. No one in Delhi hums a film song from any of the other regional cinemas—at least not until some enterprising Bollywood plagiarist nicks it. But contestants on televised regional singing competitions will break into Hindi film songs without a second thought.

The cinema plays ambassador to the language, overcoming the parochialisms to which any diverse nation can be heir. Bollywood's dominance offers an object lesson to all those who wish to legislate language. What the diktats of Delhi could not do when the government tried to impose Hindi as the national language, the seductions of Mumbai, a city that has a small claim on Hindi or any of its variants, have achieved with ease.

Bollywood is not just a film industry. It is all-pervasive: a home-grown, film-a-day dream machine that maintains a pleasant stranglehold on our imaginations. It determines—or at least shapes—how we see ourselves, how we think, how we talk, dream, speak, love, fight. It is the past perfect, the present imperfect, and the future uncertain, our national metaphor, our custom-made synecdoche, the spirit bagasse that fills the empty spaces of our lives.

We succumb to Bollywood's illusions even as we mock them. Not too long ago, a friend who works at a blood bank called in a mild panic. "I have to replace sixteen bottles by five o'clock," she said. It was nearly noon. "Any blood type. Can you come?" I could. I went. I donated my blood, ate my biscuits, drank my coffee, and went home. My friend called the next day. "*Main is khoon ki har ek boond ka keemat chukaaoongi*" (I will pay you back for every last drop of this blood), she said, riffing a Bollywood line with conscious irony. Bollywood offers Indians from all backgrounds a vast trove of shared references, a parallel language that lies just under every tongue, the sound track of our lives.

We borrow from Bollywood whenever—to describe the superficial slights of an ordinary day or to express our deepest anguish. This borrowing has no snob value. It's not like quoting Shakespeare. It is the equivalent of jumping into the village pond; anyone can do it.

We are proud of the way Bollywood has withstood the pressure of Hollywood, proud of its position as a cult cinema in the world. No one understands how Mumbai's film industry has managed this feat of cultural defiance. My own guess is India's comparative imperviousness to the charms of American-made blockbusters has something to do with the emotional tonality of cinema. In 2002, when Tarantino's *Reservoir Dogs* was remade as *Kaante*, directed by Sanjay Gupta, the thieves were given clear motives to make sense of their desire to participate in a heist. That made them moral players rather than just men who want more money. For Indian viewers, exposition is important in an old-fashioned way.

> Our movies share the ethos of Elizabethan plays. . . . They are clear about moral values: Even if the hero is a lovable crook, he goes to jail, cleans up his act, earns his redemption, touches his mother's feet, and looks forward to a blameless future.

Most Indian male stars cry unashamedly on screen; they cry most often when their mothers have had opportunity to express disappointment with them. Our movies, almost since Phalke's day, have shared the ethos of Elizabethan plays. There is a little bit of everything. They are clear about moral values: Even if the hero is a lovable crook, he goes to jail, cleans up his act, earns his redemption, touches his mother's feet, and looks forward to a blameless future. Bollywood's most successful films are patriarchal in the extreme. Women are rarely shown having careers outside the home. "In my entire career," says actor Sharmila Tagore, whose career spanned several decades, "I played a working woman twice: as a singer in one film and a doctor in another. That was because I was the heroine. A working woman was always a danger to society because she was a danger to marriage."

Bollywood taught ordinary Indians what the rich wore and how they dressed. North India is filled with houses that look like they belong on the sets of a Bollywood movie: the sweeping staircase that leads from a barnlike first floor to bedrooms on the second floor; the huge chandelier and grand driveway, even if there isn't really space inside for the former or outside for the latter. Bollywood took us abroad when foreign travel was an impossible dream for the Indian middle class. Bollywood offered romance in Paris, honeymoons in Switzerland, love affairs in Tokyo.

But popular culture remains popular only as long as it tells the stories its viewers need. There is reason to fear Bollywood may not remain the all-inclusive, all-singing, all-dancing party catered for the masses and still able to bring divas onto the floor. New films are shorter—more urban and urbane. The songs the hero and heroine once sang to each other are now part of the background score.

Some blame the nonresident Indian market, estimated to take in three times the revenue of the domestic market—not because overseas Indians buy more tickets but because they pay higher prices in dollars, pounds, and euros. Others blame the fact that the new generation of filmmakers, who speak English on the set and then go home to watch foreign films on DVD, wants to do things its own way.

As Bollywood grows slicker, the audience seems to be losing purchase. The elegant expressiveness of Urdu-inflected Hindi—in which love was declared—is losing ground to the crispness of English. The melodrama is often edited out.

The old line between performer and audience, once drawn in blood, is now drawn on class lines. On one side is the India that travels abroad, wears designer clothes, and trades real estate tips about Knightsbridge and Manhattan. On the other is the India that still watches cinema under the stars and in tents and cowsheds. If Bollywood loses touch with this other India, neither state subsidy nor nostalgia can revive it.

Or is the real threat something new? Every year, I ask students in the media class I teach how they like to relax. For twenty years, the majority said that they go to Bollywood movies. In the last two years, however, that has changed. Now it's Facebook (which allows you to generate content, not just consume it) and Twitter (which allows you to have your own followers, not just be a fan). Young Indians have taken a huge leap over books and movies to mobile phones.

But as we like to say in India, a dead elephant will still get you a hundred thousand rupees. Bollywood has a history of being able to pull itself out of ugly quagmires. It survived the ignoble 1980s and the onslaught of television and one-day cricket matches. The bound script, which was unknown to Bollywood since dialogue was often written on the set, is now the starting point of many movies. Responsible money is moving in. And at the end of the day, there isn't a bigger fame game in India.

cricket superpower
Harsha Bhogle

Cricket was first played on Indian soil in 1721 by British sailors near Cambay, a port city in what is now the state of Gujarat. In his *Compendious History of the Indian Wars*, published in 1737, Lt. Clement Downing of the British East India Company records that while anchored off Cambay, company officials and the fleet's crew "every day diverted ourfelves with playing at Cricket, and other Exercifes"—to the great amusement of local "*Culeys.*"

Indians remained spectators of the "gentlemen's game" for another century as Britain absorbed the subcontinent into its empire and whites-only cricket clubs sprang up in Calcutta, Bombay, Delhi, Poona, and Madras. The first Indians to take up the game were Parsis, wealthy and well-educated descendants of Zoroastrian exiles from Persia. In Bombay, Parsi sons took interest in the British pastime in the 1830s. In 1848, a group of leading families bankrolled the establishment of Bombay's Oriental Cricket Club. The city's Hindu elites formed a rival cricket club, the Hindu Gymkhana, in 1866. Muslims opened their cricket club in 1886. Thus, in India, religion and cricket have been mixed up from the beginning.

Cynics say the Parsis took up the game out of snobbery and a desire to ingratiate themselves with their colonial overlords. Hindus, no doubt, played to show they were just as good as the Parsis. And of course Muslims couldn't stand to be outdone by the Hindus. Still, there's no denying that there was something about the game itself. Some say cricket ap-

Harsha Bhogle is an Indian cricket commentator and journalist.

pealed to Indians because its leisurely pace—in classic test cricket, games can drag on for four or five days and often end in a draw—matched the tempo of Indian life. Others credit the game's complexity, myriad rituals, and arcane vocabulary. But maybe it was simpler than that: Cricket's great charm is that the only things you really need to play it are a plank of wood, some sort of ball, and time.

Whatever the reason for its appeal, by 1890, when Lord George R. C. Harris—himself a former captain of the British cricket team and prominent member of London's storied Marylebone Cricket Club—arrived in Bombay to take up his duties as governor, the city was crawling with cricket clubs. Each weekend the *maidan* near the ramparts of the demolished Bombay fort roared to the cheers of crowds gathered to watch the matches. So great was the clamor from Bombay residents for space to practice and play that Harris reluctantly agreed to cede large chunks of seafront real estate for gymkhanas for each of Bombay's three main religious communities.

Race and religion continued to shape Indian cricket for the next half century. The first match between Indians and the British took place in 1877, when the Zoroastrian Cricket Club played the Bombay Gymkhana in a two-day test. The Parsis lost, but twelve years later they were strong enough to defeat a British cricket team sent to tour the subcontinent. Harris instituted an annual Presidency Match between Europeans and Parsis. Soon Hindus, too, had a yearly cricket challenge with the Europeans. When the Hindu team vanquished the British in an epic test at the Bombay Gymkhana in 1906, their victory was celebrated throughout the subcontinent. In 1907, European, Parsi, and Hindu cricket teams were organized into a combined Triangular Tournament, which quickly emerged as the subcontinent's premier sporting event. A Muslim team was added in 1911 to make the contest a Quadrangular.

Among Hindu cricketers, merit clashed with caste. Palwankar Baloo, a left-handed slow bowler some have hailed as the first great Indian cricketer, was a Chamaar belonging to an "untouchable" caste near the bottom of the Hindu social hierarchy. He learned to bowl as a groundskeeper at the Parsi gymkhana in Poona and later was poached by that city's European cricket club, whose members helped him hone his bowling skills. As word of his skill spread, soon Palwankar was bowling regularly to European cricketers. He moved to Bombay and was quickly recruited to play for the Hindu Gymkhana. He and his younger brother Shivram played a key role in the Hindu team's 1906 victory over Europeans of the Bombay Gymkhana. But for years, Hindu teammates who welcomed the Palwankar brothers' talents on the pitch refused their company beyond it, declining to dine with them and even insisting that during breaks in matches the brothers take tea outside the cricket pavilion using disposable earthen mugs.

Gradually, the old prejudices gave way. In 1923, the youngest Palwankar brother, Vithal, a formidable batsman, was officially appointed captain of the Hindu team for the annual Quadrangle. The first Pan-India teams were dispatched to play informal matches in England. In 1926, India was invited to join the Imperial Cricket Council, and in 1932 an all-Indian team captained by CK Nayudu, a commoner, made its debut against England in an officially recognized Test match.

Cricket, by then, had begun to spread across the subcontinent, with clubs for Indians multiplying in Madras, Mysore, Lucknow, and Lahore. The game attracted the interest of many of India's maharajas, and Kumar Shri Ranjitsinhji, a dashing royal from Nawanagar, played briefly for Cambridge University and the English national team.

Throughout the 1930s and '40s, a rising generation of nationalist politicians—among them many prominent Hindus—condemned the habit of organizing cricket clubs on religious lines. Many decried the Bombay Quadrangular on the grounds that it fanned communal rivalries at a time when Indians of all faiths should band together in opposition to British rule. In 1934, the maharaja of Patiala inaugurated a regional contest to rival the Bombay tournament. Teams were organized by province, not religion. The Ranji Trophy, named for Ranjitsinhji, gained steadily in popularity and helped carry knowledge of cricket to small towns and villages. In 1940, Mahatma Gandhi himself condemned the Bombay tournament, forcing the Hindu Gymkhana to temporarily withdraw. After independence and the wrenching partition of Pakistan, events pitting

Hindus against Muslims fell out of favor, and in 1946, the tournament was banned.

But India's love affair with cricket itself would only grow more passionate. In the wake of independence, Indian cricket has evolved from being a vehicle for competition among different religions into a kind of national religion all its own. More than any other institution, save perhaps the army, cricket has become India's great social leveler.

> Indian cricket has evolved from being a vehicle for competition among different religions into a kind of national religion all its own.

People of all faiths, including Sikhs and Christians, have played for India's national teams. There have been many Muslim captains, such as Tiger Pataudi and Mohammad Azharuddin. Today Virender Sehwag, a Jat from Delhi, is loved in Kolkata, while Mahendra Singh Dhoni, a native of Ranchi, has been embraced with great passion by residents of Chennai, and Sachin Tendulkar is revered throughout the nation in a way that knows no geographical or cultural boundaries.

Our teams have included players from small towns as well as big cities. India's 2007 world championship team, for example, drew its captain from Ranchi, its best player from Chandigarh, and key bowlers came from Kerala, Uttar Pradesh, Vadodara, and Jalandhar. Television and the Internet have accelerated the sport's openness, allowing even small-town boys access to video of matches and expert commentary explaining the nuances of the game. And boys from rural India enjoy some critical advantages over their urban cousins: open space, ample free time, and a hunger to succeed.

Over the years, cricket has come to unite our diverse nation in ways that no other endeavor can. Indians of all faiths cheered in the 1950s, when the national cricket team won its first series in Test cricket against Pakistan, then again in the 1960s, when India beat New Zealand, the West Indians, and England all on their home pitches. Our first truly global victory came in 1983, when India's team, led by Kapil Dev, swept the Cricket World Cup in England. That victory was unexpected partly because England, the host, had changed the rules of play, moving from pure test cricket to a 60-over format designed to wind up a match in a single day. India had resisted the faster format, but after 1983, we embraced it. When India and Pakistan cohosted the next World Cup in 1987, it was shortened farther to 50 overs.

Economic reform brought further change to Indian cricket. After 1991, India's protected economy was open to multinationals, with big marketing budgets and a great hunger for the kind of advertising vehicle that could help them reach hundreds of millions of young consumers. Prior to reforms, the Board of Control for Cricket in India (BCCI) had had to pay the state broadcaster to telecast cricket matches. Suddenly, privatized networks were willing to shell out hundreds of millions for broadcast rights. As the money poured in, Indian cricket metamorphosed from a simple game with a ball and stick into very serious business.

But the blockbuster change was still to come. The innovation that has done the most to secure cricket's hold on the hearts and minds of millions of young Indian fans wasn't an Indian idea at all. England pioneered the use of 20-over format, allowing completion of a single match in under three hours. In fact, when the International Cricket Club voted to adopt the T20 format for the 2007 World Cup in Johannesburg, India was the only country to vote against the change.

> More than any other institution, save perhaps the army, cricket has become India's great social leveler.

Then came India's dramatic victory over Pakistan in the first T20 World Cup. The nation was transfixed. Immediately it dawned on India's cricket promoters that in an era of instant gratification and tiny attention spans, T20 was the perfect answer. This wasn't your father's cricket; it was every bit as exciting as soccer. What other sport could fill stadiums eight times in seven weeks?

The new format catalyzed the formation of the Indian Premier League (IPL), whose founder and first commissioner lost no time in bringing in big-time corporate investors, Bollywood glitz, and American sports-marketing savvy. Lalit Modi's genius was recognizing that what Indian cricket needed was a league of competing city teams—much like professional basketball, football, and baseball in the United States. It wasn't enough for cricket to be "organized," it had to be *promoted*—complete with fireworks, celebrity owners, and scantily clad cheerleaders.

The result was a monsoon of money.

Today the BCCI commands $1.6 billion over ten years for broadcast rights for the IPL. City-based IPL franchises—a notion that had been unheard of in cricket—now sell for hundreds of millions. And all that cash means bigger salaries for players. Overnight, an Indian cricket player who might have earned a maximum of $30,000 for the year if his team won the domestic league and captured the Ranji Trophy, could earn anywhere from $200,000 to more than $1 million for participating in an IPL tournament that wrapped up in just six weeks. For that kind of money, promoters could attract talent not just from India but from anywhere in the world. By IPL's second year, two English players, Andrew Flintoff, playing for Chennai, and Kevin Pietersen, playing for Bangalore, were earning $250,000 per week—more than some of Europe's biggest soccer stars. Cricket teams in Australia, which has also embraced the T20 format, must abide by a $1 million annual spending cap. In India, the cap is $12.5 million—so Australia's Glenn Maxwell was more than happy to turn up to play for Mumbai's IPL franchise, where he alone raked in $1 million, more money than all the players on his Australian franchise combined.

There is an element of pride also in the way India dictates to the rest of the world in cricketing matters. The Indian fan is today the most important entity in world cricket. He (and increasingly she) drives the sport globally. India gets what it wants in world cricket because people flock to the stadiums to watch a game and millions watch it on television. And while players from across the world come and play in the IPL, the BCCI does not allow Indian players to play T20 cricket in domestic leagues overseas. In cricket, as in no other field of endeavor, India is the world leader. It may have taken us

> Today India is to cricket as America is to geopolitics: the undisputed global superpower.

three centuries, but Indian cricket fans have gone from Culeys to rulers. Today India is to cricket as America is to geopolitics: the undisputed global superpower.

But the extraordinary influx of money has left cricket vulnerable to greed and corruption—as the recent wave of match-fixing allegations attests. The IPL's sixth season in 2013 was marred by police investigations which led to accusations that players in the multimillion league had tried to squeeze even more money out of the game by fixing matches. Police charged, among other things, that some players used face towels to communicate with bookies, and that not just players but also some team owners and cricket officials were deeply involved. Happily, India's national team responded to this sudden loss of confidence by winning cricket's eight-nation mini world cup, the Champions Trophy in England in June, which immediately followed the close of the IPL season. Even so, the implications of the fixing scandal are clear: cricket, now one of India's largest consumer products, is too big and too rich to be governed by well-meaning amateurs. We need professional managers, rigorous corporate-style governance, and greater transparency.

Above all, Indian cricket must continue to produce competitive teams across all the various formats. Cricket is unique in that it is the only sport played at this scale across different formats. Conditions matter more they do in any other team sport, and home and away are really that. With the resources available, India really has to be number one. India has often achieved the zenith and then slipped. In cricket, we can stand fast. We have come a long way from Cambay.

rediscovering the core
Mallika Sarabhai

In 1997 my mother, Mrinalini Sarabhai, and I found ourselves in the delightful position of being granted honorary doctor of letters degrees by the University of East Anglia. It was the first time the university had ever conferred such degrees on mother and daughter in the same year. As we waited in the dean's office for the ceremony to begin, an older gentleman with a bushy beard sat facing us. "Are you from India?" he asked. "Yes," said my mother. "We are dancers." The man's eyes brightened. "Ah, Indian dance," he exclaimed. "I will never forget the performance of the young lady I saw in London, oh, it must have been 1949—at the Piccadilly Theatre. Even today, if I close my eyes, I can see her like a vision. If only I could remember her name . . ." The dancer he remembered was my mother on her maiden classical tour of Britain and Europe. The gentleman, we soon discovered, was the celebrated British novelist John Fowles.

Indian dance traveled to the West long before Fowles saw my mother perform at the Piccadilly. The Bengali dancer Uday Shankar blazed the trail, founding Europe's first Indian dance company in Paris in 1931. Shankar, who spent much of his youth in London, had no formal training in Indian classical dance. But he was a gifted performer with a knack for adapting Indian dance forms to Western theatrical techniques. In tours of Europe and America throughout the 1930s, Shankar's *Hindu Ballet* mesmerized audiences with the idea of exotic India. Two decades earlier, the American Ruth St. Denis, who began as a vaudeville "skirt

Mallika Sarabhai is an actress, playwright, social activist, choreographer, and acclaimed Indian classical dancer.

dancer" and later emerged as a pioneer of modern dance, kindled Western fascination with the mystic Orient with
her interpretations of Indian classical dance.
St. Denis's first solo production, *Radha*, staged
at Proctor's Vaudeville House in New York
City in 1905 and featuring exotic costumes
and a trio of extras recruited from the Hindu
community on Coney Island, purported to tell
the story of Krishna and his love for a mortal
maid.

Throughout the 1930s, Uday Shankar's *Hindu Ballet* mesmerized audiences with the idea of exotic India.

But my mother's 1949 tour was the first time truly authentic Indian
classical dance had been performed outside of India. And what an impression she made. In France they called her "the Hindu Atomic Bomb";
in Spain, "the Tempest." Over the next decade, as she toured the world
with her dance company, Darpana, people across Europe, North and
South America, and Asia got their first glimpse of the riches of Indian art.

The magic of those performances lingered for decades. In 1994,
when I myself performed in Central America, part of a tour sponsored
by the Indian Council of Cultural Relations, I encountered many people who vividly remembered my mother. In Lima, Peru, we stayed in a
cavernous residence belonging to the Indian embassy. Civil war raged
and the sol seemed in freefall against the U.S. dollar. Just before our first
performance, an elderly couple asked to see me outside the green room.
They had brought with them a record that had been produced for my
mother's tour in '49, bearing the distinctive flourish of her signature on
the jacket. Was I related to her? When I said I was her daughter, they
grasped my hands and held them, their eyes wet, and told me they had
never experienced such beauty as her performance.

Throughout that tour, I had many similar experiences. In Nicaragua,
where the Sandinistas had agreed not to bomb cultural institutions in
their uprising against the government, I performed at the Rubén Darío
Theater. An old gentleman took me by the hand, walked me to a green
room, opened the lock with great care, and showed me the armchair where
my mother had rested between matinee and evening performances. In

Mexico City, a senior journalist gave me an Aztec earring. "Your mother enchanted me, and I gave her a bangle," she said. "You make her proud, so I have come to give you this."

The West's fascination with Indian culture surged in the 1960s, thanks partly to the brilliance of two Bengali classical musicians: Ali Akbar Khan, the sarod virtuoso, and the sitarist Ravi Shankar. Ravi, Uday's younger brother, had learned to dance and to play various Indian instruments as a teenager while touring with the *Hindu Ballet* at the age of thirteen. He later abandoned the tour to study the sitar in the classical manner under strict tutelage of Allauddin Khan, chief musician to the maharaja of Maihar. Of course, in popularizing Indian classic music in the West, Shankar had a little help from his friends, John, Paul, George, and Ringo. George (Harrison, that is) was so taken with the sitar that in 1966 he traveled to Srinagar to spend six weeks studying with Shankar, after which he famously used the instrument to record "Norwegian Wood." In the last frantic years of the '60s, Shankar toured with the Beatles, recorded with the violinist Yehudi Menuhin, composed a Hollywood movie score, and performed at the Monterey Pop Festival and, in 1969, at Woodstock. Shankar and Akbar opened music schools in California, and both went on to spend most of the rest of their lives in the United States. This was the heyday of flower power, and Indian music seemed a good pathway to nirvana.

In those years, several Indian classical dancers, including Indrani Rehman, Ritha Devi, and Janak Khendry, also made their homes in the West, where they did most of their performing and teaching. The painters P. Mansaram and Natvar Bhavsar created new forms with influences from the United States and Canada. Indian art gained recognition and developed a following. And yet, as the Summer of Love gave way to Altamont and the Manson murders, Indian music, dance, and art suffered from association with the counterculture and lost their hold on the imagination of Western baby boomers. By the late '70s, Indian dance and music appealed mainly to niche audiences—Indophiles already in love with or studying the country, recalcitrant flower children still grooving to ragas, and pot-smoking hippies wearing *Bandini* T-shirts sold for a song on the streets of New York and Los Angeles. In the mainstream of Western consciousness, India languished and came to be perceived once again as the land of the cow and the poor.

Revival has come slowly. One source of support came from the Indian diaspora as it spread to every country of the world. As more and more Indian students took up residence in Western universities, universities began to show more interest in India. In the United States and Europe, many leading universities introduced or expanded Indian or South Asian programs. Western interest in "things Indian" received an enormous boost when the world-famous theater director Peter Brook decided to produce the great Indian epic the Mahabharata for a world audience in late 1984. Brook had had a cult following across the world for more than four decades, and his plays sold out wherever they were produced. He was considered the twentieth century's greatest theater director. For him to take up the most complex of all Indian epics, and to want to produce it for all humanity, with an international cast, brought a frisson of expectation among theater lovers the world over. If Brook was using an Indian epic as his magnum opus, perhaps there was more to India than the cows.

As the Summer of Love gave way to Altamont and the Manson murders, Indian music, dance, and art suffered from association with the counterculture and lost their hold on the imagination of Western baby boomers.

When it opened at the Avignon Festival in July 1985, *The Mahabharata*, with me the only Indian in the cast, became the most talked of production of the decade, if not the century. It pulled in audiences who had no interest in India or its arts. Over the next five years, performing it hundreds of times in countries as diverse as France and Japan, transforming spaces like airport hangars and flower markets into venues for the twelve-hour epic, this production brought a new India to people and created a general interest in India and its arts and literature that no presentation by an Indian had ever before generated. Here was an India that was not exotic but universal—a profound and philosophical narrative that could be the story of all humankind—in a production that preserved essentials of Indian culture without fetishizing it. Audiences were taken into a deeper, truer India. Today, twenty-eight years later, the film and TV versions generate the same excitement and lead people to seek a deeper exploration of India and its arts than the occasional documentary on the drought or plague shown in the West.

The opening of India, post-1990, has seen a tsunami of collaborations, cross-cultural exchanges, tours, workshops, and concerts not only in the performing arts but also in the textile arts, design, sculpture, painting, and installation art. The Indian diaspora has produced world-renowned artists with a more global sensibility, working out of different corners of the world. The diaspora, wealthy and increasingly influential, has also ensured the growth of Bollywood, its music and dancing, with important universities now teaching Bollywood dancing. Major museums regularly present known and unknown arts, with the Musée d'Orsay shining the spotlight, for the first time, on our rich autochthonous culture. Fashion, both haute couture and prêt-à-porter, reflects many Indian strands, and our own homegrown designers are dressing the stars and the commoners alike. The growing clout of the diaspora and the continuing search for the "real and pure" on the part of Western artists, along with the rising economic prowess of India itself, have seen that these trends are financed and kept alive.

Is that enough? In the West, for many hundreds of years, the arts, especially the performing arts, were essentially entertainment. In India, for two thousand years, the arts have been rather a mirror of our lives, a medium to make us more humane, more cultured. The performing arts have spoken of what is central in life: what is good or bad, how to resist the false values of a mirage-creating world, how to remain true. They have, in fact, been the mediating, interpretive side of our philosophy, simplifying, for the uneducated or the uninitiated, the true values and meaning of life. Sculpture, as in the erotic friezes in Khajuraho, teaches us that the body is but a means to a higher self; folk music teaches rites of passage; the lyrics in the songs of dancing speak of the need to let go of the externals and focus on the essential to find the core soul; and ancient wall paintings help us realize that we need to look beyond what our eyes perceive to see the truth.

As Indian art has become a global phenomenon, Indian artists seem to have lost, for the moment, this core aspect of the arts as a socializing influence, as a centering force of life. Indian art, too, has become merely entertainment rather than the language of introspection. My mother, in her work *Memory Is a Ragged Fragment of Eternity* in 1963, attempted to bring back this relevance of art as a reflection of reality by speaking of the scourge of violence against young brides and dowry deaths. At Darpana, we continue to do so. In our arts, we have the possibility of becoming a beacon in a lost and unhappy world. India must find this core again.

making chess india's game
Viswanathan Anand

I was about six when I was first asked why I wanted to play chess. I replied, "to become world chess champion." I had only the vaguest notion of what becoming a world chess champion meant, but it seemed like a cool line. What I did understand was the bemused laughter the line elicited from grown-ups. It was a knowing put-down: "Don't children dream the most impossible, laughable things?" On one occasion I remember being asked, "Do you really think an Indian can be a world champion? Ever?"

When I began playing in chess tournaments in the early 1980s, the holy grail of Indian chess was to become a grandmaster. India had a few international masters, and there had been Indian players who had beaten world champions. But our nation had yet to produce a grandmaster. That wasn't surprising: In those days, it was virtually impossible to find good chess books in India, and few Indian chess players were able to travel beyond India to see firsthand how the game was played.

When I began to compete in international tournaments at the age of fifteen, I and the other Indian chess players competing would put our names on a waiting list with the foreign players. Then, in the few hours before our matches, we'd pore over the tournament bulletins, trying frantically to memorize each and every game that had been played. Fortunately, back then, preparation was easier since the available information was limited.

Viswanathan Anand is India's first chess grandmaster and since 2007 the reigning world chess champion.

When I first visited Moscow in the late 1980s, I was so intimidated. I thought I could be checkmated by every cabdriver. Such was the esteem in which India held the Russian chess school. I remember the trepidation with which I entered Moscow's Central House of Chess, the grand institution that had hosted the likes of Boris Spassky and Mikhail Botvinnik, and is now known as the Botvinnik Central Chess Club in honor of the great patriarch of Soviet chess who dominated the game when I was still in elementary school.

When I first visited Moscow in the late 1980s, I was so intimidated. I thought I could be checkmated by every cabdriver.

In 1991, I had to play Alexey Dreev, who was as young as I was and already one of Russia's strongest players, for a spot in the world championship cycle. The match was held in Chennai at the Trident Hotel. My friend Ferdinand Hellers doubled as my trainer. To prepare, we would work for a few hours, then watch *Terminator* (which seemed always to be playing on the hotel TV when I was about to play a match) and listen to Queen and the Pet Shop Boys on the Walkman. Dreev arrived in Chennai with a six-member delegation, complete with a physical trainer, psychologist, and manager. This was my introduction to the Russians' approach to chess. They had raised chess training to a high science with precise routines and rigorously structured strategies. But perhaps they were thrown off by my playing style, which was intuitive—and perhaps a little influenced by vodka. I ran away with the match early. The result was overwhelmingly in my favor: four wins, five draws, and only one loss—an annihilation. The Russians were stunned. I was pretty surprised myself.

By winning that match, I qualified to play later that year in the Candidates Tournament of the World Chess Championship. By then I had wised up a little. I had found my own Russian trainer, Mikhail Gurevich, who immediately said *nyet!* to the television and the Walkman. He helped me understand that training for chess was serious business. I practiced ten to twelve hours every day and did a great deal of pretournament preparation. The aim was to preserve my intuitive style but strengthen it by equipping me with a broader grasp of openings and defenses, and an ability to pick patterns based on a more detailed knowledge of chess history. In the quarter-final match in Brussels, I faced Anatoly Karpov, a formidable opponent who, throughout the 1980s and early 1990s, vied with Garry Kasparov for the title of world champion. I lost narrowly but emerged confident that with discipline and the right training, I could hold my own against any challenger at chess's highest levels.

I lost to Karpov again in 1998, in a controversial match. I had come to the table immediately after a grueling final with Michael Adams while Karpov was granted a direct seed and arrived well rested. But my training was rewarded in 2000, when I defeated Alexei Shirov at the World Chess Championship in Tehran to become the first Indian ever to win the title.

Since the mid-1990s, technology has taken some of the sheen off the Russian trainers and their methods. Access to information and efficient chess-analyzing software and databases have made chess training very different. The Russian stranglehold on the game was broken; Moscow cabbies are no longer a competitive threat (although many can still expound at length on the nuances of the Chebanenko gambit!). Players have begun to emerge from China, Norway, Armenia, Israel, and elsewhere. However, the concentration, approach, and dedication the Russians bring to their play are still their hallmark.

One of the things I bring to my play is my Indian identity—my ability to shrug off a loss as destiny and hope for a better tomorrow. I am often described as a "natural" or "intuitive" player. I agree there is something to that. I learned to play chess at high speed. At the Mikhail Tal Chess Club in Chennai, where I began playing chess, we used to play "blitz"—the shortest format of chess in which players use a timer and neither is allowed more than five minutes of total playing time. We embraced blitz to make playing fun; the club was crowded, and blitz was the best way to ensure that the max-

> One of the things I bring to my play is my Indian identity—my ability to shrug off a loss as destiny and hope for a better tomorrow.

imum number of players got time on the board. The winner stayed and the loser had to go back in queue. It made the evening more exciting. We all loved it. I learned to play fast, without agonizing about strategy or overanalyzing individual moves. Maybe this is a form of Indian ingenuity: making the most of a situation in which there isn't much structure.

And then there's God. I have what I think is an extremely Indian relationship with God. In 2010, when a volcano prevented us from traveling by air to Sofia for the world championship, we had to hire a minivan and travel forty hours through four countries. I asked God why this volcano had to erupt right then. I did not get an answer. Similarly, in Moscow before the tiebreaker of the world championship in May 2012, I again entreated God: "Just stay on my side of the board." I think this way of dealing with the divine is peculiarly Indian; everyone feels a direct connection, everyone is free to offer a deal, to ask for special favors. We appease God in victory and give him the cold shoulder in disappointment.

> I learned to play fast, without agonizing about strategy or overanalyzing individual moves.

As a young kid sprouting a wispy mustache, I was sometimes dismissed by the Russians as an upstart; I have even been referred to as a "coffeehouse player." For the Soviets, chess was in their DNA. For me, becoming the first Indian world champion brought a great sense of achievement. When I started out, Indians didn't have much interest in chess. No one talked about it. The Indian media didn't cover matches. Certainly, it wasn't the sort of thing anyone thought of pursuing as a career.

Now India seems to spawn new chess academies every day. The game is really taking off. In a sense I feel proud that many young Indians have taken to the game and are doing well in the international arena. In some small way, I believe that I may have made it possible, if only by showing that a "coffeehouse player" from Chennai without a physical trainer or psychological coach could hold his own against competitors from the Russian school.

Whenever I look at how chess has developed over the years in India, there is one project that is closest to my heart: the NIIT MindChampions' Academy, a partnership with one of India's most trusted educational brands, formed to bring children into contact with chess. Since the academy was established in 2002, we have fostered 15,600 chess clubs in schools all over India and now count more than 1.5 million students in the program. We teach in several different languages and use a combination of video tutorials, instructional software, and online matches to help participants learn chess strategies and, perhaps more important, the fundamentals of analysis and logical thinking. Apart from producing domestic champions, the schools have seen a marked increase in academic performance. Chess forces players to think spatially and keep stepping back to look at the big picture. You have to plan strategy, think ahead, engage in abstract reasoning and, at the same time, develop a keen sense of empathy. To succeed in chess, you need to work your way into your opponent's head. Perhaps because of this, many state governments have now partnered with us to introduce the program in their states.

> When I started out, Indians didn't have much interest in chess. . . . Now India seems to spawn new chess academies every day.

My dream is to see chess played in every school in India. The Soviets would include a chessboard along with the bride's wedding trousseau to ensure that the children born of that marriage knew the rules of chess. With time and effort, our more intuitive Indian way of introducing a child to chess and letting his or her mind capture the essence of the game won't do too badly either.

the paradise of the middle class
Manu Joseph

A chartered accountant, a director of strategy, and a product line manager walk into a bar in Delhi.

The friendship of men often has the quality of a feud, and it is in this way that they are friends. The three men graduated from the same college of commerce in Mumbai, where they first met as adolescents. For years they have played tennis in the same clubs in Mumbai—clubs to which their fathers belonged and passed many hours drinking single-malt whiskey and agreeing that India can be saved only by a "benign dictator." The friends are in their mid-thirties now, important men in their fields. They live in different cities but have gathered in Delhi for the wedding reception of a fourth friend, a banker who plays golf for professional reasons and has mastered the art of winning impressively against his white clients and of losing gracefully against his Asian clients.

The Accountant is the kind of man who holds the view that women should not be given important tasks in his profession. The evidence of his own intellect, he presumes, is in his power of memory. He can name the capital city of every nation in the world and deftly engineers conversations to furnish him a chance to mention the capitals of obscure countries. The Director of Strategy's preferred conversational gambit is quoting passages from the *Economist*—just as, in his college days, he reveled in quoting from newspaper editorials. The Line Manager, who works for a sports apparel manufacturer, is a good-natured athletic

Manu Joseph is editor of OPEN *magazine and a columnist for the* International Herald Tribune. *His most recent novel is* The Illicit Happiness of Other People.

man, whose only grievance with the world is that it expects people to be "knowledgeable." He finds it too taxing to read for the sake of acquiring general information.

Every time the friends reunite, they delight in retelling the same anecdotes, chiefly embellished tales of wild mischief perpetrated in their youth. But, inevitably, the conversation now turns to the state of the nation: How corrupt it has become. How inefficient. How dirty and horrible.

And yet it is a nation they adore. For them, India is a paradise. To be acknowledged by the entire nation that they are "big people," the three friends need only emerge each morning from their homes. They live their lives in a comfortable archipelago, ferrying from one sturdy middle-class island to the next, oblivious of the Other India, with its miseries, injustices, and governments of dark rustics. To minister to their daily needs, the friends rely upon drivers, house help, and nannies, whose services can be had for a pittance. Nor need they fear for their safety—at least at the hands of the poor. For citizens of the Other India, police stations and prisons are brutal places; for those suspected of crimes against the nation's "elite," extrajudicial retaliations can be severe.

> They live their lives in a comfortable archipelago, ferrying from one sturdy middle-class island to the next, oblivious of the Other India, with its miseries and injustices.

When the Accountant, the Director of Strategy, the Line Manager, and all the middle-class friends who surround them in the bar were born, the die was cast in their favor. They alone would have the opportunities to realize their talents, to succeed in a manner disproportionate to their gifts, while those from the Other India, the hundreds of millions, scrambled to eat, languished in schools without benches or roofs—and, in many cases, without teachers. In everything they did, the three old friends competed not with India's fierce millions but with just a few thousand.

For the Other Indian to lay a claim to a beautiful life, India offers not a single avenue—unless he or she is deeply corrupt or happens to be a global sports prodigy. The best-paying jobs require a bouquet of qualities and social contacts that can be seeded only at birth. Thus the upper crust of India's job market is a stratum in which places are 100 percent "reserved" for the well-born. Yet among the things that most disgust the three friends about India are the "reservations," or special quotas, in employment and education set aside by the state for what are called the nation's "backward castes."

"Merit," cry India's urban middle classes with righteous indignation. "Why can't India respect merit?" But it was not merit that took the three friends to American colleges in their early twenties after they had graduated from the college of commerce. It was a destiny foreseen and sponsored by their responsible parents.

When the friends arrived in the United States, in the mid-nineties, they were shocked by how insignificant they were. In India, girls had fawned over them and recognized them as good catches—even the portly Director of Strategy. But in America, they were condemned to chastity. All those hot girls barely cognizant of their existence; of course none of three friends had the nerve to go talk to one.

In India, the three friends were among the Chosen—good talkers, good swimmers, and good tennis players. In America, they were suddenly ordinary. Lowly shop attendants addressed them without the slightest sign of reverence. Bus drivers rebuked them for not saying "Thank you." Even waiters intimidated them. The three friends found themselves dragged from the pinnacle of India's social hierarchy to the lowest rung of the Western world's invisible caste system.

And that was when they learned to love India. Sweet home, India, where they were kings. And where they reign as kings today.

In India, the three friends were among the Chosen— good talkers, good swimmers, and good tennis players. In America, they were suddenly ordinary.

Thus we discover a major wellspring of modern Indian nationalism. The cosseted children of India's middle class have contracted a fever—a contagion born of shock that they, justly worshipped at home as kings, should in the West be so diminished. This fever then infects the entire nation, fanning one quest after another: an arsenal of nuclear weapons; the second-rate scientific institutes that have achieved almost nothing; extravagant space missions to the moon, and very soon to Mars; the clamor for election of a ruthless Hindu chauvinist. This last quest is, in essence, the modern fulfillment of their fathers' great fantasy: the "benign dictator," unfettered by the formalities of excess democracy and the absurd distractions of protecting human rights.

This same impulse animates the recent middle-class movement against the nation's political class, which was less a national anticorruption movement than a class war in drag—a conflict pitting the educated urban middle class against the rogues whom India's poor had elected leaders; the English-speaking employees of India's corporates against the usually vernacular politicians; the bribe givers against the bribe takers.

But this fever is mild in comparison to the madness that infected the earlier generation of India's urban middle class—the romance of socialism that spawned the dark ages of planned economy and the suspicion of foreign corporations, which destroyed the great republic for decades and denied India's poor the opportunity to leap beyond their circumstances. That earlier romance was consummated without a trace of irony by the beneficiaries of socialism's extraordinary inequities.

A few female acquaintances now join the three friends. The Accountant poses a question to the Line Manager that involves the word "diaphanous," confident that the Line Manager will not know its meaning. The Accountant lets out a triumphant snicker. The Director of Strategy laughs, too, to confirm that he knows the meaning of the word. The Line Manager finds himself once again on the receiving end of the humiliation that passes for friendly banter. Fortunately for him, their reunion comes to a sudden end. The Director of Strategy spies a pretty woman who had spurned him in college. He walks swiftly, his enormous buttocks bouncing. He heads not toward her but to his wife, whom he hugs and kisses in the hope that the other woman will be seared by the sight.

At other social occasions, the three friends have often sung the common middle-class lament—that India's greatness has been squandered by the Nehru-Gandhi dynasty, which has remained at the helm of the country for decades. How tragic that India's political leadership should be handed down from one generation to the next as if it were some family heirloom. And yet the three friends themselves are beneficiaries of their own families. Their parents invested huge sums to provide them with the unfair advantages that insulate them from the vast majority of boys and girls their own age—not unlike the way the Gandhi dynasty has promoted its own.

They are a part of India's inheritance economy and thus effectively recessionproof. Their lifestyle and spending choices reflect their own professional successes less than their success in cultivating the affections of their parents. In return, their parents exercise an extraordinary level of control over their lives. The Accountant remains in terrified awe of his father, just as he was in college. Should his father call him in the middle of dinner, the Accountant will rise in a half stand. He still thinks of the girl he once dated but had to stop seeing at his father's command.

The bar has filled with happy patrons. Waiters scurry here and there with silver trays. Waiters in India know how to show servility. They cast themselves as shadows because that is what is expected of them. The three friends consider this proper hospitality: The shadow comes with a tray, the master accepts its offering or flicks it away. The West will never understand true hospitality. The indignities of egalitarianism and the rituals of hospitality cannot go hand in hand. In a world that is not feudal, how can there be hospitability? If you want to see the three friends really suffer, you have only to observe them at a good New York hotel. "Where is the service?" The confidence and flamboyance of the hotel staff in New York will be interpreted by our three friends as "too much attitude." There are hierarchies all over the world, but in India they are clearly defined. That is what makes India a middle-class paradise—the clarity of the lines.

But there is trouble in paradise. While two decades of economic reforms have favored the old seasoned, highly educated urban middle classes more than any other class, there are new economic castes today created by real estate booms and the drip-down effect of massive political corruption. Expensive restaurants in India are confusing places. The refined must share the space with the uncouth. Owning a BMW is no longer evidence that one is literate. And the government's modest rural employment program has reduced the pool of cheap factory hands, drivers, and house help, raising the wages demanded by those available for hire. "Lowly" Indians have forgotten their place. Maids talk back. Drivers quit their jobs when spoken to rudely, especially by women.

There are hierarchies all over the world, but in India they are clearly defined. That is what makes India a middle-class paradise—the clarity of the lines.

And a new law passed by the government has breached the greatest fortress of the Indian middle class: schools. The law requires all private schools to reserve seats for students from "economically weaker sections." The parent groups at several schools tried their best to resist, with at least one of them even declaring in writing that they fear their children will be infected by the diseases of the poor. Another concern was that the children of the poor would be constantly reminded of their inferiority—by the comparative shabbiness of their clothes, the poor quality of their footwear, the swarthiness of their skin, or their inability to take gifts to birthday parties. A woman in the bar had a nervous moment when she took her little daughter to a birthday party and the girl asked an impoverished classmate why her mother was dressed "like a servant." Despite the cruelty of such encounters, the fact is that thousands of impoverished children today find themselves in schools they could not have otherwise attended—schools that are helping them make the leap into territory that was once strictly out-of-bounds.

The three friends, with their modest gifts, got through their lives competing against very few to achieve their beautiful lives in India. Their children will not.

But for now the paradise stays. And there is much laughter in the bar.

from statecraft to soulcraft
Vishakha N. Desai

In their all-consuming focus on economic development, are Indians missing the forest for the trees? A hundred years from now, what will Indians see as their unique contribution to the world? A century on, the world won't think much of the "India story" if it is just another saga of economic upsurge, especially if that saga culminates in the civilization's largest tangle of sprawling megacities, environmental degradation, and depletion of water tables across the entire subcontinent.

Can't we imagine another, better legacy?

In searching for a better India a hundred years hence, it helps to look back a hundred years into our past. As the twentieth century dawned with India chafing under British rule, a young Western-educated lawyer named Mohandas Gandhi stepped forward with a powerful new idea about how to liberate India from imperialism. Gandhi's call for nonviolent struggle inspired Indians and non-Indians alike. Drawing as much on indigenous Indian concepts and traditions as on Western intellectual thought, Gandhi's unique approach to fighting for freedom made it possible for oppressed peoples everywhere to demand their rights without demonizing their oppressors. When India gained independence in 1947, the world looked to India—not because it was rich or economically advanced but because of the uniqueness of its message. The world saw India as more than just another emerging market; it expected India to do great things.

In 1913, just as Gandhi was gaining recognition for his ideas, an-

Vishakha N. Desai is president emerita of the Asia Society and special adviser to the president of Columbia University, where she is a professor.

other great Indian thinker, Rabindranath Tagore, won the Nobel Prize for literature. The Nobel selection committee hailed the great Bengali poet, the first non-European ever awarded that honor, as "a new genius to the world." Tagore's message of bringing humanity together, overcoming barriers of chauvinism, jingoism, and cultural ignorance, won him admirers around the world. He celebrated the coexistence of multiple cultures—Hindu, Muslim, and British—championing the notion that India's heterogeneity was essential to the nation's identity and its unique place in the world.

Gandhi and Tagore were Indian thinkers with universal souls. Their ideas inspired, and were inspired by, the world, and were at the same time deeply rooted in the Indian tradition. These great men were open to inspiration from all sources and were passionate about projecting their message beyond India. They foresaw a modern India in a global context—a nation proud of its heritage but not a slave to it, an active member of the community of nations with something important to contribute.

Were Gandhi and Tagore with us today, they would be delighted to see that contemporary India is a flourishing democracy and remains a unified nation. Gandhi, in particular, would take comfort in the knowledge that in this century far fewer Indians suffer from hunger than in the last. But surely he would be dismayed that hundreds of millions of Indians remain illiterate and live without adequate shelter, health care, or access to clean water. He would applaud citizens' protests against government corruption and mistreatment of women. But he would be saddened that his message of nonviolent resistance is often misused in the pursuit of narrow special interests rather than to advance the greater good.

Tagore, meanwhile, might lament that the heterodox, multilayered identity of India is neither nurtured within India nor projected abroad. Both of these great men from India's past might wonder: What does India stand for today?

President Barack Obama posed a similar question at a White House briefing I participated in prior to his 2010 trip. "How does India see itself in the world?" he asked, and "Why does India's vision feel somewhat murky compared to China's?" I replied that Indians and non-Indians have focused on India's recent economic takeoff, which is barely two decades old. In political terms, India remains a young country; its sense of national identity is still evolving. But in historical terms, Indian identity has its roots of cultural traditions and philosophical ideas dating back thousands of years. This rich, multilayered history engenders a strong sense of the Indian self, always defined in relation to the family, community, the larger world, and the cosmos beyond. In today's India, I explained, neither the political nor the educational leadership has made a concerted effort to project an Indian identity combining the richness of its millennial traditions with its maturing political reality and its recent economic progress.

So how can India combine its millennial cultural and philosophical values with its modern political cohesion and contemporary economic success to create a cogent message for itself and the world? If we are to cultivate the Gandhis and Tagores of our own time, we must refocus national priorities on matters ranging from education to cultural infrastructure.

One problem is that in today's India, whether in meetings of the national planning commission or discussions around the family table, education is equated primarily with jobs and material prosperity. India's most promising students are expected to seek degrees in mathematics, science, or commerce. They are rarely encouraged to study history, philosophy, or our remarkable cultural heritage. In fact, recent reports suggest some of India's most prominent universities are closing their philosophy departments. This trend leaves me aghast and should be of deep concern to India's educational leaders. The liberal arts and the humanities should be accorded a place of prominence and prestige in national curricula at all levels, including—indeed, especially—on the campuses of the Indian Institutes of Technology, rather than dismissed as an irrelevant academic backwater upon which we set our weakest students adrift. India cannot hope to fashion a unique modern vision—a vision that combines the material and the spiritual, the rational and the intuitive, the self and the community—without the active engagement of its best and brightest students. We must inspire our sons and daughters to seek a deeper, more rigorous understanding of their extraordinary cultural and intellectual inheritance.

That objective can't be realized without significant changes in government policy and current spending priorities. India, with one of the world's oldest and richest civilizations, devotes barely 0.02 percent of its annual budget to preserving and promoting its culture—a pittance compared to France, Britain, and Japan. While some argue cultural preservation is a luxury developing nations can ill afford, India's budget for culture lags far behind that of China. In 2012, China spent $2.5 billion on cultural services, an increase of 20 percent from the previous year. China's central government allocates 0.125 percent of its annual budget to cultural services, excluding funding for free admission to cultural facilities and spending on digital libraries. Former Chinese president Hu Jintao proclaimed cultural development a top priority and pledged to build one hundred new museums in the coming decade. If India is to take matters of culture as seriously as China, India's government must raise cultural spending to a level at least comparable to that of China, not just for the maintenance of monuments and administration of museums but also to train personnel and produce and distribute educational materials for the nation's schools. The government must also explore innovative methods to support the recent emergence of private museums in India, encouraging public-private partnerships and thereby infusing a new spirit of entrepreneurialism into the cultural realm.

There is an economic dimension to this as well. By increasing its emphasis on culture, India's state and central governments will create new jobs, ranging from museum management to tourism and archaeology. We are finding all sorts of ways that traditional Indian practices of building, healing, and conserving can be applied to modern fields of endeavor as diverse as architecture, public health, and environmental preservation. More important, a stronger cultural infrastructure will foster a renewed sense of Indian identity.

The millennial civilization of India offers many gifts with relevance for our time. In all materially advanced societies, there is a deep yearning to find answers that go beyond creature comforts. The global popularity of yoga, ayurveda, and Indian spirituality suggests that the world is ready to receive a more holistic message from India. What we need now is not so much a romantic re-creation of the past but rather a rigorous study to adapt the best of the old traditions to modern times.

> What we need now is not so much a romantic re-creation of the past but rather a rigorous study to adapt the best of the old traditions to modern times.

Indians are justifiably proud of their economic progress and political resilience. But as Gandhi and Tagore knew so well, economics and politics alone cannot satisfy deeper longings in the human soul. It is time for India to reimagine its identity, rejuvenating its millennial wisdom and combining it with current material development. India can then assume its rightful place among the world's great nations, not simply because of its economic prowess but also by virtue of its vision.

beyond curry
Rohini Dey

Growing up in India, I was determined to save the world.

I still remember the dusty summer afternoon when, as a twelve-year-old, I crossed the street from school to the pristine air-conditioned environs of the UN and World Bank offices in New Delhi—an alien universe—to ask how I could one day get a job there. Incredulity gave way to derision on the faces of officials, who told me to "get a PhD in economics and come back." Which is exactly what I did.

It seems to mystify people that, after struggling to get that PhD and successfully landing my dream World Bank job, I now find myself in my tenth year as a restaurateur. It's a long way from feeding the world to upscale dining.

Why the restaurant business? Not for the glamour; trust me, I don't spend evenings, resplendent in a sari, slinging back martinis or swirling wines with customers. Nor was it for fortune; I did my due diligence on the restaurant business: a 90 percent failure rate, meager profit margins, a dearth of bank financing, daunting labor and capital demands, and myriad legal and health liabilities. And it certainly wasn't for the admiration of family and friends, who were horrified that I would abandon a perfectly respectable "brand-name" career to open a glorified *dhanda* (a favorite Hindi term for disparaging small businesses).

No, what possessed me to launch Vermilion, my Indian-Latin restaurants in Chicago and New York City, was a combination of rage, passion, and the firm conviction that I had discovered an unmet market niche.

Rohini Dey is the owner of Vermilion restaurants in New York and Chicago.

What fueled my rage was the mélange of mediocrity we Indians passed off as our cuisine abroad: the $8.99 all-you-can-eat buffets; the predictable mushy overcooked fare, swimming in oil and nuclear food dyes; the clunky table settings amid faded visuals of camels and the Taj Mahal. I was mortified by the whole pathetic repertoire. None of it bore any resemblance to what we Indians ate at home, on our streets, or in our own restaurants back in India.

As for the passion, I have always been a foodie. As a young professional in the United States with an expense account, I was dismayed to realize that finding an Indian restaurant that escaped the formulaic vibes of Bombay Palace, India House, Jaipur Club, or Royal Taj was nearly impossible.

When non-Indians think of India, what do they imagine? Legions of IT engineers? Call centers? Teeming masses and mystical yogis? It is unlikely they picture a nation with the depth of cuisine that could foster an epicurean culture. Few know of the immersion in fine dining that was my childhood in India. In our family, meals were *meals*—meticulously planned and executed, eaten together, and savored at leisure. As an Air Force brat growing up in twelve different cities around the country and traversing many more in family road trips in our beat-up Standard Herald, I relished street fare from every region: the *chaat* hawkers, *pakora* and *samosa* vendors, kebab corners, frankie stands, and *paratha* gullies of Delhi and Mumbai; *kathi* rolls, *jhal muri*, *kochuri*, fish fry, *ghugni*, *momos* in the avenues of Kolkata; *dosa*, *idli*, *upma*, *biryani* on the roads of Hyderabad and Madras; and, of course, the ubiquitous Indian-Chinese vans doling out steaming soups and chow mein noodles.

Visits to "outside" restaurants were expensive and rare. But even then,

What fueled my rage was the mélange of mediocrity we Indians passed off as our cuisine abroad: the $8.99 all-you-can-eat buffets; the predictable mushy overcooked fare, swimming in oil and nuclear food dyes; the clunky table settings amid faded visuals of camels and the Taj Mahal.

the infrequent trips to Kwality's, Karim's, Nizam's, Trishna, and Swagats or the foray to five-star hotel restaurants were magical and exposed me to new worlds of sensory adventure. At home food was subtle, fresh, and whimsical. My mother loved to experiment. She was as adept at turning out spaghetti, scones, and shepherd's pie as at Bengali fish curries, mutton curry, and *biryani*.

I've now dined on a multitude of cuisines, from the temples of haute Michelin-starred restaurants to street fare the world over, but I have yet to find a cuisine with the range and complexity offered by India. The Mughal-influenced fare from the mountains of Kashmir couldn't be more different from the hot-blooded food of tropical Bengal, or the seafood and vegetarian extravaganzas of Kerala's spice coast from the hearty earthy dishes of Punjab—and that leaves only twenty-four more states, each remarkably distinct!

Ours is one of the earliest cultures and continuous urban civilizations, rooted in the ancient Indus Valley civilization (now in Pakistan). Our food has been influenced by waves of Central Asian, Arab, and Mughal invasions; British and Portuguese occupation; Syrian Christian and Jewish immigration. It is an integral part our social fabric. Our hospitality, festivals, entertainment, family time, and religious rites revolve around meals and food.

Over the last decade, India's fine dining scene has experienced a transformation. India's burgeoning middle class is now as cuisine obsessed as counterparts in the West or Japan. Celebrity chefs jockey for position in India's largest cities; independent restaurateurs and chains compete across the country; and food TV shows, blogs, and magazines all vie for audiences. The tragedy is that, amid the global gastronomic revolution, outside India the stereotypes of Indian food remain: that it is a murky, spicy, mushy, overcooked, low-end cuisine lacking in finesse.

India's burgeoning middle class is now as cuisine obsessed as counterparts in the West or Japan.

Progress has come at an incremental pace, with barely two dozen successful Indian restaurants in metropolitan hubs such as New York,

Hong Kong, Paris, and Tokyo. London is an anomaly because of the close ties between Britain and India; as the *New York Times* has observed, Indian food rescued the British from "bland boiled nursery yuck" by lending it a previously unknown component: flavor.

Indian restaurants rarely feature in top international rankings. In the San Pellegrino Top 100, only Bukhara in Delhi regularly makes the cut. Michelin includes barely a dozen establishments serving Indian fare in its rankings of more than four thousand restaurants, and none rates more than a single star. In the United States, no Indian restaurant or Indian chef has received a James Beard Award. At Western cooking schools, students dedicate two years or more to studying French techniques, while "Asian cuisines"—including Indian—tend to be lumped into one general course.

Granted, these are Western metrics. One can rationalize the near invisibility of Indian cuisine in such rankings by arguing that few food critics outside India can be expected to appreciate the nuances of our cuisine or the vastness of the regional differences within it, or distinguish the superlative from the pedestrian. And there, smug in our parochial supremacy, we could let matters rest—case closed.

Spices from India were the single most important food product of the Middle Ages. Insatiable demand for them drew Portuguese armadas and Spanish treasure fleets, and spawned exploration missions that led to the discovery of the Americas and the New World. And yet while we still produce over 80 percent of the world's spices, the cuisine for which those spices were developed has failed to adapt to our new global age.

Can Indian cuisine ever succeed on a global level? I believe it can—and, indeed, have staked my career and financial solvency on that. But first, India and its chefs must accept the reality of our reputation today and be willing to adapt and evolve. We must rethink efforts to promote Indian cuisine and learn to market India as a preeminent culinary destination. I see no reason Indian cuisine can't achieve the popularity of French, Italian, Spanish, Japanese, Chinese, or Thai food among global diners. And why shouldn't Indian food hold its own against Nordic, Scandinavian, Vietnamese, and Korean, which are all the rage in the West these days?

The twenty-five Michelin Red Guides on restaurant ratings cover at least thirty-five destinations around the world. I've often scorned the guides for their Francophile and Japanese bias and their penchant for rewarding old-style Stockholm syndrome dining: pretentious arenas of exorbitance that turn diners into obsequious captives. But like it or not, the Michelin guides lend a stamp of legitimacy not just to individual restaurants but also to entire cities. That was certainly the case for Tokyo, Kyoto, Osaka, and Kobe, which Michelin has transformed into international gastronomic destinations.

Indians may scoff at the formulaic rigidity of Michelin ratings, safe in our insular cocoon. But if we do, we'll remain irrelevant. Instead, leading restaurateurs, culinary associations, and India's tourism industry could work together to woo the Red Guide to India. Winning over Michelin would put India on the culinary map and lure the tourism that inevitably follows food.

Michelin aside, there is much else India's restaurateurs, their lobbying channels, and indeed the food industry can do to transform our culinary profile. They might join forces with the long-running multi-million-dollar "Incredible India" campaign or partner with key Western culinary institutions (such as the James Beard Foundation or San Pellegrino) to sponsor awards for Indian-influenced restaurants across continents. They also might work more closely with India's tourism ministry to launch road shows, tasting festivals, and a network of celebrity chef exchanges to showcase our cuisine in strategic global cities.

India's vast network of embassies and consulates can assist in this process. The Indian government might sponsor young Indian chefs for on-the-job training in the West to broaden their horizons. India's food industry could develop its own global culinary awards—based on innovation, revenue, or ratings—to encourage restaurateurs to raise their profiles overseas.

Above all, Indian cuisine and all those involved in the food business must learn to embrace change. Indian chefs and restaurateurs—and diners everywhere—could use a jolt of what the economist Joseph Schumpeter called "creative destruction." Only through Darwinian mutation and variation will we survive.

Adaptation for global survival could come in many forms: enhancing the nuances of our spices, not overcooking ingredients past the point of recognition, enhancing presentation beyond brown slop in a dish, and being innovative in the ambience of Indian eateries and formats. We could introduce ambitious ingredients, broaden menu repertoires, and even infuse other global cuisines to create something provocative.

Of course, those who embrace the idea of evolution are easily branded heretics or sellouts; inevitably critics will wail that we risk diluting India's rich culinary legacy. But this is not about dumbing down flavors or restraining the vibrancy of our food. It is about drawing on the best of the traditional and the contemporary. It is about encouraging all involved in Indian food culture to develop a successful translation of our culinary traditions to relay abroad. It is about breaking free from the insular bubble in which we Indians share the glories of Indian cuisine only among ourselves.

fixing the fourth estate
Suhel Seth

India has a vibrant press with a proud history. By many measures, our nation boasts the most robust media industry in the world. India is home to 87,000 privately owned newspapers, which enjoy a combined daily circulation of 370 million—more newspapers in circulation than in any other country. Of the world's top twenty newspapers ranked by 2011 circulation, nine are Indian. The *Times of India* is the world's most widely circulated English-language daily; its circulation of more than four million is twice that of the *Wall Street Journal* and four times that of the *New York Times*. Our two largest Hindi newspapers, the *Dainik Jagran* and the *Dainik Bhaskar*, command an estimated sixteen million and fourteen million readers, respectively. India's broadcast media, monopolized by the state until 1991, now include more than eight hundred privately owned satellite channels, of which more than one hundred specialize in news.

In stark contrast to most Western nations, where the rise of the Internet has undermined the economics of traditional media, in India old and new media alike are booming. Subscriptions and advertising revenue for newspapers and magazines, as well as television viewership, have risen steadily, alongside the vigorous expansion of blogs, web-based news services, and social media.

In the 1940s, Indian-owned newspapers and periodicals played a vital role in our struggle for independence from colonial rule. Many

Suhel Seth is a writer and consultant on marketing and management, and managing partner of Counselage India. His most recent book is Get to the Top: The Ten Rules for Social Success.

newspapers aligned themselves with Mahatma Gandhi's call for freedom and defied the British government of the day. That decision cost many editors and publishers dearly, both in prison terms and monetary penalties, but harsh consequences did not deter them from following their consciences. Again, in 1975, when Indira Gandhi imposed a state of emergency that threatened our democracy, many newspapers fought for that most basic of democratic rights: freedom of expression. Many defied censorship laws by running blank columns on their front pages rather than carry government propaganda or submit their articles to censorship.

Sadly, those brave times are now a distant memory. Over the past two decades, India's press has become entangled in a corrupt nexus of politics and industry. Political pandering and commercial pressures have transformed our once-valiant fourth estate from watchdog for the public interest to lapdog of the rich and powerful.

Just how far India's news media has fallen from its national pedestal was revealed in 2010 when two Indian newsmagazines, *Open* and *Outlook*, published transcripts of recorded telephone conversations that seemed to suggest that some of India's most prominent editors and journalists had acted as lobbyists, wheeling and dealing behind the scenes on behalf of competing corporate and political interests keen on securing lucrative mobile-phone licenses. The alleged target of the recordings was Nira Radia, a high-powered corporate lobbyist who was head of Vaishnavi Communications, a public relations firm representing some of India's largest companies. Between 2008 and 2009, according to the reports, government tax authorities tapped Radia's phones in an effort to find evidence of money laundering and tax evasion. The recordings, excerpts of which were published in *Open* and *Outlook*, suggest what the surveillance effort mainly uncovered was an insidious web of political influence peddling that included some of India's most prominent producers and editors.

The transcripts appear to show several of the nation's most respected journalists offering to write pieces favoring Vaishnavi clients and obsequiously promising to cast them in the best possible light. "What kind of story do you want?" asks one prominent journalist. "It can't seem too slanted, yet it is an ideal opportunity to get all the points across." Asks another: "What should I tell them?" (Full disclosure: I know Radia well and dealt with her frequently when she was at Vaishnavi. Among the recorded conversations published in *Open* was one between Radia and me in which I explained that I would not be writing columns for a while because I was on holiday and joked with her about missing a Michael Jackson concert in London.)

The very abundance of media outlets has created competitive pressures that can make survival dependent on holding on to the advertising business of powerful corporations as well as on pandering to the lowest common denominator in audience taste.

What startled an entire nation was not the cozy relationship among the elite, but rather the cravenness with which media leaders appeared willing to morph into pliant accomplices of the commercial and political powers that be. Worse, many of India's mainstream media outlets refused to cover this burgeoning scandal at the time, and the public had to turn to social media to find out what was happening.

Why did India's fourth estate so undermine the credibility it had taken years to build? Apparently some media owners wanted to travel in the same circles as the industrialists they were meant to cover. The more fundamental cause, however, is that the very abundance of media outlets has created competitive pressures that can make survival dependent on holding on to the advertising business of powerful corporations as well as on pandering to the lowest common denominator in audience taste. In addition, many media companies have significant investments from corporate conglomerates that seem to seek not just financial returns but also influence over coverage of their companies and the issues that are central to their success. With such rampant conflicts of interest, it is little wonder that the integrity of journalism is often compromised.

In India today we have media ownership without accountability; commercial considerations and political ambitions rather than a sense of moral obligation to inform the public drive coverage. How can India's relatively young democracy thrive with a media that has so little anchoring in truth? How can the electorate make informed choices when news is often little more than thinly disguised advertising? Such is the reality of India's media that no one in government—or, for that matter, within media itself—is willing to confront this ghastly reality.

The good news is that the Radia tapes helped the public understand what has happened to the news media. At the same time, competitive pressures are pushing some media outlets to the wall. No market can sustain so many channels even if many are run for motives beyond financial return, so a shakeout and then consolidation are inevitable.

This transformation could not come at a better time. As was demonstrated in the Radia episode, the awakened youth of India are employing social media to hold the old media to account. Social media have also emerged as sources of the development stories that the mainstream media often ignores because it is either too lazy to investigate or too satisfied by the profits that come from less-serious coverage.

The Indian news media must go through a catharsis and question its basic principles, particularly its practices for both gathering and then publishing the news. More emphasis on the craft of real journalism than on craftiness of garnering profits in the short term could help trigger the second coming of Indian media. The first signs of this rebirth are already visible. Two newly launched magazines, *Open* and the *Caravan*, encourage long-form narrative journalism as well as pursuing in-depth reporting on the issues they cover.

In the long run, the true value of any media organization is the trust its customers in particular and also society in general place in it. India's fourth estate may have lost sight of that in the past decade or so, but we have every reason to hope that it can reassume its traditional role in reinforcing India's democracy.

going for olympic gold
Geet Sethi

A few weeks before the 2012 Olympic Games were due to kick off in London, the pistol ace Vijay Kumar, one of India's top shooters, felt unsure about the wooden grip on his Pardini semiautomatic pistol. Had an Indian shooter been caught in a similar situation at a previous Olympics, he might have had to write off his medal dreams. Instead, Kumar was able to call up our private organization, Olympic Gold Quest, and get the funds he needed to buy a new, customized grip. Kumar went on to win a silver medal in the twenty-five-meter rapid-fire competition—one of six medals for India at the London games.

If India is to become a true Olympic power, such private sector support for athletes will be critical. In London, Olympic Gold Quest also secured the services of the renowned coach Charles Atkinson for five-time world women's boxing champion MC Mary Kom; we funded the badminton star Saina Nehwal's stay at a hotel next door to Wembley Stadium, so she could avoid the ninety-minute commute from the Olympic Village. Such assistance may seem trivial, but for athletes competing at the highest level globally, it can mean the difference between winning and losing.

Private efforts alone, however, will not transform India's national sports culture enough to qualify India as a credible Olympic threat. Real change can come only from a unified national push.

India's Olympic record has improved steadily since the Atlanta games

Geet Sethi is an international billiards champion and cofounder of Olympic Gold Quest, a foundation for the promotion of sports in India.

in 1996, where the Bengali tennis star Leander Paes won our nation's first medal, a bronze in singles. India won its first women's medal in 2000, its first individual silver in 2004, and its first individual gold in 2008. India's six medals in London—which included two silver and four bronze—represented a new record for our nation.

And yet, relative to our size, our achievements in London were modest. Out of seventy-nine total medal rankings, India, with the world's second-largest population and tenth-largest economy, ranked fifty-fifth in the International Olympic Committee's official medal table—ahead of Mongolia with five medals, but behind Grenada, Uganda, and Venezuela, each of which won a gold medal. Even North Korea matched our total medal count.

And India's performance in London paled in comparison to that of the United States and China. The United States, with only a third as many people as India, claimed 104 Olympic medals (46 of them gold), while China, with a population roughly the same size as ours, swept 88 medals (38 of them gold).

To many, the notion that India might one day bring home as many medals as the United States or China might seem a fantasy. One in three Indians lives below the poverty line; for hundreds of millions of Indians, the quest is for *roti, kapda, aur makaan* (food, clothing, and shelter)—not Olympic gold. Even for more affluent Indians, athletic accomplishment is rarely a high priority. And democratic India will never embrace the Chinese model of selecting future athletes from infancy and pressing them into rigorous state-funded sports academies.

It's worth asking why a country still struggling to provide adequate nutrition, employment, and health care to such a large swath of its citizens should expend resources on competing in the Olympics. For rich nations like the United States, international sporting contests are an affordable indulgence financed by private sponsors. For an authoritarian nation like China, Olympic success helps bestow legitimacy and prestige on unelected ruling elites, and can be funded by official edict. But for a poor and democratic nation like India, why should the pursuit of Olympic prowess be considered anything more than an exercise in national vanity?

The most obvious answer is that enthusiasm for the Olympics can help foster a national culture of sport, contributing to the general health of all. As far back as 1951 India's first prime minister, Jawaharlal Nehru, lamented the fact that the country had largely neglected athletic competition as a national and social activity. "Athletic contests are good from the point of view of developing friendly rivalry among the youth of the nations," he said. "We have to aim at the physical fitness of the entire nation and, more especially, of the youth of the nation. This fitness can only be achieved if we aim high." Yet after six decades, India's policy makers continue to ignore the importance of physical education and sport in our schools.

No less important, in my view, is that Indians, as much as the citizens of any other nation, need heroes and role models—champions whose achievements affirm our collective identity, encourage us to transcend our myriad differences in religion, caste, ethnicity, and language, and inspire us to greatness as a nation. Sport, like almost nothing else, has the power to unite us. It brings us all to the arena where, as fellow Indians, we can rally around our athletes, cheer them on as one, and take common pride in their achievements.

Indians from all walks of life can take pride in—and draw hope from— stories of Indian athletes like Mary Kom, the daughter of rural laborers from a poor tribal community in the northeastern state of Manipur, whose discipline and determination enabled her to win a bronze medal in women's boxing in London; or Saina Nehwal, the daughter of a middle-class Jat family in Haryana, who won a bronze medal in badminton in London and has become India's highest-paid athlete outside of cricket.

Competitive sports have finally become accessible to all strata of Indian society—not just the rich. Our hockey players emerge from the slums of Mumbai, archers from lower- and lower-middle-class backgrounds from the tribal belts, boxers and wrestlers from the rural heartlands. Many have realized that success in sports is a passport to upward social mobility.

India's young and rapidly growing population is creating an unparalleled pool of potential Olympic athletes. One in three Indians is younger than twenty years old. By 2020, it is expected that 325 million people will reach working age. If even half a percent of India's young population decides to play recreational sports, India will boast a pool of 1.62 million kids from which to draw potential athletes. If 10 percent of that pool could be inspired to play at the competitive level, and if 10 percent of those athletes then could be trained for global competition, India would have more than sixteen thousand potential Olympic athletes. And the pool could be far larger if we make sport a way of life for the majority of the country.

India's young and rapidly growing population is creating an unparalleled pool of potential Olympic athletes.

How much might India hope to improve its Olympic performance? It is not impossible to imagine that in the 2020 summer games, India could claim twenty medals. That achievement, though more than triple our London record, would equal the London medal counts of the Netherlands and Ukraine—and should be sufficient to place India comfortably into the top fifteen medal-winning nations in 2020.

Of course, Olympic medals do not come cheaply. It is difficult to measure precisely the correlation between how much countries spend to train and support their Olympic athletes and how many medals those athletes bring home from the games. As a general rule, however, middle-tier performers at the London games invested a minimum of about $2 million per medal. For Olympic powerhouses like the United States, Australia, and China, the investment per gold medal was probably $6 million, and for some countries, such as Australia, the amount was likely four to five times higher.

If India is to claim twenty medals in the 2020 Olympic Games (with at least seven to eight golds), I believe the implied funding level is at least $120 to $200 million. That's a big jump up from the $30 million we invested in athletes in London, but it is a sum that should be easily within India's means.

The best way for India to fund the development of its Olympic athletes is through a public-private partnership model along the lines of

Great Britain's Olympic support entity, UK Sport. I advocate the establishment of an independently administered Indian Olympic Fund, which could be supported by both the private sector and the Indian government. The fund would be charged with channeling money to short-term programs such as training and competitions, but also for investing in long-term development projects such as building stadiums and training facilities and purchasing equipment. The fund should be governed by an independent committee composed of members drawn from a variety of different backgrounds, including sports, administration, and the business world. Members should serve four- to eight-year terms that rotate in tandem with the Olympic games. An organization of this type would enable funding athletes in a transparent, modern way in keeping with widely established auditing practices.

Great Britain's experience suggests a promising model for India. Unsatisfied with their nation's record of just fifteen medals in the 1996 summer Olympics in Atlanta, Great Britain created UK Sport, a national sports fund, and resolved to support the new entity with money from the national lottery. UK Sport took a hardheaded strategic approach to allocating funds, prioritizing sports in which British athletes excelled or had promise, such as rowing, sailing, cycling, and track and field. Within each sport, the fund focused on support for the most promising athletes. This effort to pick winners was not without controversy. But funding levels for individual athletes were determined by professional, transparent methods using clear performance targets for athletes and teams. At the same time, the agency set aside funds to develop promising newcomers, both sports and athletes.

For Britain, this more rigorous approach to Olympic competition has clearly paid off. Since Atlanta, Britain has steadily improved its medal count, winning twenty-eight medals in Sydney in 2000, thirty in Athens in 2004, and forty-seven in Beijing in 2008. At the London games in 2012, Team Britain hauled home a record-shattering sixty-five medals.

For India's would-be Olympians, the funding landscape could not be more different. Currently all elite Indian athletes other than cricketers must rely on government funding for the chance to train and compete at an Olympic level. Private groups like Olympic Gold Quest, Mittal Champions Trust, and the Lakshya Sports Foundation have begun to reduce athletes' dependence on the state, but the quantum of private funding must be increased dramatically—ideally to around 50 percent, up from the current ratio of less than 10 percent. This will free government moneys to be used for the more basic task of developing sports facilities around the country. Despite an expanding budget, the Ministry of Youth Affairs and Sports has not been able to build a sports infrastructure in India at an adequate pace. We need to embark on a systematic building program comparable to India's effort in 2010, when crews rushed to upgrade training facilities before the Commonwealth Games in Delhi.

> The leaders of India's Olympic community must make some tough, unemotional choices about where to invest scarce resources.

The leaders of India's Olympic community must make some tough, unemotional choices about where to invest scarce resources. Archery, shooting, wrestling, boxing, track and field, and badminton are good starting points since there are more medals at stake in these disciplines, and India has a promising pool of talent. Athletes, coaches, officials, the government, and private benefactors all need to unite behind these priorities.

More broadly, India must develop a more supportive national attitude toward sports. The media—electronic and print alike—should pay greater heed to domestic sporting events. Outside of cricket, which has not been an Olympic sport since Britain defeated France in the Paris games of 1900, there has been a drastic decline in the coverage of Indian athletes, with even national championships drawing precious little attention. International figures from football, tennis, golf, and motorsports are household names across the country, while those Indians taking their first steps in competitive sport struggle to get even a mention in the media. Only after an athlete has become internationally known can he or she break through at home.

The government, at the central, state, and local levels, also needs to make sports a crucial part of the school and college curriculum. Interscholastic competitions need to become part of TV schedules. National sports federations need to take college and university programs under their wing and reenergize them.

Throughout all these changes, we must keep the athletes at the forefront of our minds. Everything we do must be designed to reflect their interests and to encourage widespread participation in competitive sports. That's how we'll develop one of the biggest, best talent pools in the world. That's how India will strike Olympic gold.

india in the world

asia's pivotal power
Bill Emmott

With independence from Britain still a few months away, one of the early foreign-policy acts of India's first prime minister–designate, Jawaharlal Nehru, was to convene in March 1947 a big "Asian Relations Conference" in Delhi. It was a momentous gathering, bringing together official delegates from across the continent, ranging from the Arab world in West Asia to the very different far eastern and southern reaches of the shortly to be liberated continent. The implication of the event seemed clear: With the end of imperialism would come a new diplomacy, uniting the countries of Asia in a spirit of peace and prosperity. Free, democratic, and developing India would be at the heart of those diplomatic connections. But it never happened.

The dream today of a new, reimagined Indian place in the world over the next twenty or thirty years ought to be that Nehru's original vision will at last be implemented. Not, for sure, in the form of regional hegemony, but rather with India forging for itself a central role in keeping Asia an open, peaceful, prosperous continental space in which nations agree to follow rules and pursue cooperation rather than unilateralism or conflict.

India's traditions of democracy and the rule of law, its sheer size in economic and demographic terms, and its geographical location all combine to give it a natural potential role as one of Asia's leaders. It could

Bill Emmott is the author of Rivals: How the Power Struggle Between China, India, and Japan Will Shape Our Next Decade. *He was editor of the* Economist *from 1993 to 2006.*

serve as a vital bridge to West Asia—Iran and the Gulf—while also balancing the vast emerging power of China. And from such a role in Asia, as a leading preserver of regional security, stability, and economic progress, India would inevitably emerge as a global leader. After all, Asia is already half of the world's population and by midcentury may well be producing half of the world's economic output.

That dream can begin, as Nehru's did, in a mood of idealism. But the best argument for translating Nehru's dream into reality is that doing so is overwhelmingly in India's national interest. The reasons involve both opportunity and danger.

Opportunity arises from the growth of India's economy and the expanding role of trade and foreign investment in the country's development. Just like China during the 1990s and the first decade of the twenty-first century, India over the next few decades will rapidly extend its sphere of economic influence, building an interconnected array of international interests both to foster and to protect. As with China, those interests are likely to be global, given India's size, complexity, and sophistication, but geography, culture, regional economic dynamism, and cost advantages will assure that India's deepest interests can and will be local to Asia.

Danger arises precisely because in this open, global economy, India is not the only country whose interests and exposure are expanding. So are those of China and of many smaller powers within the region. Moreover, India is fifteen to twenty years behind China in this process and is the weaker nation in economic and military terms.

In Asia, three great regional powers—India, China, and Japan—now have overlapping and often competing interests, with the United States standing alongside as a global power with extraordinarily strong regional interests and presence. As was demonstrated in Europe during the nineteenth and twentieth centuries, competition among regional powers can help foster economic progress and technological innovation, but it can also foster military and strategic conflict.

It is tempting to believe that the desire for economic progress will forever trump military and strategic concerns. After the end of the wars surrounding Vietnam in the 1970s, peace across East Asia coincided with regional prosperity—virtually everywhere except, unfortunately, the borders of India itself. But faith that this broader Asian peace will always and inevitably prevail has been destroyed by the friction during 2012 and 2013 between Asia's two largest economic powers, China and Japan, over a group of small islands in the East China Sea, known as the Diaoyu to the Chinese, who claim them, and the Senkakus to the Japanese, who have sovereignty over them.

These barren and seemingly irrelevant rocks have become a foreign policy flashpoint both for strategic reasons (they potentially affect the control of important sea-lanes and access to the Chinese coast) and for reasons of national pride and memory. With military radars being locked on one another, and rival ships and aircraft patrolling the area, the chance of actual conflict, whether accidental or deliberate, cannot be discounted. The two countries are jeopardizing one of the world's most critical trade relationships because each fears looking weak before the other.

India has its own equivalents to this Sino-Japanese dispute, places of long-standing territorial disagreement of great strategic and historic significance. There are many flashpoints in the Himalayas, where India disputes borders with China in Kashmir and the Tibetan region of Aksai Chin, while China disputes Indian sovereignty over the vast northeastern state of Arunachal Pradesh.

India also has wider concerns over the actual and potential Chinese military presence in the Indian Ocean, especially thanks to Chinese aid for the building of new harbors in Pakistan and Sri Lanka that could become naval bases in the future. Indian defense strategists see China as laying a "string of pearls" around the subcontinent with which to encircle or contain India.

Far better for India than years of grinding, attritional competition with China in Asia, punctuated by friction over these territorial disputes, would be the development of a framework of regional cooperation—

Far better for India than years of grinding, attritional competition with China in Asia would be the development of a framework of regional cooperation.

one that deters all sides from aggression and provides incentives for the peaceful resolution of conflicts. The seeds of such a framework were sown in 2005 with the establishment of the curiously named "East Asia Summit"—curious because key participants included the non–East Asian countries of Australia, India, New Zealand, and the Southeast Asian nations, along with China, Japan, and South Korea. In 2011, summit membership was expanded to include the United States and Russia. So far, the group's meetings have proved little more than photo opportunities. If the forum is to develop into a serious regional body—one commensurate with Nehru's 1947 vision—two things must change.

First, China must be persuaded that consensual, multilateral decision-making and dispute resolution are more in its interest than dealing with issues bilaterally, or simply between China and other regional blocs such as the Association of Southeast Asian Nations. For now, however, China's leaders view the region very differently. They believe their nation's rising economic power makes it a natural economic hegemon, a hub country for flows of trade and investment. They reckon that rising economic influence will provide political leverage over their regional neighbors, whose only alternatives for counterbalancing are unappealing: the outsider the United States, or the weakening, constitutionally constrained force of Japan.

The second requirement for the East Asian Summit to become a meaningful forum is that India emerge fully as the third balancing power of Asia—one with a much bigger Asian presence than it has today, and a much clearer policy of its own seeking such collective decision-making. The growth of India's economy has made that plausible. Even so, India's trade and investment connections to the rest of Asia remain relatively weak. Most of all, though, India's foreign policy, both political and economic, has not shifted toward Asia or collective Asian solutions in a convincing or coherent way.

Such a policy wasn't quite Nehru's 1947 vision, of course. It was too soon after the Second World War for that, and independence for both India and other Asian nations was too new. Not even the European Coal and Steel Community had been founded by then, let alone the European

Union, so there was also no comparable supranational body elsewhere to take inspiration from—although, at the moment of shedding European colonialism, he might anyway have been disinclined to follow a European model. But he wanted unity, and did call for Asian countries to end their isolation from one another and meet together to carry out common tasks.

Nehru's 1947 vision never had a chance. Like many postwar dreams, it was thwarted by the onset of the cold war and, more locally, by the Communist takeover in China in 1949. Despite paying initial lip service to their mutual interests as liberating leaders of great civilizations, Mao Zedong saw India and Nehru as standing in the way of China's strategic interests: its desire to achieve sovereignty over Tibet and to secure its western frontiers in the Himalayas. The Chinese seizure of Tibet in 1949, the escape into exile in India of the Tibetan spiritual and political leader, the Dalai Lama, in 1959, and then a short border war with India over the Himalayan territory of Aksai Chin in 1962 all proved that any notions of an India-China rapprochement as coleaders of a new, liberated Asia were entirely fanciful.

India's domestic policy choices further complicated Nehru's Pan-Asian outlook. India's decision to close its borders to most foreign investment and trade, adopting an import substitution model rather than the Japanese-style export-led development, guaranteed the country's isolation. So, too, did India's often bitter relationships with its South Asian neighbors Pakistan, Ceylon, Bangladesh, and even Nepal, Bhutan, and Burma.

Since the early 1990s, India has, of course, abandoned that isolationist, protectionist economic policy, becoming far more open to trade and foreign direct investment. The hope for 2030 must be that India will by then match China in its willingness to receive foreign capital and technology and to maintain tariff levels close to those of European countries. India already is on a path toward such an outcome. If it can stay the course, India will greatly increase its attractiveness to other Asian countries as a trading, cultural, and diplomatic partner. New Delhi's foreign policy, on the other hand, has not yet shifted decisively toward Asia and toward collective Asian solutions. India's main security preoccupations remain domestic: preserving stability at home, guarding against internal terrorism, and girding for the risk of renewed conflict with Pakistan. This insularity has been exacerbated by Delhi's unwillingness to expand its meager diplomatic corps, which remains roughly the size of that of Singapore.

Alas, there remains one region with which India's relations have not improved and to which it is not especially attractive: that is the rest of South Asia. India's poor relationships with its neighbors are, together, the biggest obstacle to its playing a bigger role in Asia.

India's acrimonious relations with its neighbors hurt first and foremost because they weaken India's own economy. They also tarnish India's global image. Fractious ties with Bangladesh, Nepal, Sri Lanka, and, above all, Pakistan undermine diplomatic trust in India among East and Southeast Asia and with the Gulf, and constrain India's soft power. Fairly or not, India has allowed itself to be perceived by its neighbors as the new regional hegemon, in some ways the modern equivalent of Britain, the region's former colonial power. Such tensions are a huge distraction. They signal that as long as India is focusing on military competition with Pakistan, it will never play a full part in Asian regional security. India's failure to establish cooperative and consensual relations inside South Asia sends a message that India will never be a committed partner or participant on a grander, Asian scale.

> India's poor relationships with its neighbors are, together, the biggest obstacle to its playing a bigger role in Asia.

The notion that India might emerge as a regional and even global power is presumptuous, perhaps grandiose. But we need such visions to drive and give inspiration to policy and thinking today. Nehru was keenly aware of that need when he convened his 1947 conference with the aim of giving inspiration and leadership to the newly independent nations of a changing Asia. Geopolitical realities and domestic frailties meant that the inspiration and the leadership could not achieve what Nehru hoped. Now there is both another chance, and another need, for that inspiration and leadership finally to become real, sustained, and effective.

india and america: redefining the partnership
Stephen P. Cohen

As India changes and grows, so naturally do the security threats the nation confronts. Before Indian strategists can properly order their responses, they need to map out this changed landscape, to understand who or what their real enemies are—and just as important, who are their friends.

The first thing to acknowledge is that domestic affairs must be treated as a major component of security policy. Conflicts over water, ethnic and linguistic tensions, and the pressures of widening income disparities all threaten India's stability from within. Yet other than the Maoist uprisings in eastern India, these issues are generally relegated to the bottom of the threat hierarchy.

Similarly, the split between "foreign" threats and domestic problems is an artificial one. The internal politics of India's neighbors have to be part of its political calibrations because they inevitably resonate within the country's diverse linguistic and ethnic groupings. The reverse is also true: India's treatment of its minorities, whether Muslims, Christians, tribals, or scheduled castes, are naturally of concern to the rest of the region. Delhi must not only acknowledge these linkages but also take advantage of them. Several long-standing border and water disputes—with Pakistan, China, Nepal, and Bangladesh—could be solved much faster if they were considered within a regional framework, rather than country by country.

Even the more obviously "hard" security issues need to be consid-

Stephen P. Cohen is a senior fellow at the Brookings Institution and the author of Shooting for a Century: The India-Pakistan Conundrum.

ered in a new light. For the next half dozen years at least, India's most pressing problem will continue to be Pakistan. Over the longer term it might—but only might—be China.

The fashion in Delhi now is to assert that Pakistan no longer counts, that India has surpassed it once and for all. This attitude is a manifestation of the "invincible India" syndrome and is unrealistic. Pakistan is not a trivial state, and a failing Pakistan could do great damage to Indian interests. First, there is the finite risk of future terror operations. As in the past, these could lead to broader crises involving both militaries, and in all of their recent crises each country made a serious policy or intelligence misjudgment. Given their combined arsenal of nearly two hundred nuclear weapons, the consequences of such a mistake are potentially enormous. Militarily, Pakistan is a low-risk but high-cost problem.

Second, even if an armed crisis can be avoided, a failing Pakistan is a drag on India. The main purpose of India's national defense is to ensure that the country's growth and development continue undisturbed. Yet although India and Pakistan are natural trading partners and culturally similar in multiple ways, their rivalry has helped to make South Asia one of the least integrated regions in the world. Continued tensions between them will prevent the Indian economy from achieving its full potential.

The best approach for India and other states is to view Pakistan in the same terms the West saw the Soviet Union: a state to be contained militarily, when necessary, but also a state that can be transformed over time (this was the view of George F. Kennan). Pakistan is no Stalinist state, so the prospects for internal reform are theoretically better. Indians must be patient with Pakistan's difficult process of reform, as the West was patient with that of the former Soviet Union. Given the existence of a large Pakistani nuclear arsenal, there really is no other choice.

India is in sync with the rest of the world regarding China. Most countries welcome trade with and investment in the dynamic Chinese economy. But they also see the People's Republic as a potential long-term problem, with everyone unsure of China's future direction. For India, with a long and contested border with China, this is a grave issue, as are China's expansive territorial claims.

India's response is moderated by two considerations: its weakness on the ground, where China has developed its military capabilities along the border and bolstered infrastructure on the Tibetan plateau; and, as with Pakistan, the existence of a bipolar nuclear balance of terror. India's military response to provocations from Beijing is also restrained by the knowledge that, were it to push against China militarily, it would be vulnerable to a nightmarish two-front crisis—all the more reason to pursue strategic normalization with its weaker ally, Pakistan.

Above all, India must refrain from seeing the Chinese challenge as a "race." This is a horribly weak metaphor. If it is a race it has no end point, it ranges across many dimensions, and there will never be a clear winner or loser. All objective analyses note the differences between India and China—they pursue different political models and have different economic systems, and they are also vastly different societies. India must remain true to its core values, which are widely shared with the most powerful states in the West and Asia, and not be tempted by the totalitarian shortcut. (At the same time, this doesn't mean that the present high levels of corruption and venality should be tolerated.) India has little counterleverage to the Chinese presence in Pakistan. But it can offer the prospect of economic normalization, which gives hope that Pakistan can be weaned away from China over the long run.

> India has little counterleverage to the Chinese presence in Pakistan. But it can offer the prospect of economic normalization, which gives hope that Pakistan can be weaned away from China over the long run.

In both its containment of Pakistan and its steady course vis-à-vis China, India now finds a new and surprising partner, the United States. In this, American calculations parallel Indian ones, and the two countries are evolving a congenial working relationship. It is well short of an alliance but more than happenstance. This new ability to talk to each other is reinforced by growing economic and social links.

This is a major development in both countries. Until the 1980s, the

United States and India were strategically hostile: Indian elites had come to regard America as part of an encircling ring crafted to "keep it down," and Americans regarded India's nonalignment as phony at best. The change was ushered in by the Clinton administration's criticism of Pakistan for the 1999 Kargil adventure and the Bush administration's bold recasting of nuclear policy. The latter may never power any lightbulbs in India, but it represents a turning point, summarized in the phrase "natural allies," first used by Prime Minister Vajpayee more than a decade ago and echoed by American officials. The term preserves India's nonaligned status and provides cover for a strategic change of course by both states.

> In both its containment of Pakistan and its steady course vis-à-vis China, India now finds a new and surprising partner, the United States.

On other security issues, such as stability in the Indian Ocean region, there is general agreement between Washington and New Delhi, and for the same reason. Both are status-quo powers, and both are wary of a China that might seek regional dominance. Cooperation in stabilization operations is in the interest of both, and the United States has backed up its policy by selling India several weapons systems—landing craft and long-range airlift—that are explicitly designed to enhance India's overseas capabilities.

For the next decade at least, the world will be multialigned, with one major world power and several states on the next rung. India is one of those states, and it knows that it's not yet ready to lead an alliance of the other countries in its tier. "Partner" thus aptly describes the India–United States relationship, implying a situation that is profitable to both sides but not necessarily one of perfect equality. Full understanding may lag until the cold war generation passes in both countries. But in the meantime, the two countries' economies, societies, cultures, and educational systems will continue to interpenetrate. This has already facilitated some breakthrough agreements and the understanding over such countries as Pakistan and China.

In some ways the strategic cooperation between India and America will resemble that between America and France, only India is expanding its power, not shrinking it. Paradoxically, India also depends more now than ever on the United States, not for aid but for defense technology and modern organizational models. The relationship will differ markedly from the single-issue rapprochement between Nixon and China over the Soviet Union. It could be a precursor to normalization between India and Pakistan, which would be as big a transformation as that heralded by the United States–India nuclear agreement.

Americans and Indians alike must bear in mind that for both countries, domestic issues have to take precedence over foreign and security policy. This will dominate the concerns of their leaderships for at least two years for America, perhaps longer for India. The idea of a formal alliance fits neither their cultural temperaments nor the threats that they face. But their new partnership looks to be very long-lasting.

butter chicken at birla
Kumar Mangalam Birla

Mahatma Gandhi was killed in my great-grandfather's home. Near the end of his life, India's founding father used to stay at Birla House when he came to Delhi, and in January 1948 an assassin shot him point-blank as he walked out into the grassy courtyard where he held his daily prayer meetings. The house and garden are now a shrine and museum, visited by tens of thousands of admirers every year.

Growing up, I hardly needed to visit the memorial to be reminded of the values held by my close-knit Marwari family. Our tiny community, originally from Rajasthan, has had spectacular success in business in part because we have maintained tight familial relations and traditional values—including many of those promoted by Gandhi himself. Marwari traders apprenticed their sons to other Marwari firms, loaned each other money, and insured one another's goods, confident that their partners held to these same codes. To some in the West, our ways probably looked old-fashioned: When I took over the company in 1996 at age twenty-nine, after the sudden death of my father, no meat was cooked in Birla cafeterias; no wine or whiskey was served at company functions.

> Our newest employees were understandably worried about how life might change under Indian ownership. Would they have to give up their Foster's and barbecues at company events?

Seven years later we bought a small copper mine in Australia. The

Kumar Mangalam Birla is chairman of the Aditya Birla Group.

deal wasn't a huge one, worth only about $12.5 million, but it presented me with a unique challenge of the sort I had not yet faced as chairman. Our newest employees were understandably worried about how life might change under Indian ownership. Would they have to give up their Foster's and barbecues at company events? Of course not, we reassured them.

But then several of my Indian managers asked why *they* should have to go meatless at parties, if employees abroad did not. At Marwari business houses, including Birla, the top ranks of executives traditionally have been filled with other Marwaris. I had introduced some managers from other firms and other communities, and they had a valid point. I was genuinely flustered. My lieutenants were relentless: I had never faced a situation where my own people felt so strongly about something. Yet at the same time I knew vegetarianism was a part of our values as a family and as a company. A core belief! I had broken a lot of family norms, but I thought this one was going to be multidimensionally disastrous for me.

> Vegetarianism was a part of our values as a family and as a company. I had broken a lot of family norms, but I thought this one was going to be multidimensionally disastrous.

Fortunately, my grandparents merely laughed when I approached them with my dilemma: They understood better than I did that our company had to change with the times. If we wanted to make our mark on the world, we had to be prepared for the world to leave its mark on us.

The Aditya Birla Group is now one of India's most globalized conglomerates. We have operations in thirty-six countries on five continents and employ 136,000 people around the world. Over 60 percent of our revenues come from overseas. In the 1970s, my father, frustrated by the heavy-handed and corrupt license raj at home, expanded widely in Southeast Asia. Since I took over as chairman, we've made a dozen acquisitions overseas worth a total of more than $8 billion, in sectors as varied as mining, pulp, aluminum, and insurance. We've branched out into Australia, America, Canada, and Europe. For the moment our top management remains all-Indian, even if not all-Marwari. But I would guess that within a decade, half of our seniormost staff will be non-Indian.

We have expanded internationally for many reasons—sometimes to spread our bets, sometimes because we found it impossible to open a plant in India as fast and as cheaply as we could abroad. In each case we've made our decision based on whether or not the deal would increase shareholder value. Yet when I look around me, I see too many Indian companies eager simply to be written about as global players. Sometimes that clouds the fundamentals of making an overseas acquisition or having an overseas presence. To globalize for the sake of globalizing—as a matter of ego—is perilous. Expanding internationally is hard, risky work. And as I was reminded the first time I saw butter chicken being served in a Birla canteen, the most difficult challenges turn out to be the ones you least expect.

One thing I've learned throughout this process of international expansion is that if Indian companies want to reinvent themselves as world-beaters, they should be prepared for some humbling experiences. Birla is a sixth-generation industrial concern; we sponsor hundreds of schools and temples around the country. Virtually every Indian recognizes our name. But when we decided to acquire a Canadian pulp mill in 1998, none of the twelve hundred residents of Atholville, New Brunswick, had any idea who we were. We had to present ourselves, our credentials, our philosophy to everyone from the local shopkeepers to the unions and provincial government. The team I'd sent to Canada to sign the deal was initially quite upset; they felt demeaned, as if they were being treated like fly-by-night operators.

The process of building trust does not end once the deal goes through. With any foreign acquisition, the new employees watch for signals to see if you are walking the talk, if your decisions match your promises. You have to be very careful that people don't read into things more than they should—how many people have been sent out from India, how often they report back to headquarters, whether they're treated any differently from non-Indian employees. All these things can make the difference between a company that integrates well into the larger group and one that resents being taken over.

Globalization is not just about putting up a plant. It's not about making an acquisition. It's much, much more. One has to tread cautiously, patiently. It has to be an evolutionary process. Before we made our biggest purchase to date—the $6 billion buyout of aluminum giant Novelis in 2007—I asked the due diligence team I sent out to give me substantive feedback about the attitudes of the company's American employees. I told them to engage the Novelis people in deep conversations, to find out how they felt about working for an Indian conglomerate, what questions they had about our culture. The deal would be the second-largest Indian acquisition ever in North America, and would make us the biggest producer of rolled aluminum in the world. But these "soft" concerns were as important to me as statistics about plant machinery, profitability, productivity. I don't know if I'll ever write a check that big again; I certainly didn't want it to buy me a hostile, disgruntled workforce.

Integrating all these global operations is obviously a challenge in itself. Some Indian companies prefer to leave their foreign acquisitions to operate on their own, almost as independent outposts. But if you want all your employees to share the same values and to feel a sense of kinship with one another, as we do, you've got to work at creating an emotional bond—the kind of thing that an Indian growing up hearing the name Birla, or attending a Birla school, would take for granted. By the same token, you have to be prepared to treat all your employees and managers—Indian and non-Indian—equally. The views of those outside India have to count as much as those here at home. It might take them longer to bond with the parent company, to think about the larger good rather than maximizing their silo operations. But the effort is worth it.

What's even more difficult for a tradition-bound company like ours—but just as valuable—is learning and importing values from the new acquisitions. This goes well beyond the food in the cafeteria. Before we started expanding overseas, the corporate presentations in our commodities businesses never discussed safety and the environment. Then we saw how our new employees operated. Their first slides always dealt with safety. They talked about near misses, fatal accidents. It was a huge deal—it came before any discussion of the competitive environment or profitability. Now we do the same. We have a deeper appreciation for the value of environmental sustainability.

Some lessons surprised me even more. Ironically, before we became more international, I used to be much more impressed by someone who could speak the Queen's English than, say, a chartered accountant from Jodhpur whose spoken English required some effort to understand. Now when I look across all our operations in places like Brazil or Egypt or Thailand, I see a whole host of people who aren't comfortable in English, who need interpreters, but who are very, very good at what they do. Sadly, it took that experience for me to respect an accountant from Rajasthan—my home state—as much as a graduate of St. Stephen's in Delhi. At one time we even wanted to run English classes for some of our employees! Now it's not an issue in my mind. If you can get your point across, if you are adding value, if you are competent, then bloody hell to your English.

More concretely, as we've grown we've also had to learn new ways of structuring our organization. We've created positions for sector heads who control billions of dollars' worth of business, rather than hundreds of millions—just as some of our foreign acquisitions did.

The good news is that globalization gets easier over time: There is a snowball effect. The next time we bought a pulp mill in Canada, we were known. The New Brunswick government was comfortable with us; the mill workers knew who we were. Interestingly, as we become more global, people have real feedback to fall back on. When we acquired Columbian Chemicals in 2011, executives at Columbian headquarters in Atlanta were able to go across town to Novelis headquarters and ask about us—what we were all about, how we're run, what sort of autonomy we encouraged. They were talking to people to whom they could relate easily and who could give them honest and accurate information. Maybe not all of it was positive, of course, but at least it was real.

Now, when we want to recruit expat talent to move to India, it's much easier as well because they know about our global operations. They know that opportunities across the group are getting bigger and more interesting. It's made us a more attractive employer to non-Indians. As we are "going global," we're also finding that global executives are becoming more willing to "go Indian."

As I've said, this has taken years of painstaking work. It's not an overnight process, and it's not as easy as writing a check. There are opportunities out there for ambitious and well-run Indian companies—as long as they remember that the world will change them as much as they hope to change the world.

can india inc. go global?
Alok Kshirsagar and Gautam Kumra

What comes to mind when you hear the name or see the image of Coke, Disney, Siemens, Toyota, or Samsung? You know where they are from and what they do. They have transformed the lives of customers and employees and served as powerful ambassadors for their home countries. For the United States, it was the 1950s and 1960s that saw the first generation of these global companies, in Japan it was the 1970s and 1980s. In the 1990s and 2000s, it was South Korea and increasingly China (think Lenovo and Huawei).

Now it's India's turn.

We can readily imagine India brands' journey toward global prominence because it has already begun. In the last decade, Indian companies have expanded their international footprints. Birla, a conglomerate that is a top ten global cement manufacturer as well as Asia's biggest aluminum producer, gets 60 percent of its revenues from outside India. Airtel, an integrated telecom-services provider founded in 1995, already operates in nineteen countries and has the world's fourth-biggest subscriber base. Mahindra, the world's largest tractor company, operates in one hundred countries.

Today, more than 30 percent of the revenues of India's top fifty listed nonbanking companies come from international sources—more than double the percent in 2006.

Alok Kshirsagar is a senior partner in McKinsey's Mumbai office. Gautam Kumra is a senior partner in McKinsey's Delhi office.

344

And India has made inroads in ways that few readily appreciate. Generic drugs by companies such as Dr. Reddy's, Sun Pharma, and Zydus are sold all over the world.

Today, more than 30 percent of the revenues of India's top fifty listed nonbanking companies come from international sources—more than double the percent in 2006. Outward investment has been above $9 billion in each of the past six years.

That said, India still punches well below its weight. There are only eight Indian companies in the *Fortune* Global 500 and only three of these are private (Reliance Industries, Tata Steel, and Tata Motors). That is fewer than Australia (nine) and many fewer than South Korea (thirteen) and China (seventy-three). To be fair, the *Fortune* 500 is a measure more of "bigness" than of "globalness," but India's low representation is still striking.

india inc. in 2028

If there were to be a fifteenth anniversary edition of *Reimagining India*, however, we think the position will have changed substantially. We believe that over the next fifteen years, India can develop at least fifty world-class multinationals. These companies will have progressed from increasing their exports and overseas investments to establishing global platforms and brands.

Why is this idea more than an act of imagination? Because India already has a critical mass of firms with the aspirations, strong capabilities, and balance-sheet strength from which to build truly global companies.

For a start, most of today's managers grew up in a multicultural country with a complex, dynamic, and competitive environment. The price sensitivity of the Indian consumer has forced companies to innovate and challenge established global models. For example, in the 1990s,

Airtel was among the first mobile-phone companies to outsource IT and network management. This allowed it to develop a "minute factory" that drove volume up while driving costs down.

Moreover, in many ways India does not operate as a single market. The complexity of competing across state borders with different tax systems, consumer habits, and local government policies is akin to competing across national borders. Indian executives have learned to be resilient and know how to adapt in a volatile business environment. These capabilities can now prove very valuable as they venture out, particularly to other emerging markets that share some of the same conditions. There is not much that any country can throw at Indian managers that they cannot cope with.

It's also worth noting that unlike in China, it is entrepreneurs and private firms, not state-owned enterprises, that are driving the globalization of Indian business. TCS, HCL, Infosys, Wipro, and similar firms like to say they were "born global," and they were. The younger scions of the family dynasties have also proved important to the broad-based spread of Indian business. Almost all top Indian managers are fluent English speakers (and there is an increasing number who are Spanish and Mandarin speakers, too).

Finally, Indian companies will continue to pursue international expansion as a way to diversify their risk away from the domestic economy and the challenges of doing business in an uncertain political and policy environment.

getting globalization right

McKinsey research that studied companies across Asia has proved that those that globalized with a clear purpose, business model, and capabilities have been much more successful than those that expanded just because they could.

The ambition to acquire must be matched with the ability to create value; aspirations need to mesh with capabilities. A study of cross-border deals from Japan between 1980 and 2000 found that most of them failed due either to weak strategy or poor governance. There have been many fundamental changes in how the Japanese manage their outbound forays. In India, for example, they are spending more time thinking about how to manage global partners and in general going for stronger local talent than they did in the 1980s.

Korean companies have followed the same path. Many had a very difficult time when they first sought to go global in the 1980s and 1990s. Like the Japanese, the Koreans often bought weak companies and then were unable to turn them around. But they shifted focus and learned how to invest organically, how to build global brands, and how to get high returns on their investments.

Hyundai, for example, initially struggled when it entered the United States (as did Toyota), and its cars suffered from a reputation for poor quality. So Hyundai improved its products, backed that up with generous warranties, and has now become a competitor to be reckoned with.

There is good reason to be optimistic that India can learn from the experiences of its Asian neighbors and step up its own game. Although there have been some well-known missteps, most Indian companies know what they want to achieve. In an analysis of more than three hundred deals in which Indian companies bought foreign players, McKinsey found that 43 percent of them were to access new markets (the figure for China was 20 percent) and 24 percent were to access new technologies.

But it will take more than imagination and a few case examples for success. It will require many acts of will, calculated daring, and new capabilities. Drawn from McKinsey's experiences working with Indian companies, here are four imperatives for the successful globalization of India Inc.

1. Deepen market insights: think local, while going global.
Many Indian companies have grown internationally via a combination of opportunistic export-led growth and product-driven sales. Some in the pharma and IT industries have developed tailored services for different customer segments, but most companies have faltered when it comes to developing deep local insights. Increasing international market share requires much greater levels of investments in segment and market insight. Indian companies have to tailor their offerings, not just replicate their business model. For some, this requires a big mind-set shift.

The approach Tata Motors took with Jaguar Land Rover in China is a good example of the rewards of doing this right. Since the acquisition of JLR in 2008, Tata has made substantial investments in China and built a new factory, which it operates with a local joint venture partner. In the financial year ending March 2012, sales for JLR China surged nearly 50 percent. China is now JLR's largest market and a big factor in its turn-around.

2. Create and institutionalize global processes.

Founders and entrepreneurs have led India's globalization. These kinds of leaders made their mark via intuition, inspiration, and navigation of personal networks. But what works in India does not necessarily work overseas. The need is for a more process-driven form of management that can be rolled out in different countries. To create order and consistency across their global operations, Indian companies need to create systems for everything from how to get supplies to their factories to how they operate their plants.

In particular, there needs to be much greater emphasis on managing unfamiliar risks. Most Indian companies, especially those in the top one hundred, are very good at managing domestic risks on an intuitive and reactive basis. Their ability (with the help of one or two phone calls) to understand the underlying reason for regulatory changes, commodity price shifts, the lack of suppliers, and labor union troubles is extraordinary. When they go abroad, however, they encounter unfamiliar challenges. They do not know the regulator, the unions, the policy makers, or the nature of the local partners. A much more disciplined process to identify and manage these risks is required—not just to check a box for compliance or regulatory purposes but as a critical way to increase value and build resilience.

3. Be an active owner to create value from M&A.

Traditional M&A involves consolidation and back-office synergies, but when acquiring an asset overseas, it is essential to increase revenues. Indian acquirers often buy an asset that is already distressed, troubled, or starved of investment. It is necessary to focus on revenue growth by bringing in new technology, attracting new customers, and finding new markets. These will make a big difference to the morale of the acquired organization.

Unfortunately, some senior Indian leaders have the view that Indian companies are preferred because they are relatively passive investors who are apt to leave the acquired company alone. This is not always the right view to take. Being passive can mean losing value. And being active does not necessarily mean slash and burn; it can be about bringing in three or four new managers to improve performance in a disciplined fashion and to work on mind-sets and capabilities.

4. Develop and recruit global talent.
Global business needs people with global perspectives—and these are in short supply. Most successful global companies have a cadre of one hundred (some even have five hundred) executives who are able to carry their culture, processes, and standards around the world. Indian companies are often remiss in this regard. When asked who will manage international expansion, they usually come up with the same set of five or ten trusted people who have been managing everything for them in the domestic market.

Indian executives can readily recite the challenges that foreign companies have faced in finding their feet in India. Among them: They were not committed to the long term; they didn't have the right people; they changed their (expatriate) bosses every three years; they didn't know how to manage a local joint venture; and they were not integrated into society. There is truth in this critique. There is also irony because Indian companies often make the exact same mistakes in their own overseas ventures.

Not only does India lack internationally experienced leaders, but many companies don't consider giving outsiders a real shot either. It's not hard to find firms that get more than three-quarters of their revenues from outside India—and have 95 percent Indian senior leadership. The CEO of Coke was born in Turkey, the CEO of Pepsi in India, the former CEO of Sony in Britain. At the moment, it is hard to imagine any Indian company of similar stature selecting a non-Indian for the top spot. Sure, there might be an outsider with a leadership position in sales, but not in operations or finance. This glass ceiling, coupled with the fact that few Indian companies have great global brand names, prevents top talent from joining even the best Indian firms. They need to show executives that there are clear, performance-based career paths and no impediments to advancement.

At the same time, it's important to develop India's own best and brightest to global standards. Depending on the segment and business model, this needs to go beyond just the United States and Europe to also encompass important markets in Latin America, Asia, and Africa. It is typical in the Indian C-suite for executives never to have held an international assignment or even to have worked outside their companies or business units. These leaders may be brilliant at managing domestic businesses, but that does not mean they are well prepared to run global ones. One key priority for global Indian companies, then, is to start to build a cadre of fifty to one hundred internationally oriented middle to senior managers now so that their leadership capabilities can match their global ambitions.

why does it matter?

Even after twenty years of liberalization, some people question whether market-led international competition is the road that India should travel. Surely, they say, India should concentrate more on its domestic priorities. We argue that the two are intimately connected, that India's health and prosperity cannot be sundered from the world. Consider how India's IT services industry, perhaps the country's most global, has created millions of high-skilled, high-paying jobs in India.

Globalization is also crucial to the health of the corporate sector. With more and more global companies treating India as an important market, Indian companies that do not learn how to be globally competitive will lose at home, too. Failure is certainly an option; staying on the sidelines is not. This is not a rising tide for all boats—those Indian companies that have developed the right capabilities and business models have already been much more successful than their peers.

Finally, there is an element of national interest. Business success on a global scale is an expression of soft power. Successful companies exert influence in a way that may not be possible for those confined to the Indian market alone. Consider how important, say, Coke or Apple is to the perception of the United States. Or think of it this way: Has South Korea ever had more effective ambassadors than Samsung and LG? Already, India's success in industries like IT and pharma has changed the country's image in a profoundly positive way.

We can imagine the world fifteen years hence and envision the skylines of major cities lit with names of leading Indian brands. And we can imagine dozens of Indian companies that will be not only leaders in their sectors but also pioneers in creating new businesses.

the closing of the indian mind
Kishore Mahbubani

The United States is the greatest human laboratory in the world. America welcomes immigrants from all over the globe, offers them a level playing field, and encourages them to test themselves against world-class competition. Mexican bodega owners fight for customers against Korean grocers. Israeli coders challenge Russian hackers. Chinese microbiologists compete for funding against Swiss geneticists.

And who has come out ahead in this unparalleled global free-for-all? Indians. Their per capita income now ranks as the highest of any ethnic group in the States: In 2010, Indians earned $37,931 annually, compared to a national average of $26,708. If India's population of 1.2 billion could achieve only half of the per capita income of Indian immigrants in America, the country's GDP today would be $24.65 trillion instead of a relatively trifling $1.85 trillion, less than Italy's. The gap between India's potential and its actual performance is huge, perhaps the biggest of any country in the world.

Yet remarkably, even though Indians themselves have often noted how much better their countrymen perform overseas, that fact has not spurred a more intense debate at home. More than three decades ago, China's Deng Xiaoping looked around the region, saw how much richer the Chinese in Taiwan, Hong Kong, and Singapore were than those on the mainland, and asked the obvious question: Why? The equally obvious answer was that China's economic system was flawed. That led him

Kishore Mahbubani is dean of the Lee Kuan Yew School of Public Policy at the National University of Singapore.

to the bold decision to smash the iron rice bowl that Mao Zedong had provided and to open up the Chinese economy. For the next thirty years, mainland China delivered the fastest-growing economy in the world. Before his death, Deng could claim to have lifted more people out of poverty than any other leader in human history.

The Indian business leader Ratan Tata commented at a public symposium in Singapore that he'd similarly urged Indians to learn from the success of their counterparts in the Southeast Asian city-state. According to him, most of them scoffed at the idea that huge India could learn anything from tiny Singapore.

That reaction helps explain India's performance gap. One of India's leading intellectuals, Pratap Bhanu Mehta, has framed the problem this way: Although China has a closed society, it has an open mind. The country's leaders are pragmatic rather than ideological, focused intently on which policies work rather than which ones reaffirm their preconceived worldviews.

By contrast, India has a wonderfully open society—but as a nation, a very closed mind. In contrast to China, which has studied the world intensively and realizes it has to adjust, India is still clinging to outdated and misguided concepts. The country has become one of the most ideologically hidebound societies in the world. It continues to be nearly impossible to challenge conventional wisdom and sacred cows, particularly economic ones.

> India has a wonderfully open society—but as a nation, a very closed mind.

Where Deng happily cast aside decades of Communist dogma, Indian politicians are still repeating shibboleths like "multinational corporations with deep pockets will hurt the interests of the poor," as Sanjay Singh, an MP from Uttar Pradesh, claimed in 2011 during the parliamentary debate on whether to allow foreign direct investment (FDI) in India's retail sector. This is, as has been pointed out often, arrant nonsense. FDI in retail will actually help poor farmers and lower food costs for consumers.

In 1991, when Narasimha Rao and Manmohan Singh opened up the

Indian economy, their hand was forced by an acute balance of payments crisis. Two decades later, obvious reforms remain stalled, and every new measure proposed runs into a storm of political protest. Politicians fearfully block measures like allowing in foreign retailers, as though Indian shopkeepers could not possibly compete against them. (Thankfully, a reform package allowing some FDI in retail passed in the parliament in late 2012 with a slim majority.) I come from a Sindhi family that emigrated from Karachi in 1947. Our community has thrived in the retail sector around the world—surely we can do so at home, too.

India could, in fact, learn quite a bit from its diaspora. My mother had a close shave fleeing Karachi, so I fully appreciate the traumas of partition. But go to the trading floors of any of the world's major banks today, and you will see Indians and Pakistanis happily working together, oblivious of the supposedly insurmountable divide between their nations. When I sit down to write in Singapore, I always put on a recording by Mohammed Rafi—an Indian Muslim singer brought up in Lahore in what is now Pakistan. Such cultural connections come naturally to South Asians abroad.

Indian strategists will cry that I'm being simplistic, that India lives in a dangerous neighborhood and must remain vigilant against outside threats. Fair enough. But China has had an equally complex, if not tougher, problem with Taiwan. In some ways its challenge has been greater: While all mainland Chinese believe Taiwan is an integral part of China, the island has for decades been protected by a rock-solid defense treaty with the United States and its incomparable military. Pakistan has no such treaty, and in fact, tensions with Washington have grown in recent years.

Yet China has almost entirely neutralized the Taiwan problem. Lately, Beijing has pursued a brilliant strategy of isolating the Taiwanese government and engaging with the Taiwanese people. China has laid out the red carpet for Taiwanese investors and tourists. By now, with the

Chinese and Taiwanese economies inextricably linked, the Taiwan Strait is no longer considered a major geopolitical flash point.

India could be pursuing a similar policy of economic and people-to-people engagement with Pakistan, replicating what the Indian and Pakistani diasporas do overseas, often spontaneously and effortlessly. Today, none of its neighbors, not even Pakistan, can seriously threaten India. China has wisely made its neighbors stakeholders in its own economic growth and prosperity, and even traditional American allies like Japan, South Korea, and Australia now trade more with the mainland than with the United States. India should similarly be fostering greater trade and economic interdependence with all its South Asian neighbors. In some cases, unilateral concessions may be in order, as India's economy dwarfs those of its neighbors. Various vested interests will naturally oppose such giveaways. But the long-term geopolitical gains will far surpass the short-term economic losses.

In fact, by rights India should be one of the world's leading champions of globalization rather than an insecure and fearful opponent of it. For several decades after World War II, both the United States and Europe provided the impetus for liberalizing trade around the world, believing correctly that as free markets and demand expanded globally, most of the new jobs created would go to Americans and Europeans. Now they've begun to retreat from globalization because of fears—also correct—that the new jobs are going to go to Chinese and Indians. As the new "winners" of globalization, China and India should join forces to promote the process and keep up its momentum. Instead hoary ideological suspicions have thus far prevented India from playing such a leadership role.

> India should be one of the world's leading champions of globalization rather than an insecure and fearful opponent of it.

One could blame India's underperformance on a host of factors: overpopulation, corruption, illiteracy, political incompetence, stubbornly persistent poverty. But the real failure is, to a large extent, one of imagination. Many Indian leaders still seem unable to conceive of their country as a confident, open-minded, rising power—one that can afford to take risks and can be generous with its supposed adversaries. At one time the legacy of two hundred years of British colonialism had undoubtedly damaged Indians' cultural self-confidence. In recent years Indians abroad have proved that they've shed that burden. It's time for their leaders to follow them.

the village people
Suketu Mehta

I am a city dweller, like my father and my grandfather. My great-grand-father lived and worked, like his forefathers, in the villages of rural Gujarat—as did the forefathers of Mahatma Gandhi, who declared, "The future of India lies in its villages." This is no longer true for my family or my motherland or, for that matter, most of the planet.

We have become an urban species, living in a globe of cities. For the first time in human history, just over half the world's population now lives in cities. In 1900, only 10 percent of us did; by 2050, 75 percent of us will. There is, properly speaking, a stampede to cities.

Never have we moved so much, so continuously. Economists are grappling with this shift, as are urban planners, demographers, sociologists, anthropologists, civil engineers. But what about the rest of us? What does it mean to the individual human being to go from village to city? What does it do to his or her mind?

Gujaratis like my family have been migrating for centuries to trade—to the East Indies, to Africa, to Britain, to North America. Indians have been in the vanguard of this restless migration—for reasons as varied as colonialism, indentured labor, economic want, or just the unexpected benefit of colonialism: the acquisition of the English language. Increasingly, people like us don't just go from a village in India to a city in India; we go from a village in Punjab direct to Paris. There is no acclimation station. Within twenty-four hours, a villager from Gujarat is transported—

Suketu Mehta is the author of Maximum City: Bombay Lost and Found.

not to Bombay, but to New York. Jet-lagged, he tries to make sense of the subway, white women in short skirts, the Empire State Building. Everything is different in the city, but the city makes no accommodation for this difference. He is expected to adjust, immediately, even though he has traveled not just through countries but also through centuries.

The attraction of the urban is more successful than the attraction of religion; it is the one thing that most of us can agree on—that we like to live in cities. We are voting with our feet. The greatest mass conversion of our time isn't to any religion; it is to the cult of the city. The story of the city has prepared the young people in the villages to inhabit the cities; they are no longer foreign to them when they arrive.

And how do we pay tribute for this conversion? How are we tithed? We give up: personal space, homogeneity, and nature. We live in ant colonies and commute in cattle cars. We mingle promiscuously with people unlike us. We walk on the hot concrete and miss the passing of the seasons.

These are huge things to give up. For all our history, for the entire duration of our collective memory, we have lived close to where we grew our food, with our caste, and with large spaces where we could be alone at midday. We flocked to medieval city-forts when we felt threatened in the countryside. When the threat passed, we went home to the land.

The central question of cities in our time is this: Within these enormous, historically unprecedented, and continuously mobile agglomerations of people, how do we form a community? Whom do they belong to, these twenty or forty or sixty million people living side by side, on top of each other?

These city dwellers are not local, not international, not internal, but what I call "interlocal." The dictionary defines the word as "situated between, belonging to, or connecting several places." Interlocals can be between the here and the there, belong to both and, most important, connect them all.

The communities of people that move from locality to locality, from village to city, or across countries are not exactly transnational; they owe no allegiance to nations. It is possible to identify yourself—as I do—as an Indian, an American, a resident of Greenwich Village and Bandra, a Hindu, a professor, a writer, a straight male, a father, middle class, a Democrat. All these identities are rooted in the local, the specific. To be a nationalist, you must exclude the international; a nation-state is often defined by what it's not, like the BJP's version of Hinduism.

It is possible to identify yourself—as I do—as an Indian, an American, a resident of Greenwich Village and Bandra, a Hindu, a professor, a writer, a straight male, a father, middle class, a Democrat.

Because of this plethora of identities, I find it impossible to hate or exclude the totality of a human being—because at least some of our identities overlap. If I meet a Pakistani, I may not like the part of him that is a nationalist Pakistani. But I will like the part of him that is a father. I will like the part of him that enjoys a samosa. I will like the part of him that is a brown man.

The trick to overcoming strife is not to melt into any sort of pot but to proliferate our identities. We are composed of many circles, many bubbles, within ourselves. Some are larger, others very small. Some of these bubbles touch, overlap. When we meet another person—when the Mexican busboy from Sunset Park meets the patrician from Park Avenue—a good predictor of whether two disparate people will find a likeness is how many circles intersect.

The interlocal can be quite firmly fixed in his localities. I live in Greenwich Village and Bandra, and I am attached to both of these places. But that doesn't mean that I am globalized. Being interlocal is also something subtler, finer, than being globalized. It means that I can be a Bombayite Gujubhai and a Jackson Heights homeboy simultaneously. There's also an international class of rich corporate flotsam, who move among the business hotels and convention centers of the world without ever being conscious of what is local in the cities they move amid.

The interlocal migrant, on the other hand, is keenly aware of his immediate physical surroundings and conducts commerce with them. He may be defined by his locality, but he is not limited by it. He plays a role in connecting the places he travels between. It is hard for the interlocal to conceive of going to war on behalf of his locality, unless it's for a soccer game. America and India might conceivably go to war, but Jackson Heights could never go to war against Andheri, or the Upper East Side against Malabar Hill. That is because they are too alike and contain a large population of interlocals, who bring news of the humanity of one to the other.

There is a difference between being interlocal and translocal. The former implies connection, the formation of a bridge. The latter involves flying over. Someone who is interlocal does not travel *above* localities, transcend them, or flit about from place to place. He traverses *between* localities. He is keenly rooted in each to varying degrees.

To be interlocal is to be grounded. You may feel very much at home on the Lower East Side of New York, as well as in your parents' community in Florida, as well as in your aunt's home in Bandra. You may not even be conscious of nationality when moving between these very different places. But you are acutely aware of the texture of the neighborhoods; you have certain transactions with the people around you, you know where to eat, where to shop. You feel a strong allegiance to these places, but it is an open, even promiscuous sort of allegiance that allows for multiple, heterogeneous belonging. You can be an interlocal and a patriot—but, unlike the usual definition of patriotism, you can feel patriotic toward more than one country.

Interlocals bring news of food and music to the localities they travel between. Thus, in Jackson Heights, my family became aware of pizza, tacos, and falafel. And when we went back to India, we cooked it for our relatives, so that they could relish it, too. In multiple ways, interlocals enrich the places they connect.

The interlocal also lives in a state of longing. When he is in one of his localities, he dreams of the other. This makes him restless. He cranes his neck and looks at a flock of birds and his heart stirs. As a result, inter-locals often live in a state of continuous transit. The villager who moves to the city doesn't just stay there. He migrates back to the village when necessary, stays to seed his ground (his farm, his wife), and then migrates back when there is need of money. The villagers who come to the city do not forget the village. They bring village rhythms, trees, roosters, gods with them to the city. The slums of the developing cities are interlocal communities: villages in the city.

The new interlocals are part of the cities and city borders they move to, without totally surrendering themselves to the new places. They feel no inclination to be fully an "American" or a "New Yorker" like previous migrants were under pressure to do. Their children might, to varying degrees. But even the children retain strong ties to the countries or cities their parents were born in. The children, too, are interlocal and better equipped for the twenty-first-century world. Where is home for them—for me?

I am one of the tribe that Stalin and then Hitler called "rootless cos-mopolitans." We have always been the target of hostility by nationalists, since we don't have one overriding loyalty that can be exploited. But we are growing in number, every day, every year. My notion of home now—this geographically dispersed entity—will increasingly be home for all of us in the years to come. Most of my friends travel in this orbit. I meet people in New York this week whom I saw in Bombay last week and will see in London next week, but I am unlikely to ever run into them in St. Louis, Lucknow, or Liverpool. I do not live in America but I do live in New York. I am of the twenty-first century: a city dweller, a megalopolis dweller. I can move easily between Paris and New York and Bombay, but I am not at home for long in Fargo or Gorakhpur or Tours.

The first and third worlds are distributed over the cities of the world, and in each one, they live side by side. There are people who live in Mal-abar Hill as they do on the Upper East Side or in the Eighth Arrondisse-ment; in each of these cities, their neighbors are the universal fraternity of the poor. There are sections of Harlem that have a higher infant mortality rate than Bangladesh. The distance between Malabar Hill and the Dharavi slums, or between the Upper East Side and gritty East New York, is much greater than between Malabar Hill and the Upper East Side.

> The distance between Malabar Hill and the Dharavi slums, or between the Upper East Side and gritty East New York, is much greater than between Malabar Hill and the Upper East Side.

Sometime before I came back to Bombay, I had stopped thinking of the city as home. Home is not a geographically intact entity; it is where my people are. My map of home is composed of a living room in New York, a bedroom in Paris, another in Bombay, and a long-locked storeroom in Calcutta. I shuttle between these cities, to the houses and apartments of my friends and relations, and I am equally comfortable in all of these well-known spaces. The country outside these rooms is kept at bay; the furnishings and the routines of these rooms resemble each other. In all these cities, I have Colombian coffee in the morning, an Indian vegetarian lunch, and pasta and wine in the evening. If any component of this entity is missing, I long for it. But it is no longer an anguished longing, especially since the birth of my sons. Most of the time, home is pretty much wherever they happen to be.

I went to Bombay to find out if I could go home again. After two and a half years, I knew the answer: cursing it, complaining about it, hating it passionately sometimes, wanting to go back to America all the time, yes. I could live there and be accepted back into the country in every significant way—as an Indian, a Bombayite. They push you out, but they also pull you in. And, having made that discovery, having established that to my satisfaction, I was free to leave again—with confidence, once more into the world. I can be cosmopolitan because I know that I am Indian.

And so I came back to New York, twenty-three years after I first stepped out into the lobby of JFK Airport, with the knowledge that I will always be moving to and fro. I can live neither in New York nor in Bombay, but in a personal hybrid of both. I have decided, or the decision has been made for me, that I am going to live a distributed existence. I will not choose. I assert, with confidence, with pride, that I am not rooted in any one city. I refuse to live in one room. My home has many rooms. My home is a palace; it is Earth.

stumbling toward peace
Ahmed Rashid

Although the 1947 partition of the Indian subcontinent deprived India and Afghanistan of a common border, the two nations remained close to each other all the same. Both countries cast a wary eye on the newly formed nation of Pakistan; whenever Afghan king Zahir Shah felt too much pressure from his southern neighbor, or from Iran on his western border, he would hop on a plane to Delhi. There he would be received rapturously, reminding everyone in the region that Afghanistan had powerful friends and that India could exert influence well beyond its borders.

Delhi squandered this influence by supporting the Soviet invasion of Afghanistan in 1979. India was the only state in the region and the only democracy in the world to support the Soviet-backed Afghan communist regime in Kabul. The mujahideen fighters who toppled that regime had been funded by the CIA and the Saudis, and armed and trained by Pakistan's Inter-Services Intelligence (ISI) agency. They bore little goodwill toward India. Delhi closed its embassy at the height of the civil war in the Afghan capital. When the Pakistan-backed Taliban captured Kabul in 1996, they made clear that Indian diplomats were not welcome back. Pakistan celebrated the severing of the link between India and Afghanistan as a great strategic victory.

Treating Afghanistan as another battleground in their long-standing rivalry has served neither Pakistan nor India well—and especially

Ahmed Rashid is a journalist and the author of five books, including Taliban *and* Descent into Chaos.

not Afghanistan. At the end of 1999, Pakistani and Kashmiri terrorists humiliated and enraged Delhi by hijacking an Indian Airlines plane and flying it to Kandahar in southern Afghanistan. India had to release several dangerous militants from jail in order to get the passengers freed. After the World Trade Center attacks and fall of the Taliban just two years later, India retaliated by cozying up to the new, Western-backed government in Kabul.

> Treating Afghanistan as another battleground in their long-standing rivalry has served neither Pakistan nor India well.

In the decade since, India has given nearly $2 billion in aid to Afghanistan—substantially more than richer donors such as China or Saudi Arabia have offered. The money has been spread out among all Afghan ethnic groups from the Tajiks, Hazaras, and Uzbeks of the Northern Alliance—India's traditional friends—to the majority Pashtuns in the south, homeland of the Taliban. India has provided planes for the national airline Ariana and buses for mass transport in Kabul. Its most visible project is a new parliament building in Kabul costing over $125 million; its most popular is a midday meal program for two million Afghan schoolchildren.

Pakistan's military faces an Afghanistan friendly with India again, and an India deeply entrenched in the Afghan government, military, and economy. Indians train the Afghan army. Indian contractors have built seven hundred kilometers of roads, worth a quarter billion dollars, throughout the country. Once, all of Afghanistan's imports and exports had to flow through the Pakistani port of Karachi. Since 2001, Iran and India have built an alternative road network that connects Afghanistan to the Iranian ports of Chabahar and Bandar Abbas on the Gulf. More than 60 percent of Afghanistan's trade and imports now travels on this route, as does an ever-increasing flow of goods from Central Asia.

In effect, Pakistan now confronts on one border exactly what it does on the other: a territory that Islamabad is convinced should be in its sphere of influence but that its archrival India threatens to dominate. Kabul has become the new Kashmir.

What's worse, from Pakistan's perspective, is that tensions over Afghanistan are making it harder to sustain the progress India and Pakistan had finally begun to make over Kashmir—the open wound that has prevented peace on the subcontinent ever since independence. In 2004, the two countries agreed to a cease-fire in the contested region, over which they have fought three wars. For the first time since 1947 they initiated a diplomatic back channel, which in 2008 came extremely close to settling the intractable dispute. Both armies have dramatically reduced the crossfire between them, and the number of Pakistani militants crossing over into Indian Kashmir have dropped considerably. Yet further advances have stalled.

At the same time, the jockeying between India and Pakistan on the ground in Afghanistan threatens to flare into a new proxy war, especially as U.S. forces prepare to withdraw from the region. In some ways such a battle has already begun. Pakistanis accuse India's intelligence agency, the Research and Analysis Wing (RAW), of providing funds, training, and arms from camps in southern Afghanistan to separatist insurgents in Pakistan's Balochistan province. Indians accuse the ISI of sponsoring Taliban attacks on India's embassy in Kabul and on Indian doctors and contractors working in the capital and elsewhere. Dozens of Indians and Pakistanis have died already in this shadow war.

Rather than trying to tamp down the growing violence, Delhi and Islamabad continue to vie for dominance over Afghanistan. Pakistan has blocked India from any role in power-sharing talks between the Afghan government and the Taliban, hoping to ensure that its allies and not India's hold the upper hand in Kabul. That strategy is foolishly shortsighted: India has invested too much in Afghanistan to be cut out of the loop entirely, and Delhi could easily encourage its friends in the Northern Alliance to sabotage such talks.

None of the players in the region can afford another Afghan civil war. The fighting could easily swell into a regional proxy war, with Pakistan enlisting the aid of the Chinese, and India working with Iran, Russia, and the Central Asian republics. The chaos could dwarf the long-simmering war in Kashmir.

None of this is inevitable, of course. In fact, India and Pakistan should be able to find common ground much more easily in Afghanistan than in Kashmir. Disorder in Kabul serves neither of them.

The most obvious arena for cooperation is the Afghan economy. Right now both sides are acting against their own interests. Pakistan blocks Indian exports from traveling across Pakistan to Afghanistan. That means Islamabad is losing out on lucrative transit fees. More important, the restrictions have led the Indians to encourage alternate trade routes through Iran. Tehran has offered to build a railway line connecting the Afghan city of Herat with the Iranian rail network—a development that could cut Pakistan off from even more of the trade from Afghanistan and the Central Asian republics.

> India and Pakistan should be able to find common ground much more easily in Afghanistan than in Kashmir. Disorder in Kabul serves neither of them.

For their part, major Indian companies that have bid for oil and mineral exploration rights in Afghanistan could benefit immensely from hiring Pakistani service companies to help them. And perhaps the most significant missed opportunity is in energy. Since 1993, a critically important pipeline known by the acronym TAPI, which would carry gas from Turkmenistan across Afghanistan to Pakistan and India, has been stuck in the planning stages. Pakistan desperately needs the gas and TAPI could prove to be a major bridge builder between India and Pakistan. But no institutional funding for the pipeline will be available until fighting in the region ends and the world sees greater cooperation among the South Asian rivals.

The real failure on both sides is their refusal to discuss their current status and aims in Afghanistan. Remarkable as it may sound, neither country has ever talked about the situation in Afghanistan with the other. According to Pakistan, India is not a direct neighbor of Afghanistan, so there is nothing to discuss. India says it sees no need to explain to Pakistan its relations with third countries. This attitude has helped fuel the worst suspicions and fears about the other's role in Afghanistan.

India and Pakistan need to institute a series of bilateral meetings on the Afghan situation at several levels, from the diplomatic to intelligence and military. Such talks would make their missions more transparent and create greater trust. Much greater openness is needed on issues such as the number of intelligence agents each embassy maintains in the country and the alleged support given to Baloch dissidents by India and to Taliban fighters by Pakistan.

Such trust-building measures could have an impact well beyond Afghanistan. Kashmir will be a much tougher problem to resolve, of course, after decades of suspicion and tens of thousands of deaths and disappearances. But almost everyone acknowledges that the key to closer ties between India and Pakistan is greater economic cooperation. In 2011, the two countries began reducing the list of goods that could not be traded between them, and India offered Pakistan most-favored-nation status—a gesture that Islamabad is expected to reciprocate. Partnering on development projects in Afghanistan would benefit both countries economically and provide a model for closer cooperation in other sectors. India and Pakistan could stumble their way toward another war in Afghanistan. Or they might just find a path to peace.

what friends are for
Bruce Riedel

America and India have taken to describing themselves as "natural allies." The label is apt. Our two nations have never had any quarrels over territory since we sit on opposite sides of the globe. We are both democracies that prize our citizens' civil liberties and freedoms. (And as democracies, we like to tell the rest of the world that we know best.) Both of us have bred a host of entrepreneurial geniuses and have built thriving middle classes.

> America and India were born from the same mother, the British empire. Yet when India finally won its freedom from the British, our relationship was far from friendly.

Our nations were born from the same mother, the British empire that ruled more of the world than any other in history. America won its independence just as India was losing its: Soon after his decisive defeat at Yorktown, Cornwallis moved to the other side of the world to become governor-general of India, where he laid the foundations of British rule on the subcontinent. Yet when India finally won its freedom from the British (with a little backstage help from Washington), our relationship was far from friendly. For most of its first fifty years, India was as much an adversary of America as anything else.

Bruce Riedel is director of the Intelligence Project at the Brookings Institution and a senior fellow at the Saban Center for Middle East Policy. He is the author of Avoiding Armageddon: America, India, and Pakistan to the Brink and Back.

India's freedom fighters had not liberated India from a failing superpower in order to fall into the clutches of a rising one. The nation's first prime minister, Jawaharlal Nehru, admired America's freedoms and dynamism yet was driven by his socialist dogma to mistrust its capitalist ambitions. Above all, India resented Washington's relationship to its sister nation, also carved out of the former British Raj in 1947—Pakistan.

Throughout the cold war, India believed—all too often rightly—that America favored its South Asian rival. Pakistan assiduously cultivated the relationship with the United States, joining the global chain of anti-communist allies encircling the Soviet Union from Norway to Japan. The Pakistanis signed up to so many pro-Western defense organizations that they described their nation proudly as America's "most allied ally."

Depending on who happened to be in the White House at the time, this ostentatious show of support worked. Richard Nixon, who once said Pakistan was "a country I would do anything for," detested the Indian leader Indira Gandhi, Nehru's daughter. (She returned the sentiment, once asking in Hindi during a meeting with the American leader, "How much longer must I talk to this man?") In 1971, when the Indians helped East Bengal to break away from Pakistan and form an independent nation, Bangladesh, Nixon tried to brush back Gandhi by sending a U.S. carrier battle group into the Bay of Bengal. The iron lady of South Asia was not amused.

Indians understandably still blame the United States for spending billions to support the Pakistani-backed mujahideen fighting the Soviets in Afghanistan, a policy that ended up fostering the jihadist culture that now infects the region. Even in the last decade, as relations between New Delhi and Washington grew much closer, the $25 billion that America poured into Pakistan for its dubious support in the war against the Taliban and Al Qaeda rankled deeply across the border.

I have spent much of my professional life working to understand India and trying to build ties between our countries. I've spent an equal amount of time trying to find common ground with Pakistan and hoping for an enduring partnership with America to emerge. I have had the honor of working for four presidents as they grappled with India and Pakistan in the White House. I am the first to admit that U.S. policies over the years have often been misguided, shortsighted, and ineffective. Even now, despite all the talk about our common interests, the relationship between America and India remains dismayingly flimsy.

Still, the answer is not for either of us to disengage. Indians need to appreciate that the United States has legitimate interests in South Asia—not least in seeing that two of the world's nuclear powers do not go to war again. American policy makers should likewise accept that they cannot "dehyphenate" the relationship to India and Pakistan, to use the current jargon, and hope simply to deal with each on its own merits. The goal may be laudable, but geography makes it a mirage. Instead, Washington must plunge directly into the most difficult, long-lasting, and dangerous issue that bedevils relations between the South Asian rivals: Kashmir.

> Despite all the talk about our common interests, the relationship between America and India remains dismayingly flimsy.

India and Pakistan began fighting for control over the former Himalayan kingdom of Kashmir within weeks of becoming independent nations. Both claim the entirety of the state, although India—which controls the most populated areas, including the lush Kashmir Valley—has shown willingness to accept the line dividing the two sides as a de facto border. Pakistan has traditionally and unrealistically sought outside support for its claim to all of Kashmir; India has by the same token bitterly resisted any intervention in what it insists is a bilateral issue. American presidents have accordingly put the Kashmir problem in the "too hard" category and left it to simmer.

This hands-off policy has clearly failed. As part of its asymmetric war against India in Kashmir, Pakistan continues to sponsor some of the world's deadliest jihadist groups. Operations launched by organizations like Lashkar-e-Taiba (Army of God)—including the 26/11 attacks in Mumbai—have pushed the two rivals close to outright war several times in just the last decade. If anything, Kashmir presents an even more dangerous flashpoint today than fifty years ago, as both India and Pakistan rapidly expand their nuclear arsenals.

On the other hand, Indo-U.S. relations have probably never stood on a steadier, more enduring footing. The civil nuclear agreement first announced in 2005—by which some Indian nuclear reactors would be put under an international safeguard and inspection regime, and in return India would be able to purchase reactor technology from America and other countries—was a landmark in relations between the two countries. It has effectively taken one of the thorniest issues between them—nuclear proliferation—off the table. American support for India's bid to become a permanent member of the United Nations Security Council has further eased doubts about America's reliability as a strategic partner. An extremely rare bipartisan consensus in Washington now backs closer ties with India.

> The civil nuclear agreement first announced in 2005 was a landmark in relations between the two countries.

Quietly but forcefully, Washington should now push New Delhi to be more flexible on Kashmir. India is right to argue that it should not be asked to give up its portion of the state. But Indians also need to recognize that their hopes and aspirations for the future are unlikely to materialize as long as a state of near war continues to plague relations with Pakistan. As the stronger power in the equation, with a far more stable and predictable political system, India is much better equipped to make the kind of diplomatic moves needed to break the logjam over Kashmir. It can reduce the size of its military footprint in the state and encourage more dialogue about the future; it also can and must take greater action to prevent human rights abuses.

There is a way to resolve the Kashmir problem along the lines of Indian thinking—focusing less on territorial adjustments than on making the state a zone of peace and prosperity between India and Pakistan, like the Saar region between France and Germany. The Line of Control would have to become both a permanent, conventional international border (perhaps with some minor modifications) and a permeable frontier between the two parts of Kashmir. A special condominium might be created—a zone where India and Pakistan shared sovereignty—to allow Kashmiris on both sides of the border to work together on issues like transportation, the environment, sports, and tourism. Indian and Pakistani currencies could become legal tender in both parts of the state—an idea recently floated in India.

As a symbol of reconciliation, such an arrangement could set the tone for a broader rapprochement across the region. Formal and informal trade barriers should be lowered. Most visa requirements should be lifted, so that average citizens can travel between countries in the region as easily as Spaniards, Greeks, and Germans do across the European Union. As transit and trade grow, so will cooperation on the environment, water resources, and other crucial issues.

I'm not suggesting that Washington lecture India on what's in its best interests. But a discreet, sustained American effort led by the U.S. president to promote a solution is probably necessary to any effort to move the parties toward an agreement. The United States can help concretely by making clear to Pakistan that some red lines on terrorism are real; if Indian leaders see proof that their neighbor is taking action to dismantle Kashmiri jihadist groups, they will have much more flexibility to pursue a breakthrough peace deal. Where American influence falls short, Washington can encourage allies like Saudi Arabia and the Gulf states to nudge Pakistan toward a rapprochement. There might even be an opportunity for the United States and China—a strong supporter of Pakistan—to work together in the interests of a deal. That would relieve fears among some in New Delhi that America wants to use India to counter the rise of Asia's other superpower.

Of course Indians and Pakistanis have to be the primary actors in efforts to shape their future. History has shown that American actions can make a bad situation worse, and there is only limited evidence

> History has shown that American actions can make a bad situation worse, and there is only limited evidence that they can make things fundamentally better.

that they can make things fundamentally better. Still, this is what friends do: encourage difficult but necessary moves and provide the reassurances needed to make such actions less risky. America must be more ambitious and assertive about this problem than it's been, and India should be more receptive to U.S. prodding. Success will only strengthen the bonds that have at long last begun to link our two nations.

incredible india, credible states
Christopher J. Graves

Mark Twain came to India in 1896, propelled by debt and honor. He was sixty years old and a global celebrity—the best-known and most beloved author of his day. But his business judgments were as poor as his writing was brilliant. A year earlier, ill-considered investments in book publishing and a newly invented typesetting machine had wiped out Twain's considerable personal fortune and left him with debts of more than $70,000 (about $2 million today). To repay creditors, Twain embarked on a hundred-date, round-the-world lecture tour that took him from Cleveland, Ohio, to Hawaii, Fiji, Australia, New Zealand, Ceylon, India, Mauritius, South Africa, and England.

Of the many stops along Twain's extraordinary year-long odyssey, no destination seized his imagination like India. In a whirlwind three months, he visited a score of Indian locales, including Bombay, Poona, Benares, Lucknow, Baroda, Jaipur, Calcutta, and Darjeeling. Twain was exhilarated. He found India a land so vast, so colorful, and so diverse that it almost defied characterization. In *Following the Equator*, the popular travelogue Twain published after his return, reflections on India spill across nearly half the book's 712 pages. In some passages, Twain sounds almost breathless as he extols the country's wonders:

> This is indeed India! the land of dreams and romance, of fabulous wealth and fabulous poverty, of splendor and rags, of pal-

Christopher J. Graves is global CEO of Ogilvy Public Relations.

aces and hovels, of famine and pestilence, of genii and giants and Aladdin lamps, of tigers and elephants, the cobra and the jungle, the country of a hundred nations and a hundred tongues, of a thousand religions and two million gods, cradle of the human race, birthplace of human speech, mother of history, grandmother of legend, great-grandmother of tradition. . . . So far as I am able to judge, nothing has been left undone, either by man or nature, to make India the most extraordinary country that the sun visits on his rounds.

Twain owed his fame to his folksy, intuitive writing style and gift for crafting simple phrases that perfectly captured the essence of places and people. And yet, in India, this master wordsmith was so awestruck he could catalog only the country's enormity and contrasts. "There is only one India!" he exclaimed. "Its marvels are its own; the patents cannot be infringed; imitations are not possible."

Twain's inability to succinctly sum up India foreshadowed the challenge faced by those struggling to develop a "brand" for modern India. How does one brand a nation that defies description? Indian leaders wrestled in earnest with that question in the early 1990s after a balance of payments crisis forced the government to abandon stultifying regulations and open the economy to outside trade and investment. Attracting tourists from overseas was an obvious solution for bringing in the foreign currency India needed to stabilize its economy. And yet, in the four decades since independence, India's government had made virtually no effort to woo visitors from abroad. Sprawling India drew fewer foreign tourists than tiny Singapore. Travelers in key target markets in Western Europe saw India as destitute, dirty, and dangerous. Marketers knew that an ad campaign that merely pronounced India modern, clean, and comfortable would clash with foreign travelers' long-held perceptions and risked dismissal or even ridicule.

In 2002, Ogilvy & Mather, working with the Indian government, helped fashion a branding solution that embraced the nation's extraordinary diversity. At the heart of that strategy was the slogan "Incredible

!ndia." The exclamation point replacing the "I" was meant to capture the feeling of wonder—even astonishment—expressed by Twain ("There is only one India!") and many other first-time visitors. The campaign simply and elegantly portrayed the natural beauty of India. The key phrase was often paired with breathtaking visuals in which the exclamation mark was represented by natural sights or landmarks of similar shape—the finial spire atop the dome of the Taj Mahal, for example, or the taut calf of a yogi balanced on one leg. Piyush Pandey, chairman of Ogilvy & Mather India, says the goal of the Incredible !ndia campaign was to "change the image of India as a land of just snake charmers and bullock carts. We concentrated on a few destinations such as the Taj Mahal or the Red Fort. With rising awareness and much better infrastructure, we were able to expand the vision to include adventure tourism, nature, and wildlife tourism, a Buddhist tour for Japanese and medical tourism for Middle Eastern visitors."

> In 2011, India welcomed roughly the same number of foreign tourists as Bulgaria.

Overall, Incredible !ndia proved a great success. The campaign has endured for more than a decade under the oversight of several different advertising agencies. Its core message has seeped into every corner of India's communications; even the immigration forms at India's airports call out Incredible !ndia. Tourism receipts leaped to $18 billion in 2012, up from $3.5 billion in 2003 (catapulting India to sixteenth place globally, up from thirty-eighth). Foreign tourists have risen to 6.3 million in 2011, up from 2.7 million in 2003 (moving India to thirty-eighth place, up from fifty-third).

For all that, however, India still punches below its weight, attracting only two-thirds as many foreign tourists as Singapore, less than half as many as Thailand, and only a quarter as many as Malaysia. In 2011, India welcomed roughly the same number of foreign tourists as Bulgaria.

More important, as a vehicle for promoting important things other than tourism—trade and investment, to name two—the campaign has clear limitations. "Incredible" may be alluring and enchanting for tourists, but it is worrisome for foreign investors, who crave stability, consistency, and opportunity. Investors don't want India to be *in*credible. They want it to be *credible*.

A further complication: As India's individual states grow and develop, many are exploring new brand identities of their own. The time has come for India to make a fundamental decision about its branding architecture: Will it be a "branded house" or a "house of brands"? Or will it try to be a bit of both?

"Incredible" may be alluring and enchanting for tourists, but it is worrisome for foreign investors, who crave stability, consistency, and opportunity.

A branded house refers to large, multi-product companies that brand every product with the same parent company name. For example, Apple is a branded house. Everything the company makes and markets is clearly labeled as an Apple product. Even if a product has its own identity, such as the iPad, everyone knows it comes from Apple. In contrast, Unilever is a house of brands. The consumer giant's thousands of products—from personal care (Dove, Lux, Pond's) to foods (Lipton, Hellman's, Chef Boyardee)—are each promoted under the name of its own product line rather than their larger Unilever provenance. Of course, both Unilever and its rival Procter & Gamble want consumers to be able to distinguish which products come from which parent company, so increasingly both also brand their products with marks identifying the corporate parent; even so, branding for individual product lines remains the primary aim.

Incredible !ndia started as a branded house approach. Increasingly, however, India's states are finding the one house too confining and looking for ways to differentiate themselves as travel destinations. Some have opted to go it alone. Kerala is promoting itself as "God's Own Country." Bengal wants to be known as "Beautiful Bengal," while Haryana touts itself as "A Pioneer in Highway Tourism." Some states—such as Goa and Tamil Nadu—have added the parent brand of Incredible !ndia on top of their own state brands and slogans, while others have embraced a hybrid approach. Rajasthan, for example, sports its own logo featuring a red, green, orange, and yellow sun, while calling itself "The Incredible State of !ndia." Madhya Pradesh, not to be outdone, claims to be the "Heart of Incredible !ndia." States employing this hybrid approach hope to weave their own distinctive identity into the larger tapestry of the national brand.

The danger, of course, is that all these locally distinctive patterns threaten the integrity of the tapestry as a whole, confusing foreign travelers and undermining efforts to consolidate Brand India abroad. "Incredible !ndia" has endured for over a decade. To abandon it, or even compete with it, doesn't make much sense. In marketing to overseas travelers, India's tourism industry as a whole will be far better off if states can resist the temptation to defect and go alone. Instead, they should work together to maintain the consistency of an overarching, outward-facing national brand effort in which local state tourism brands are permitted but with secondary emphasis.

Successful destination branding must go beyond slogans, however; it demands the hard work of pulling together an array of entities, from regulators, to hotels, to airlines, to travel agencies and trade associations. At a January 2013 panel of aviation and travel industry experts in New Delhi, many foreign panelists bemoaned the lack of collaboration across India's travel and tourism industry. Gerard Brown, an international airline tourism development executive with UBM Aviation, decried the fragmentation of India's travel industry as "overwhelming."

Brand India faces an even greater challenge when it comes to attracting investors, who arrive looking to spend on far more than just a dazzling week's holiday. The metrics that matter to India's business visitors are far from reassuring. On the World Bank's ease of doing business ranking, India sits at 132 out of 185 countries. On the Heritage Foundation and *Wall Street Journal*'s economic freedom index, India ranks 119th out of 177 (below Malawi, Greece, and Senegal). On the Corruption Perception Index published by Transparency International, India is tied for 94th (with Benin, Colombia, Djibouti, Greece, Moldova, Mongolia, and Senegal) out of 174.

The narrative in the global press is no less discouraging. A March 2012 article in the *Economist*, for example, warned that after a burst of high growth in the 2000s, India's economy was slouching back toward over-regulation and torpor. "Like a Bollywood villain who just refuses to die," the article intoned, "the old India has made a terrifying reappearance."

Such dire assessments suggest that when it comes to business and foreign investment, India's best strategy for nation branding is to abandon nation branding altogether. In travel and tourism, cooperation is the most sensible course. But in seeking to attract global investment, competition among states may be the most effective route.

> When it comes to business and foreign investment, India's best strategy for nation branding is to abandon nation branding altogether.

Already some are doing exactly that. In Gujarat, Chief Minister Narendra Modi has launched "Vibrant Gujarat," a Davos-style conference aimed at marketing the state to Indian and foreign investors.

Certainly, foreign experts and investors have learned to distinguish between Indian states that are probusiness and those that are not; few global executives buy into a Brand India. In his book *Inside Out: India and China, Local Politics Go Global*, the Brookings Institution scholar William Antholis explicitly differentiates India's "forward states" (including Maharashtra, Gujarat, and Tamil Nadu), "backward states," and "swing states." "Companies need to align themselves with states with strong leadership," says U.S.-India Business Council president Ron Somers, an executive with more than two decades' experience operating "state-by-state, dialect-by-dialect" in India. He envisions "a kaleidoscope of these chief ministers, awash in colors of their native dress, speaking their state dialect, and all saying 'We're open for business.'"

Aparna Dutt Sharma, who heads the India Brand Equity Forum, argues that a national umbrella brand and segmented subbrands can successfully coexist. "Umbrella branding needs to remain a distinct and visible part of a nation brand promotion strategy," she says. "As nation brand strategies are generally geared to attract trade, investment, and tourism, both umbrella nation branding and sectoral/segment-oriented branding have their own distinct relevance."

India's challenge now demands it embrace two distinctly different branding approaches simultaneously. To attract first-time foreign travelers, it must continue to create an alluring, emotionally bonding campaign for India as an overall concept. At the same time, to attract serious foreign investors and business builders, it must encourage its states to compete, each with its own distinct business-friendly brand, born of local strengths and segmentation, perhaps metaphorically replacing the exclamation point with a dollar sign.

Mark Twain found synergy in the two ideals. The lecture fees and book royalties he earned from his adventures in Incredible India earned him more than enough money to repay his debts and restore his own credibility. India, too, must find a way for the twain to meet.

acknowledgments

Many people, inside and outside McKinsey, shared their time, talent, and enthusiasm to make *Reimagining India* a reality.

In McKinsey's India office, special thanks are due Barnik Maitra, who played a central role in making the dream of this book a reality. He helped keep the trains running on time and on the right tracks, worked tirelessly to coordinate with contributors, and saved us all from innumerable errors of fact, analysis, and judgment. Kulsum Merchant shared insight, ideas, and contacts at every juncture. Aparna Krishnan and Adhiraj Alai assisted with logistics and project management.

In New York, Rik Kirkland, head of McKinsey Global Publishing, reprised the role he played for *Reimagining Japan*, providing editorial direction, encouragement, and inspiration. McKinsey senior editor Cait Murphy worked closely with all the McKinsey authors. We also are indebted to McKinsey colleagues James Manyika and Brian Salsberg, who went the extra mile in putting us together with crucial contributors.

We benefited enormously from the skill, knowledge, and professionalism of an extraordinary team of outside editors: Nisid Hajari (now in Singapore), Paul Blustein (Kamakura), Rick Hornik (New York), and Gwen Robinson (Bangkok). Thanks, too, to John Sparks, who served as lead editor for our info graphics.

Moomal Mehta, deputy director of the Asia Society in Mumbai, championed our cause, shared her insights, and graciously put us in touch with many wonderful authors.

Priscilla Painton and her team at Simon & Schuster embraced the spirit of this project from its inception, reviewed every essay, and provided wise and detailed counsel on how to translate our vision into a final format that would engage readers and be worthy of our distinguished contributors.

Finally, we wish to express our deep gratitude to all members of McKinsey's India offices, now celebrating the firm's twentieth year in India. McKinsey's India partners have championed this project wholeheartedly from start to finish. Without their unwavering commitment, *Reimagining India* could never have been imagined.

Clay Chandler, Adil Zainulbhai, Editors
August 2013

contributors

ANIL AGARWAL is executive chairman of the Vedanta Resources PLC, a global metals and mining producer with operations in seven countries. Headquartered in London, Vedanta is the world's largest integrated zinc lead producer and among the top producers of copper, iron ore, and silver.

MUKESH AMBANI is chairman and CEO of Reliance Industries, India's largest private sector company. He is a member of the Indian Prime Minister's Council on Trade and Industry, a member of the board of governors of the National Council of Applied Economic Research, and chairman of the Indian Institute of Management, Bangalore. Ambani has a degree in chemical engineering from the Mumbai University Indian Institute of Chemical Technology and an MBA from Stanford University.

VISWANATHAN ANAND, India's first chess grandmaster, has been the world chess champion since 2007. He was also the Fédération Internationale des Échecs world rapid chess champion in 2003. In 2007, he received the Padma Vibhushan, the first sportsman so honored.

DOMINIC BARTON is a senior partner and the global managing director of McKinsey & Co.

HARSHA BHOGLE is a journalist who is considered "the voice of Indian cricket." He began his sports commentary career in 1980 on All

India Radio and worked for the BBC for eight years. Since 1995, he has been presenting live cricket for ESPN STAR Sports. Bhogle earned a degree in chemical engineering from Osmania University and attended the Indian Institute of Technology in Ahmedabad.

KUMAR MANGALAM BIRLA is chairman of the Aditya Birla Group, a global conglomerate founded in 1857 by his great-grandfather. The Birla Group is among the world's top rolling aluminum, cement, and textile producers. Birla is also chancellor of the Birla Institute of Technology and Science, a university focusing on engineering and the sciences, and a member of the Central Board of Directors of the Reserve Bank of India. He authored India's first report on corporate governance (1999) and has served as the chairman of the Securities and Exchange Board of India's Committee on Insider Trading.

JOHN CHAMBERS is chairman and CEO of Cisco Systems. He has received a number of awards, including the Clinton Global Citizen Award and the Woodrow Wilson Award for Corporate Citizenship.

CLAY CHANDLER is McKinsey's Asia editor. He is former Asia editor of *Fortune* magazine and has held a variety of other journalistic assignments, including chief economic correspondent and Hong Kong bureau chief for the *Washington Post* and Tokyo correspondent for the *Wall Street Journal*. Chandler is a graduate of Harvard University, where he studied politics, economics, and East Asian history. He is coeditor, with Heang Chhor and Brian Salsberg, of *Reimagining Japan: The Quest for a Future That Works* (Shogakukan, 2011).

MADHAV CHAVAN is cofounder, president, and CEO of the Pratham Education Foundation. Founded in 1994 to provide preschool education to children living in the Mumbai slums, Pratham is now the largest education NGO in India, reaching three million primary school children in nineteen states. In 2012, Chavan won the WISE Prize for Education, considered the Nobel Prize for education.

LOUIS R. CHÊNEVERT is the chairman and CEO of United Technologies, whose business units include Otis elevators, Pratt & Whitney aircraft engines, and Sikorsky Aircraft. Chênevert is a member of the Business Council, the US-India CEO Forum, and Business Roundtable.

PHILIP CLARKE became CEO of Tesco in 2011, thirty-seven years after he first started to work stacking shelves at the British grocer. Today Tesco is one of the world's largest retailers, with sixty-seven hundred stores in twelve markets. Clarke graduated from the University of Liverpool with a degree in economic history.

STEPHEN P. COHEN, a senior fellow in foreign policy studies at the Brookings Institution, is an expert on South Asian security and nuclear proliferation. He has served as a consultant to the Department of State, the RAND Corporation, and the Lawrence Livermore Laboratory, and has been a member of the Council on Foreign Relations' task force on South Asia and the Asia Society's committee on U.S.–South Asian relations. He is the author of *Shooting for a Century: The India-Pakistan Conundrum* (2013), *Beyond America's Grasp: A Century of Failed Diplomacy in the Middle East* (2009), coauthor, with Sunil Dasgupta, of *Arming without Aiming: India's Military Modernization* (2010), and a contributor to *The Future of Pakistan* (2011).

VIKASH DAGA is a partner in McKinsey's Delhi office.

GURCHARAN DAS is a regular columnist for six Indian newspapers (in English, Hindi, Telugu, and Marathi), and he has written for the *New York Times*, the *Wall Street Journal*, *Financial Times*, *Foreign Affairs*, and *Newsweek*. His literary works include a novel, *A Fine Family* (2001), and an exploration of the Mahabharata epic, *The Difficulty of Being Good: On the Subtle Art of Dharma* (2009). He is best known for his books on modern India, including *India Unbound: From Independence to the Global Information Age* (2000), a narrative history of twentieth-century India, which was filmed by the BBC, and *India Grows at Night: A Liberal Case for a*

Strong State (2012). Das became a full-time writer in 1995, after a successful business career, rising to become CEO of Procter & Gamble India.

SONALDE DESAI is a professor of sociology at the University of Maryland and a senior fellow at the National Council of Applied Economic Research in New Delhi. A demographer, Desai studies comparative social, educational, and economic inequality. In collaboration with the NCAER, she recently helped to complete the India Human Development Survey, which collected detailed information on forty thousand households. The data will be used to study the relationships among poverty, gender inequality, and public policy. Desai earned a PhD in sociology from Stanford University. She is the author of *Gender Inequality and Demographic Behavior: India* (1994) and a contributor to *Human Development in India: Challenges for a Society in Transition* (2010).

VISHAKHA N. DESAI, president and CEO of the Asia Society from 2004 to 2012, is special adviser for global affairs to the president of Columbia University and senior adviser for Global Policy and Programs at the Guggenheim Foundation. A scholar of classical Indian art, she was curator of Indian, Southeast Asian, and Islamic art at Boston's Museum of Fine Arts and has served as an adviser and juror for numerous international projects on contemporary art, including the Venice Biennale. Desai has taught at the University of Massachusetts, Boston University, and Columbia University.

ROHINI DEY is a restaurateur and former economist and management consultant. She is the owner and founder of Vermilion, Indo-Latin restaurants in New York and Chicago. She founded the Vermilion James Beard Foundation for Women in Culinary Leadership Scholarship to create more women leaders in the dining industry, and is an active member of the Chicago Network, the International Women's Forum, and the Women's Forum of New York. She writes a monthly column for the *Chicago Sun-Times*.

FRANK D'SOUZA is the cofounder and CEO of Cognizant, a global consulting and information technology provider. Born in Nairobi, D'Souza earned an MBA from Carnegie Mellon University. D'Souza is a director of the U.S.-India Business Council.

BILL EMMOTT is a writer and consultant on international affairs. From 1993 to 2006, he was editor of the *Economist*. He writes about current affairs for the *Times* of London and *La Stampa* in Italy. Emmott is the author of numerous books, including *Rivals: How the Power Struggle Between China, India, and Japan Will Shape Our Next Decade* (2008) and *Good Italy, Bad Italy: Why Italy Must Conquer Its Demons to Face the Future* (2012). He earned a first-class degree in philosophy, politics, and economics from Magdalen College, Oxford.

SONIA FALEIRO is the author of *Beautiful Thing: Inside the Secret World of Bombay's Dance Bars* (2010), which was the London *Sunday Times* Travel Book of the Year in 2011. Born in Goa and raised in New Delhi, she studied at St. Stephen's College and the University of Edinburgh. She has written for *India Today*, *Tehelka*, the *New York Times*, and the *International Herald Tribune*.

MALCOLM FRANK is executive vice president for strategy and marketing at Cognizant. He has a degree in economics from Yale University.

PATRICK FRENCH is an award-winning British historian. His books include *Younghusband: The Last Great Imperial Adventurer* (1994), *Liberty or Death: India's Journey to Independence and Division* (1997), *Tibet, Tibet* (2004), *The World Is What It Is: The Authorized Biography of V. S. Naipaul* (2008), and *India: A Portrait* (2011). A founding member of the intergovernmental India-UK Round Table, he has lectured at Oxford, Harvard, the Royal Geographical Society, the Asia Society, the American Enterprise Institute, and many other institutions.

BILL GATES is the cofounder and chairman of Microsoft and cochair of the Bill & Melinda Gates Foundation.

ANAND GIRIDHARADAS is the author of *India Calling: An Intimate Portrait of a Nation's Remaking* (2011). A former McKinsey consultant, he writes the "Currents" column for the *New York Times* and its global edition, the *International Herald Tribune*. Born in Cleveland, Ohio, and educated at the University of Michigan, Oxford, and Harvard, he has reported and lectured around the world. In 2011, he was named a Henry Crown fellow of the Aspen Institute.

NISABA GODREJ is the executive director of Godrej Consumer Products and a member of the board of directors and president of Human Capital & Innovation for Godrej Industries. Godrej, a diversified conglomerate founded in India in 1897, today has a presence in more than sixty countries. Nisaba Godrej's focus is on innovation, human capital, and strategy, particularly as related to consumer products. She is also responsible for the group's corporate social responsibility practices. She earned a BSc degree from the Wharton School at the University of Pennsylvania and an MBA from Harvard. She is on the board of Teach for India and the Heroes Project.

CHRISTOPHER J. GRAVES is global CEO of Ogilvy Public Relations Worldwide. Before joining Ogilvy, he worked in business news for twenty-three years, including cofounding the long-running TV show *Wall Street Journal Report*. He was also vice president of news and programming for CNBC in Europe and Asia. Graves is a frequent public speaker and moderator, appearing on CNBC's *Squawk Box* and at events such as the Clinton Global Initiative, World Economic Forum, and the World Islamic Economic Forum.

RAMACHANDRA GUHA is a professor of history at the London School of Economics whose interests include environmentalism and cricket. He is a columnist for several Indian newspapers and a regular contributor to

Caravan and *Outlook* magazines, and is the author of *India After Gandhi: The History of the World's Largest Democracy* (2007) and *How Much Should a Person Consume? Environmentalism in India and the United States* (2006), and the editor of *The Picador Book of Cricket* (2001). Guha is managing trustee of the New India Foundation, a nonprofit body that funds research on modern Indian history.

RAJAT GUPTA joined McKinsey in 1992 and is a full-time director in McKinsey's Mumbai office.

SHEKHAR GUPTA is editor-in-chief of the *Indian Express*, which is known for its investigative journalism. He writes the weekly column "National Interest" for the newspaper and hosts the interview-based television program *Walk the Talk*.

YASHENG HUANG is a professor of political economy and international management at the MIT Sloan School of Management and holds a special-term professorship at Fudan University's School of Management. He founded and heads MIT's China Lab and India Lab, which help entrepreneurs improve their management skills. He is the author of several books on globalization, emerging markets, and foreign direct investment, including *Capitalism with Chinese Characteristics: Entrepreneurship and the State* (2008), a history of economic reforms in China.

MANU JOSEPH is the editor of *OPEN* magazine. His novel *Serious Men* (2010) won *The Hindu* Literary Prize in 2010 and the PEN Open Book Award in 2011.

NOSHIR KAKA is a senior partner in McKinsey's Mumbai office and managing director of McKinsey India.

MUHTAR KENT is chairman and CEO of The Coca-Cola Company. He answered a newspaper ad in 1978 and was hired to drive a truck selling

Coke. The rest is history. Kent is active in the global business community; he is cochair of the Consumer Goods Forum and a fellow of the Foreign Policy Association, and is on the boards of Special Olympics International, Ronald McDonald House Charities, and Catalyst.

SALMAN KHAN, a former hedge fund analyst, is the founder of Khan Academy, a nonprofit organization that produces video lessons for viewing on YouTube. He has three degrees from MIT (mathematics, electrical engineering, and computer science) and an MBA from Harvard. In 2012, *Time* named Khan one of the one hundred most influential people in the world. He is the author *of The One World Schoolhouse: Education Reimagined* (2012).

VINOD KHOSLA is an entrepreneur, investor, and technology fan. He is the founder of Khosla Ventures, a venture capital firm that focuses on clean technology and information technology investments. Khosla was a cofounder of Daisy systems and founding CEO of Sun Microsystems, where he pioneered open systems and commercial RISC processors. Khosla is mentor to many entrepreneurs seeking to build technology-based businesses. Khosla holds a bachelor of technology in electrical engineering from IIT, New Delhi, a master's in biomedical engineering from Carnegie Mellon University, and an MBA from the Stanford Graduate School of Business.

ALOK KSHIRSAGAR is a senior partner in McKinsey's Mumbai office.

GAUTAM KUMRA is a senior partner in McKinsey's Delhi office.

RAJIV LALL is the executive chairman of Infrastructure Development Finance Company, which was founded in 1997 to promote private sector infrastructure finance in India. Lall chairs the Global Agenda Council on Infrastructure of the World Economic Forum and the Infrastructure Council of the Confederation of Indian Industry; he is also a former president of the Bombay Chamber of Commerce and Industry. Before joining IDFC, Lall worked with Warburg Pincus, Morgan Stanley, the World Bank, and the Asian Development Bank. He earned a BA in politics, philosophy, and economics from Oxford University and a PhD in economics from Columbia University.

EDWARD LUCE is Washington columnist for the *Financial Times* and former South Asia bureau chief based in New Delhi. He is the author of *In Spite of the Gods: The Strange Rise of Modern India* (2007) and *Time to Start Thinking: America in the Age of Descent* (2012).

ANU MADGAVKAR is a senior fellow at the McKinsey Global Institute.

KISHORE MAHBUBANI is dean of the Lee Kuan Yew School of Public Policy at the National University of Singapore. A diplomat for more than three decades, he was twice Singapore's ambassador to the United Nations and president of the Security Council in January 2001 and May 2002. Mahbubani is a regular contributor to *Foreign Affairs*, the *National Interest*, the *New York Times*, the *Financial Times*, and other publications. He is the author of *Can Asians Think?* (2001), *The New Asian Hemisphere: The Irresistible Shift of Global Power to the East* (2008), and *The Great Convergence: Asia, the West, and the Logic of One World* (2013).

ANAND MAHINDRA is chairman and managing director of the Mahindra Group, a Mumbai-based Indian multinational conglomerate with interests in diverse sectors, ranging from real estate and hotels to cars and aerospace components.

BARNIK C. MAITRA is a partner in McKinsey's Mumbai office.

VICTOR MALLET is the South Asia bureau chief for the *Financial Times* and former Asia editor (2006–2008) and chief Asia correspondent (2003–2006). He is the author of *The Trouble with Tigers: The Rise and Fall of South-East Asia* (1999).

KIRAN MAZUMDAR-SHAW is chairman and managing director of Biocon Limited, India's biggest biotechnology company. Mazumdar-Shaw serves on the government of India's advisory council on biotechnology and is a member of the Prime Minister's Council on Trade & Industry and the US-India CEO Forum. In 2005, the Indian government awarded her the Padma Bhushan, the third-highest civilian award. A graduate of Bangalore University, Mazumdar-Shaw qualified as a master brewer at the University of Ballarat, Australia, and was India's first woman brewmaster.

SUKETU MEHTA is the author of *Maximum City: Bombay Lost and Found*, which was a finalist for the 2005 Pulitzer Prize. Born in Calcutta and raised in Mumbai and New York, he is a professor of journalism at New York University. He has written for many publications, including the *New Yorker*, the *New York Times Magazine*, *National Geographic*, *Granta*, *Harper's*, *Time*, and *Newsweek*.

VIKRAM SINGH MEHTA is chairman of Brookings India and former chairman of the Shell Group of Companies in India. He writes a monthly column for the *Indian Express*. He earned a master's degree in economics from Magdalen College, Oxford University, as well as a master's from the Fletcher School of Law and Diplomacy at Tufts University.

SUNIL BHARTI MITTAL is the founder, chairman, and group CEO of Bharti Enterprises and chairman of Bharti Airtel, which operates in twenty countries in Africa and South Asia. By number of subscribers, Bharti Airtel is one of the world's largest mobile operators and the largest in India. A former president of the Confederation of Indian Industry, Mittal is a member of the Prime Minister's Council on Trade & Industry and a recipient of the Padma Bhushan. He also serves on the boards of the International Telecommunication Union and Harvard University's Global Advisory Council, and is a member of the India-US, India-UK, and India-Japan CEO forums.

ZIA MODY is the founder and managing partner of AZB & Partners, one of India's largest law firms, which specializes in mergers and acquisitions. She is a nonexecutive director of the HSBC Asia-Pacific Board, a member of the World Bank Administrative Tribunal, and a vice president of the London Court of International Arbitration. She studied law at Selwyn College, Cambridge, and has a master's degree from Harvard Law School.

NANDAN NILEKANI is cofounder and former cochairman and CEO of Infosys. Since 2009, he has served as chairman of the Unique Identification Authority of India, which seeks to give every resident of India a digital identification. He is the author of *Imagining India: The Idea of a Renewed Nation* (2009).

NITIN NOHRIA was named dean of the Harvard Business School in 2010, where he had been on the faculty for twenty-two years. His areas of interest include human motivation, leadership, and corporate transformation and accountability. Nohria has coauthored or coedited sixteen books, including *The Handbook for Teaching Leadership: Knowing, Doing, and Being* (2012), *Paths to Power: How Insiders and Outsiders Shaped American Business Leadership* (2006), and *Changing Fortunes: The Rise and Fall of the Industrial Corporation* (2002). He earned a degree in chemical engineering from the Indian Institute of Technology, Bombay, and a doctorate in management from MIT.

VIVEK PANDIT is a senior partner in McKinsey's Mumbai office.

JERRY PINTO is a journalist, poet, and novelist. He writes frequently on Indian cinema, including the books *Helen: The Life and Times of an H-Bomb* (2006), about the actress Helen Jairag Richardson, and *Leela: A Patchwork Life* (2010), about Leela Naidu. He published his first novel, *Em and the big Hoom*, in 2012. Pinto is a guest lecturer in social communications media at the Sophia Polytechnic and is a committee member of the Indian chapter of PEN and a member of the Poetry Circle, Mumbai. He has degrees from the University of Mumbai and the Government Law College, Mumbai.

AZIM PREMJI is chairman of Wipro Ltd., founded in 1945 by his father. Since the 1960s, Premji has led Wipro's diversification from a hydrogenated cooking fat company into information technology, and Wipro is now one of the largest IT companies in India. Premji is nonexecutive director on the Board of the Reserve Bank of India, a member of the Prime Minister's Councils for National Integration and for Trade & Industry, as well as a member of the Indo-UK and the Indo-France CEO's Forum. In 2011, he received the Padma Vibhushan from the government of India and the Legion of Honor from France.

SUKUMAR RANGANATHAN is the editor of *Mint*, a New Delhi–based business newspaper founded in 2007 as a collaboration with the *Wall Street Journal*, and *LiveMint.com*, its online counterpart. He is also the former managing editor of *Business Today* magazine.

AHMED RASHID has been the Pakistan, Afghanistan, and Central Asia correspondent for Britain's *Daily Telegraph* for more than twenty years. He also writes for the *Wall Street Journal*, the *Nation*, *Daily Times* (Pakistan), and numerous academic journals. He appears regularly on international TV and radio networks, including CNN and BBC World. He is the author of *Taliban: Militant Islam, Oil, and Fundamentalism in Central Asia* (2000), *Descent into Chaos: The United States and the Disaster in Pakistan, Afghanistan, and Central Asia* (2008), and *Pakistan on the Brink: The Future of America, Pakistan, and Afghanistan* (2012). Rashid attended Government College in Lahore and Fitzwilliam College, Cambridge.

K. SRINATH REDDY, MD, is a founding member of the Public Health Foundation of India, an independent foundation launched by Prime Minister Manmohan Singh in 2006, president of the World Heart Federation, and a consultant to the World Health Organization and the World

Bank. In recognition of his commitment to preventing heart disease and improving public health, he has received the prestigious Padma Bhushan, the Queen Elizabeth Medal from the Royal Society for the Promotion of Health in the United Kingdom, and the WHO Director General's Award for Global Leadership in Tobacco Control.

BRUCE RIEDEL is a director of the Intelligence Project at the Brookings Institution and a senior fellow at the Saban Center for Middle East Policy. He also teaches at the Johns Hopkins School of Advanced International Studies and is a senior adviser with the Albright Stonebridge Group. As a staff member of the National Security Council, he has advised the last four U.S. presidents on Middle East and South Asian issues, following a long career at the Central Intelligence Agency. Riedel is the author of *The Search for al Qaeda: Its Leadership, Ideology, and Future* (2008), *The Deadly Embrace: Pakistan, America, and the Future of the Global Jihad* (2011), and *Avoiding Armageddon: America, India, and Pakistan to the Brink and Back* (2013).

SHIRISH SANKHE is a senior partner in McKinsey's Mumbai office.

MALLIKA SARABHAI is a choreographer, Kuchipudi and Bharata-natyam dancer, and longtime codirector, with her mother, the acclaimed dancer Mrinalini Sarabhai, of the Darpana Academy of Performing Arts in Ahmedabad. She played the role of Draupadi in Peter Brook's play *The Mahabharata* for five years, performing in France, North America, Australia, Japan, and Scotland. Sarabhai earned an MBA from the Indian Institute of Management in Ahmedabad and a doctorate in organizational behavior from Gujarat University. She received a Padma Bhushan in 2010.

ERIC SCHMIDT joined Google in 2001 and helped grow the company from a Silicon Valley start-up to a global leader in technology. He served as Google's CEO from 2001 to 2011, overseeing the company's technical and business strategy alongside founders Sergey Brin and Larry Page.

Under his leadership Google dramatically scaled its infrastructure and diversified its product offerings while maintaining a strong culture of innovation. He is the coauthor, with Jared Cohen, of *The New Digital Age: Reshaping the Future of People, Nations and Business* (2013).

HOWARD SCHULTZ is chairman, president, and CEO of Starbucks Coffee Company. His inspiration for Starbucks came during a trip to Milan, where he noticed that there were coffee bars on almost every street. They sold not only excellent espresso, but also served as a local meeting place. Today there are Starbucks in all corners of the world—almost nineteen thousand of them.

SUHEL SETH, a writer and consultant on marketing and management, is managing partner of Counselage India, a strategic brand consultancy, and founder of the advertising and marketing agency Equus. He sits on the global advisory boards of British Airways and Cavendish and on the regional boards of Citibank India, Coca-Cola India, and STAR TV. Seth attended Harvard Business School's Advanced Management Program. His most recent book is *Get to the Top: The Ten Rules for Social Success*.

GEET SETHI is a five-time World Professional Billiards champion and four-time winner of the Indian National Snooker Championships. He is cofounder of Olympic Gold Quest, a program to identify and support promising Indian athletes to compete in Olympic sports. He is a recipient of the Rajiv Gandhi Khel Ratna, India's highest sporting award.

RUCHIR SHARMA is head of the emerging markets equity team at Morgan Stanley Investment Management. His articles have appeared in *Newsweek*, the *Wall Street Journal*, *Foreign Affairs*, the *New York Times*, the *Washington Post*, *Forbes*, and the *Economic Times*. He is the author of *Breakout Nations: In Pursuit of the Next Economic Miracles* (2012).

SHANTANU SINHA is president and COO of the Khan Academy. A former McKinsey consultant in Silicon Valley, he has three bachelor's degrees (electrical engineering and computer science, mathematics, and brain and cognitive sciences) and a master's in electrical engineering and computer sciences, all from MIT.

ARVIND SUBRAMANIAN is a senior fellow jointly at the Peterson Institute for International Economics and at the Center for Global Development. He is author of *India's Turn: Understanding the Economic Transformation* (2009) and *Eclipse: Living in the Shadow of China's Economic Dominance* (2011), and coauthor of *Who Needs to Open the Capital Account?* (2012). Subramanian has published widely in academic journals, contributes frequently to the *Financial Times*, and is a columnist for India's leading financial daily, *Business Standard*. He advises the Indian government in various capacities, including as a member of the Finance Minister's Expert Group on the G-20.

NAVEEN TEWARI is the founder and CEO of InMobi, a mobile-based network that sells, distributes, and helps to produce mobile ads. A former McKinsey consultant, he worked with Charles River Ventures to develop its Indian investment strategy. In 2013, *MIT Technology Review* named InMobi one of that year's fifty disruptive companies ("organizations at the forefront of radical change, displaying 'disruptive innovation' that would . . . transform industry and change our lives"). Tewari is also the founder and chairman of the India School Fund, which establishes schools in rural areas. He earned an undergraduate degree from the Indian Institute of Technology, Kanpur, and an MBA from Harvard.

JEAN-PASCAL TRICOIRE is president and CEO of Schneider Electric, a French-based global electricity, energy, and infrastructure company.

ASHUTOSH VARSHNEY is the Sol Goldman Professor of International Studies and the Social Sciences at Brown University. He is a consultant to the World Bank and has served on the former UN secretary general Kofi Annan's Millennium Task Force on Poverty (2002–2005). He also has worked with the UN Development Programme, Human Rights Watch,

Freedom House, and Britain's Department for International Development. Varshney has written or contributed to several books, including *Ethnic Conflict and Civic Life: Hindus and Muslims in India* (2002) and *Democracy, Development and the Countryside: Urban-Rural Struggles in India* (1995).

MILES WHITE is chairman and CEO of Abbott Laboratories, a leading manufacturer of products and medications for diabetes, eye care, heart disease, nutrition, and animal health.

ADIL ZAINULBHAI is a senior partner in McKinsey's Mumbai office and chairman of McKinsey India.

FAREED ZAKARIA is a journalist, author, and television commentator who specializes in international affairs. He is editor-at-large for *Time* magazine and is the host of CNN's *Fareed Zakaria GPS* (Global Public Square). Zakaria is the author of four books, including *The Post-American World* (2009) and *The Future of Freedom: Illiberal Democracy at Home and Abroad* (2004). Born in Mumbai, Zakaria earned a BA from Yale and a PhD in political science from Harvard. In 2010, he received the Padma Bhushan from the Indian government.